SIMON FRASER UNIVERSITY
W.A.C. BENNETT LIBRARY

Transition

Transition

The First Decade

Edited by
Mario I. Blejer and
Marko Škreb

The MIT Press
Cambridge, Massachusetts
London, England

This book was set in Palatino on 3B2 by Asco Typesetters, Hong Kong.

Printed and bound in the United States of America.

Library of Congress Cataloging-in-Publication Data

Transition : the first decade / edited by Mario I. Blejer and Marko Skreb.
    p.   cm.
Includes bibliographical references and index.
ISBN 0-262-02505-1 (alk. paper)
1. Privatization—Europe, Eastern—Case studies. 2. Privatization—Europe,
Central—Case studies. 3. Europe, Eastern—Economic policy—1989—Case studies.
4. Europe, Central—Economic policy—1989—Case studies. 5. Post-communism—
Europe, Eastern—Case studies. 6. Post-communism—Europe, Central—Case studies.
I. Blejer, Mario I. II. Skreb, Marko, 1957–
HD4140.7 .T735   2002
338.943′009171′7—dc21   2001044332

Contents

I   Introduction

1   A Decade of Transition in a Variety of Settings: A Comparison of Country Experiences

Mario I. Blejer and
Marko Škreb

The turn of the century is a time when the world is reflecting on the first decade of one of the most momentous transformations in modern history. During this unique decade, a major component of the world economy has been changing from one system of economic organization to a completely different one. The postsocialist transition, symbolically inaugurated by the fall of the Berlin Wall, has been an immense undertaking, and its outcome is still in the making. However, a decade constitutes, at least psychologically, an important benchmark and affords an opportunity to take stock of achievements, setbacks, and outstanding challenges, and there have been, indeed, many attempts to use this opportunity to draw conclusions on transition.[1]

Although the state of transition encompasses a number of features common to all countries undergoing the process, the pace and degree of success to date have been largely determined by country-specific conditions and political configurations. Although most transition strategies are based on a three-pronged approach—liberalization, institution building, and macroeconomic stabilization—countries have, in practice, adopted distinctive reform agendas and achieved varying degrees of success. Whereas some countries have moved decisively ahead with their transformation, others are making a steady effort to catch up, and although it is possible to affirm that the very worst period of transition is now behind us in virtually all the economies involved, the picture that emerges at the end of the first decade is, indeed, far from uniform.

It can be said, without hesitation, that across the whole region progress has definitely been made in many respects. The essential pillars of a market economy have been built, prices have been largely liberalized, and inflation has been conquered. Growth has, in general, resumed, and living conditions are improving. The pace of improvement, however, is slow and uneven. In fact, we can detect a widening gap among the transition economies, with increasing divergence in performance, structure, and institutions. Whereas some have asked whether it is still useful to analyze the transition countries as a single homogeneous group under these circumstances, we believe that this variety of policies, intensity of effort, and outcomes calls for a comparative study of the experiences of all the countries involved over the first ten years to understand what has worked, what has failed, and the nature of the challenges that lie ahead.

The object of this volume is to attempt such a task. It starts by presenting two general studies, the first of which reviews and summarizes the major accomplishments as well as the deficiencies of the transition process and covers a wide set of issues in a comparative country setting. In chapter 2, entitled "Ten Years of Transition in Central Europe and the Former Soviet Union: The Good News and the Not-So-Good News," Johannes Linn identifies seven major lessons. The first (obviously good) is that changes in the countries involved are fundamental and far reaching, encompassing all aspects of life, notably social, political, economic, and institutional. The second is that the Central European and Baltic countries have managed to stabilize their economies and bring them back to market-oriented systems. The third is that poorer, small countries of the Caucausus and Central Asia are vigorously continuing economic and political reforms, despite the enormous initial shock caused by the breakup of the Soviet Union. The fourth is that despite the breakup of the former Yugoslavia and the warfare that ensued, the countries in that region have managed to rebuild. The fifth is that the neglect of institutional reforms can be detrimental to further economic reforms (as the case of Russia clearly demonstrates). The sixth is that although the Russian and Ukrainian economies did not perform well, which had a serious impact on the political and social conditions in those countries, the influence of these events on the world economy remained very limited. The final lesson that Linn draws is that market-oriented reforms, together with institutional strengthening and social reforms, have worked and have put the formally centrally planned economies (at least a large part of them) on a sustainable growth path.

Chapter 3, "Postcommunist Transition and Post-Washington Consensus: The Lessons for Policy Reforms," by Grzegorz Kolodko, elaborates on the details of implementing major policy reforms and recapitulates the experiences of various countries, with the aim of deriving policy lessons. Kolodko criticizes the "belief that a market economy can be introduced by 'shock therapy'" and emphatically points out the deficiencies in the implementation of the Washington consensus on transition economies. His contention is that for a market economy to operate normally, strong institutional structures and appropriate behavior are needed. The need for institution building is the strongest policy conclusion of his analysis. However, institution building is, by its nature, a very gradual process. Therefore, he concludes that transition must be gradual. This, of course, represents a strongly and well-articulated view of one of the sides in the old debate between shock and gradualism in transition.

Following these two broad and comparative articles, the second part of the volume turns to a detailed study of eleven specific country cases. It covers the experiences of countries at various levels of transition, which could be divided into four groups.

Chapter 4, "East Germany: Transition with Unification, Experiments, and Experiences," constitutes a category by itself, since it deals with the unique case of transition cum reunification. According to the chapter's authors, Jürgen von Hagen and Rolf R. Strauch, East Germany's transition presents, after ten years, a mixed picture. Today East Germany's economy has characteristics such as consumption and savings, purchases of durables, and active employment that are very much like those in West Germany. Local governments are also similar in the provision of public services. Nonetheless, huge differences in incomes, output, and local tax capacities remain. In the view of the authors, the instant adoption of the regulatory framework from West Germany and massive public transfers had less successful results than anticipated at the time of reunification. The inflexible East German labor market remains the main problem. Moreover, in the authors' view, it will be very difficult to phase out the existing industrial support programs and transfers. They fear that East Germany may remain transfer dependent for the foreseeable future.

The chapters concerning the second group of countries analyzed detail the developments in the five Central and Southern Europe countries considered to have made the most progress in the transformation process: Poland, Hungary, the Czech Republic, Croatia, and Slovenia. Marek Dabrowsky begins chapter 5, "Ten Years of Polish Economic Transition, 1989–1999" by stating that Poland was the first postcommunist country to begin the transition to a market economy. The pace of the changes in the country was uneven. After the first two years of rapid and comprehensive reforms, the reform movement slowed, but in 1998–1999, reforms picked up pace again. Poland's transition can generally be considered as successful and effective, but the process has been more complicated than sometimes perceived. Although the basic foundations of a modern market economy have been formally established, much remains to be accomplished: bringing inflation down to the EU level, fiscal consolidation, labor market reforms, completion of privatization, and so on. The author concludes that future reforms will be dictated by the requirements of EU membership.

In chapter 6, "Fiscal Foundations of Convergence to the European Union: The Hungarian Economy toward EU Accession," László Halpern and Judit Neményi analyze the challenges Hungary has faced in negotiating EU membership. In their view, countries on their way to EU membership face difficult choices, and real and nominal convergence still require substantial adjustment in Hungary. Although the first period of nominal convergence is, in practical terms, achieved when it is possible to peg the exchange rate credibly, policymakers are then confronted with the question of what the most efficient form of a real appreciation trend is. Assuming a real appreciation trend of 2–3 percent per year, countries may either have higher inflation than the 2 percent observed in the EU or, if price stability is preferred, face nominal appreciation of the exchange rate. The latter option is feasible, however, only if prices and wages are flexible downward, which is not the case in advanced associated countries. In short, if the currency cannot appreciate and price stability is required, then all the adjustment must be made on the fiscal side. This could translate into a requirement for a budgetary surplus requirement, which is not easily achievable (especially if needed pension system reform may increase the deficit).

In chapter 7, "The Czech Republic: Ten Years of Transition," Vladimír Dlouhý identifies three main periods in the Czech Republic's transition: The first period, from 1990 to 1994, was marked with successful initial reforms. In the second period, from 1994 to 1997, reforms first slowed down and then stopped completely. The third period, 1997–1999, was dominated by the reaction to the currency crisis of May 1997. As a result, growth over that period was negative, and the solvency of the banking sector became uncertain. Dlouhy identifies the main cause of the 1997 crisis as a lack of microeconomic adjustment, which was particularly needed in the Czech case because of the hypertrophy of its heavy industry at the beginning of transition. More specifically, he thinks that the recession suffered by the Czech Republic was caused by the dearth of strong private financial institutions (banks), the lack of enterprise restructuring, the inadequate regulation of the capital markets, and the monopolistic structures of some markets. The policy implications are obvious. The author is optimistic, however, about the future, because Czech policymakers are learning from their past mistakes.

The next two case studies cover countries formerly part of Yugoslavia and involve a completely different methodological approach. Velimir Šonje and Boris Vujčić focus on "Croatia in the Second Stage of Transition: 1994–1999" in chapter 8. For various reasons, the authors assert that the first five years of transition in Croatia have many specific features (e.g., the war, a legacy of more liberal socialism) that make it difficult to compare this period with the transition periods of other economies. Following a brief review of economic data for Croatia up to 1994, they cover in an appealing and comprehensive way a wide variety of topics. The first issue discussed is the well-known relationship between inflation and monetary growth. This is followed by a comprehensive analysis of interest rate policy, capital inflows, and the banking crises in Croatia. Subsequently, the relationship among banking supervision, central bank credibility, and the exchange rate system is examined. The important problem of the causes and consequences of the domestic payment system arrears in Croatia is given special attention, as are the linkages between monetary and fiscal policy. In the last two sections the authors investigate the reasons for poor export performance (three are identified: the war, exclusion from trade associations, and the lack of foreign direct investment) and labor market developments.

Chapter 9, "Fiscal Impulse of Transition: The Case of Slovenia," by Velimir Bole, focuses, like the Hungarian case study in chapter 6, on the fiscal aspect of transition. The author argues that in socialist countries before transition, some "normal" government functions, such as the social safety net, were performed by enterprises or were considered unnecessary (regulatory infrastructure). Therefore, transition created a heavy one-time burden on government expenditures (and revenues), making it very difficult to evaluate the sustainability of the long-term fiscal stance. Acknowledging that there are strong arguments against analyzing the "transition fiscal impulse" (the impact of transition on a fiscal position), the author estimates that the overall transition impulse to a fiscal position in Slovenia was highest during the second and third year of transition, at more than 3 percent of GDP. Interestingly enough, Bole's view is that the impulse, which leveled off in 1996, is still strong after ten years of transition and can be estimated at 1 percent of GDP.

In the third group of countries studied in the volume, the experience of the more advanced countries is sharply contrasted with that of the three Slavic republics of the former Soviet Union. Progress, or the lack thereof, in Russia, Belarus, and Ukraine is the subject of the third section.

Chapter 10, by Yegor Gaidar, is entitled "The Legacy of the Socialist Economy: The Macro- and Microeconomic Consequences of Soft Budget Constraints." The chapter is divided into four main parts. First, Gaidar evaluates countries that have managed to counteract fiscal crisis (a common feature of transition) with tight monetary policy and to achieve rapid disinflation. In his terminology, they are called "monetarist" countries. For those countries to embark on a sustained path of reform, they had to impose severe budget constraints on their enterprises. Second, Gaidar speaks about countries whose monetary policy was soft and where high inflation was prolonged, calling them "populist" countries. Such countries combine soft budget constraints on enterprises with weak fiscal constraints. Third, the author examines the problem of incentives and norms of behavior for formerly state-owned enterprises. Finally, Gaidar turns to the economic and political problems of the postsocialist transition in Russia. Both macroeconomic stabilization and general economic reforms in Russia were slow. The main problem in reducing the budget deficit was the lack of political support. Gaidar concludes that the government's attempts to impose severe budgetary constraints on enterprises failed and that this, combined with the monetary financing of the budgetary deficit, resulted in the perpetuation of soft budgetary constraints in Russia. In his view, the only way out of stagnation and high inflation for Russia is to ensure durable financial stabilization. For this to happen, Russia needs to rid itself of the "nomenklatura of the capitalist sector," free resources, and facilitate developments in the private sector.

Domenico Mario Nuti starts chapter 11, "Belarus: A Command Economy without Central Planning," by challenging the conventional wisdom that Belarus is a transition economy. Politically, Belarus is led by a Communist Party monopoly. Economically, it is a command economy where state enterprises are dominant. There are price controls, monetary overexpansion, and multiple exchange rate regimes. There is no economic stabilization. Paradoxically, this backwardness in reforms has, so far, sheltered Belarus from the negative consequences of transition observed in Russia. Obviously, Belarus's policies are not sustainable and cannot lead to the needed continued growth in the country. The author argues that it might be better for Belarusian authorities to admit openly that they are not willing to move toward a market economy instead of making promises on which they do not deliver. He concludes that at this stage of reform (or lack thereof), even a proposed monetary union with Russia would not work. Nuti's chapter is of particular interest because there is very little available literature on Belarus and it contains relatively rare statistical data on the country.

The second most populous country of the former Soviet Union, Ukraine, is examined by Anders Åslund chapter 12, entitled "Problems with Economic Transformation in Ukraine." Åslund begins by noting that Ukraine is one of the least successful countries in transforming itself into a market economy. As he writes, "to summarize, Ukraine suffers from a poor sense of direction, a weak state, a corrupt bureaucracy, corrupt businessmen, and a weak civil society." Corruption and rent seeking are predominant in all aspects of the ruling trinity in Ukraine: the government, businessmen, and the parliament. The problem is that Ukraine is in a bad equilibrium that results in a vicious cycle. The question is, what can free the country from that situation? The author concludes that the stalemate can be broken either by a major economic crisis or by the attrition of rents as competition over their distribution gradually increases. Ukrainian problems are not so much problems of economic reforms as political tribulations. Therefore, Åslund claims, only the democratic process can resolve Ukraine's present situation.

The fourth and final group of case studies in the volume contrasts dissimilar developments in two major Balkan countries: Bulgaria and Romania. Chapter 13, by Ilian Mihov, entitled "The Economic Transition in Bulgaria, 1989–1999," provides an analysis of the major economic developments in Bulgaria over the last decade. Bulgaria's transition has indeed been difficult, as the cumulative decline in its

GDP over the period was 37 percent. Part of the problem was the slowness of the privatization process, which did not stop the accumulation of losses by state-owned companies. Banks continued throwing good money after bad so that companies could continue to operate. This resulted in a rising share of bad loans on the balance sheets of commercial banks. The central bank continued injecting liquidity via refinancing so that the banks could operate, and the system, surely enough, ended up in hyperinflation: a scenario familiar to many other countries as well. The introduction of a currency board in 1997 signaled a new era. As a consequence, the country was successful in bringing down inflation, improving the quality of the banks' balance sheets, and closing down big loss-making enterprises. Nevertheless, serious challenges lie ahead for Bulgaria. First, privatization has not been completed (especially of the banks and big state-owned enterprises). Second, and despite the initial success, Milhov asks whether Bulgaria will choose to keep its currency board in the future and whether this is the most suitable regime for Bulgaria.

The final study is presented by Daniel Daianu in chapter 14, "Strain and Economic Adjustment: Romania's Travails and Pains." Daianu's conclusions are much in line with Kolodko's general statement in chapter 3 that institutions ultimately determine economic performance. Institution building takes time. It would therefore be naïve to assume that institutions in postcommunist economies could quickly achieve the same results as those in the West. In addition, the author stresses the need for structural reforms, without which no macroeconomic stabilization can be sustainable. Finally, he pleads for realism, not only in designing policies, but also in making judgments on what constitutes good performance and what must be done in the future.

The volume closes with a chapter by Jacques de Larosière. A former managing director of the International Monetary Fund and president of the European Bank for Reconstruction and Development, he is certainly the right person to present an overview of ten years of transition. In chapter 15, entitled simply "Transition Economies," de Larosière has divided his remarks into two sections. The first section asserts that the initial success of transition in a particular country depends on a combination of macroeconomic stabilization and structural reforms; the second argues that the continuation of the success of transition after the initial phase is largely dependent on a legal environment and building strong institutions. In discussing structural reforms, de Larosière strongly emphasizes the need to liberalize prices, open the country up to foreign trade, open up its capital markets, and ensure the freedom of enterprises. On the subject of macroeconomic stability (after briefly analyzing why inflation derails reforms), the author turns to the issue of the need for a new monetary policy, concluding that fiscal policies were often to blame for the problems transition countries encountered and that monetary policy had to bear the bulk of stabilization, with repercussions for the interest rates and exchange rate system. It is well known that structural reforms and macroeconomic stabilization are indispensable transition pillars, but we know today that they are not enough for a well-functioning market economy. After explaining why a legal framework is important for any market economy, more details are given on the role of the government. In de Larosière's view, despite all the success of transition, much remains to be done. Political freedoms in transition countries are much higher than before, but in some of the countries corruption, rent seeking, insider privileges, and other similar problems are gaining ground. What can be done to combat the ills that hamper economic growth? The author concludes as follows: "My hunch ... is that education and openness to world information will eventually help the people of those countries attain better governance."

In summary, the fifteen chapters in this volume go a long way toward providing elements for a thorough and comprehensive evaluation of the radical changes brought about by the process of transition that started a decade ago. These studies also contribute to an assessment of the prospects for the medium and long term. As a whole, it is becoming more evident that the transition countries as a group have experienced dramatic changes. Their responses, although different and distinct, have prepared most of them for further progress and growth.

Some of the results confirmed in the country studies in this volume, such as the fact that macroeconomic stability is a necessary prerequisite for growth, are already well known and documented in transition literature (Blejer and Skreb 1997), as is the need for substantial financial-sector reform in transition economies (Blejer and Skreb 1999a). It is also common knowledge that transition is a lengthy and very costly process that affects all aspects of a country's economy and, more generally, an entire society (Blejer and Skreb 1999b, 1999c).

What is very clearly evident from this volume is the need for greater emphasis on institutional building and the enforcement of contracts (as stressed by de Larosière, Linn, Kolodko, Daianu, and Gaidar). If countries do not pay attention to the legal and institutional frameworks of a market economy, corruption, rent seeking, and the protection of vested interests may seriously hamper economic growth, as is presently the case in countries of the former Soviet Union.

Finally, it is clear that there is no single pattern of transition, nor are the prospects for their futures the same. The countries most advanced in their approach to the European Union (Hungary, Poland) and physically closer to Brussels will obviously have different outlooks than those that are more distant from the European capital (Bulgaria, Romania). Small countries (Slovenia, Croatia) will have to embark on a different development path than big ones (Russia, Ukraine). The "one size fits all" approach does not work on the complex, multifaceted and dynamic structures of each individual economy. We strongly believe, however, that sound macroeconomic policies combined with structural reforms and institution building ultimately cannot fail. Such policies are not necessarily popular with the electorate; they are not simply understood or explained to the public at large, rendering policymaking even more challenging. When "practicing transition," policymakers have to think not only about sound economic principles but also about the economic, social, and political realities in any given country. It is true that sound economic principles should ultimately mean good politics, but this is not necessarily the case in the short run. It is important to bear in mind that, as Dlouhy stresses in chapter 7, "markets do not fail, only policymakers do."

References

Blejer, M., and M. Skreb, eds. 1997. *Macroeconomic stabilization in transition economies.* Cambridge: Cambridge University Press.

Blejer, M., and M. Skreb, eds. 1999a. *Financial sector transformation: Lessons from economies in transition.* Cambridge: Cambridge University Press.

Blejer, M., and M. Skreb, eds. 1999b. *Balance of payments, exchange rates and competitiveness in transition economies.* Boston/Dordrecht/London: Kluwer Academic.

Blejer, M., and M. Skreb, eds. 1999c. *Central banking, monetary policies, and the implications for transition economies*. Boston/Dordrecht/London: Kluwer Academic.

European Bank for Reconstruction and Development (EBRD). 1999. *Transition Report*. London: Author.

Fischer, S., and R. Sahay. 2000. The transition economies after ten years of transition. Working Paper, International Monetary Fund, Washington, D.C.

Wyplosz, C. 2000. Ten years of transformation: Macroeconomic lessons. Policy research working paper no. 2288, World Bank, Washington, D.C.

2

Ten Years of Transition in Central Europe and the Former Soviet Union: The Good News and the Not-So-Good News

Johannes F. Linn

The transition in Central Europe and the former Soviet Union can alternatively be viewed as a great success or a dismal failure. In fact, the picture is very differentiated, depending on the aspects of the transition process and on the countries under consideration. This chapter attempts to provide a broad overview of the good news and not-so-good news of transition in the region after ten years. It is structured in three sections. The first section looks at the broad aggregate economic, social, and institutional trends. The second explores country-specific experiences in key countries and groups of countries. The final section draws some overall conclusions relevant for policy and reform in the future. The chapter is exploratory and as such is intended to provide a basis for discussion and research.

Aggregate Trends

Looking at Central Europe and the former Soviet Union in aggregate, the good news is that progress has been made toward macroeconomic stabilization. Median inflation rates dropped from three-digit levels in the first half of the 1990s to the teens and below in the late 1990s (table 2.1). The median fiscal balance, after having reached some 7 percent of GDP in the early 1990s, had stabilized at about 3 percent of GDP in the late 1990s (table 2.2). Foreign direct investment grew from low levels of barely over $3 billion to about $20 billion over the same period (table 2.3).

The bad news is that the region lost about 25 percent in terms of real GDP in the period 1990–1999 (figure 2.1).[1] Only for two years (1997 and 1999) did GDP in the region grow (or is it projected to have grown) (figure 2.2 and table 2.4). Unemployment rose rapidly from near zero in 1989 to an average of over 10 percent in the mid-

Table 2.1
Annual inflation in Europe and Central Asia (change in period-average consumer price index, in percent)

	1990	1991	1992	1993	1994	1995	1996	1997	1998	1999a
ECA Region[b]	10	92	678	355	137	33	24	14	11	9
Central Europe and Baltic States[b]	16	120	211	85	36	19	15	10	9	7
Albania	0	36	226	85	23	8	13	33	22	7
Bosnia	—	—	—	—	—	7	-8	11	3	3
Bulgaria	64	239	83	73	96	63	123	1,082	22	7
Croatia[c]	—	123	664	1,517	98	2	4	4	6	4
Czech Republic	10	57	11	21	10	9	9	8	11	5
Estonia	23	211	1,069	89	48	29	23	11	11	6
Hungary	29	35	23	23	19	28	24	18	14	9
Latvia	11	172	959	109	36	25	18	8	5	3
Lithuania	16	224	1,163	291	72	40	25	9	5	3
FYR Macedonia	—	—	1,975	355	55	9	-1	3	2	—
Poland	586	70	43	35	32	28	20	15	12	7
Romania	5	161	211	255	137	32	39	155	41	35
Slovak Republic	10	61	10	23	13	10	7	6	7	10
Slovenia	550	118	201	32	21	13	10	8	8	8
Community of Independent States[b]	5	89	1,109	1,222	1,498	247	43	17	18	20
Armenia	10	80	678	3,732	5,273	177	19	14	9	9
Azerbaijan	8	83	1,351	981	1,428	412	25	4	-1	3
Belarus	5	94	970	1,188	2,221	709	53	64	73	150

Georgia	3	79	637	3,125	15,607	163	39	7	4	20
Kazakhstan	19	87	1,623	1,256	1,158	35	39	17	7	6
Kyrgyz Republic	5	114	1,007	782	228	52	31	25	10	15
Moldova	15	136	1,780	2,707	2,405	24	15	11	18	35
Russia	6	93	1,354	895	305	189	47	15	28	100
Tajikistan	—	—	—	—	350	635	443	88	64	12
Turkmenistan	—	—	—	—	1,748	1,005	992	84	17	25
Ukraine	4	91	1,210	4,735	891	377	80	16	20	20
Uzbekistan	3	82	645	534	1,568	305	54	71	29	29
Turkey	60	66	70	66	106	94	79	86	84	65

Source: World Bank staff estimates, December 1998.

[a] Projected.

[b] Median of countries included.

[c] RPI.

Note: Missing data due to lack of information.

Table 2.2
Fiscal balances in Europe and Central Asia (as a share of GDP, in percent)

	1990	1991	1992	1993	1994	1995	1996	1997	1998	1999[a]
ECA Region[b]	0.8	-4.6	-7.2	-7.0	-6.1	-3.7	-4.2	-2.8	-3.2	-3.0
Central Europe and Baltic States[b]	0.5	-4.6	-4.9	-3.4	-2.9	-2.8	-1.7	-1.7	-2.6	-2.6
Albania	-3.7	-43.7	-20.3	-14.5	-12.9	-10.4	-12.1	-12.6	-10.4	-13.6
Bosnia	—	—	—	—	—	-7.0	-27.0	-25.0	-20.0	-16.0
Bulgaria	-9.1	-8.2	-7.2	-10.9	-6.4	-5.2	-15.4	2.1	2.5	-1.1
Croatia[c]	—	-4.6	-3.4	-1.5	1.7	-0.7	-0.4	-1.1	0.9	-2.1
Czech Republic	—	—	-1.0	1.4	0.5	-0.7	-1.0	-1.7	-2.1	-2.6
Estonia	—	—	—	-0.7	1.3	0.4	-1.9	2.0	-0.2	-1.5
Hungary	0.5	-2.1	-5.4	-6.6	-7.5	-3.1	0.8	-1.8	-4.0	-3.8
Latvia	—	—	—	0.6	-4.0	-2.9	-1.2	1.7	0.0	-2.8
Lithuania	—	—	—	-5.5	-5.0	-4.7	-4.5	-1.8	-5.9	-3.5
FYR Macedonia	—	—	—	-13.8	-2.9	-1.2	-0.4	-0.4	-1.7	—
Poland	3.7	-6.7	-4.9	-3.4	-3.2	-3.3	-3.6	-3.3	-3.0	-2.5
Romania	1.2	3.2	-4.6	-0.4	-1.9	-2.7	-4.1	-3.9	-3.3	-2.1
Slovak Republic	—	—	-11.9	-7.0	-1.3	0.2	-1.4	-4.5	-5.5	-3.0
Slovenia	—	2.6	0.2	0.3	-0.2	0.0	0.3	-1.1	-1.2	-0.7
Community of Independent States[b]	1.8	-3.4	-15.8	-11.1	-8.9	-5.5	-5.2	-4.1	-3.8	-3.3
Armenia	—	-1.8	-8.1	-56.1	-16.4	-9.0	-8.6	-5.5	-5.5	-6.1
Azerbaijan	-5.5	-5.0	-4.1	-14.0	-16.4	-4.1	-4.3	-1.7	-4.5	-3.5
Belarus	—	—	-2.0	-5.6	-3.6	-2.8	-2.0	-2.3	-1.1	-1.8

Georgia	—	—	—	-26.2	-16.5	-5.2	-4.5	-4.6	-4.5	-2.1
Kazakhstan	—	-9.0	-6.9	-0.7	-6.5	-3.2	-3.2	-3.7	-3.7	-4.8
Kyrgyz Republic	—	4.0	-17.4	-13.5	-7.7	-17.3	-9.5	-9.0	-8.1	-6.5
Moldova	2.8	0.0	-27.3	-8.4	-9.7	-5.7	-6.3	-6.2	-2.9	-2.6
Russia	—	—	-21.8	-8.7	-11.3	-5.8	-8.7	-7.6	-7.9	-7.6
Tajikistan	—	—	-30.3	-24.8	-10.2	-11.2	-5.8	-3.3	-3.8	3.0
Turkmenistan	1.8	2.5	—	-0.4	-2.0	-3.0	-1.0	0.0	-3.0	-3.0
Ukraine	—	-13.8	-14.3	-11.8	-8.2	-7.0	-4.4	-6.7	-2.7	-1.0
Uzbekistan	—	-4.9	-18.5	-10.4	-6.1	-4.1	-7.3	-2.1	-3.0	-5.4
Turkey	-7.5	-9.6	-10.7	-12.4	-7.7	-4.8	-9.0	-8.7	-10.2	-8.7

Source: World Bank staff estimates, December 1998.
[a] Projected.
[b] Median of countries included.
[c] State budget, cash deficit.
Note: Missing data due to lack of information.

Table 2.3
Foreign direct investment in Europe and Central Asia (in millions of U.S. dollars)

	1991	1992	1993	1994	1995	1996	1997	1998	1999
ECA Region	3,100	5,096	7,073	6,341	14,360	13,923	20,016	20,282	17,557
Central Europe and Baltic States	2,392	3,309	4,338	3,901	9,644	8,085	9,331	13,684	12,546
Albania	—	32	45	65	89	97	42	45	43
Bosnia	—	—	—	—	0	0	0	100	150
Bulgaria	56	42	55	105	98	138	491	364	300
Croatia	—	13	78	106	96	513	231	763	550
Czech Republic	600	1,103	654	749	2,526	1,388	1,275	2,480	1,915
Estonia	—	56	154	212	199	110	130	132	147
Hungary	1,462	1,479	2,350	1,146	4,453	1,987	1,653	1,450	1,500
Latvia	—	—	51	279	245	379	508	220	339
Lithuania	76	10	30	31	73	152	355	926	600
FYR Macedonia	—	—	—	24	10	11	16	126	—
Poland	117	284	580	542	1,134	2,741	3,041	4,500	5,000
Romania	40	77	94	341	417	263	1,224	2,040	1,300
Slovak Republic	—	100	134	170	134	129	70	382	499
Slovenia	41	113	112	131	171	178	295	157	203
Community of Independent States	−75	1,008	2,114	1,881	3,944	5,226	10,131	6,057	4,261
Armenia	—	—	—	3	19	18	51	138	100
Azerbaijan	—	—	60	20	275	601	1,047	1,154	926
Belarus	—	—	18	11	15	73	198	142	120
Georgia	—	—	1	8	6	54	236	221	95

Kazakhstan	—	100	473	820	964	1,137	1,320	1,132	1,100
Kyrgyz Republic	—	—	10	38	96	47	83	52	45
Moldova	25	17	14	18	73	53	79	80	120
Russia	-100	700	1,211	637	2,017	2,478	6,241	2,182	900
Tajikistan	—	—	0	0	13	20	20	12	29
Turkmenistan	—	11	80	103	233	129	108	—	—
Ukraine	—	170	200	151	257	526	581	718	600
Uzbekistan	—	9	48	73	-24	90	167	226	226
Turkey	783	779	622	559	772	612	554	541	750

Sources: World Bank staff estimates, December 1998.
Note: Missing data due to lack of information.

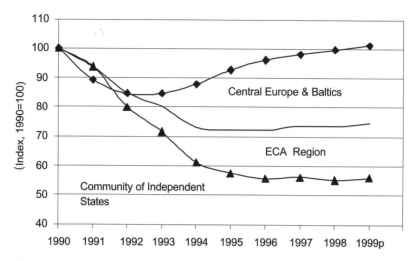

Figure 2.1
Real GDP

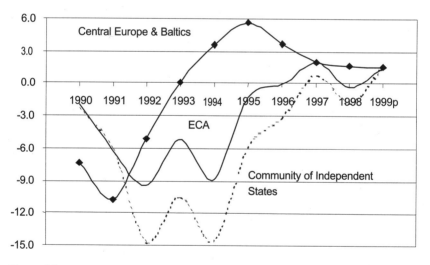

Figure 2.2
Real GDP growth

and late 1990s (Wyplosz 1999, figure 2.4). At the same time, median current account deficits have increased over the decade, reaching 6–8 percent of GDP during the second half of the 1990s (table 2.5). This reflects, on the one hand, an increased access to capital inflows, including foreign direct investment, but on the other, unsustainability of external accounts in some countries.

The aggregate numbers hide substantial differences across countries. Perhaps the most significant difference is between the countries of Central Europe and the Baltics (CEB) and those of the Commonwealth of Independent States (CIS). For CEB, average GDP growth rates turned positive in 1993 and have remained so since (figure 2.2 and table 2.4). As a result, real GDP in CEB in 1999 returned to about the level of 1990, and continued growth will soon raise GDP levels in the region above those in existence prior to the onset of the transition. For the CIS, only one year of positive growth (1997) and a cumulative decline in real GDP of about 45 percent since 1990 reflects the depth of the recession experienced in this part of the region (figure 2.1). As a result of this dramatic difference in growth performance, the relative size of the GDP of countries of CEB and of the GDP of the CIS has undergone a striking reversal: In 1990 the GDP of the CIS was about three times that of CEB; in 1999, the GDP of the CIS is projected to have been only two-thirds of that of CEB (table 2.6). And whereas in 1990 the nominal GDP of Russia was more than six times that of Poland, which in turn equaled that of Ukraine, by 1999 Russia's nominal GDP hardly exceeded that of Poland, which in turn is now four-and-a-half times that of Ukraine.[2]

The differences in other areas of macroeconomic performance between CEB and the CIS appear less striking: median inflation, fiscal balances, and current account deficits were broadly comparable in the second half of the 1990s across these two subregions, although inflation rates and fiscal imbalances tended to be somewhat higher in the CIS. The difference in economic performance across the two subregions therefore appears to result less from major differences in the macroeconomic area than from differences in the quality of the fiscal adjustment underlying those macroeconomic balances (sustainability, efficiency, etc.), in the structure of their economies, and in the quality of their policies and institutions. This hypothesis is broadly consistent with the pattern of foreign direct investment in the two subregions. Foreign direct investment was consistently much higher in CEB than in the CIS (except in 1997, which saw a major, but

Table 2.4
GDP growth in Europe and Central Asia (in percentage change)

	1990	1991	1992	1993	1994	1995	1996	1997	1998	1999[a]
ECA Region[b]	-2.0	-6.3	-9.5	-5.3	-8.9	-1.2	0.0	2.0	-0.3	1.5
Central Europe and Baltic States[b]	-7.4	-10.8	-5.1	0.2	3.6	5.6	3.7	2.0	1.6	1.6
Albania	-10.0	-27.7	-7.2	9.6	9.4	8.9	8.2	-7.0	8.0	8.0
Bosnia	—	—	—	—	—	33.0	69.1	29.5	17.7	15.4
Bulgaria	-9.1	-11.7	-7.3	-1.5	1.8	2.1	-10.9	-6.9	3.5	1.5
Croatia	-5.4	-21.1	-11.7	-8.0	5.9	6.8	6.0	6.5	2.7	-1.0
Czech Republic	-1.2	-14.2	-6.4	0.6	2.7	6.4	3.8	0.3	-2.3	-1.0
Estonia	-8.1	-11.0	-25.8	-8.5	-2.7	4.3	4.0	11.4	4.3	2.0
Hungary	-3.5	-11.9	-3.1	-0.6	2.9	1.5	1.3	4.6	5.1	4.0
Latvia	-3.5	-8.0	-35.0	-16.0	0.6	-0.8	3.3	8.6	3.6	0.5
Lithuania	-6.9	-5.7	-21.3	-16.2	-9.8	3.3	4.7	7.3	5.1	0.3
FYR Macedonia	—	—	—	-9.4	-1.7	-1.2	0.8	1.5	2.9	—
Poland	-11.6	-7.0	2.6	3.8	5.2	7.0	6.1	6.9	4.8	3.5
Romania	-5.6	-12.9	-8.8	1.5	3.9	6.9	4.1	-6.6	-7.3	-2.0
Slovak Republic	-2.5	-14.6	-6.5	-3.7	4.9	6.8	6.6	6.5	4.4	2.0
Slovenia	-4.7	-8.1	-5.4	2.8	5.3	4.1	3.5	4.6	3.9	3.5
Community of Independent States[b]	-2.4	-6.2	-14.7	-10.5	-14.7	-5.9	-3.1	0.8	-1.7	1.5
Armenia	-8.5	-8.8	-52.3	-15.0	5.4	6.9	5.8	3.1	6.9	4.5
Azerbaijan	-12.0	-0.7	-22.7	-23.1	-19.7	-11.8	1.3	5.8	9.6	3.7
Belarus	-1.9	-1.2	-9.6	-7.6	-12.6	-10.4	2.8	11.4	8.3	1.0
Georgia	-11.1	-28.1	-43.4	-39.4	-11.4	2.4	10.5	10.7	2.9	2.0

Kazakhstan	-1.1	-11.8	-13.0	-12.9	-18.0	-8.2	0.5	1.7	-2.5	-1.5
Kyrgyz Republic	3.2	-5.0	-19.0	-16.0	-20.0	-5.4	5.6	9.9	1.8	1.0
Moldova	-2.4	-16.0	-29.1	-1.2	-31.2	-1.4	-1.8	1.3	-8.6	-5.0
Russia	-3.6	-5.0	-14.5	-8.7	-12.6	-4.1	-3.4	0.9	-4.6	2.0
Tajikistan	-0.6	-8.7	-28.9	-11.1	-21.4	-12.5	-4.4	1.7	5.3	5.5
Turkmenistan	1.5	-5.0	-5.0	-10.0	-19.0	-8.2	-8.0	-26.0	5.0	19.0
Ukraine	-0.9	-8.7	-9.9	-14.2	-22.9	-12.2	-10.0	-3.0	-1.7	-1.5
Uzbekistan	4.3	-0.9	-9.5	-2.3	-4.2	-0.9	1.6	2.4	3.4	3.0
Turkey	9.3	0.9	6.0	8.0	-5.5	7.2	7.0	7.5	2.8	1.5

Source: World Bank staff estimates, December 1998.
[a] Projected.
[b] Population-weighted averages. Excludes Bosnia.
Note: Missing data due to lack of information.

Table 2.5
Current account balances in Europe and Central Asia (as a share of GDP, in percent)

	1990	1991	1992	1993	1994	1995	1996	1997	1998	1999[a]
ECA Region[b]	0.4	-2.5	-1.0	-3.3	-2.2	-4.4	-7.1	-6.1	-7.8	-5.5
Central Europe and Baltic States[b]	-1.9	-4.5	0.0	-1.6	-1.7	-5.0	-7.7	-6.8	-7.8	-5.8
Albania	-5.8	-25.7	-62.3	-29.7	-14.3	-7.5	-9.2	-12.1	-6.1	-11.4
Bosnia	—	—	—	—	—	-10.3	-27.3	-32.3	-24.4	-19.5
Bulgaria	-5.9	-7.2	-9.3	-12.8	-2.1	-1.0	-0.8	4.1	-2.2	-2.6
Croatia	—	-10.1	5.3	0.9	0.7	-9.5	-7.6	-12.5	-7.6	-5.8
Czech Republic	—	—	-1.7	2.2	-0.1	-2.9	-8.7	-6.0	-1.5	-1.3
Estonia	—	—	-1.0	1.3	-7.1	-4.4	-9.1	-12.0	-8.7	-8.0
Hungary	1.0	0.8	0.9	-9.0	-9.5	-5.6	-3.7	-2.1	-4.8	-5.0
Latvia	—	—	15.2	19.7	5.5	-0.4	-5.5	-6.1	-11.0	-9.0
Lithuania	—	—	5.4	-3.1	-2.1	-10.2	-9.2	-10.2	-12.1	-11.4
FYR Macedonia	—	—	—	—	-9.4	-5.7	-6.5	-7.4	-8.4	—
Poland	1.1	-1.0	-0.3	-0.1	2.3	3.3	-1.0	-3.1	-4.5	-5.3
Romania	-4.7	-4.5	-7.5	-4.7	-1.7	-5.6	-7.8	-6.7	-7.9	-6.5
Slovak Republic	—	—	0.4	-5.0	4.8	2.3	-11.1	-6.9	-9.7	-4.5
Slovenia	3.0	1.5	7.4	1.5	3.8	-0.1	0.2	0.2	0.0	-0.2
Community of Independent States[b]	0.4	2.8	-4.6	-4.9	-5.1	-4.0	-6.5	-5.5	-7.8	-6.1
Armenia (excluding grants)	—	—	-84.1	-54.6	-35.5	-16.9	-15.0	-15.8	-17.3	-15.9
Azerbaijan	—	9.8	—	-2.8	-15.8	-10.1	-18.2	-23.7	-33.1	-28.0
Belarus	—	—	—	-11.9	-9.1	-4.3	-3.7	-5.9	-7.1	-8.3
Georgia (excluding grants)	—	—	-21.0	-11.0	-22.3	-7.5	-6.0	-7.6	-8.4	-5.6

Kazakhstan	—	—	-0.4	-1.8	-6.0	-2.7	-3.6	-4.1	-5.6	-5.0
Kyrgyz Republic	—	—	-4.6	-3.4	-3.3	-7.0	-15.5	-6.2	-15.1	-11.3
Moldova	—	—	-1.4	-6.3	-4.2	-3.7	-9.1	-14.9	-20.1	-20.6
Russia	0.4	2.8	0.1	0.7	2.7	1.9	2.1	0.6	0.3	8.9
Tajikistan	—	—	-18.0	-31.0	-21.0	-15.0	-7.0	-5.0	-10.2	-6.6
Turkmenistan	—	—	—	18.5	8.0	1.3	0.5	-4.7	-6.8	-4.0
Ukraine	—	-3.9	-0.7	-1.2	-2.2	-2.3	-2.7	-2.2	-3.1	-3.1
Uzbekistan[c]	—	—	-11.8	-8.4	0.5	-0.2	-7.2	-4.0	-1.4	-2.0
Turkey	—	0.2	-0.6	-3.5	2.0	-1.4	-2.6	-2.5	0.0	-1.8

Source: World Bank staff estimates, December 1998.
[a] Projected.
[b] Median of countries included.
[c] Figures for 1995 and 1996 include estimate of nonregistered trade surplus.
Note: Missing data due to lack of information.

Table 2.6
GDP (in millions of current U.S. dollars)

	1991	1992	1993	1994	1995	1996	1997	1998[a]	1999[b]
ECA Region	1,012,861	1,007,892	969,167	864,884	975,269	1,092,588	1,128,245	968,891	847,535
Central Europe and Baltic States	233,126	233,161	244,075	272,402	338,178	363,498	359,515	379,375	377,276
Albania	1,128	1,037	1,216	1,988	2,480	2,753	2,335	3,112	3,829
Bosnia	—	—	—	—	1,867	2,741	3,423	4,082	4,853
Bulgaria	10,944	10,352	10,831	9,787	13,100	9,830	10,085	12,489	14,832
Croatia	18,180	10,241	10,870	14,591	18,811	19,872	19,947	21,320	19,862
Czech Republic	24,292	27,951	31,185	39,882	50,894	56,554	52,035	55,100	54,700
Estonia	6,020	4,226	4,004	4,028	4,789	4,358	4,821	5,561	6,013
Hungary	33,445	37,249	38,610	41,491	44,662	45,176	45,725	47,747	49,175
Latvia	11,025	6,358	5,315	5,461	4,904	5,134	5,638	6,394	6,948
Lithuania	—	1,831	2,662	4,227	6,026	7,892	9,585	10,685	11,468
FYR Macedonia	2,116	1,861	2,768	3,320	4,413	4,391	3,690	3,457	—
Poland	73,631	82,702	84,701	91,233	118,181	134,111	132,500	130,528	135,097
Romania	28,847	25,090	27,252	28,242	31,903	33,079	32,070	38,100	31,000
Slovak Republic	10,837	11,742	11,984	13,766	17,401	18,752	19,461	21,200	19,200
Slovenia	12,660	12,521	12,678	14,387	18,746	18,853	18,201	19,600	20,300
Community of Independent States	627,733	612,967	543,473	462,127	465,019	544,875	578,485	392,397	264,167
Armenia	3,065	1,132	1,065	1,145	1,276	1,631	1,751	1,964	2,127
Azerbaijan	9,724	5,851	4,738	3,865	3,751	3,595	3,852	4,127	4,106
Belarus	25,541	23,089	23,103	20,095	18,192	18,564	20,744	22,559	22,785
Georgia	—	5,782	4,188	3,570	2,801	4,519	5,093	4,973	4,159

Kazakhstan	31,765	27,409	24,956	19,461	19,525	20,759	22,336	22,179	15,688
Kyrgyz Republic	2,818	2,169	2,587	2,541	3,336	2,743	2,243	1,704	1,304
Moldova	4,047	2,823	4,463	2,709	3,037	1,624	1,808	1,489	1,223
Russia	466,167	441,988	393,370	325,904	347,471	429,264	443,040	275,648	166,993
Tajikistan	4,209	2,984	2,933	2,163	2,146	2,030	1,087	1,290	1,178
Turkmenistan	5,547	6,246	5,708	4,374	4,424	2,060	2,392	—	—
Ukraine	74,850	91,505	71,285	52,292	49,061	44,558	59,756	42,400	30,400
Uzbekistan	—	1,989	5,076	24,007	10,000	13,530	14,383	14,065	14,205
	152,002	161,763	181,619	130,355	172,071	184,215	190,246	197,120	206,092
Turkey									

Source: World Bank staff estimates, December 1998.
[a] Preliminary data.
[b] Projected data.
Note: Missing data due to lack of information.

temporary, expansion of foreign direct investment in Russia). In 1998 and 1999 foreign direct investment in CEB exceeded that in the CIS by two to three times (table 2.3). Comparative indicators of structural and institutional performance confirm the notion that the difference in growth performance between the two subregions is grounded in substantial differences in structural and institutional parameters and reforms. The European Bank for Reconstruction and Development's (EBRD's) estimates show that countries in the CIS have levels of structural distortion substantially higher than those of the countries in CEB (EBRD 1998, 29). Also, estimates by the World Bank of differences in public-sector governance and corruption show that the countries of the CIS have particularly weak public institutions and high levels of corruption, whereas the countries of CEB tend to perform better in these areas (World Bank 1997, 35). Some of these differences are certainly due to stronger and more persistent efforts of reform in many of the countries of CEB, but they are likely also to be due to the more favorable starting positions of these countries relative to those of the CIS: The length and depth of socialist, centrally planned rule tended to be less in CEB, and the distortions in economic structure were less severe also as regards the wide geographic dispersion of key industries and heavy reliance on military production and the disruption of public institutions associated with the breakup of the Soviet Union. The legacy of history certainly matters.

A key question is whether we can also find a link between reform policies and growth given (i.e., after accounting for differences in) the initial institutional and economic structure of countries. Some empirical evidence shows such a link even within these two groups of countries (CEB and CIS) (Selowsky and Martin 1997). Moreover, this evidence shows that growth responds with a longer lag in the CIS countries, including some negative impacts during the first few years of the transition. This could be consistent with the more adverse initial conditions in the CIS countries discussed earlier, that is, a higher share of negative value added and military output; a wider dispersion of industries, impairing labor mobility; and so on.

A key lesson of macroeconomic management has been confirmed in the transition economies of CEB and the CIS: A sustained combination of tight monetary and loose fiscal policies and fixed exchange rates is a prescription for macroeconomic stagnation and eventual financial crisis. A number of countries, among them Russia and Ukraine, managed to bring down inflation through tight monetary policies and fixed exchange rates in the mid-1990s but failed to establish a reasonable fiscal balance. The resulting macroeconomic stability proved more apparent than real: Persistently loose fiscal management combined with tight monetary policy resulted in high interest rates and overvalued exchange rates and hence the stagnation of the real economy, of exports, and of private investment and contributed to a weak financial sector and the emergence of a foreign debt trap, making these countries very vulnerable to external shocks and financial crises.

Along with the economic changes that have accompanied transition in Central Europe and the former Soviet Union has come a major and often neglected dramatic deterioration in the social conditions of the population. One of the great achievements of the socialist system was the great improvement in and the wide access to social services (education and health) and to safety nets. As a result, the incidence of poverty in the region was low, and the social indicators at the onset of transition were generally very good. Inequality and the incidence of poverty have since increased throughout the region and especially in the CIS. Income distribution and poverty data are weak for most countries, but the divergences are clearly substantial. For example, absolute poverty (as measured by the share of population living on less than two dollars per day) is as high as 80 percent in Moldova but less than 10 percent in Hungary. Social indicators (especially life expectancy) have also deteriorated substantially in many countries of the CIS, whereas they have tended to remain steady in CEB.

More generally, many areas, especially in the CIS, have suffered severe social dislocations. Aside from rising un- and underemployment, interregional inequities have been on the increase, especially in and around one-company towns, which were prevalent for major industries in remote areas of the former Soviet Union, as well as in rural areas, where the pervasive decline of agricultural production and nonfarm rural employment opportunities has resulted in the rise of a new class of rural landless poor. Related to these social trends, both as a cause and a result, have been increasing ethnic and religious tensions in the region, which had previously been forcibly submerged under the veneer of socialist integration.

In the environmental area, transition has brought some significant benefits. The widespread disregard of environmental damages and costs associated with the heavy industrial and energy-intensive development in the region before 1990 and the lack of incentives for environmental protection and energy conservation (in industry, agriculture, housing, and transportation) had led to serious declines in environmental quality throughout the region, especially in some areas of the former Soviet Union. These declines in environmental quality had led in turn to a significant incidence of environmentally related health problems in the region, which were threatening the sustainability of achievements in terms of improved indicators of health and life expectancy. Environmental conditions in many areas began to improve after 1990 for two important reasons: First, the decline in economic activity, particularly in the heavily polluting industries, resulted in reductions in levels of air and water pollution. Second, improved policies and institutions began to lead to better incentives through market-determined prices and more effective regulation. Of course, in many countries there are still major weaknesses in these areas, with reforms and institutional capacity still far from fully developed.

Country-Specific Experiences

It is important to step beyond the broad trends for the region and two subregions that we have explored so far to look briefly at the experiences of individual countries and country groups within the region and subregions. It is notable that whereas CEB countries grew each year between 1993 and 1999 at average annual rates of about 2.5 percent, four out of the fourteen CEB countries experienced at least one year of negative growth during 1997–1999. Conversely, among the CIS countries, which overall were characterized by negative growth trends throughout the 1990s, seven of twelve countries experienced three or more years of uninterrupted growth during the second half of the 1990s (table 2.4). But the differences among the countries in these two regions extend much beyond their differing growth experiences.

Central Europe and the Baltics

In CEB it is useful to consider the following five groups of countries:

1. Countries that keep growing at steady rates, without major fluctuations and little affected by the recent external shocks of the inter-

national financial crisis (Poland, Hungary, and Slovenia): These are countries with sound macroeconomic (especially fiscal) policies and sustainable external balances, supported by high inflows of direct foreign investment. They also carried out substantial structural reforms and significant improvements in legal and institutional capacity during the 1990s. Of course, these countries still face challenges of structural, social, and environmental reform (e.g., restructuring of declining industries and of uncompetitive agricultural sectors, pension and health-sector reforms, meeting the environmental standards of the European Union).

2. Countries that have good policies but are small and still strongly linked to the CIS and hence experience stronger fluctuations in growth, current account deficits, and export performance (Estonia, Latvia, Lithuania): These countries have developed a solid growth record based on good reforms but experience relatively high and volatile current account deficits as a result of large fluctuations in foreign direct investment and large borrowings from the private sector. A main challenge for these countries is to strengthen the regulatory framework in the financial sector and to ensure that they manage their external vulnerability by maintaining fiscal prudence, sound financial systems, and strong international competitiveness.

3. Countries where spurts of growth have taken place intermittently because of large amounts of foreign direct investment, remittances, tourism, and better utilization of existing capacity, but where insufficient financial discipline and soft budget constraints in the enterprise and banking sectors have generated excessive borrowing abroad, quasi-fiscal contingent liabilities, interenterprise arrears, and banking sectors with a very high share of bad debts (Bulgaria, Croatia, Czech Republic, Romania, Slovak Republic): Although these countries remain relatively vulnerable to external shocks and internal economic and political dislocations, the good news is that they have been (Bulgaria) or are now (the other four countries) confronting these problems through strong reductions in quasi-fiscal expenditures, limiting external borrowing by state banks and public enterprises, and targeted restructuring of their banks and public enterprises. Some of these countries (Bulgaria, Croatia, and Romania) are also significantly affected by the disruption in trade, tourism, and foreign investment resulting from the Kosovo crisis.

4. Countries in the Balkans that were emerging from civil strife after the breakup of the former Yugoslavia but are now severely affected by the impact of the Kosovo crisis (Albania, Bosnia and Herzegovina, and FYR Macedonia): These countries experienced strong economic recoveries in the second half of the 1990s after years of economic and social crisis but in 1999 were set back economically because of the severe impact of the refugee influx and trade disruption related to the Kosovo crisis. This crisis has demonstrated that an overall settlement of the regional political situation, including that in the Federal Republic of Yugoslavia, is a prerequisite for long-term economic and social recovery and stability in Southeast Europe. The Southeast Europe Stability Pact concluded in the summer of 1999 may provide a basis for political stability in the region in the future.

5. Countries that are on the path to EU accession: Cutting across the above taxonomy of countries are the ten EU accession countries, all of which face special challenges and opportunities associated with the prospects for accession. They need to go through major efforts to strengthen their policies and institutions and need to carry out major investments (e.g., in the environmental area) to bring their economies in line with EU requirements (*acquis communautaire*). At the same time, the accession process reinforces their incentives to keep reforms on track, provides domestic and foreign private investors with the confidence that these countries are, or are becoming, more secure places for investments, and will result in substantial flows of concessional financial resources from the EU.

CIS Countries

The CIS countries also form a heterogeneous group, although united by a common history of communist and precommunist integration in the Soviet Union and, before that, the Czarist Russian Empire. Together they experienced over seventy years of uninterrupted socialist economic and political control, an absence of democratic and pluralist institutions and civil society, and a very rigid and distorting allocation of resources, across sectors, geographically and socially. The current heterogeneity among the countries concerned is due to many factors: differences in natural resource endowment, in size and internal decentralization, in the prevalence of ethnic and religious fragmentation, in the extent of economic, institutional, and political development, in differing progress with market-oriented reforms, and in the degree of continued dependence in their economic relations on Russia. Russia's impact on its neighbors has gradually declined, as newly independent countries of the former Soviet Union have increasingly reoriented their economic structures away from trade with Russia and each other and toward the world economy and as flows of finance (budgetary grants and state enterprise investments) between the CIS countries have dried up. Nonetheless, Russia still represents a dominant economic force in the CIS, as the heavy impact of Russia's economic crisis in 1998 has demonstrated. Hence, it is appropriate to look first at the developments in Russia.

Russia

Russia experienced negative growth throughout the 1990s, with the exception of a small positive growth rate in 1997, and it has seen a significant increase in poverty (some 40 percent of Russians are now characterized as poor, according to World Bank estimates). There is a lively debate about the reasons for Russia's poor performance and recent crisis (e.g., Aslund 1999; Stiglitz 1999). Without trying to resolve this debate or even to summarize it, the main factors certainly include the legacy of the Soviet era (mentioned above); internal political fragmentation across political factions and regions; external shocks (low energy and other commodity prices, the international financial crisis following the East Asian collapse); and most importantly a lack of effective domestic reforms, including the persistence of high fiscal deficits, incomplete structural reforms, lack of attention to social needs, weak governance and pervasive corruption, and a lack of consistent, sustained government action at all levels of government (national, subnational, local). Aside from the question of where Russia is heading now and what the international community can do to help, perhaps the most interesting question is whether without the East Asian financial crisis in 1997 and the resulting commodity price collapse and without the domestic political upheavals of 1998 the Russian crisis of August 1998 could have been avoided.

There were a number of important positive trends in Russia in mid-1997:

• The economy was bottoming out, with positive growth in 1997 (table 2.4).

• The fiscal situation improved after July 1997 (figure 2.3).

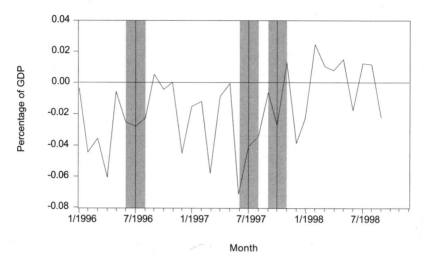

Figure 2.3
Federal budget primary balance

• Foreign reserves increased through July 1997 (figure 2.4).

• Domestic interest rates and spreads on Eurobonds declined through October 1997 (figures 2.5 and 2.6).

Without a fully developed counterfactual model, it is not possible to demonstrate that these trends were sustainable in the absence of the external shock and the internal political upheaval (removal of the prime minister in April 1998) and if sustained would have been sufficient to prevent a crisis from occurring. The point to be made here, however, is that there is at least a good chance that without these shocks Russia might have not only avoided a crash but also entered a virtuous cycle, in which sustained growth and continued economic reforms could have reinforced each other. If this is correct, the bad news is that the external and internal shocks interacted to throw Russia off a potentially sustainable path of recovery and reform, because of still pervasive vulnerabilities.

The good news, on the other hand, is that Russia had made substantial progress by 1997 and that its economic fate in 1997–1999 was not inextricably sealed. At this point, where Russia's economic and political future is at best uncertain, it is perhaps reassuring that a path of recovery appeared feasible so recently and might again appear, particularly if reasonably stable and supportive external and

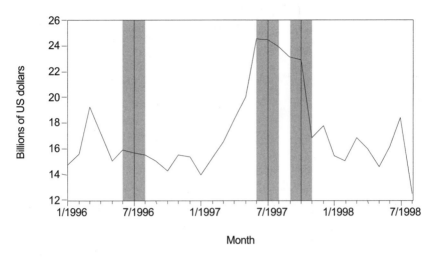

Figure 2.4
Gross international reserves

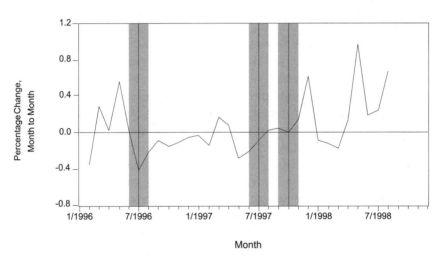

Figure 2.5
GKO secondary market yields

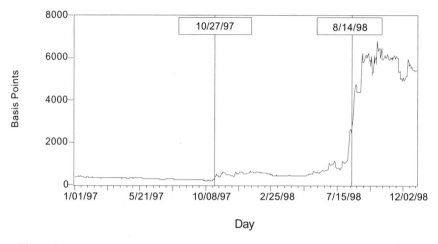

Figure 2.6
Daily spreads on Russian Eurobond, January 1, 1997–December 31, 1998

internal conditions were to prevail. Indeed, Russia weathered the crisis better than might have been expected: Inflation has moderated because of restrained monetary policy, and output is expanding (2 percent growth likely for 1999) because of improved prices on key commodities and because of strong export growth and import substitution resulting from devaluation of the exchange rate. In this connection, it is important to remember that savings, either international or domestic, are not the constraint to increasing investment and private-sector activity in Russia. Foreign direct investment remains low in Russia (the peak US $6 billion achieved in 1997 is still one-third the level in Brazil), given its natural endowment and human capital. Domestic savings prior to the crisis were a healthy 24 percent of GDP. But capital flight remains high: about $1 billion per month. Improving the environment for investment, including that by Russia's own citizens, remains the major constraint to increasing investment in Russia, and this constraint can be reduced or eliminated only by improving domestic policies and institutions.

Ukraine
In many ways the Ukraine experience resembles on the surface that of Russia, with a similar, albeit even more severe multiyear recession and similar external and domestic factors explaining its protracted difficulties. Of course, there are differences, including the fact that

Ukraine does not have the energy resources of Russia and hence is conversely affected by energy price changes; Ukraine suffered more from the Russia crisis than from the East Asian crisis; Ukraine had made less progress by 1997 with structural reforms than had Russia, although it, too, was making some progress at the time. Like Russia it paid insufficient attention to the social impacts of the crisis, did much to hinder the development of its tremendous agricultural potential, threw up many hurdles to foreign and domestic private investments, and was cursed with a dysfunctional public sector. Like Russia, there was too little consensus and ownership of the reform agenda in key public and civic institutions, and the decentralized subnational power centers in the regions were able to undermine the reform process at every corner. Like Russia's economy in 1997, Ukraine's was poised to bottom out in 1998, although its chances for a sustained recovery were slim in the absence of significant structural reforms. The good news is that, in contrast to Russia, Ukraine was able to avoid a financial meltdown in 1998 by a shrewd handling of its macroeconomic policies and debt management and by keeping a slow reform process on track that permitted continued assistance from international financial institutions. The chances for a sustained recovery now hang in the balance and depend much on whether, after the presidential elections late in 1999, a strong, reform-oriented political consensus can be built.

Other CIS Countries
It is again useful to consider the remaining CIS countries in several groups:

1. Resource-rich countries with a reasonable history of reform who are now hit by the fallout from the Russia crisis and by the gyrations in the world energy prices (Azerbaijan, Kazakhstan): Having struggled with the transition process but having advanced macroeconomic stabilization and structural reforms (privatization, agricultural reforms, etc.) reasonably well so far, these two countries in the medium term will depend heavily on their ability to develop their substantial energy resources effectively and transport to them international markets, which will depend, among other things, on regional economic and political stability in the Central Asian and Caucasus regions and in Russia. Equally important will be the ability of both countries to manage the potential financial windfall from developing these en-

ergy resources, so that boom doesn't turn into bust, as has happened
to so many resource-rich countries. The development of effective,
transparent public institutions and governance will be key here.

2. Small, less well endowed, poor countries with good recent histories of reform but very fragile economies and finances and subject
to the fallout from the Russia crisis, troubled by domestic political
and ethnic strife, or both (Armenia, Georgia, Kyrgyz Republic, Moldova, Tajikistan): The good news from the transition experience of
these diverse countries has been that they managed in the last few
years of the 1990s to promote some significant reforms in the
economic and political sphere, despite many odds, and that, with the
exception of Moldova, they had managed to turn around their economies on an apparently sustained basis, with economic growth continuing for a number of successive years (table 2.4). The bad news is
that the Russia crisis hit all these countries hard because of their
continued significant dependence on economic relations with Russia
(trade, remittances, investments, etc.). Also, because of porous borders and tax evasion, these countries are collecting low tax revenues
relative to their social expenditures. The economic impact of the
Russian crisis and tougher-than-expected domestic policy adjustment
requirements in turn have made it more difficult to maintain the domestic political consensus around reforms and hence have slowed
the progress of reforms, which in turn has limited the amount of essential external financial support from the international community.
It is crucial that these countries reduce tax evasion, which is significant and must be forcefully addressed in order for these countries to
be able to maintain key social services. The key challenge for these
countries and for the international community now is to prevent a
vicious cycle of economic and political downward spiraling from
taking hold.

3. Countries that have deliberately followed a slow or nonreform
course in moving from the centrally planned, Soviet system to a
market-oriented approach (Belarus, Turkmenistan, Uzbekistan): These
countries represent something of a conundrum to the outside ob-
server. All three have deliberately chosen a course of very slow,
partial and limited structural reforms; hence they score lowest on the
EBRD's liberalization index (EBRD 1998, 26) and have benefited only
to a very limited extent from financial assistance by the international
community. Nonetheless, all three countries have shown some suc-

cess in avoiding the steep and prolonged cumulative decline in economic activity that has characterized many other countries in the CIS. In fact, Belarus managed to propel a growth spurt lasting at least three years (until the impact of the Russia crisis put an end to it, apparently) based on highly interventionist industrial policies that have preserved and utilized existing industrial capacity (through directed credit and direct allocation of foreign exchange), predominantly for exports to Russia. The key question for all three countries is whether this approach is sustainable as a basis for continued growth, for a gradual integration into the world economy, for a reduced dependence on Russia, and for the development of a flexible, modern economy, let along an open, pluralistic society. A deliberate and sustained reform effort, the broadening of the social consensus around such a path, and increased reliance on external and domestic private initiative and investment seems essential, however.

Conclusion: Good News and Not-So-Good News of the Transition Process

Perhaps the best place to start a summary of the implications of the ten years of transition is to recall how fundamental, far reaching, and deep has been the change in political, economic, social and institutional paradigms that most countries in Central Europe and the former Soviet Union have undertaken. Modern history offers no parallels, save perhaps the Soviet revolution in Russia and the introduction of the communist-socialist paradigm after World War I. Therefore, perhaps the best news so far of the ten years of transition is that it has proceeded overall in a relatively orderly fashion, compared to the potential downside scenarios one might have conjured up in the late 1980s and early 1990s as the breakup of the Eastern Bloc and of the Soviet Union became a reality. Certainly, if one sees the events in and around the former Yugoslavia in the wake of its breakup as a model of what might have occurred farther east, one must be grateful for the relatively peaceful and even orderly process of transformation that has occurred in the countries of Central Europe and the former Soviet Union.

Second in the good news department is the remarkable success of many of the Central European and the Baltic countries in stabilizing their economies and in returning them quickly to a market-oriented path, to the point where many have been able to place themselves on a path of sustained recovery and are now readying themselves for full integration into the European Union. The fact that many of these economies were able to withstand the international financial crisis following the collapse of East Asia and Russia is a remarkable testimony to the success and durability of market-oriented reforms in the Central European context.

The remarkable ability of some of the smaller, poorer countries of the region, particularly those in the Caucasus and Central Asia, to pursue determined political and economic reforms against many odds and, with such reforms, to revive their economies after the initial shock of the breakup of the Soviet economy is another highlight of the transition experience. On the downside remains, of course, the continuing fragility, both political and economic, of these countries, as demonstrated now in the wake of the crisis in Russia and its serious impact on the economies of these countries. Particularly troublesome is the potential linkage between economic and political fallout from the external shock, with the potential for disrupting the reform consensus and momentum in these countries, which in turn could derail their economic recovery and the scope for external support. Clearly, maintaining the positive and mutually reinforcing momentum in these countries along with external support will be a critical challenge.

The ability of the fragile countries of the Balkans to rebuild after the breakup of the former Yugoslavia also was one of the positive features of the late 1990s. This experience shows how good will on the part of key political partners, combined with well-coordinated and purposeful assistance from the outside, can restore a sense of stability, hope, and renewed economic and social recovery in war-torn countries. Perhaps the greatest challenge, but also one of the success stories to date, has been the post-Dayton reconstruction of Bosnia-Herzegovina. Of course, that the stability of entire Balkan region continues to hang in the balance and that widespread death and destruction were once again the order of the day in 1999 are sad testimony to the fact that economic and social well-being and prospects matter little when countries and their people engage in a self-destructive path of internal or external aggression.

The importance of advancing, on the institutional front, pari passu advances in economic policies has also become apparent, particularly in the case of the CIS. Some observers (e.g., Stiglitz 1999) believe that a lack of attention to institutional reform was at the heart of Russia's 1998 economic crisis. One can also point to the legacy of Czarist and Soviet history and the fact that institutional change requires much time and political cohesion for implementation. Certainly, efforts were made from the outside to support institutional reform, for example, in the areas of public-sector management, legal and regulatory reform, and financial-sector institution building. But it is fair to say that these efforts did not, and perhaps could not, suffice in building the necessary market institutions in good time to assure effective governance and private-sector development in many of the countries of the CIS. Much more work and understanding is required to advance more forcefully in this area. Can we unbundle institutional reforms to identify those that, at the margin, have the biggest complementarity with the next stages of economic policy reforms? How much can these institutional reforms be pushed from the outside? Can institutional reforms be promoted successfully before markets and private-sector activity begins to emerge, that is, ahead of the effective demand for such institutions?

Although the persistent and dramatic decline of the Russian and Ukrainian economies is likely to have only a limited impact on the world economy—beyond the initial impact of the August 1998 Russian financial collapse, which did shake international financial markets—its impact on the social and political conditions for the Russian and Ukrainian people, and for the surrounding countries of the CIS, is potentially very serious. There are few obvious prospects for a rapid turnaround in both countries, given the interplay of economic and political uncertainties and dynamics at this time. For the longer term, the hope must be that both countries, with their great natural and human resources, will find ways to develop a political consensus that makes it possible to turn the economies of these countries around, as has been the case in much of Latin America after decades of uncertain and counterproductive economic and political fortunes. Unfortunately, developing such a consensus tends to be a slow process, spread over years rather than months. Although the two countries are different in important ways, there are also striking similarities in the problems that Russia and Ukraine face as large, politically fragmented transition economies. This may provide a basis for analysis into the political and economic causes of their extraordinary, and in many regards exceptionally severe, difficulties.

Finally, the lesson for the international community that one can draw from the ten years of transition in Central Europe and the former Soviet Union is that market-oriented reforms, combined with social reforms and institutional strengthening, have worked to turn former socialist, centrally planned countries around and can put them on a sustainable path of economic growth and social inclusion. However, this process tends to be slow and costly, and slower and more costly and uncertain in the CIS than in Central Europe and the Baltics. External shocks expose basic vulnerabilities and make the challenge of resuming growth that much harder. External assistance is important, but it has only limited leverage in helping to speed up reforms and their beneficial results and in making them stick. Financial and technical assistance needs to be combined with efforts to build broad-based political understanding and support, a task that is neither easy nor always welcome in the countries concerned.

References

Aslund, Anders. 1999. Why has Russia's economic transformation been so arduous? Paper presented at World Bank ABCDE Conference, Washington, D.C., April.

European Bank for Reconstruction and Development (EBRD). 1998. *Transition report 1997*. London.

Selowsky, Marcelo, and Ricardo Martin. 1997. Policy performance and output growth in the transition economies. *American Economic Review* (May): 349–53.

Stiglitz, Joseph E., 1999. Whither reform? Paper presented at World Bank ABCDE Conference, Washington, D.C., April.

World Bank. 1997. *World development report 1997*. Washington, D.C.

Wyplosz, Charles, 1999. Ten years of transformation: Macroeconomic lessons. Paper presented at World Bank ABCDE Conference, Washington, D.C., April.

3

Postcommunist Transition and Post-Washington Consensus: The Lessons for Policy Reforms

Grzegorz W. Kolodko

Introduction

The centrally planned economy has ceased to exist. Even in countries still considered socialist (communist), like China and Vietnam, the mechanism of economic coordination has shifted to a great extent from state intervention to market allocation. Thus, during the 1990s the process of postsocialist transformation has advanced significantly. About thirty countries in Eastern Europe, the former Soviet Union, and Asia are involved in vast systemic changes. Undoubtedly, these changes are leading to full-fledged market economies, though the precise outcome of transformation will not be the same for all countries involved. Whereas some, leaders in transition and well-placed geopolitically, are bound to join the European Union in the near future, others, lagging behind in systemic changes, will remain hybrid systems with the remnants of central planning alongside elements of market regulation and a growing private sector. Whereas some countries will expand quickly and catch up with their developed neighbors within a generation, others will experience sluggish economic growth and a relatively low standard of living.

Transition to a market economy is a lengthy process that comprises various spheres of economic activities. New institutional arrangements are of key importance for successful transformation. A market economy requires not only liberal regulation and private ownership, but also adequate institutions. For this reason transition can be executed only in a gradual manner, since institution building is a gradual process based on new organizations, new laws, and the changing behavior of various economic entities. The belief that a market economy can be introduced by "shock therapy" has been proven wrong, and in several cases, when attempted, has caused more problems than it has solved. Only liberalization and stabilization measures can be introduced in a radical manner, and even this is not a necessity. The need for such radical measures depends on the scope of financial destabilization, and they are possible only under certain political conditions.

The main argument in favor of transition has been a desire to put the countries in question on the path of sustainable growth. It has been assumed that the shift of property rights from state to private hands and the shift of allocation mechanism from state to free market would soon enhance saving rates and capital formation as well as allocative efficiency. Thus it ought also to have contributed to high-quality growth. Unfortunately, for a number of reasons this has not occurred. In all transition economies, before any growth has occurred (and in some countries there is no growth yet) there has been severe contraction, ranging from 20 percent over three years in Poland to more than 60 percent in nine years in Ukraine (table 3.1). These unfavorable results are the consequence of both the legacy of the previous system and the policies exercised during transition, though it is obvious that the latter are of major importance.

These transition policies were based to a large extent on the so-called Washington consensus. The set of policies designed in accordance with this consensus has stressed the importance of liberalization, privatization, and opening of postsocialist economies as well as the necessity of sustaining financial discipline. Having been developed for another set of conditions (i.e., the structural crisis in Latin America in the 1980s), however, initially this approach was missing crucial elements necessary for systemic overhaul, stabilization, and growth: institution building, improvement of corporate governance of the state sector prior to privatization, and the redesign of the role of the state, instead of its urgent withdrawal from economic activities. The erroneous assumption that emerging market forces can quickly substitute for the government in its role in setting up new institutions, in investing in human capital, and in developing infrastructure has caused severe contraction and growing social stress in transition countries.

The need to manage the institutional aspects of transition has been recognized and addressed only in later stages. The technical assistance of the International Monetary Fund (IMF) and the World Bank in dealing with these issues may have an even more important positive influence on the course of transition and growth than their financial involvement. Lending by these organizations is often called "assistance," despite the fact that such assistance is just commercial credits with tough accompanying terms. This assistance enforces far-reaching structural reforms in the countries that receive it and pushes them towards policies that are supposed to bring durable growth.

Hence, there is a need to search for a new consensus about what policy reforms are necessary for sustained growth. The East Asian contagion, Eastern European transition, and the Brazilian crisis do suggest that for recovery and durable growth healthy financial fundamentals and liberal, transparent deregulation are not the only decisive factors: Sound institutional arrangements, reregulation of financial markets, and wise governmental policy are also essential. Against the recent experience with the crises of several emerging markets (including the ones in transition countries) the outline of a new consensus—a post-Washington consensus—can be drawn. This new consensus not only points to the need for liberal markets and open economies but also stresses the new role of the state, the fundamental meaning of market organizations and the institutional links among them, and the need for more equitable growth.

After losing over a quarter of GDP between 1990 and 1998, a majority of the postsocialist transition economies are now gaining momentum. This is not yet true in the two most sizable, Russia and Ukraine, but they too have the potential to become growing economies (Kolodko 1998). In the coming years, the postsocialist emerging markets will become not only rapidly growing economies, but also—owing to the East Asian turmoil—the fastest growing region in the world. Yet how fast they will grow depends on policy reforms implemented in particular countries. The direction these reforms take will also depend on cooperation with international organizations and their technical advice and financial support, which are conditionally linked to execution of market-friendly policies and implementation of sound structural reforms. Thus these organizations' influence upon the course of reforms and chosen policies is much stronger than their actual financial engagement and the actual risk they undertake.

Policy without Growth: Missing Elements

Since the beginning of the 1990s the so-called Washington consensus has been accepted as conventional wisdom on policies for movement from stabilization to growth. It has been assumed that tough finan-

Table 3.1
Recession and growth in transition economies, 1990–1997

Countries	Years of GDP decline	Did GDP fall after some growth?	Average annual rate of GDP growth			1997 GDP index (1989 = 100)	Rank
			(1990–1993)	(1994–1997)	(1990–1997)		
Poland	2	no	-3.1	6.3	1.6	111.8	1
Slovenia	3	no	-3.9	4.0	0.0	99.3	2
Czech Republic	3	yes*	-4.3	3.6	-0.4	95.8	3
Slovakia	4	no	-6.8	6.3	-0.3	95.6	4
Hungary	4	no	-4.8	2.5	-1.1	90.4	5
Uzbekistan	5	no	-3.1	-0.3	-1.7	86.7	6
Romania	4	yes	-6.4	2.1	-2.2	82.4	7
Albania	4	yes	-8.8	4.9	-2.0	79.1	8
Estonia	5	no	-9.7	4.1	-2.8	77.9	9
Croatia	4	no	-9.9	3.0	-3.4	73.3	10
Belarus	6	no	-5.4	-2.6	-4.0	70.8	11
Bulgaria	6	yes	-7.4	-3.6	-5.5	62.8	12
Kyrgyzstan	5	no	-9.3	-2.4	-5.8	58.7	13
Kazakhstan	6	no	-6.7	-6.0	-6.3	58.1	14
Latvia	4	yes	-13.8	2.2	-5.8	56.8	15
FYR Macedonia	6	no	-12.9	-0.8	-6.9	55.3	16
Russia	7	yes*	-10.1	-5.3	-7.7	52.2	17
Turkmenistan	7	no	-4.5	-12.5	-8.5	48.3	18
Lithuania	5	no	-18.3	0.5	-8.9	42.8	19
Armenia	4	no	-21.4	5.4	-8.0	41.1	20

Azerbaijan	6	no	−14.5	−5.7	−10.1	40.5	21
Tajikistan	7	no	−12.2	−8.4	−10.3	40.0	22
Ukraine	8	no recovery	−10.1	−12.1	−11.1	38.3	23
Moldova	7	yes*	−12.6	−10.2	−11.4	35.1	24
Georgia	5	no	−24.1	2.9	−10.6	34.3	25

Sources: National statistics, international organizations, and author's own calculations.

*GDP contracted again in 1998.

cial policy accompanied by deregulation and trade liberalization is sufficient to conquer stagnation and launch economic growth, especially in the less developed countries toward which the Washington consensus was addressed. Despite the fact that the policy reforms advised by this line of thought were at that time mostly relevant to the Latin American experience, they were applied to structural crisis issues in other regions, including transition economies. Later, interaction between the theories and the practice resulted in a process of learning by doing. On one hand, the orientation of these policy reforms has had an important influence upon the course of postsocialist transition. On the other hand, the transition process has had an impact on policy as well.

A summary of the 1989 Washington consensus given by John Williamson (1990) delineated the proposed set of policies, stressing the importance of the organizations involved. Williamson later (1997) enumerated ten points that at the time influential financial organizations, political bodies, and professional economists seemed to agree on:

• Fiscal Discipline. Budget deficit ... should be small enough to be financed without recourse to the inflation tax....
• Public Expenditure Priorities. Expenditure should be redirected from politically sensitive areas ... toward neglected fields with high economic returns and the potential to improve income distribution....
• Tax Reform. Tax reform involves broadening the tax base and cutting marginal tax rates. The aim is to sharpen incentives and improve horizontal equity without lowering realized progressivity....
• Financial Liberalization. The ultimate objective of financial liberalization is market-determined interest rates, but experience has shown that, under conditions of a chronic lack of confidence, market-determined rates can be so high as to threaten the financial solvency of productive enterprise and government....
• Exchange Rates. Countries need a unified (at least for trade transactions) exchange rate set at a level sufficiently competitive to induce a rapid growth in nontraditional exports and managed so as to ensure exporters that this competitiveness will be maintained in the future.
• Trade Liberalization. Quantitative trade restrictions should be rapidly replaced by tariffs, and these should be progressively reduced until a uniform low tariff in the range of 10 percent (or at most around 20 percent) is achieved....
• Foreign Direct Investment. Barriers impeding the entry of foreign firms should be abolished; foreign and domestic firms should be allowed to compete on equal terms.

• Privatization. State enterprises should be privatized.
• Deregulation. Governments should abolish regulations that impede the entry of new firms or that restrict competition, and then should ensure that all regulations are justified by such criteria as safety, environmental protection, or prudential supervision of financial institutions.
• Property Rights. The legal system should provide secure property rights without excessive costs and should make such rights available to the informal sector. (Williamson 1997, 60–61)

Later, mainly under the influence of experience with overhauling the Latin American economies over the first half of 1990s and taking into consideration the lessons learned from Eastern Europe and the former Soviet Union, a new agenda was presented. Whereas it included obvious points from the earlier consensus, there were certain new concerns and accents. Again, ten points were raised:

• Increase saving by (inter alia) maintaining fiscal discipline.
• Reorient public expenditure toward (inter alia) well-directed social expenditure.
• Reform the tax system by (inter alia) introducing an eco-sensitive land tax.
• Strengthen banking supervision.
• Maintain a competitive exchange rate, abounding both floating and the use of the exchange rate as a nominal anchor.
• Pursue intra-regional trade liberalization.
• Build a competitive market economy by (inter alia) privatizing and deregulating (including the labor market).
• Make well-defined property rights available to all.
• Build key institutions such as independent central banks, strong budget offices, independent and incorruptible judiciaries, and agencies to sponsor productivity missions.
• Increase educational spending and redirect it toward primary and secondary school. (Williamson 1997, 58)

The new items on this agenda correctly address the issues of institution building, environmental protection, and investment in education, yet they are still missing some points of great importance that are especially pertinent to transition economies. First of all, dealing with corporate governance reform in the state sector before privatization is not mentioned, nor is the behavioral aspect of institution building. Also the necessity of equitable growth is still overlooked. The shortest point on the agenda of the early Washington consensus ("State enterprises should be privatized") is in reality a long-term policy challenge. Even if there is a strong commitment to privatizing quickly and extensively, which is not always the case, it is not feasible, for both technical and political reasons. Issues also arise involving sequencing, pace, distribution of costs and benefits, and the efficient exercise of corporate governance.

As for the institutional aspect of reform, in postsocialist transition economies, unlike in distorted developing market economies, it is not enough merely to establish organizations, for instance, an independent central bank or comprehensive tax administration. Cultural changes are also necessary to facilitate efficiency and growth, changes in behavior within organizations and changes in the interactions among them.

The early Washington consensus was actually aiming at countries that already had market economies and were not just in a transition to such a system. Joseph Stiglitz (1998a), although stressing the importance of governments as a complement to markets, points out that the experience of Latin America in the 1980s catalyzed the consensus achieved in the late 1980s and early 1990s between the U.S. Treasury, the IMF, and the World Bank, as well as some influential think tanks. Stiglitz claims that for this reason, countries facing challenges different from those that presented themselves to the Latin American countries have never found satisfactory answers to their most pressing questions in the Washington consensus. Its simplified interpretation vis-à-vis the postsocialist economies implied that it would be sufficient to fix the appropriate financial fundamentals and privatize the bulk of state assets. Subsequently, growth should begin and continue for the long term. Because this has not happened as presumed, the Washington consensus must be reconsidered.

There has always been a question as to the actual existence of a Washington consensus. Was a consensus in fact really achieved, or was the effort just a well-intentioned and well-motivated attempt? In fact, the latter is the case. There is no standard terminology for the doctrines presented in the Washington consensus, and various practitioners advocated these doctrines with varying degrees of subtlety and emphasis. Though the set of views is often summarized as the "Washington consensus," to be sure, there never was a consensus even in Washington (let alone outside of Washington) on the appropriateness of these policies (Stiglitz 1998b, 58).

The partial failure of the Washington consensus with regard to transition economies must be linked with its neglect of the significance of institution building for the beginning of growth, even if economic fundamentals are by and large in order. Such oversight explains why so many Western scholars initially did not properly understand the real problem in the transition economies. Institutions change very slowly, but they have a strong influence on economic performance. As the 1993 Nobel laureate in economics states, since "Western neo-classical economic theory is devoid of institutions, it is of little help in analyzing the underlying sources of economic performance. It would be little exaggeration to say that, while neo-classical theory is focused on the operation of efficient factor and product markets, few Western economists understand the institutional requirements essential to the creation of such markets since they simply take them for granted. A set of political and economic institutions that provides low-cost transacting and credible commitment makes possible the efficient factor and product markets underlying economic growth" (North 1997, 2).

Expectations of growth in transition economies were based on the assumption that market institutions, if they had not yet appeared automatically, would somehow rise up soon after liberalization and stabilization measures were executed. It was believed that if policies were put in place to secure the progress of stabilization and enhance sound fundamentals, the economy should regain momentum and start to develop quickly. What actually happened, however, was much more depressing. Because of a vacuum with neither plan nor market system, productive capacity was utilized even less than previously, savings and investments began to decline, and instead of fast growth there was deep recession. A lack of institutional development turned out to be the missing element in transition policies based on the Washington consensus. Instead of sustained growth, liberalization and privatization without a well-organized market structure led to extended contraction. This was not only the legacy of a socialist past, but also the result of current policies.

Under some circumstances, though not in every case, the manner of reasoning characteristic of the Washington consensus may be relevant to the challenges faced by distorted, less-developed market economies, in which certain market organizations have always been in place—contrary to the experience of postsocialist economies. In postsocialist countries, organizations essential to a market economy were either distorted or did not exist, so the economy could not expand. Some institutions in these economies needed to be developed from scratch, since they did not exist under the centrally planned regime. Hence, even with progress in liberalization and radical privatization, there was still no positive supply response. Misallocation of resources and investments has therefore continued during transition, although now for different reasons than under socialist economic structures.

At the outset of transition the only relatively developed part of a market infrastructure in transition economies was a commodities trading network, but even this was operating under chronic shortages. A capital market structure was nonexistent. The lack of financial intermediaries discouraged accumulation and worsened allocation of savings. Thus, immediately after the collapse of socialism, the lack of proper regulation of the emerging capital market and the dearth of such key organizations as investment banks, mutual funds, a stock exchange, and a security control commission, caused distortions that liberalization and privatization could not offset.

These key organizations and institutional links must be developed gradually. Considering the point of departure, this also calls for a process of retraining many professionals to enable them to work in a market environment. This takes years, and thus it would be much wiser to manage the processes of liberalization and privatization at a pace compatible with the speed of human capital development. Otherwise, loosed market forces will not be able to shape economic structures and processes and raise competitiveness and ability for growth. A dissonance between liberalization measures and institution building has actually occurred in a number of countries that took a more radical approach toward transition. In these cases "creative destruction," popular in Poland at the beginning of 1990s, failed to deliver, because there was too much destruction and not enough creation.

Socialist countries were full- or over full-employment economies, that is, economies with labor shortages. Thus a social security system protecting against unemployment did not exist, because it was not needed. All countries in this region therefore had to develop such a safety net from scratch.[1] In the meantime, before such systems could be implemented, in addition to the misallocation of capital, there was the misallocation of labor.

Since the mid-1990s, the Bretton Woods organizations have started to pay more attention to the way market structures are organized as well as to the behavioral aspects of market performance. A number of less developed and transition economies learned quickly that there is no sustained growth without sound fundamentals. They later also learned that the market and growth need both liberalization and organization. Now, because of transitional contraction and because of conclusions drawn from the East Asian crisis, it has become evident that even with sound fundamentals, that is, a balanced budget and current account, low inflation, a stable currency, liberalized trade, and a vast private sector, growth will not be sustained if these favorable features are not supported by an appropriate institutional setup. Actually, without such a setup, the fundamentals themselves will become unsound and unsustainable, as time and again is proven by actual developments, for instance, in the Czech Republic or more recently in Brazil.

There seems to be a growing agreement that the early Washington consensus must be revised and adjusted toward actual challenges and new circumstances. If the consensus is going to work, elements so far missing must be included. These elements are linked with institutional arrangements, though they are not universal. Certain elements are missing regarding the overhauling of the Latin American debt crisis, others in the case of counteracting the East Asian contagion, and still others in fighting the Eastern European transitional depression. In this last category, eight elements are of key importance:

• The lack of organizational infrastructure for a liberal market economy.

• Weak financial intermediaries unable to allocate efficiently privatized assets.

• A lack of commercialization of state enterprises prior to privatization.

• Unqualified management unable to execute sound corporate governance under the conditions of a deregulated economy.

• A lack of institutional infrastructure for competition policy.

• A weak legal framework and judiciary system and a consequent inability to enforce tax code and business contracts.

• Poor local government unprepared to tackle the issues of regional development.

• A lack of nongovernmental organizations (NGOs) supporting the functioning of the emerging market economy and civil society.

Hence, policies that under other conditions might have worked have not been effective in overcoming the crisis in the postsocialist economies. Even if the targets and instruments as such were well defined, they could not be reached and used as envisaged, since they were put into use within a systemic vacuum.

Toward a New Consensus

Rather than a permanent agreement between principal partners, the process of developing new consensus must involve a constant search for such agreement as well as a quest for new partners. These features are indispensable for its ultimate success. From time to time, when the situation changes and our knowledge about it evolves, new documents and programs, accentuating additional points of concern and examining old points in a different light, come to the fore. A good example of such progress is the World Bank's 1996 *Annual Development Report*, devoted entirely to the transition from plan to market (World Bank 1996), and the September 1996 IMF Interim Committee Declaration, *Partnership for Sustainable Global Growth* (IMF 1996).

The latter statement may be seen as a modified version of the early Washington consensus. Among eleven points, six are of special relevance to the situation of transition economies. Point 1 stresses that monetary, fiscal, and structural policies are complementary and reinforce each other. Point 3 claims a favorable environment for private savings needs to be created. Point 7 emphasizes that budgetary policies have to aim at medium-term balance and a reduction in public debt, and point 9 says that structural reforms must be supplemented, with special attention paid to labor markets. Point 10 stresses the importance of good corporate governance, and point 11 cautions against corruption in the public sector and money laundering in banks, warning that monitoring and supervision of these two areas must be strengthened. Other points, also important for sustainable development, address the issues of exchange rate stability, disinflation, resisting protectionist pressure, progress toward increased freedom of capital movement, and fiscal adjustment by reducing unproductive spending while ensuring adequate investment in infrastructure.

The Washington consensus, however, is not an official position taken by any particular organization or institution. It is rather a gathering of policy options being agreed upon by important partners to such an extent that the agreement may be considered a consensus.

Yet there is still a search for agreement among the organizations involved as well as among policymakers, policy-oriented researchers, and advisors. Because I was personally involved in all three, that is, research, advice giving, and policymaking, it was quite interesting for me to receive a reaction to the outcome of my involvement from the author of the Washington consensus. As John Williamson[2] put it:

I was particularly pleased that you have tried to define an alternative to big bangery in terms of a more careful design of individual policy components rather than generalized go slow ("gradualism").[3] On just about all the individual items you identify, certainly including protection and privatization, I agree with you in retrospect, and indeed I would have agreed with you at the time.... But in all honesty I have to confess that I still worry that had I been in the place of Balcerowicz [who was the minister of finance in Poland in 1989–1991] I might not have put together the decisive package that I think in retrospect Poland needed at the time, and that laid the foundation for your successful period in office. Perhaps one needed a little bit of overkill to make it emotionally possible for your allies to accept that the world had changed, and even to give you the opportunity of correcting their excesses and in the process winning their acceptance of the new model? It reminds me of the situation in my home country: I am much more comfortable with Tony Blair than with Mrs. Thatcher, but I am not sure that we could have had him without her.

In this instance, psychological and political rather than economic and financial arguments are given as decisive factors favoring the radical set of policies undertaken at the beginning of the 1990s. Nonetheless, it seems that Williamson and I still differ as for the evaluation of the scope and costs of that overkill. Was it only "a little bit" of otherwise necessary measures, as one may still believe, or was it a serious excess of unnecessary radicalism, as it seems to be proved elsewhere (Kolodko 1991; Nuti 1992; Rosati 1994; Poznanski 1996; Hausner 1997)? When ideas and strategies involving more gradual change and the active involvement of the state in institutional redesign in postsocialist transition economies were expounded for the first time (Kolodko 1989, 1992; Laski 1990; Nuti 1990; Poznanski 1993) and when they were later implemented in Poland (Kolodko 1993, 1996, 2000), they were unorthodox and controversial with respect to the Washington consensus. In fact, these new ideas did not so much endorse more gradual change as recognize that the necessary changes would be time-consuming by their very nature. In 1997 and 1998, however, even in official international circles, there were widespread signs that a new consensus is emerging, and that it is, to a certain extent, based on the ideas implemented in Poland in 1994–1997 (Kolodko and Nuti 1997). Thanks to its multitrack approach, Poland is now recognized as having avoided the adverse experience of other transition economies. The new ideas and policies developed under Strategy for Poland were to some extent elaborated against the mainstream of the early Washington consensus and now have contributed importantly to its revision.

In the aftermath of the East Asian crisis, as it has spread beyond anybody's expectation, the train of thought has also begun to change track among the most influential opinion leaders in the international financial community, thanks to a much belated raising of doubts regarding the accuracy of the recipe proposed for postsocialist emerging markets, especially for the most important, Russia. A consensus has not yet been agreed upon, but lessons are gradually being learned. It is now more broadly acknowledged that "the benefits brought by short-term international lenders are questionable: they do not provide new technology, they do not improve the management of domestic institutions; and they do not offer reliable finance of current account deficit. In countries with high savings rates, they also increase already excessive investment rates. To manage the inflows, borrowers may have to accumulate huge reserves.... The Asian saga proves, once again, that liberalization of inadequately regulated and capitalized financial system is a recipe for disaster" (Wolf 1998, 5). All the while, the Bretton Woods organizations were insisting upon, and determining their financial involvement based on, tough fiscal and monetary policy. If it was a period of 10 percent GDP decline, or a period of 10 percent expansion, there was always political pressure on the government and finance minister to bring the fiscal gap down and keep the real interest rate up. Even when a country's budget deficit was smaller than that of industrial countries and its real interest rate was so high that it was not possible to contain the deficit further because of the soaring costs of servicing the public debt, continuing fiscal and monetary tightness was a permanent requirement. A high real interest rate facilitates the portfolio investors (through interest rate differentials) but at the costs of both budget (taxpayers) and the business sector, owing to the crowding-out effect.

The importance of a change in corporate governance, as opposed to a sheer transfer of property titles, is now being recognized even by early keen supporters of rapid, mass privatization. There is no clear evidence that privatized enterprises perform better than state enterprises in the immediate aftermath of privatization. Nicholas Stern (1996, 8) points to the process of restructuring, which "itself will be a major and fundamental task involving investment, hard decisions and dislocation. It will be much less painful if economic growth, effective corporate governance and well-functioning safety nets are established. Thus good corporate governance of the public enterprises and sound competition policy are at least as essential for recovery as privatization and liberalization."

After the laissez-faire of the early transition, values of cooperation and solidarity are being rediscovered. Even billionaire financier George Soros has readily acknowledged these values: "although I have made a fortune in the financial markets,[4] I now fear that the untrammeled intensification of laissez-faire capitalism and the spread of market values into all areas of life is endangering our open and democratic society. . . . Too much competition and too little cooperation can cause intolerable inequities and instability" (Soros 1997). Yet although it should be obvious from the outset that transition based upon a sort of laissez-faire must bring "intolerable inequities and instability" (Kolodko 2000), it is still not acknowledged widely enough, and such an obvious conclusion is still challenged.

The World Bank's 1996 *World Development Report* emphasizes very strongly the need for social consensus, though it has been very difficult to reach such consensus in transition economies, considering their falling output and growing inequality between income groups within a society. Establishing a social consensus, however, will be crucial for the long-term success of transition: Cross-country analyses suggest that societies that have very unequal distributions of income or assets among the population tend to be politically and socially less stable and to have lower rates of investment and growth than those in which the income and asset distributions are more uniform (World Bank 1996).

It is now more or less accepted that in economies still affected by structural rigidities, such as formal and informal indexation and sluggish supply response, once inflation had fallen well below a threshold of about 20 percent, attempts at speeding up disinflation would have had significant, perhaps intolerable costs—as for instance in Romania in 1998–1999—certainly higher than the moderate but steady falling inflation actually experienced by some countries leading in transition and those recently following Poland's path.

What is most important is that inflation should continue to fall steadily and noticeably without accelerating again. Such a steady, gradual process of disinflation not only contributes to the growing credibility of the government and monetary authorities but also makes economic developments predictable and creates a better business environment and confidence on the international scene.

The prerequisite for an enhanced saving ratio, that is, one that is faster than the income increase, is a growth in real income, stabilization, and optimistic expectations. Only against such background can the propensity to save steadily increase. The 1996 European Bank for Reconstruction and Development (EBRD) *Transition Report*, which is devoted to infrastructure and savings, stresses the equal role of increasing government savings—especially through the overhaul of social security and pension systems and more broadly based taxation at lower rates—and developing of contractual savings and life insurance. From this perspective, the pressure to maintain high and positive real interest rates has been grossly misplaced. The fiscal and quasi-fiscal activities of central banks, notably in the emerging economies and especially in postsocialist countries, have attracted considerable attention (Fry 1993). In particular, the costs of sterilization policies, which are the result of excessive interest rate differentials and/or of undervalued currencies, have come to the fore, for example, the Organisation for Economic Cooperation and Development (OECD) country study of the Czech Republic (OECD 1996). It turns out that for a considerable time, the central banks of both the Czech Republic and Poland have wasted about 1 percent of GDP in their unfortunate sterilization policies (Nuti 1996).

There is yet one more key feature of the emerging consensus: Along with the continuous leading role of the Washington-based organizations, especially the IMF and the World Bank, it must encompass more partners than the previous consensus did. Other international organizations, like the United Nations, OECD, World Trade Organization, International Labor Organization, and EBRD, should play a bigger role than they have thus far. Also, regional organizations, like the Association of South East Asian Nations (ASEAN) in Asia, Central European Free Trade Agreement (CEFTA) in central Europe, or the Commonwealth of Independent States in the former Soviet Union, should be better prepared to present their purpose in the global forum and try to influence the process of changing the international financial and economic order. Some international nongovernmental organizations (NGOs) ought to be more influential too.

Thus the search for the new consensus must rely not only on the quest for new policies agreed on in Washington, but also on the policies agreed on between Washington and other important places in different parts of the global economy. There are many hints that such process is on the way, but much more is yet to be accomplished.

The Means and Ends of Economic Policy

The lack of success of policies based on the early Washington consensus is also due to confusion of the means of the policies with their ends. A sound fiscal stance, low inflation, a stable exchange rate, and overall financial stabilization are only the means of economic policy, whereas sustained growth and a healthier standard of living are its ends. Yet after several years of exercising these means, neither growth nor a higher standard of living has been achieved in transition countries. Important changes like privatization and liberalization are merely instruments, not targets. So it is strange that so often these instrumental processes are presented as a core of economic policy, if not its ultimate end. Too much attention is focused on the means that hypothetically should lead to improvement of efficiency and competitiveness, instead of concentration on the outcome of these exercises. Such bias leads to the distortion of policy, and the tools become the goals themselves, without sufficient concern about their impact on the real economy.

In economic policy, intellectual oversimplification sometimes assumes that, from a certain point and under certain circumstances, things should run themselves, so there is no need to think about how to manage them. An extreme example of such thought is the supposition that "the best policy is no policy."[5] But considering the distinction between ends and means, it should be obvious to all those involved in economic research, advice, and policy that such confusion cannot be attributed merely to the naiveté and laziness of economists and politicians: Actually, they do work hard. These intellectual misunderstandings result instead from political antagonism, and the difference is more about conflicts of interests than about alternative theoretical concepts and scientific explanations.

Of course, policy mistakes do sometimes occur because of a lack of experience and proper knowledge, but more often they stem from obedience to a particular group of interests or to "theoretical schools" that happen to be ideological and political lobbies too. This is why there are no leftist or rightist doctors or engineers, but there are leftist and rightist economists and policymakers. John Williamson (1990) points to "political" and "technocratic" Washington, stressing their different priorities and policy options. There are important divisions not only *between* the political and technocratic parts of Washington, however, but also *within* them.

What makes the picture still more complex is the fact that some of the actors on the so-called technocratic side of the scene do play, even if unintentionally, political roles as well. This is also true with regard to the Bretton Woods organizations, especially the IMF. Their influence and the consequences of their policies simply have such serious implications for particular countries and regions, if not the entire global economy, that sometimes they have much more to say— and decide—than what may be seen as purely technocratic concerns. The position of the IMF towards such big countries in transition as Russia and Ukraine are the best points in case here.

But the issue is even more complex than that, because, aside from intellectual controversies and different normative values, there are also different political, economic, and financial interests involved. Otherwise it would be impossible to interpret why erroneous policies had continued, in many cases, even after it was obvious that they were wrong—as, for instance, with early liberalization and stabilization policy in Poland in 1989–1992; the neglect of corporate governance in the Czech Republic in 1993–1996; the Russian privatization of 1994–1998, executed with the active involvement of politically connected informal institutions and with fraudulent Albanian financial intermediaries in 1995–1997, which were tolerated until the whole economy eventually collapsed.

Such events serve only as examples of the confusion of economic policy's targets with its instruments. Economic policy is to be judged not by the pace of privatization, but by its efficiency, measured first by the increase of competitiveness and budgetary proceeds, and then by the increase in contribution to national income. The strong insistence on privatization's acceleration coming from some lobbies and their political allies is merely a means to sell the state-owned assets producing privatization more cheaply. Thus entities are able to buy these assets not faster, as is publicly suggested through political connections and dependent news media, but more cheaply than under a more reasonably paced procedure. The ones that sell fast, sell cheap too. And the ones who buy fast, buy cheap as well.

There have been warnings about, criticisms of, and intellectual and political opposition to all these unwise policies, but still they have gotten through, not because of a lack of good economic ideas or a deficit of sound policy programs, but because of pressure from strong lobbies and interest groups. Therefore, in designing good policy, it is important not only to be right but also to be able to enforce the preferred policies. Often the strongest lobby is not where truth and logic are, but where power and money are.

Therefore, true reforms, those that facilitate the public interests of many as opposed to the particular interests of a few, must always be thought of as a means to long-term targets, such as sustained growth. Otherwise, there will be fictitious "progress" reflected in an artificial improvement of situation. If the share of the private sector, the scope of trade liberalization, or the deregulation of capital transfers is bigger than it would be without these policies, but at the same time economic contraction is deeper or growth more sluggish and the standard of living is deteriorating, then the overall situation is worse, not better. Yet often, economic status is judged from the perspective of a particular group of interests, and this perspective is presented as a picture of the general economic situation.

So while evaluating the actual standing of an economy and policy, one must consider not only what is examined, and by what means it is scrutinized, but also who is carrying out such an evaluation. With this in mind, it is obvious that, for instance, the evaluations of Moody's rating agency and the Russian trade unions must be as different as the interests of the Morgan Stanley investment bank and the Siberian miners.

Hence, the aims of development policy are more comprehensive and their interpretation is changing as well among those who previously subscribed to the Washington consensus, primarily the World Bank. Not only should a balanced economy and sustained growth be of serious policy concern, but also standard of living improvement, distribution of income, the environment, and last but not least, democracy itself. Our understanding of the instruments to promote well-functioning markets has also improved, and we have broadened the objectives of development to include other goals, such as sustainable development, egalitarian development, and democratic development (Stiglitz 1998a, 1).

True, the World Bank always was more inclined toward social issues and development of human capital than other international financial institutions and other banks. Usually banks look to profits, not to the human development index, as an indicator of their success. It must be acknowledged that the World Bank has become involved in a number of projects, not only in transition economies, that serve to increase standards of living and decrease poverty.

Yet now even the IMF is trying to join the club and claim that it too would like to aim at a more fair distribution of the fruits of growth, if only the advised policies would deliver some. Stanley Fischer, the IMF's First Deputy Managing Director, himself concerned about equitable growth for a long time, has raised the question, Why do equity considerations matter for the Fund? and then has answered that "first, as a matter of social justice, all members of society should share in the benefits of economic growth. And although there are many important arguments about precisely what constitutes a fair distribution of income, we accept the view that poverty in the midst of plenty is not socially acceptable. But, second, there is also an instrumental argument for equity: adjustment programs that are equitable and growth that is equitable are more likely to be sustainable. These are good enough reasons for the IMF to be concerned about equity considerations—whether it be poverty reduction or concerns about income distribution in the programs the IMF supports" (Fischer 1998, 1).

Undoubtedly, the experience of transformation has contributed significantly to these changes Fischer mentions. We still have to deal with the difficult road from contraction to growth in postsocialist economies, but we have also experienced fast growth in Asian reformed socialist economies, which, unlike the transition economies of Eastern European and the former Soviet Union, did not follow many early Washington consensus suggestions. Now these experiences, together with the aftermath of the East Asian crisis and its contagion, are working as a catalyst for the emergence of "the post-Washington consensus" the same way that the Latin American debt crisis of the 1980s ignited the formation of its predecessor. There is still a long distance to travel, however, from the emerging intellectual consensus to a real political agreement about appropriate policy reforms and actions. And of course, even if intellectual consensus is closer than before, controversies regarding different normative values and contradictory interests do remain.

Transition as a Process of Systemic Redesign

The only chance for the ultimate success of economic transformation is to design suitable institutions, which often must be developed from the beginning. Such design is more difficult in post-Soviet republics than in Eastern Europe, because the former lacked even such basic institutions as a sovereign central bank or national currency, and private ownership of the means of production was virtually non-existent. In Asian reformed socialist economies the process of transformation is going at a much slower pace, and yet it also is directed at further liberalization and opening up.

As for postsocialist countries, some follow a path of rapid change; others have taken a course of gradual, perhaps even too slow liberalization and privatization. Though that course was followed by a relatively milder contraction, it delayed crucial structural reforms. Nevertheless, if the given time is used for appropriate institution building, it can pay off later. If, however, the time of gradual liberalization is wasted from the perspective of institutional reforms, then the chance for a long-term expansion is indeed small.

Although under these circumstances contraction has been more severe in early stages, later, institution building has often been more advanced. In the long run, after learning the bitter lesson that market economies do not expand without a wise, government-led development policy and well-designed institutions, both types of economies, that is, European and former Soviet economies in transition as well as the reformed economies of China and Vietnam, have a chance to succeed in their market endeavors.

Government involvement is of vital importance in the process of comprehensive institution building. Truly this, as much as liberalization, is the essence of transition. In other words, without taking adequate care of institutional arrangements, liberalization and privatization alone cannot deliver what the nations that undertake them expect from their economies. Thus, if the state fails to design a proper institutional setup for liberalization and privatization, then market failures prevail and informal institutionalization takes over. Instead of a sound market, in the words of the chief economists at the World Bank and EBRD, a "bandit capitalism" emerges: "It is easy to identify institutional arrangements that work well: each partner does what it is supposed to do, there is good coordination, little conflict and the economy grows smoothly and rapidly. We can also recognise ill-functioning institutional arrangements: change is inhibited by bureaucratic requirements or there is 'bandit capitalism' with pervasive corruption and deceit" (Stern and Stiglitz 1997, 20). Such institutional pathologies could arise as a result of transition-by-chance, as opposed to transition-by-design. In a number of cases inappropriate transition policy has led to these pathologies. A system in which "only the stupid pay taxes," contracts are not executed as agreed, or payments are not made on time is hardly a market economy. It is rather chaos stemming from institutional disintegration.

Without the knowledge of how a new system works and without a vision of how to get to that system, there is no way to accomplish this goal on time and in good shape. Transition becomes protracted: Costs are higher than necessary, results are not as good as they could be under alternative scenarios, and the whole process lasts longer than would otherwise be necessary. And as the advocates of transition-by-design stressed, contrary to the supporters of transition-by-chance, the ensuing recession lasts longer, recovery comes later, and output expands more slowly (Poznanski 1996). Thus proper institutional design is a paramount task during the time of transition. At the same time, its accomplishment is more difficult in transition economies than elsewhere, because of their institutional discontinuity. The old setup, for instance, central price regulation, or investment's allocation by Gosplan and branch ministries, no longer works, but the new one, for instance, investment banking or stock exchange, is not yet in place. Thus a systemic vacuum prevails.

A foundation for market capitalism requires the dominance of private property and also a competitive enterprise sector, functioning markets, and respect for the rules of market allocation. Well-performing financial intermediaries are necessary to facilitate trade transactions and investment deals as well as to promote savings. But the market, its introduction notwithstanding, also needs a proper legal environment, one that is able to support execution of market rules, enforcement of contracts, and the appropriate behavior of economic agents (firms, households, organizations, and the government). For these reasons transition calls not for a dismissal of government, but for its streamlining and adjustment to the new circumstances. The World Bank, unlike the advocates of market fundamentalism, acknowledges that

the state makes a vital contribution to economic development when its role matches its institutional capability. But capability is not destiny. It can and must be improved if governments are to promote further improvements in economic and social welfare.... Three interrelated sets of institutional mechanisms can help create incentives that will strengthen the state's capability. These mechanisms aim to:
• Enforce rules and restraints in society as well as within the state
• Promote competitive pressures from outside and from within the state, and
• Facilitate voice and partnership both outside and within the state (World Bank 1997).

This is true for all economic systems and countries with differing scopes of economic activity, various GDP levels, and odd institutional advancement, so it is even truer for transition economies. In countries where the rules were previously fundamentally different from current postsocialist regulations, the introduction of new behaviors and the enforcement of new regulations for economic entities calls for even harder and more determined state effort than elsewhere.

Unfortunately, a state's ability to attack the issue of law enforcement is much weaker during transition than under state socialism. It is also weaker than under the governments of traditional market economies, with mature civil societies and well-working institutions. Postsocialist states have been deliberately weakened by neoliberal policies, often with the official support of the governments of leading industrial countries and that of international organizations. For example, the Russian government is weak and unable to collect taxes due not because of the legacy from the communist period, but because of an ill-advised liberal approach and inappropriately executed deregulation and privatization. Now it is difficult to bring things under the sovereignty of the new state, because they have been allowed to get out of control in the old state, mainly because of mismanaged liberalization and the manner in which the institutional redesign occurred.

As for new partnerships between market players, that is precisely what gradual institution building is about. In the long term, such partnerships enhance the environment for growth in a country, but at the initial stages ongoing changes can destabilize existing links between partners involved in economic activities. The old relationships cease to exist, whereas the new ones are only *in statu nascendi*. Thus active state participation is needed in institution building, since market relations are often associated with inappropriate events owing to activities of various lobbies and informal organizations, including organized crime.

Transition as an Instrument of Development Strategy

The new institutional setup in a transition economy must be founded on the basis of new organizations that did not exist—since they were not needed—under the previous, centrally planned state economy. Transition calls not only for a new legal system, but also for learning a new type of behavior. Enterprises, banks, the civil service and state bureaucracy, even households—all must quickly learn how to perform under the circumstances of new reality: the emerging market system. Political leaders in postsocialist countries do not have, as Moses did, forty years to turn their people around. Accelerating this process and cutting the costs of institutional and cultural adjustment require special training and education efforts by political and intellectual elites and NGOs. The Bretton Woods institutions have begun contributing to such acceleration in postsocialist countries. After seeing that sometimes providing new skills and knowledge is more important than just lending money, they have started to pay much more attention to offering technical assistance and professional training to countries undergoing economic transformation.

In countries that enjoyed a relatively liberal system under socialism, the process of learning how the real true market economy works goes much faster. If a particular country had a private sector and decentralized management of state companies under its previous economic system, learning new methods of corporate governance goes more smoothly. If there was already a two-tier banking system, learning sound commercial banking is easier. If an anti-trust body existed, this previously relatively useless organization (because of the shortages) now must regulate well-supplied markets to make them truly competitive.

In countries that had traditional centrally planned regimes until the late 1980s, however, learning takes place more slowly. This factor explains the differences in the economic performance of such neighbors as Hungary, on one hand, and Romania, on the other. The faster is the process of institution building in a country, the better is the environment there for business activity and hence for growth. Government guidance and intervention can hasten the whole process, as in Poland in the 1990s, but if mismanaged, as it was over the same period of time in Russia, it can spoil it too. Nonetheless, such a risk cannot be an excuse for state withdrawal from institution-building activities. The risk involved in economic transition calls for wise guidance and rational intervention.

In the very long term, transition should be seen as a major instrument of development policy. Systemic changes that do not lead toward durable growth and sustainable development do not make sense. There are, however, ideologically motivated efforts at change that are made without deep concern about their pragmatic implications for the society involved. Such motivation must not be disregarded, since it can be very strong, especially during a period of revolutionary change. And postsocialist transformations are of such a nature, regardless of their pace.

Yet the situation is more complex than can be explained by mere ideology, because behind political motivations there are always some particular interest groups. To counterbalance these interests with lobbies oriented toward long-range progress and development is not easy, since such groups would need to resist strong pressures coming from other interest groups. In other words, there are lobbies that fight for their own current, short-term interests using any and all means at their disposal, but there are currently few lobbies fighting with equal determination and force in favor of long-term development and remote policy targets. Actually, the only visible and somewhat effective lobby of the latter type is the environmental lobby.

However apparent it should be that systemic transition is not the target but merely the path to a more important goal, there is still some confusion on this point, in particular about the interdependence among institutional changes and real economy expansion. Can a system be perfect while growth is not satisfactory, or can it be praised at a time when its ability to expand is weak? Of course it should not be, yet peculiarly, it often is. In professional discourse, reforms are apparently appreciated for their own sake, with insufficient attention paid to their real outcomes.

Thus the enormous contraction in Eastern Europe and the former Soviet Union has been a result of, on one hand, deficiencies in development policy and exaggeration of the significance of transition as such and, on the other, a confusion of transition with liberalization and privatization. Policies have focused mainly on stabilization measures, trade liberalization, and privatization, without paying enough attention to events in the real economy, such as output, consumption, investment, and unemployment. This approach has changed the initial conditions of these economies (though not always for better) and caused contraction instead of growth. From a very long-term viewpoint, an economic system's design plays an instrumental role in a nation's capacity for expansion and development. As one generation passes away, the next takes its place. When one set of solutions has ceased to serve the purpose, another must replace it and take over. Hence, the system ought to be flexible enough to meet the challenge of a country's changing circumstances. The economic systems in the countries of Eastern Europe and the former Soviet Union have adjusted several times in the past and will change again many more times in the future, given its service (i.e., supporting for development) role and new, often unpredictable circumstances. Therefore, the entire process of transformation should be seen only as a historical episode, albeit a very important one, that may serve development needs well, if policies are managed in an appropriate way.

Contrary to the experience in Eastern Europe and the former Soviet Union, attention to development policy and treatment of market-oriented reforms as the means for successful development have contributed significantly to the high rate of growth in China and Vietnam (Montes 1997). This is indeed interesting, because there is not yet any example of such flourishing in terms of durable growth in the postsocialist economies of Eastern Europe and the former Soviet Union. The reforms of the socialist system that failed in Europe still work in Asia. In the latter, it has been feasible to distinguish between system design and policy guidance, that is, to take advantage of the existing system and adjust it as necessary to new challenges for the sake of further growth. This offers the ability to use the system and its modification as a means of expansion and not as a target.

Hence, each political system has room for some variation, for distinct policies and exercises. The system itself cannot serve as a substitute for good policy. History shows that it is most frequently sufficient to improve policies, without overhauling an entire system. Of course, during transition there is also room for better or worse economic policy, for wise or not-so-wise government action, and for various forms of involvement by the international community.

Institution Building

We speak of building institutions, but in reality, institutions must be learned rather than built. This is the process. Since the failure of shock therapy—and it did fail—because the systemic vacuum and deep recession, the process of postsocialist change has been managed in a more reasonable way, by deliberate measures carried out at a somehow slower pace than previously. By the very nature of this long-term and complex process, it cannot be carried forward in a radical way. It takes time and is costly in both financial and economic senses. It is risky and can expose the country that undertakes it to social and political tensions. Only part of the multilayer transition process, namely, liberalization linked with stabilization, can be executed—if political conditions permit—in a radical manner. Even this is not an imperative, but a policy choice depending on the scope of monetary and fiscal disequilibria in the country, and on the range of social tolerance for hardship.

As for structural adjustment, institutional reform, and behavioral change, they will take a long time under any conditions. For example, in Eastern Europe about 77 percent of computer software is estimated to be pirated, whereas in the United States the level of such illegal practices stands at about 20 percent: still not insignificant, but four times less common than in transition economies. Such a difference cannot be explained solely on the basis of more efficient law enforcement and better marketing in the United States. The more important distinction is that between a weak market culture and a mature one. Yet even in mature markets such as that of the United States the process of behavioral change must be ongoing if, despite the sophistication of market institutions and established market culture, as much as a fifth of computer software is still simply stolen.

Surely, from the viewpoint of the societies concerned and their political elites, it must seem that economic transformation will be a very lengthy process, but in reality it should be seen as a very short historical incident, considering the mighty and comprehensive changes that are taking place. Establishing traditional market economies, although accomplished under different circumstances, took much longer than the current transformations in socialist and postsocialist countries. Ten years is really a very short time to turn an economy around. So the postsocialist transition, despite the hardship it has brought, should be seen as a relatively quick process involving complex changes in structures, institutions, and behaviors.

The difficulties incurred in the current transitions have derived, however, not from a lack of knowledge of how the market works, but from a difficulty in knowing how to get to a market system from the specific situation of each of the late socialist economies. The most challenging problem has not been finding a target design for new organizations and institutions, but identifying the appropriate process of transition leading toward those targets. The most difficult question to be answered, therefore, is not how the system should look and work at the very end, but how to get from here to there.

Simultaneously, a process of learning by doing is taking place. In both the East and West previous theoretical explanations and pragmatic approaches have evolved significantly. Professionals from transition countries have gained knowledge of market performance. Great political and intellectual debates, training at home and abroad, and simple experience of the process have brought tremendous progress vis-à-vis the qualifications of researchers, entrepreneurs, and political elites. Professionals from developed countries, including government representatives dealing with transition, experts from international organizations, and the business community, have learned about the specific circumstances of transition. They have been able to absorb knowledge on various features of postsocialist realities and have realized that one should attack the challenges presented by postsocialist economic transition in a somehow different, rather unorthodox way. Major lessons about the significance of institution building for durable growth have been learned at last, and the proper policy conclusions seem now to have been drawn.

Unfortunately, the process of learning by doing has been very costly for the Eastern European and post-Soviet nations. To be sure, future growth should not be counted as compensation for the past slump. It has already been expected and forecast several times that the production over the whole region would grow, yet in several cases this has not become a reality so far. Worse, output in some postsocialist economies is still shrinking and even further contraction, at least in the year 2000, is foreseen (table 3.2). During the first ten years of transition, GDP in postsocialist economies contracted more than at the time of the Great Depression in 1929–1933. This severe contraction was not necessary, and its intensity could have been diminished if existing knowledge about the possible alternative methods of transformation had not been neglected and Western economic thought and policy advice had adjusted more quickly to actual challenges.

More recently, better-orchestrated attempts have aimed at gradual, but steady institution building. By institutions I mean not only organizations and the links among them, but also proper behavior of actors on the economic stage. Thus, with much better coordinated international assistance, transition policies have shifted in the right direction in a number of countries. Market organizations have been created, new law has been drafted and adopted, and new skills have been taught. Indeed in the late 1990s Eastern Europe, and to a lesser degree the former Soviet Union, looked quite different than they did in the early 1990s. Yet there was and is still a long road to travel.

Policy Conclusions

The course of events in postsocialist economies has been greatly influenced by policies based on the Washington consensus. But the transformation to a market economy and occurrences accompanying this process have also had a significant impact on the revision of these policies and the consensus underlying them. On the one hand, the line of thought typical for the Washington consensus has had important meaning for the direction of systemic reform and policy attempts in Eastern Europe and the former Soviet Union. On the other hand, the fact that policies suggested by the consensus and subsequently executed did not bring the expected results led to a search for alternative policy means. As a consequence, the range of issues upon which there is consensus among the major partners on the global financial, economic, and political scene has actually expanded over the years.

The postsocialist transformation in Eastern Europe and the former Soviet Union has contributed to this evolution of attitudes. New issues and problems have emerged together with the emerging postsocialist markets, and hence there are new concerns, toward which views differ and are far from being agreed upon. Nevertheless, there are numerous symptoms of an urgent need for a new consensus.

Table 3.2
Forecast of Economic Growth in Transition Economies, 1998–2002

	GDP index, 1997 (1989 = 100)	Rate of growth						Average Ranking[a]	GDP index, 2002	
		1998[b]	1999	2000	2001	2002	1998–2002		(1997 = 100)	(1989 = 100)
Poland	111.8	4.8	4.5	5.0	5.4	5.7	5.6	9	128.4	143.2
Slovenia	99.3	4.3	3.7	4.3	4.4	4.8	4.7	15	123.4	122.6
Slovakia	95.6	5.3	2.2	4.0	5.6	6.9	5.3	10	126.3	120.8
Hungary	90.4	5.2	4.3	4.1	4.0	4.1	4.7	13	123.7	111.8
Albania	79.1	4.3	6.2	8.9	8.0	4.4	7.2	4	136.0	107.6
Uzbekistan	86.7	4.5	4.5	4.3	3.8	4.2	4.6	16	123.2	106.8
Czech Republic	95.8	-2.5	0.5	3.3	3.9	5.2	2.1	23	110.6	106.0
Estonia	77.9	6.4	6.1	5.9	6.9	5.9	7.1	5	135.3	105.4
Romania	82.4	-4.7	2.2	4.9	4.8	5.1	2.5	22	112.5	92.7
Croatia	73.3	4.2	2.9	4.3	4.1	4.3	4.3	19	121.4	89.0
Bulgaria	62.8	3.5	2.7	4.6	5.2	5.2	4.6	17	123.0	77.3
Yugoslavia	62.7	5.4	1.3	3.9	4.7	5.5	4.5	18	122.5	76.8
Latvia	56.8	6.6	5.4	4.4	3.9	5.4	5.7	8	128.5	73.0
Kyrgyzstan	58.7	3.0	3.0	4.7	5.2	5.7	4.7	14	123.5	72.5
Turkmenistan	48.3	4.7	12.1	16.0	3.5	4.2	9.4	2	146.8	70.9
Kazakhstan	58.1	1.4	0.6	3.0	5.5	8.3	4.0	20	120.0	69.7
FYR Macedonia	55.3	5.3	4.7	4.6	4.1	4.1	5.0	12	125.0	69.1
Belarus	70.8	4.2	-9.3	-5.8	1.5	2.9	-1.4	26	93.0	65.8
Azerbaijan	40.5	7.9	7.9	9.0	9.9	10.7	10.9	1	154.4	62.5
Lithuania	42.8	7.4	4.5	3.7	3.8	4.1	5.2	11	125.8	53.8
Armenia	41.1	5.7	4.4	5.0	5.7	6.1	6.0	6	129.9	53.4

Tajikistan	40.0	4.3	4.3	5.8	5.5	5.9	5.7	7	128.6	51.4
Russia	52.2	-4.7	-5.3	-2.6	3.9	4.1	-1.0	25	95.1	49.6
Georgia	34.3	7.2	5.1	7.9	9.4	8.0	8.7	3	143.6	49.3
Moldova	35.1	-2.2	0.7	4.1	5.2	6.2	2.9	21	114.5	40.2
Ukraine	38.3	-2.0	-5.2	-1.1	4.0	4.6	0.0	24	100.0	38.3

Sources: PlanEcon 1998a and 1998b and author's calculations based on table 3.1.
[a] Ranking is according to the 2002 GDP index (1997 = 100) and 1998–2002 average rate of growth.
[b] Preliminary evaluation.

Additionally, several new elements of what has been agreed upon in the past must be emphasized. There are twelve major policy conclusions to be drawn:

1. The main policy conclusion—and the key implication of the post-Washington consensus—is that the institutional arrangements in an economy are the most important factor in determining its progress toward durable growth. What is taken for granted in some market economies—an institutional setup sufficient for ongoing liberalization and free market performance—must be created, often from the outset, in countries moving from statist, centrally planned economies. If there is a choice between developing these institutional arrangements spontaneously (by chance) or in a way directed by the government (by design), then the latter option is more suitable in the case of postsocialist countries. Yet the governments of industrial countries and international organizations must assist some governments in these attempts. Those countries that, because of strong government commitments, have been able to handle such design are doing much better than those that have not. Recovery has come sooner, growth is robust, and they have the prospect of sustainable development. Those that have tried to trust that major institutional overhaul can occur by itself—that is, by chance—or have not been able to guide this complex process adequately are lagging behind in both transition advancement and pace of growth.

2. The size of the government is less important than the quality of its policy and the manner in which changes of government size are brought about. In transition economies the issue is not just downsizing the government, but a deep restructuring of the public finance system and a change in the policy targets and means. Basically, fiscal transfers should be redirected from noncompetitive sectors toward institution building (including behavioral and cultural changes), investment in human capital, and hard infrastructure. Attempts to downsize the government through cuts in budgetary expenditure can cause more harm than good in terms of launching recovery and growth. Even if a small government is sometimes better than a larger one, often government cannot be downsized without causing economic contraction and deterioration in the standard of living. The idea must be considered that creative downsizing in a country's government should occur only when its economy is on the rise, even though most often the strongest attempt to downsize government

has been undertaken over a period of deep contraction. Thus, the general problem lies in restructuring expenditures rather than cutting them for an illusion of concurrent, albeit unsustainable, fiscal prudence.

3. Unlike certain liberalization measures, institution building by its nature must be a gradual process. Thus feedback between specific "inputs" to this process and its "output" must be monitored constantly, and the policies must be adjusted and corrected. In postsocialist transition there are many uncharted waters where one should not rely on misguided analogies with experience from distorted market economies. One must instead consider the specific features of the type of emerging market in each particular economy. Therefore it is necessary to orchestrate some institution-building innovation in a way that may not previously have been used in other places. This is true in particular regarding privatization and development of capital markets.

4. If institutional building is neglected and left to the spontaneous processes and unleashed forces of liberalized markets, then informal institutionalization fills the systemic vacuum. The negligence of government in organizing market infrastructure with active policy is causing a situation in transition economies of Eastern Europe and the former Soviet Union in which informal organizations and institutional links among them are taking over. In extreme cases, these involve widespread corruption and organized crime, the two main maladies in countries after liberalization and privatization under weak governments. Sometimes governments are too weak not because they are too large, but because they were forced to become smaller too early, that is before the infant market in the country was able to substitute for the state. Prematurely or too extensively downsized government is not strong enough, and then the market expands in the informal sector (shadow economy), while difficulties mount in the official economy. Then profits accrue to the informal sector, but revenues fall in the official sector, with all the negative consequences for the budget and social policy. Thus the market works in such a way that profits are privatized, but the losses are socialized in a politically unsustainable way.

5. Policies in transition economies must transform and streamline the judiciary system to serve the needs of the emerging market econ-

omy. Accomplishing this is a great challenge, since the old system of contract execution under planned allocation has ceased to exist, but a new system of contract implementation under market rules and culture has not yet matured. The establishment and development of new law (e.g., trade and tax code, capital market regulation, property rights protection, competition and antitrust rules, banking supervision, consumer protection, environmental protection) are even more important than and ought to be addressed before privatization of state assets. Creation and advancement of a legal framework for the market economy should be much higher on the agenda of international financial organizations. It must be put in front, as a more urgent and important issue than liberalization and privatization, since the latter can contribute to sound growth only if the former has already been secured.

6. A shift of competence and power from the central government to local governments is necessary for deregulation of a postsocialist economy. Such a shift means moving the public finance system toward decentralization and streamlining local governments by giving them greater fiscal autonomy. Otherwise the process of weakening the central government is not matched by a proportionate enhancing of the strength of local governments. Both levels of government must be seen as an integrated entity needed for the sake of gradual institution building. If local governments are not sufficiently enhanced while the central government is simultaneously weakened too much and market forces are not yet supported by new institutional arrangements, then liberalization and privatization will not necessarily improve capital allocation and will not raise economic efficiency.

7. Accelerating the development of NGOs in transition economies is an urgent necessity. Next to the private sector and the state, NGOs are the third indispensable pillar of a contemporary market economy and civic society. With a lack of a range of NGOs, which are supposed to take care of various aspects of public life, there is a continued tension in the relation between the state and society, and the expanding private sector does not provide a sufficient or satisfactory solution to this matter. Certain spheres within the public domain must depend neither on the state nor on the profit-oriented private sector. A growing part of international technical, financial, and political assistance to transition economies must be channeled into enhancing NGOs.

Otherwise the infant market economy and democracy in postsocialist countries will not evolve fast enough and the transition to a market economy will be incomplete. The lack of the institutional infrastructure provided by NGOs then becomes a progressively larger obstacle to successful systemic changes and high-quality growth.

8. During transition, income policy and government concern for equitable growth has great meaning. Whereas increasing inequity is unavoidable during the initial years of transition, the state must play an active role, through fiscal and social policies, in controlling income dispersion. Beyond a certain limit of disparity, further expansion of overall economic activity becomes constrained and growth starts to slow or recovery is delayed. If disparity growth is tolerated for a number of years during contraction, when the standard of living is improving for a few and declining for many, then the political support for necessary reforms will evaporate. Hence, large inequities turn the population against crucial institutional and structural reforms.

9. Postsocialist transition to the market is taking place at a time of worldwide globalization, hence opening and integration with the world economy is an indispensable part of the whole endeavor. Yet these processes must be managed carefully, with special attention to short-term capital flow liberalization, which must be monitored and controlled by the countries' fiscal and monetary authorities with the support of international financial institutions, such as the IMF and the Bank for International Settlement (BIS). It is better to liberalize capital markets in a transition economy later rather than sooner. First institution building must be advanced enough to serve its purpose, and stabilization ought to be consolidated into stability. Only then should financial markets be liberalized, and then in a gradual manner. Otherwise the societies of young emerging markets and democracies are not going to be supportive of the introduction of market mechanisms or integration with the world economy, and they may even become hostile toward such changes.

10. International organizations should not only support, but also insist on, further regional integration and cooperation. If a country's growth is expected to be durable and fast, it requires export expansion, which will depend on strong regional links. Thus it calls for institutional support, such as export-import banks, commodity ex-

changes, and credit insurance agencies. This should be the main
institution-building concern of the EBRD, supported by directed
lending from the EBRD and technical assistance from it. This type of
market infrastructure is still underdeveloped in transition economies; thus regional trade and cross-country foreign direct investment
are lagging behind overall changes that transition implies. What
should be one of the driving forces of sustainable growth in transition economies is actually one of the main obstacles to it.

11. The Bretton Woods organizations should reconsider their
policies toward transition economies. If the IMF mainly takes care of
financial liquidity, currency convertibility, fiscal prudence, and monetary stabilization, the World Bank should further focus attention
mainly on conditions for equitable growth and sustainable development. For obvious reasons these two kinds of economic policy aims—
or rather the means in the former case and the ends in the latter—are
often contradictory. There is an inclination to confuse the ends with
the means of the policy, to subordinate long-term development policy to short-term stabilization policy. Yet the record of transition so
far has shown neither much development nor much stability. Hence,
in the future fiscal and monetary policies must be subordinated to
development policy, not the other way around. There is a need for
the World Bank's performance criteria describing socioeconomic development as much as there is such a need for the traditional IMF
fiscal and monetary criteria. The new set of criteria should always
stress the implication, for growth, capital allocation, income distribution, and the social safety net, of the financial policies a country is
being advised to adopt and implement. The World Bank should not
accept and support policy reforms and actions that, while aiming at
financial stabilization, may lead to social destabilization resulting
from lack of growth, spreading poverty, increasing inequality, and
divestment in human capital.

12. These interactive processes of learning-by-monitoring and learn-
ing-by-doing continue and will last for several years in economies in
transition. After all, even if there is—as indeed there seems to be—a
growing chance for some kind of the post-Washington consensus,
this must be seen as a process, and not as a single act that can
be completed. Such an emerging consensus must also be developed
among many more partners than just the important organizations
based in Washington. Otherwise, the policies agreed to in Washington

will not be able to deliver what they assume elsewhere. This is also an important policy conclusion that should be obvious in the era of globalization. Furthermore, what may be agreed on currently must be revised often if conditions and challenges change, as they have done recently and undoubtedly will do again and again in the future. Thus the quest for a comprehensive and implementable consensus on policies facilitating sustainable growth must continue.

References

European Bank for Reconstruction and Development (EBRD). 1996. *Transition report.* London.

Fischer, Stanley. 1998. Opening remarks. Presented to the International Monetary Fund conference "Economic Policy and Equity," Washington, D.C., June 8–9.

Fry, Maxwell. 1993. *The fiscal abuse of central banks.* Working paper no. 93/58, International Monetary Fund, Washington, D.C.

Hausner, Jerzy. 1997. The political economy of socialism's transformation. Paper presented at United Nations University/World Institute for Development Economics Research project meeting, "Transition Strategies, Alternatives and Outcomes," Helsinki, May 15–17.

International Monetary Fund (IMF). 1996. *Partnership for sustainable global growth* (Interim Committee Declaration, September 29). Washington, D.C.

Kolodko, Grzegorz W. 1989. Reform, stabilization policies and economic adjustment in Poland. Working paper no. WP 51, World Institute for Development Economics Research of the United Nations University, Helsinki.

Kolodko, Grzegorz W. 1991. Inflation stabilization in Poland: A year after. *Rivista di Politica Economica,* no. 6 (June): 289–330.

Kolodko, Grzegorz W. 1992. *From output collapse to sustainable growth in transition economies—The fiscal implications.* Working paper, Washington, D.C.: International Monetary Fund.

Kolodko, Grzegorz W. 1993. A strategy for economic transformation in Eastern Europe. *Most* 4, no. 1: 1–25.

Kolodko, Grzegorz W. 1996. *Poland 2000: The new economic strategy.* Warsaw: Poltext.

Kolodko, Grzegorz W. 1998. A plan for Russia. *The Harriman Review* (Special Issue: *The Russian Economy in Crisis*), Columbia University, New York, December 24–27.

Kolodko, Grzegorz W. 2000. *From shock to therapy: The political economy of postsocialist transformation.* Oxford: Oxford University Press.

Kolodko, Grzegorz W., and D. Mario Nuti. 1997. *The Polish alternative: Old myths, hard facts and new strategies in the successful transformation of the Polish economy.* WIDER Research for Action 33. Helsinki: United Nations University World Institute for Development Economics Research.

Laski, Kazimierz. 1990. The stabilization plan for Poland. *Wirtschaftspolitische Bläter* 5: 414–58.

Montes, Manuel. 1997. Vietnam: Is there a socialist road to the market?. Paper presented at United Nations University/World Institute for Development Economics Research project meeting, "Transition Strategies, Alternatives and Outcomes," Helsinki, May 15–17.

North, Douglass C. 1997. *The contribution of the new institutional economics to an understanding of the transition problem*. WIDER Annual Lectures 1. Helsinki: United Nations University World Institute for Development Economics Research.

Nuti, D. Mario. 1990. Crisis, reform and stabilization in Central Eastern Europe: Prospects and Western response. In *La Grande Europa, La Nuova Europa: Opportunita e Rischi*. Sienna: Monti Dei Paschi Di Sienna.

Nuti, D. Mario. 1992. Lessons from stabilization and reform in Central Eastern Europe. Working papers no. 92, Council of the European Community, Brussels.

Nuti, D. Mario. 1996. Exchange rate and monetary policy in Poland 1994–96, or the case for privatising the National Bank of Poland. Paper presented at United Nations University/World Institute for Development Economics Research project meeting, "Transition Strategies, Alternatives and Outcomes," Helsinki, May 15–17.

Organisation for Economic Cooperation and Development (OECD). 1996. *Czechoslovakia 1996*. OECD Economic Surveys. Paris: Author.

PlanEcon. 1998a. *Review and outlook for the former Soviet Union*. Washington, D.C.: Author.

PlanEcon. 1998b. *Review and outlook for Eastern Europe*. Washington, D.C.: PlanEcon, Author.

Poznanski, Kazimierz. 1993. Poland's transition to capitalism: Shock and therapy. In *Stabilization and privatization in Poland*, ed. K. Poznanski. Boston: Kluwer Academic.

Poznanski, Kazimierz. 1996. *Poland's protracted transition: Institutional change and economic growth*. Cambridge: Cambridge University Press.

Rosati, Dariusz. 1994. Output decline during transition from plan to market. *Economics of Transition* 2, no. 4: 419–42.

Soros, George. 1997. The capitalist threat. *Atlantic Monthly* (February).

Stern, Nicholas. 1996. The transition in Eastern Europe and the former Soviet Union: Some strategic lessons from the experience of 25 countries over six years. Paper presented at OECD/CCET colloquium, Paris, May 29–30.

Stern, Nicholas, and Joseph E. Stiglitz. 1997. A framework for a development strategy in a market economy: Objectives, scope, institutions and instruments. Working paper no. 20. European Bank for Reconstruction and Development, London.

Stiglitz, Joseph E. 1998a. *More instruments and broader goals: Moving toward the post-Washington consensus*. WIDER Annual Lectures 2. Helsinki: United Nations University World Institute for Development Economics Research.

Stiglitz, Joseph E. 1998b. Economic science, economic policy, and economic advice. Paper presented at annual conference on development economics, "Knowledge for Development," World Bank, Washington D.C., April 20–21.

Williamson, John. 1990. What Washington means by policy reform. In *Latin American adjustment: How much has happened?* ed. John Williamson. Washington, D.C.: Institute for International Economics.

Williamson, John. 1997. The Washington consensus revisited. In *Economic and social development into the XXI century*, ed. Louis Emmerij. Washington, DC: Inter-American Development Bank.

Wolf, Martin. 1998. Ins and outs of capital flows. *Financial Times*, June 16.

World Bank. 1996. *From plan to market.* World Development Report 1996. Washington, D.C.: Author.

World Bank. 1997. *The state in a changing world.* World Development Report 1997. Washington, D.C.: Oxford University Press for World Bank.

II

The Country Experiences

4

East Germany: Transition
with Unification,
Experiments, and
Experiences

Jürgen von Hagen and Rolf
R. Strauch

Introduction

East Germany remains unique among the transition economies. Soon after the fall of the Berlin Wall in 1989, it became part of the Federal Republic of Germany. German union meant the transplantation of West Germany's legal, administrative, and economic infrastructure to the five new federal states. Perhaps the most visible aspects of this from the outside were East Germany's adoption of the deutsche mark (DM), the integration of East Germany into the fiscal framework of the Federal Republic, and the immediate and full participation of East Germany in the trading system of the European Union.

At the time, the rapid integration of East Germany into the Federal Republic was met with high hopes, but also with warning criticism. Optimistic views, including those of the West German government under Chancellor Helmut Kohl, held that East Germany would be rapidly reconstructed and transformed into a thriving, modern economy and that East Germany would quickly converge with West Germany in terms of economic performance. In fact, the federal government's economic policy toward the new states rested on the assumption that the transition phase would be successfully completed in a matter of a few years. In contrast, those who were more skeptical warned that East Germany risked becoming Germany's "mezzogiorno," a region permanently lagging behind in economic development and dependent on transfers from the West.

More than a decade after the fall of the Berlin Wall, we can ask how successful East Germany's transition has been and to what extent convergence has occurred. This chapter gives an account of East Germany's economic development since 1990. In the second section, we review East Germany's macroeconomic transition. In the third section, we consider its progress in economic restructuring. The fourth section is devoted to the adjustments in the labor market and the fifth to public finance aspects of East Germany's transition. The final section delineates our main conclusions: First, there has been significant convergence in the administrative and economic realm, though persistent differences remain in the level of output and incomes as well as local capacities. Second, the risk that East Germany will become a transfer-dependent economy is considerable for the foreseeable future. Endogenous institutional change in the labor market showing its first signs in East Germany may become important in overcoming these problems.

Macroeconomic Performance

Table 4.1 summarizes East Germany's macroeconomic performance since 1991.[1] Between 1991 and 1997, East Germany's total population fell by almost 3 percent, although net migration between East and West Germany was low after 1990. Real GDP had already started to decline prior to German union in 1990; after German union, the decline accelerated. The total drop in real GDP between 1989 and 1991 amounted to 35 percent. From 1992 on, real GDP increased by a total of 41 percent. In 1989, East Germany's real GDP stood at 13 percent of West German GDP; by 1991, it had decreased to 8 percent, but between 1991 and 1997, it rose from 8 percent to 10 percent of West German GDP. Real economic growth in East Germany was vigorous only in the first half of the 1990s; it fell to levels close to the low West German growth rates after 1995. Thus East Germany seems to be closely tied to the West German business cycle in the second half of the 1990s. Per capita real GDP started out at 31 percent of West Germany's level in 1991 and rose to 44.5 percent during the 1990s.

In 1991, East German industrial production fell by 33 percent compared to the annualized level of the first half of 1990. Table 4.1 shows that the recovery in this area did not take off before 1993, and it quickly slowed again in the German recession of the mid-1990s. Today, industrial production in East Germany barely exceeds pre-transformation levels.

Table 4.1 indicates how different the development of per capita consumption in East Germany was during this period. Per capita consumption reached 51 percent of the West German level in 1991; that is, the gap between the two parts of Germany was much smaller

Table 4.1
Economic performance, Germany, 1991–1998

	Real GDP (billions)		Real GDP growth rate		Per capita real GDP		Population (thousands)	Consumption per capita		Industrial production (growth rate)	
	East	West	East	West	East	West		East	West	East	West
1991	206.0	2,647.6	−22.9	5.1	12.9	41.3	15,910	11,527	22,582	−33.0	3.7
1992	222.2	2,694.3	7.9	1.8	14.1	41.5	15,730	12,501	22,813	0.8	−0.1
1993	242.4	2,639.1	9.8	−0.2	15.5	40.3	15,645	12,778	22,565	6.0	−7.7
1994	265.6	2,694.0	10.4	2.1	17.1	40.9	15,564	13,255	22,644	14.5	2.9
1995	277.3	2,718.2	4.7	0.9	18.1	41.1	15,505	13,755	—	4.8	0.0
1996	286.4	2,747.6	3.8	1.1	18.5	41.4	15,451	13,837	—	1.1	−0.6
1997	292.2	2,809.5	1.9	2.3	18.8	42.2	15,405	13,548	—	2.5	2.6
1998	297.5	2,919.1	2.0	3.9	19.4[a]	—	15,350[a]	—	—	—	—

Sources: Council of Economic Advisors, various issues, and von Hagen 1997.
Note: Dashes indicate data are not available.
[a] Estimated.

in consumption terms than in production terms. By 1994, East German per capita consumption had advanced to 58 percent of the West German level.[2]

East and West German consumption figures are difficult to compare during this period, because of the remaining distortions of relative prices. For example, housing prices remain much lower in East Germany than in West Germany. Thus the differences in standard of living in East and West Germany are likely significantly smaller than the consumption data suggest. Microeconomic data (DIW, IfW, and IWH 1999) indicate that average household incomes in East Germany had advanced to 80 percent of West German levels in 1995 and that households in East Germany could in that same year purchase a representative bundle of goods, for which West German consumers paid DM 100, for DM 91. This suggests that East German real household incomes were approximately 90 percent of West German levels in 1995. Household ownership rates were similar for most categories of consumer durables in East and West Germany in the mid-1990s. This convergence is consistent with the observation that net migration from East to West Germany virtually stopped in the early 1990s.

Table 4.2 reports the uses of GDP in East Germany for the years for which data are available. This table reveals perhaps the most stunning aspect of East Germany's transition process: its ability to consume and invest far above the level of domestically produced

Table 4.2
East Germany: Uses of GDP

	Consumption	Private investment	Government purchases	External balance	Public transfers	Foreign investment
1991	89.0	44.5	43.5	−75.0	67.5	15.5
1992	81.7	47.7	42.0	−70.8	56.9	20.0
1993	74.2	47.2	37.6	−59.5	51.7	20.4
1994	68.0	50.4	34.9	−55.5	46.0	21.1
1995	64.9	48.4	33.1	−44.2	46.5	—
1996	65.9	46.2	32.8	−43.7	45.3	—
1997	62.3	43.5	31.0	−36.8	43.4	—

Source: Federal Statistical Office.
Note: All entries are percentages of East German GDP. Dashes indicate data are not available.

output and incomes. The external deficit of East Germany amounted to 75 percent of its GDP in 1991. In 1994, it still stood significantly above 50 percent. By 1997, the external deficit amounted to 37 percent of GDP, but the 1995–1997 figures may be biased downward, as they do not include all investment. As the table shows, public-sector transfers from West Germany financed between 80 and 100 percent of that deficit.

To put these numbers in perspective, note that West German consumption amounted to 55 percent of West German GDP in 1991, investment amounted to 21.3 percent, and government purchases to 18 percent. The ratio of consumption to GDP thus was higher by two thirds in East Germany than in West Germany. Private household saving ratios (saving in relation to disposable income), however, were almost the same in the two parts of Germany. Thus the higher consumption ratio is not an indication of a higher propensity of East German households to consume out of a given income, but rather the result of a higher ratio of disposable incomes to GDP, which was facilitated by the public-sector transfers.

Another interesting observation comes from combining the data on foreign investment from table 4.2 with those concerning the investment subsidies paid by the federal government to firms investing in East Germany during the 1990s, reported in table 4.12. Combining the two series yields a ratio of investment financed by external funds to GDP of 23.8 percent in 1991, 25.7 percent in 1992, 25.2 percent in 1993, and 25.2 percent in 1994. Subtracting this from the ratio of investments to GDP in table 4.2 yields an internal investment rate for East Germany of 25.0 percent, 23.2 percent, 22.2 percent, and 22.9 percent, respectively, for the same years. Except in 1991, this rate is not much different from West Germany's rate of investment, which hovered around 20 percent in these years. Again, the data suggest that the very large investment rate is due to expansion of the budget constraint rather than a significantly different pattern of economic choices in East Germany compared to West Germany. This suggests that without the public transfers, East German investment would have been lower by the amount of direct investment subsidies.

The observation of similar investment and consumption propensities in East and West Germany is puzzling in view of the fact that because of the scarcity of modern capital equipment in East Germany, the real rate of return on capital should have been high and induced East Germans to save and invest more out of their incomes.

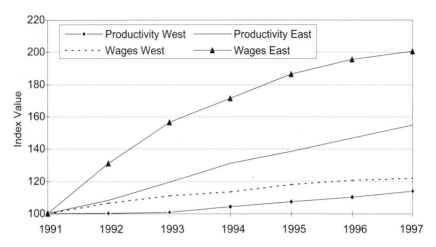

Figure 4.1
Wages and productivity in East and West Germany, 1991–1997
Source: Deutsche Bundesbank.
Note: Wages indicate the collective bargaining agreements computed as real hourly earnings; productivity is the GDP produced by a worker per hour.

The solution to the puzzle lies in the discrepancy between wage cost and productivity in East Germany. The conversion of East German wages into DM wages at a rate of one to one implied that wages initially were much higher relative to productivity in East Germany than in West Germany.

Figure 4.1 illustrates the subsequent movements in wage and productivity levels. Between 1990 and 1991, East German wages rose by 18 percent, followed by 32 percent in 1992 and 19 percent in 1993. Later on, the wage hikes became more moderate, and from 1995 onward real wage growth actually fell below labor productivity gains. Productivity increased during the process, but far less than wages during the initial phase. Productivity gains peaked at 10 percent in 1993 and have been around 6 percent since then. Unit labor cost in East Germany started out at 150 percent of West German levels in the early 1990s. A strong improvement in this area in the first years of the 1990s came to a halt after 1993. At the end of the 1990s, unit labor cost stood at 130 percent of the West German level. Thus, at the end of that decade, East Germany's economy suffered from a severe and persistent disadvantage in competitiveness relative to that of West Germany.

Table 4.3
Investment support programs in East Germany (in billions of DM)

	1991	1992	1993	1994	1995	1996	1997	1998[a]
Tax allowances	1.04	4.19	4.89	4.44	3.62	2.41	1.74	1.32
Depreciation allowances	3.40	4.90	6.30	7.10	9.10	9.50	6.82	7.00
Investment subsidies	7.52	6.38	6.98	6.70	5.08	6.27	4.48	2.37
ERP loans	8.15	6.12	6.02	4.10	3.58	3.58	3.17	1.52
KfW loans	5.92	6.34	3.79	2.05	2.14	2.14	1.91	0.72
DtA loans	3.52	3.88	3.19	3.16	2.47	2.47	2.07	0.83

Sources: ERP (European Reconstruction Program), KfW (Kreditanstalt für Wiederaufbau), and DtA (Deutsche Ausgleichsbank).
[a] First six months only.

The Kohl government's justification for the initial conversion rate for East German wages and its subsequent support for rapid nominal wage equalization was that East German labor, even if priced high, would soon attract capital and modern technology because of the high level of training of East German workers and that this would fill the productivity gap. Obviously, this "wage-pull" argument, though it bought the government popularity with the labor unions, makes no economic sense, as it disregards the importance of the rate of return on capital for capital investments. The data suggest that the government's policies failed to mobilize internal savings and investment in East Germany. Put simply, the return on capital was too low given the excessive wage cost.

To spur investment nevertheless, the Kohl government paid massive investment subsidies of various forms, as shown in table 4.3. Sinn (1995) estimates that, as a result, the cost of capital in East Germany became negative for industrial investments and the renovation of buildings and very low, though positive, for other types of investments. But since much of this investment support was based on saving taxes, it could be obtained only by firms that were mature enough to earn sufficient profits already. East German businesses were therefore less able to enjoy such benefits than West German businesses (DIW, IfW, and IWH 1999). Sinn (1995) argues that these subsidies therefore favored the acquisition of East German firms by West German businesses, without necessarily leading to the building of new production facilities. They seem to have done little to stimulate investment by East German companies in East Germany.

Table 4.4
Distribution of investment in East Germany

	Manufac-turing	Trade and transpor-tation	Services without residential housing	Residential housing	Govern-ment
1991	32.3	22.0	10.3	17.1	17.0
1992	31.1	21.1	9.7	18.1	18.9
1993	27.8	19.5	14.1	20.2	17.7
1994	23.8	18.0	16.1	24.2	17.4
1995	22.6	15.7	18.0	27.7	15.8
1996	21.2	15.7	17.5	29.5	15.5
1997	21.0	16.3	16.3	30.5	15.2
1998	21.4	16.2	16.4	29.4	15.9

Source: Council of Economic Advisors, various issues.
Note: All entries in percentage of total annual investment.

Table 4.4 reports the sectoral distribution of investment in East Germany during the 1990s. In the early years of transition, manufacturing attracted the largest part of investment, followed by trade and transportation. This is consistent with the need to rebuild the productive capital stock of the East German economy, which was largely worn out at the end of the 1980s (von Hagen 1997; DIW, IfW, and IWH 1999). Over time, however, residential housing became the main attractor of new capital, a result of tax incentives that the federal government set in favor of residential housing. At the same time, investment in the service sector excluding residential housing increased its share in total investment significantly.

Between 1991 and 1998, an estimated DM 1,300 million were invested in new capital equipment and structures in East Germany (DIW, IfW, and IWH 1999). The capital stock, which initially was reduced significantly by the dismantling of old production sites, grew at an annual rate of 7 percent over the same period, compared to 2.5 percent in West Germany. As a result, the average age of capital equipment had fallen by 1994 to 25.3 years, compared to 32.6 years in 1991 and 21.3 years in West Germany in 1994.

Because of monetary union with West Germany, inflation was never a problem in East Germany's transition phase.[3] Under the strict price stability orientation of the German Bundesbank, the relative price adjustments required by the deregulation of the East German

Table 4.5
Inflation and unemployment in Germany, 1991–1997

	PPI inflation (percent per year)		CPI inflation (percent per year)		Unemployment (percent)	
	East	West	East	West	East	West
1991	—	2.5	78.0	105.8	10.7	5.5
1992	2.3	1.4	78.6	105.3	14.8	5.8
1993	1.9	0.0	83.3	97.2	14.9	7.3
1994	1.3	0.6	95.4	100.0	14.6	8.3
1995	1.4	1.7	100.0	100.0	13.5	8.4
1996	1.4	−0.1	101.1	99.4	15.0	9.1
1997	1.8	1.1	103.6	102.0	17.5	9.9

Source: Council of Economic Advisors, various issues.
Note: Dash indicates data are not available.

markets were never allowed to feed into general inflation, and the conversion of monetary assets from East German mark to deutsche mark succeeded in avoiding an inflationary monetary overhang. Table 4.5 shows that consumer prices still rose considerably faster in East than in West Germany in the early 1990s, peaking at 12.1 percent in 1992. The strongest price increases were for housing (the rental price of apartments increased by 369 percent between 1991 and 1997), health care and cosmetics (53 percent), and energy (35 percent); the smallest price increases occurred for textiles (3 percent) and furniture and household goods (5.8 percent). In the late 1990s, the rate of price increase in East Germany decreased to the West German level.

After an initial drop of about 30 percent, producer prices in East Germany remained flat throughout the 1990s, moving pretty much in line with West German producer prices, as shown in table 4.5. This close comovement indicates the high degree of market integration between the two parts of Germany, which did not leave much room for deviations of producer prices in East Germany from those in West Germany. The largest price increase in this category was that for electricity, gas, and water supply, with a total increase of 17.8 percent between 1991 and 1997.

Unemployment in East Germany started off at 4.7 percent in the second half of 1990, increasing quickly to an average of 10.7 percent in 1991. After three years of stagnant unemployment rates above 14 percent, those rates declined slightly to 13.5 percent in 1995 but

Table 4.6
Sectoral structure of production

	East Germany, 1991	East Germany, 1997	West Germany, 1997
Agriculture, forestry	3.3	1.7	1.1
Manufacturing	36.1	34.2	32.6
Construction	11.8	14.5	4.6
Energy, water, mining	7.7	4.1	2.2
Industry	16.7	15.1	25.7
Trade, transportation	14.6	13.2	14.8
Services	21.4	30.8	38.2
Government	24.6	19.9	13.3

Source: Federal Statistical Office.
Note: All entries are percentages of total output.

returned to even higher levels in the late 1990s. Note, however, that West Germany saw a rising unemployment rate at the same time.

Economic Restructuring

The 1990s witnessed strong structural adjustments in the East German economy. Table 4.6 shows that the agricultural sector, which was still relatively large in 1991, declined by 1.6 percentage points and at the end of the 1990s was approaching the West German share of a mere 1.1 percent of GDP. The share of manufacturing fell from 36.1 percent to 34.6 percent from 1991 to 1997, remaining slightly higher than in West Germany. Whereas trade and transportation started off and remained at a similar position in East and West Germany over the period, the service sector in East Germany rose almost 10 percentage points but remained 8 percent below the share of services in West Germany as of 1997. The government sector in East Germany declined by 4.7 percentage points over the period but remained 6.6 percent higher than in West Germany as of 1997.

A closer look at these data reveals a dramatic process of de-industrialization in East Germany. The industrial sector shrank by almost 2 percent of GDP from 1991 to 1997, nonconstruction manufacturing by over 4.5 percent. Its share in 1997 was below 20 percent of GDP, much lower than that of industry in West Germany. The large and growing share of construction also reflects the East German construction boom of the 1990s. Compared to West Germany, the size of this sector seems hardly sustainable, signaling a further need for restructuring.

Overall, table 4.6 indicates a strong shift in East German production from industry to services. To some extent, this is because under the old socialist regime, many services typically offered by specialized institutions in market economies and therefore counted as part of the service sector were offered by the state-owned industrial companies and implicitly counted as industrial output. Typical examples are social services offered by East German firms. Groebel (1996) estimates that this difference between the institutional division of labor in the economy results in an overestimation of the share of the manufacturing sector in East Germany by 17 percent and an underestimation of the service sector by 25 percent relative to official statistics.[4] More generally, however, the move from a manufacturing-based to a service-based economy is a common sign of a modernizing society. In this regard, West Germany has lagged significantly behind her West European partners over the past twenty-five years. Assuming that some of the productive activity at least that is currently in the construction sector in East Germany will move into services over time, the data in the table predict that East Germany will lead West Germany on the way to a more modern, service-oriented economy in the longer run.

Table 4.7 indicates that the restructuring process in East Germany has been accompanied by strong changes in productivity. Overall, productivity in the East caught up from a third to half of the West German level between 1991 and 1997. The relative gains were strong in the early 1990s but slowed in the late 1990s; as West Germany realized significant productivity gains, too, after 1994, East German productivity increased in parallel. The strongest productivity gains were realized in the manufacturing sector, whereas relative productivity in the service sector remained low in East Germany. Combining the information in tables 4.5–4.7 suggests that productivity gains in East Germany in the early 1990s were realized predominantly through the shedding of labor and only later through the improvement of the capital stock (see Dietrich et al. 1998).

Hidden behind these aggregate figures for the industrial sector are some very strong relative changes in production across East German industries, as table 4.8 shows. Mining and quarries, leather production and processing, energy and water supply, and machinery were

Table 4.7
Productivity trends in East and West Germany

	Total economy		Manufacturing		Trade, banking		Services	
	West	East	West	East	West	East	West	East
1991	100.0	32.6	100.0	28.8	100.0	35.1	100.0	33.8
1992	100.8	39.9	99.3	41.4	99.9	41.2	100.1	37.0
1993	100.6	44.5	96.9	50.1	99.4	47.6	100.9	36.6
1994	103.8	46.3	102.4	53.9	101.7	50.2	101.3	36.0
1995	105.7	46.9	104.2	54.8	104.3	51.3	101.7	36.1
1996	108.4	48.3	105.8	58.8	106.9	52.1	104.2	36.6
1997	112.4	49.1	111.6	60.3	110.9	51.8	106.2	37.1

Source: Council of Economic Advisors, various issues.
Note: West: 1991 = 100. East: Current productivity in percentage of productivity in West Germany.

Table 4.8
Relative change in industrial output in East Germany, 1991–1997

	Total industry	Mining, quarries	Manufacturing	Food, tobacco	Textiles and clothing	Leather
Output[a]	32.8	−63.7	58.9	97.9	8.4	−54.7
Productivity[b]	61.3	95.3	—	71.9	57.5	66.5

	Wood processing	Paper and printing	Mineral oils, etc.	Chemicals	Rubber, plastics	Glass, ceramics
Output[a]	248.3	112.0	29.0	10.0	221.6	143.8
Productivity[b]	68.2	93.9	26.4	36.1	71.1	73.6

	Metal, metal goods	Machinery	Office machinery, optics	Furniture, musical instruments	Energy, water
Output[a]	156.2	−26.0	99.9	80.6	−11.5
Productivity[b]	66.5	51.7	69.3	58.3	—

Source: Federal Statistical Office.
Note: Dashes indicate data are not available.
[a] Relative change, 1991–1997.
[b] East Germany in relation to West Germany (percentage), 1996.

the losing industries of the 1990s. In contrast, production in the wood processing industry, rubber and plastics, metal goods, glass and ceramics, and office machinery and optics were the expanding industries during that decade. This restructuring of East German industry occurred simultaneously with similarly strong shifts in employment and in labor productivity (von Hagen 1997).

Reviewing these structural changes in the industrial sector, Ragnitz et al. (1998) and Dietrich et al. (1998) note a number of tendencies. First, the relatively fast-growing industries in East Germany tend to be those that are intensive in transportation cost and produce primarily for the regional markets rather than the German and international markets. This is consistent with the observation that East Germany today had a ratio of exports to GDP of less than 10 percent at the end of the 1990s. Industries that are less protected by transportation costs apparently find it too hard to compete with Western European countries because of the combination of low productivity and high wages.

Second, the relatively fast-growing industries in East Germany at the end of the 1990s are those that, according to West German experience, tend to have a limited growth potential only in the longer run and those that have a relatively low intensity in high-skilled labor. A continuation of this trend would imply a slowdown of East German growth in the long run, with only limited chances to catch up with West Germany in terms of per capita output and labor productivity. These trends together signal a risk that East Germany may develop a lasting dependency on income transfers from West Germany, if comparable standards of living are to be maintained in both East and West Germany.

Labor Market Adjustment

In 1989, the East German economy had 9.56 million employees; as table 4.9 shows, this number fell to 7.59 million in 1991. By 1997, the number of jobs in East Germany had further decreased to 6.43 million. Thus, the economy lost about one third of its jobs during the 1990s. Note that the process of job destruction in the 1990s was parallel in East and West Germany, though less pronounced in the latter.

The decisive factor in East Germany's labor market crisis was the immediate and full extension of West Germany's labor market institutions to East Germany, including an unemployment insurance

Table 4.9
German employment (in thousands of jobs)

	East	West
1991	7,590	28,973
1992	6,725	29,135
1993	6,544	28,677
1994	6,656	28,316
1995	6,736	28,081
1996	6,603	27,769
1997	6,425	27,848

Source: Council of Economic Advisors, various issues.

characterized by generous unemployment benefits. Until 1994, the income replacement rate in German unemployment insurance was 68 percent for an unemployed individual with at least one child, and 63 percent for an unemployed person without children. These rates were lowered to 67 percent and 60 percent, respectively, in the Consolidation Act of 1993. The duration of benefits varies from one year for individuals under the age of 45 to 32 months for individuals above the age of 57. Upon expiration, unemployment benefits are replaced by unemployment aid, which has no maximum duration for individuals below age 65. In 1994, income replacement rates under unemployment aid were lowered from 58 percent to 56 percent for individuals with at least one child and from 57 percent to 53 percent for an unemployed person without children (BMA 1998; Steffen 1995).

The rules of unemployment insurance in East Germany defined the rules of wage bargaining in East Germany. They allowed West German employers and labor unions to fend off the competition of low-wage workers from East Germany. Whereas unions feared such competition for the pressure it might exert on the high wage level in West Germany, employers were equally dismayed with the prospect of low-wage competitors from the new parts of the country. Their collusion was facilitated by the fact that West German unions soon took over wage negotiations in East Germany. Western union leaders presented themselves as acting on behalf of the East German workers, as East German unions had fallen into political disrepute for their association with the communist regime. To eliminate wage competition from East Germany, employers associations and unions in 1991 agreed on a stepwise adjustment of East German wages to Western

levels. Several industries—most importantly the steel industry—
envisaged having the same wage levels in East and West Germany
by 1994 (Council of Economic Advisors 1992: 107–10). Moreover,
unions striving for a very rapid adjustment of wages signed contracts only for less than a year to facilitate renegotiations and a quick
upward adjustment of wages.

The result of this could only be to price East German labor out of
the market. But high wage levels secured high unemployment benefits, which left the unemployed better off staying in the East than
moving to the West to find employment. Massive unemployment in
East Germany was the result (Sinn 1995; von Hagen 1997).[5] Instead
of creating jobs in the East, the adjustment process triggered huge
social transfers from West Germany. Elsewhere, we explain that the
Kohl government, which was trailing far behind in the polls running
up to the election in 1990, allowed this to happen in the hope of improving its reelection chances (von Hagen and Strauch 1999).

The federal government responded to the rise in unemployment
with an unprecedented level of labor market interventions. Table 4.10
reports the number of participants in different labor market schemes
and the unemployment rate for East Germany. Between 2 and 5 percent of the German labor force participated in public-works programs
from 1991 to 1997; a similar number of employees were enrolled in
training programs. This number fell to 171,000 by 1997 from its peak
of 428,000 in 1992. Early retirement and provisional retirement
schemes were a third kind of labor market policy. At their peak, some
11 percent of the total labor force benefited from these schemes. An
even larger number of individuals were included in programs supporting part-time work during the initial stage of the transition process (BMA 1998). In 1991, 19.6 percent of the labor force received
such transfers, but the number of recipients was significantly smaller
in subsequent years. The combined full-time work equivalent of
these measures amounted to almost 20 percent of the labor force
in 1991 and approximately 11 percent in more recent years. Taken
together, they created what became known as a "secondary labor
market" in Germany.

Empirical evidence on the effectiveness of these measures in terms
of a reintegration of participants into the labor market is rather
disappointing.[6] Only on-the-job training or training demanded by
enterprises seem to have a positive effect on an individual's chances
to find employment. In particular, the programs have failed to rein-

Table 4.10
Labor market policies in East Germany, 1991–1997

	1991	1992	1993	1994	1995	1996	1997
Employees in part-time work	1,616	370	181	97	71	71	50
Employees in job creation schemes	183	388	260	281	312	278	235
Employees in training schemes	169	428	351	248	250	238	171
Employees in early retirement or transitional old-age schemes	554	811	853	650	374	186	58
Employed persons	7,321	6,387	6,219	6,330	6,396	6,259	6,053
Unemployed persons	913	1,170	1,149	1,142	1,047	1,169	1,363
Unemployment rate	11.1%	14.4%	15.1%	15.2%	14%	15.7%	18.1%

Sources: Deutsche Bundesbank 1998, Autorengemeinschaft 1998.
Note: Employment figures in thousands of employees.

Table 4.11
German labor market participation

	Participation rate			Employment rate	
	East 1991	East 1998	West 1998	East 1998	West 1998
All male	59.9	58.2	57.0	48.2	52.1
All female	50.0	48.6	39.7	37.3	36.3
Female, unmarried	27.6	34.4	33.5	28.1	30.9
Female, married	73.0	67.1	49.4	51.4	45.4
Female widowed, divorced	30.7	29.3	25.6	20.0	22.3

Source: Federal Statistical Office.
Note: Participation rate: Self-employed, employed, and unemployed persons as percentage of total working-age population (in group). Employment rate: Self-employed persons and employees as percentage of total working-age population (in group).

tegrate the long-term unemployed into the labor market (Berthold and Fehn 1997). Thus they were unable to overcome the structural weaknesses of Germany's highly administered labor market.[7]

Table 4.11 considers the labor market participation rates of different groups of the East and West German population. Participation of East German males started the decade at almost 60 percent in 1991. It declined somewhat and approached the West German rate as the decade progressed. Female participation, which was traditionally higher in East Germany than in West Germany, remained so in 1998. An interesting observation from this table is that the differences in employment rates between East and West Germany are much more limited than the differences in unemployment rates from table 4.5 would suggest. This similarity of employment rates in the two parts of the country suggests that labor supply choices in East Germany are becoming much like the West German ones. In this sense, we observe convergence of the two labor markets. However, convergence does not imply integration, which would suggest a narrowing of regional unemployment rate differentials. In 1998, West German unemployment rates varied between 8.7 percent and 13.6 percent among the non-city-states; East German unemployment rates varied between 18.4 percent and 21.7 percent. These large differences between the two parts of the country suggest that the unemployment insurance and welfare systems create sufficiently strong disincentives to moving to prevent the equalization of unemployment rates expected in an integrated market.

If we accept the hypothesis of similar employment choices in East and West Germany, table 4.11 suggests that the difference in unemployment rates in the two parts of the country largely reflects differences in the response to institutional incentives to register unemployed. Specifically, East German individuals who effectively chose to leave the labor market decided to remain registered unemployed to receive unemployment benefits, while their West German counterparts leave the market without registering. Assume that instead, East Germany had started with participation rates similar to those of West Germany in 1998. Under this assumption, the same observed employment rate in East Germany in 1998 would have implied a registered rate of unemployment of 16.2 percent instead of 17.2 percent for all males in 1998, but only 7.4 percent instead of 23.2 percent for all females. These estimates imply a reduction of the number of registered unemployed males by 90,000 and unemployed females by 657,000, or a total of 747,000 individuals, more than 50 percent of the 1.4 million registered unemployed in East Germany.[8] The resulting unemployment rate would then be similar to West Germany's. Admittedly, this is a rather mechanistic calculation, but one that illustrates the large consequences of the adverse incentive effects of Germany's labor market institutions and the low quality of unemployment rates as welfare indicators for East Germany.

Eventually, a wage policy conducted largely according to the economic interests of West German unions and employers associations could not remain without an institutional response. The response has been an increasing erosion of the traditional German wage-setting institutions in East Germany. Traditionally, wages in East Germany have been negotiated between unions and representatives of the employers association, with settlements binding for all employers who are members of the association. Thus, a firm can withdraw from the settlement only if it leaves the association. Recent data (DIW, IfW, and IWH 1999) show that at the end of the 1990s only 15 percent of all firms were members of an association and intended to remain members, down from 26 percent in 1993; 79 percent were not members, up from 64 percent. Only 36 percent of all employees in East Germany were working in firms that were members of an association, down from 62 percent in 1993. Of those employed, 55 percent worked for firms that were not members of an employers association, up from 24 percent in 1993. Those who still received wages under union contracts accounted for 67 percent of all employees in the late

1990s, down from 83 percent in 1993. An important long-term consequence of the labor market adjustments may thus be that East German wage-setting arrangements will gain more flexibility than those in West Germany.

Public Finance Aspects

As noted in previous sections of the chapter, government spending programs were the backbone of several macroeconomic developments and distortions in East Germany in the 1990s. The following subsection will describe how the East German Länder were integrated into the West German fiscal system and analyze the fiscal magnitude and implications of massive state intervention. Then we will turn to the more specific aspect of local public finances, because the peculiarities and problems of institution building and fiscal integration can be illustrated particularly well in this area. Despite clear convergence toward West German patterns, marked differences continued to exist in the fiscal position of local governments in East Germany at the end of the 1990s.

West-East Transfers

German unification implied the extension of West Germany's social security and assistance institutions to East Germany and inclusion of East Germany in its federal grant system. German fiscal federalism establishes a system of horizontal and vertical resource flows among different layers of government, complemented by centralized pensions and unemployment insurance administered by independent federal agencies.

All German states participate in a horizontal equalization system that aims at reducing differences in their tax revenues. Because of the weakness of their tax bases, the immediate integration of the new states into this system would have turned all West German states into net contributors. As the West German states resisted this, the East German states were initially excluded from equalization and supplementary federal grants paid under this scheme. The federal government shouldered the bulk of the responsibility for fiscal equalization by transferring large amounts of funds to the new states. The German Unity Fund, originally devised to cover the deficits of the GDR government during the interim period until unification, soon became the main financial arrangement for these transfers (Schwinn 1997, 51–54; Rensch 1997). Beyond their contributions to this fund, West German states paid only small transfers to those in East Germany.

A 1993 consolidation program dissolved the German Unity Fund and integrated the new states into the equalization system from 1995 on. To facilitate this step, the federal government ceded 7 percent of its value-added tax (VAT) share to the states and agreed to cover most of the revenue shortfalls remaining for the East German states after the transfers within the horizontal equalization scheme. Additional federal grants, to governments with less than proportional tax power and for states with a low population density suffering from diseconomies of scale in public administration, were instituted to compensate for the fiscal burdens caused by the socialist regime. In addition, a financial package was approved providing grants for the new states to support economic growth and investment.

Table 4.12 reports the transfer flows paid to East Germany by various parts of the German government during the 1990s. Total gross transfers rose from DM 139 billion in 1991 to DM 189 billion in 1997, and the federal government's share in these transfer flows increased over time. The table also reports the functional distribution of these transfers. The largest share were transfers to private households. Social security payments rose from DM 56 billion to DM 84 billion between 1991 and 1996, accounting each year for between 40 and 46 percent of total gross transfers. A large part of these expenditures were payments from the federal government, which were channeled through the social security system to overcome its financing shortages in East Germany (see table 4.13). Moreover, the federal government directly paid for East German social security benefits under early retirement schemes and unemployment support. Subsidies to East German enterprises were the third largest transfer category, amounting to 8 billion in 1991 and 16 billion in 1997.[9] Importantly, transfers to finance public investment amounted to much less than transfer payments to individuals, clearly refuting the tax-smoothing interpretation of German fiscal policy after unification.

Federal support to the social insurance system would have been even larger without the transfers from within the system to East Germany. As table 4.14 indicates, in 1990, East Germans contributed 50 percent of the unemployment insurance benefits paid in East Germany. This share had fallen to 7.1 percent in 1993 and remained at a comparably low level through 1997. Similarly, as the table also

Table 4.12
Public gross transfers to East Germany, 1991–1998 (in billions of DM)

	1991	1992	1993	1994	1995	1996	1997	1998
Federal budget	75	88	114	114	135	138	131	139
German Unity Fund	31	24	15	5	—	—	—	—
EU	4	5	5	6	7	7	7	7
Pension fund	—	5	9	12	17	19	18	18
Labor office (BfA)	25	38	38	28	23	26	26	28
Länder and local governments in West Germany	5	5	10	14	10	11	11	11
Total	139	151	167	169	185	187	183	189
Social security benefits	40.3%	45.0%	46.1%	43.7%	42.7%	44.9%	44.2%	44.4%
Subsidies to firms	5.8%	6.6%	6.6%	10.0%	9.7%	8.0%	7.7%	8.5%
Investment	15.8%	15.2%	15.6%	15.4%	18.3%	17.6%	17.5%	17.5%
Cash transfers (not classifiable)	38.1%	33.1%	31.7%	30.8%	29.2%	29.4%	30.6%	29.6%

Sources: Deutsche Bundesbank 1997 and Federal Ministry of Finance 1998.
Note: Figures for 1998 are from preliminary budget. Dashes indicate data are not available.

Table 4.13
Financial transfers of the federal government, 1991–1997 (in billions of DM)

Transfers to East Germany	1991	1992	1993	1994	1995	1996	1997
Private households	27.2	32.9	52.6	44.6	44.5	46.3	—
Unemployment aid	0.3	1.5	3.5	4.9	5.7	6.8	—
Early retirement	5.7	5.1	5.0	7.2	8.2	5.6	2.1[a]
Unemployment ins.	5.9	8.9	24.4	10.2	6.9	13.8	9.6
Pension system	7.7	8.7	10.7	13.5	15.1	16.2	17.4[b]
Others	7.6	8.7	9.0	8.8	8.6	3.9	—
Firms	19.7	22.9	20.2	25.3	25.0	21.6	—
States and communities	9.5	6.6	7.6	7.3	32.6	32.3	—

Sources: Boss 1998 and Federal Ministry of Finance 1998.
Note: Dashes indicate data are not available.
[a] Preliminary budget figure.
[b] Includes preliminary budget figure.

Table 4.14
Ratio of contributions to expenditures for unemployment insurance and pension fund in Germany, 1990–1997

	Unemployment insurance		Pension fund	
	West	East	West	East
1990	92.6	50.4	86.0	—
1991	148.7	15.2	85.0	80.9
1992	154.4	7.2	83.4	69.4
1993	129.4	7.1	78.9	65.4
1994	133.6	9.0	81.0	62.2
1995	131.1	11.1	80.7	57.8
1996	120.5	10.2	81.8	55.6
1997	127.5	9.5	84.0	56.0

Source: Deutsche Bundesbank.
Note: Dash indicates data are not available.

shows, the ratio of pension contributions to expenses in East Germany fell from around 81 percent in 1991 to 56 percent in 1997, a result of rising unemployment, rising early retirement benefits, and rising wage levels. Thus although social security and unemployment insurance have no explicit geographical dimension, these schemes became channels of massive regional income distribution in Germany in the 1990s (Czada 1995).

Meanwhile, the governments of the new East German states continuously spent in excess of their tax revenues (Seitz and Peters 1999). Although their indebtedness was low at the time of unification, the level of state debt in East Germany reached DM 96.3 billion at the end of 1998, and East German municipalities had incurred DM 30 billion debt at that time. The combined debt thus corresponded to about one-third of GDP. In per capita terms, East German states and municipalities had incurred debt totaling DM 8,940 per capita by the end of 1998, slightly more than the DM 8,900 of West German states and municipalities.

Municipal Government in East Germany

Under the socialist regime, East Germany had lost its traditional federal structure consisting of a central government, state governments, and local governments (villages and counties). States were abolished as administrative and political units in 1952 (Stamm 1990) and replaced by fourteen district administrations (and East Berlin). Local administrations deteriorated to purely administrative bodies.

With the transplantation of the "ready-made state" from West to East Germany (Rose et al. 1993) shortly after unification, district governments were abolished, and the traditional structure was reinstalled. Municipalities were granted autonomy in local matters in May 1990. Before unification, the management of local state enterprises had been an important activity for city governments. As this task became obsolete, these governments assumed a number of new tasks, such as administering social, cultural, and sports activities and the management of hospitals and public schools. New administrative fields such as social assistance, the registration of citizens, and property and environmental protection were ascribed to municipalities and county governments (see Wollmann 1996, 117–18; 1997, 269–71).

Local governments were generally ill-equipped to fulfill these new tasks, as core administrations were heavily understaffed. Counties

Table 4.15
Local government staff in Germany (per thousand inhabitants)

	New länder (including East Berlin)		Old länder
	1991	1996	1991
General administration	3.91	4.07	3.08
Financial administration	0.61	1.05	0.69
Public security service	1.15	1.65	1.29
Schools	4.18	2.27	1.93
Science, research, and culture	1.47	1.48	0.96
Social security	10.96	6.02	2.71
Aid for young people	8.91	4.53	1.18
Health, sports, and recreation	8.20	2.02	1.32
Hospitals	5.15	0.00	0.02
Construction and housing	1.73	2.05	2.12
Public facilities and industrial services (*Wirtschaftsförderung*)	1.50	2.00	1.71
Public enterprises	0.16	0.06	1.17

Source: Federal Statistical Office 1991, 1996a, and 1996b.

were in a better position at the beginning but lost parts of their staff, particularly in tax administration, either to state governments or the private sector. At the same time, the transfer of tasks and personnel formerly belonging to subordinated agencies or state-owned enterprises created a large overhang of personnel in areas such as social affairs and sports,[10] as table 4.15 illustrates. In contrast, financial administration, construction and housing, and local industrial development were understaffed in East Germany compared to West German states. In subsequent years the number of personnel in schooling and health was drastically reduced, but the number of employees in the social area remained relatively large.

The small size of many communities was another liability of the former system. Preunification East Germany was divided into 7,640 communities, of which 87 percent had fewer than 2,000 inhabitants and 47 percent fewer than 500 inhabitants; only 7 percent had more than 5,000 inhabitants (Bizer and Scholl 1998, 41). In contrast, the minimal size of a viable community was estimated at 5,000 inhabitants in West Germany prior to unification. Similarly, the average county population in the new states was 60,000 inhabitants, against 150,000 in West Germany (Wollmann 1997, 289.) Undersized communities promoted parochialism,[11] planning uncertainty, and short-sighted action. The new East German states undertook local government reforms during the first postunification electoral term, and these reforms became effective with the start of the second electoral term, between December 1993 and December 1994.

Municipal Finances

Table 4.16 shows the evolution of municipal revenues in East Germany from 1991 to 1998. After a sharp rise between 1991 and 1992 due to higher tax rates, revenues continued to increase until 1995. Since then, revenues have deteriorated as federal and state grants to the operating budgets have decreased.

The treaty that governed German unification decreed that local governments should receive at least 40 percent of the grants from the German Unity Fund and 20 percent of state tax revenues. Municipalities became eligible for grants financing "joint policies" (*Gemeinschaftsaufgaben*) such as higher education, regional development, and coastal protection and could draw from a range of special programs financed by various federal ministries.[12] Under the 1993 consolidation program, municipal debts for public housing inherited from the past were assumed by the federal Debt Processing Fund (Bohley 1995, 213).

As indicated in table 4.16, municipal governments continuously ran operating surpluses during the 1990s. Initially, large wage payments due to the excess staff inherited from the socialist regime were an important resource drain for local authorities, making up more than 50 percent of their operating budgets. The large wage hikes in the private and public sector aggravated the problem during the first years after unification. Although local authorities were successful in reducing numbers of staff, the problem was slow to go away because, in contrast to state governments, local authorities could not dissolve entire organizations but had to remove all staff members individually. This often provoked lawsuits, which prolonged the process (Karrenberg and Münstermann 1999, 212). As a result wage payments declined steadily between 1992 and 1998, but continued as of 1998 to command more than 40 percent of local operating budgets. In contrast, social transfers increased fourfold from 1991 to 1995 and declined only afterward.

As indicated by table 4.17, capital budget revenues in East German local governments remained fairly stable after an initial rise between

Jürgen von Hagen and Rolf R. Strauch

Table 4.16
Revenues and expenditures of East German local governments—Operating budget (in billions of DM)

	1991	1992	1993	1994	1995	1996	1997	1998
Taxes	2.51	4.31	5.40	6.73	7.52	6.23	6.68	7.57
Profit tax (net)	0.50	0.71	1.15	1.99	1.70	1.97	2.59	2.78
Profit tax (gross)	0.51	0.71	1.24	2.24	1.91	2.20	2.61	2.83
Local share of value-added tax	—	—	—	—	—	—	—	0.69
Local share of income tax	1.12	2.57	3.06	3.43	4.31	2.54	2.24	2.12
Grants of federal government and länder	26.69	23.22	23.93	23.94	25.33	22.90	21.27	20.44
Transfers to families (*Familienlastenausgleich*)	—	—	—	—	—	0.57	0.32	0.21
Charges	3.25	4.70	5.10	5.00	5.28	4.95	4.51	4.28
Other revenues	6.00	9.08	8.70	8.22	8.25	7.75	6.17	5.72
Total operating revenues	38.45	41.32	43.14	43.89	46.38	42.40	38.97	38.23
Wage payments	17.39	21.32	20.13	18.23	17.97	16.76	15.45	14.91
Purchases	10.72	11.64	11.05	10.83	10.69	10.16	9.63	9.40
Social transfers	2.20	4.33	5.96	7.60	8.70	7.86	6.38	6.27
Interest payments	0.23	0.60	1.03	1.28	1.53	1.70	1.70	1.71
Payments to public sector	0.85	0.78	0.92	0.91	0.68	0.97	1.00	0.68
Other expenditures	3.20	2.10	2.31	2.50	2.97	3.01	3.06	3.31
Total operating expenditures	34.59	40.78	41.40	41.35	42.54	40.45	37.21	36.28

Note: All nominal data are from *Der Städtetag* (April 1999), deflated by the Deutsche Bundesbank's price index for government consumption (1995 = 100). Figures for 1991, 1997, and 1998 are estimates.

Table 4.17
Revenues and expenditures of East German local governments—Capital budget (in billions of DM)

	1991	1992	1993	1994	1995	1996	1997	1998
Investment grants of federal government and länder	11.55	10.28	10.00	7.15	8.00	7.72	7.95	7.51
Privatization proceeds	0.57	1.44	2.68	3.08	3.07	2.96	2.71	3.07
Contributions	0.05	0.24	0.40	0.52	0.62	0.56	0.59	0.57
Other revenues	0.32	0.76	0.61	0.70	0.61	0.63	0.60	0.76
Total capital revenues	10.84	12.72	13.68	11.45	12.30	11.87	11.84	11.91
(Fixed) investment	13.67	20.08	18.95	17.94	16.13	14.26	13.10	12.60
Construction	11.74	17.16	16.32	15.63	14.03	12.30	11.32	10.94
Purchase of fixed assets	1.92	2.92	2.62	2.32	2.10	1.95	1.78	1.66
Other expenditures	0.77	0.95	1.25	1.49	2.09	2.19	2.15	2.05
Total capital expenditures	14.44	21.03	20.21	19.43	18.22	16.44	15.25	14.65

Note: All nominal data are from *Der Städtetag* (April 1999), deflated by the Deutsche Bundesbank's price index for government consumption (1995 = 100). Figures for 1991, 1997 and 1998 are estimates.

Table 4.18
Structure of East and West German local government budgets

Year	Revenues			Expenditures		
	Taxes	Charges and contributions	Grants	Wage payments	Social transfers	Investment
East German local governments						
1991	5.1	6.7	77.6	35.5	4.5	27.9
1992	7.0	8	54.2	34.5	7.0	32.5
1993	8.8	8.9	55.1	32.7	9.7	30.8
1994	11.1	9.1	51.1	30.0	12.5	29.5
1995	12.8	9.7	54.9	29.6	14.3	26.6
1996	10.9	9.7	53.8	29.5	13.8	25.1
1997	12.7	9.7	55.7	29.4	12.2	25.0
1998	14.9	9.5	54.9	28.3	12.3	24.7
West German local governments						
1998	38.8	15.4	27.0	27.0	19.9	15.4

Note: All nominal data are from *Der Städtetag* (April 1999). Figures indicate the ratio of the revenue or spending category to total expenditures without special transactions (*besondere Finanzierungsvorgänge*), in percent. City-states are excluded.

1991 and 1993. Aggregate capital expenditure, on the other hand, rose sharply in 1991 and 1992, mainly for financing construction projects. Expenditures decreased from then onward, reaching DM 14.7 billion in 1998. East German municipalities continuously ran deficits on the capital budget during the 1990s; these deficits peaked at DM 8.3 billion in 1992. The deficits of the initial years after unification led to a strongly rising debt level throughout the 1990s, which in per capita terms converged to the level in West German states.

Table 4.18 illustrates the structure of revenues and expenditures in East Germany and compares it to that of West German municipal governments. The numbers indicate the ratio of revenues accounted for by various sources and the ratio of disaggregated spending categories in total expenditures.[13] The share of expenditures financed through tax revenues increased steadily over the decade but remained much smaller than in the West. In 1998 it reached 14.9 percent for East German municipalities, whereas it stood at 38.8 percent for their Western counterparts. After 1991, the overall contribution of grants from higher levels of government to local government revenues remained fairly stable around 54 percent, with a shift from investment to operating grants not depicted in the table. Hence, the contribution to local expenditures still doubled the level of support to Western local governments. On the expenditure side, the share of wage payments declined from 35.5 percent in 1991 to 28.3 percent in 1998, which was close to the West German level in that same year. At the same time the importance of social transfers increased significantly in the local government budgets, rising from 4.5 percent in 1991 to 14.3 percent in 1995 and leveling off gradually at about 12 percent thereafter.

To explain the low tax revenues of East German local governments, one must recognize, apart from the weakness of the economic structure discussed above, that taxes are largely exogenous at the local level because the federal government, together with the states, determines the relevant legislation. The states set forth their own statutes of local public finances determining the share of revenues transferred to the local level and their functional distribution.[14] Local governments have discretionary authority over the rate of local profit and property taxes as well as service charges, the second most important source of own revenues. But East German municipalities were not allowed to raise a capital levy on local enterprises (*Gewerbekapitalsteuer*) until 1995, and special measures were introduced to reduce the tax burden on profits (Bohley 1995, 199).[15] Moreover, states urged local governments not to raise the tax rate on property above a maximum rate during the initial years after unification (Bizer and Scholl 1998). Thus, the legal authority of East German local governments to raise taxes was even more constrained than that in West Germany.

In addition, limited administrative capacity at the local level contributed to the limited taxing power. Property taxation illustrates the point.[16] Property tax in Germany has two versions: type A, applying to agricultural enterprises, and type B, applying to noncommercial real estate, houses, and apartments. State tax administrations collect type A tax, and local tax administrations collect type B. This includes the entire process from generating property registers and assessing property values to the computation of the tax liability and tax collection. Property tax data show large differences between West and East German municipalities in the per capita collection of type B tax revenues and their growth during the 1990s. In contrast, type A collections in East and West Germany performed in a very similar way. Noting that state governments were able to build efficient administrations in a much shorter time than local governments suggests that limited administrative capacity is behind the weak tax collections at the lower level. Furthermore, type B tax collections grew faster and reached higher levels per capita in large compared to small communities. If size is taken as a rough proxy for administrative capacity—large communities are more established links to outside experts and can attract tax personnel from a more diversified pool of employees—this observation suggests again that limited administrative capacity is at the root of the weak taxing power of East German local government.

Social transfers in Germany, like revenues, are largely removed from the discretion of local authorities (Seitz 1999). Entitlement to social assistance is generally granted by federal law, which specifies two types of assistance programs, subsistence aid and emergency aid. Subsistence aid is granted to families unable to maintain a socially or culturally defined minimum subsistence level. Each state government decides upon the minimum amount of aid that must be given to recipients. In addition, subsistence aid includes supplementary payments for housing, clothes, and the like, which are not covered by the base payment. Emergency aid is granted to those affected by extraordinary hardships, for example, handicapped people suddenly in need of special care. States determine the basic amount of social aid and how its financing is to be shared between the state and the local authorities, and local authorities often end up bearing the lion's share of social aid expenditures. The total flow of resources under these programs is by and large determined by local living conditions and social infrastructure, the age and gender structure of the population, employment, and migration.

During the initial years after reunification subsistence aid expenditures in East Germany increased, from DM 1 billion in 1991 to DM 1.5 billion in 1993, and continued to increase somewhat afterward.[17] The average expenditures per recipient were DM 1,680 in 1993, 44 percent of the West German level. Moreover, the risk of becoming a recipient was 1.6 percent on average in that year, which was 0.9 percentage points lower than in West Germany at the time. The reason for the relatively low level of per capita expenditures is the relatively high fluctuation in the number of recipients and, among others, the low housing prices in East Germany. The low level of risk in East Germany compared to West is primarily the result of the very high participation ratio inherited from the past and the labor market policies discussed above, which secured other sources of support for individuals who would otherwise have been eligible for subsistence aid.

In contrast, emergency aid spending more than doubled in East Germany between 1991 and 1994. The number of emergency aid recipients increased from 167,000 in 1991 to 255,000 in 1993. The average expenditures per recipients were about 30 percent lower than in West Germany, which may be due to East Germany's lower average wages. With the convergence of the East German health care sector to West German standards and costs, however, expenditures rose sharply. The increase in spending was attributable in particular on the contribution to health care, which accounts for half of the total aid, and the social reintegration of the handicapped. The growth of social assistance spending was curbed by the introduction of emergency care insurance in 1995–1996. This new system covers a large part of the hardships formerly producing the eligibility for social aid. The new arrangement has helped East German local governments avoid a further growth in expenditures.

Conclusions

More than a decade after the fall of the Berlin Wall, East Germany's transition presents a mixed picture. On the one hand, economic choices in the private sector, such as consumption and saving, purchases of durables, and active employment look very much like those of West Germans. Similarly, local governments look much like local governments in the West as regards the provision of public services. On the other hand, these similarities do not correspond to the persistent differences in the levels of output and incomes earned in East Germany or to the differences in local tax capacities in the two parts of Germany. Investment has been strong in East Germany in recent years, but this investment seems to have been largely dependent on financial incentives provided by the federal government, and investment choices often do not seem to promise the development of a modern industrial base with high labor productivity.

Overall, the combination of an immediate adoption after unification of West Germany's regulatory and transfer system with the receipt of huge public transfers primarily used to finance consumption has been much less of a blessing for East Germany than many optimistic observers hoped at the time of unification. The failure of the

Kohl government to address in due time the incentive issues in the labor market and for stimulating investment has kept East Germany's economy from entering into a sustainable recovery. Today, the risk that East Germany will remain a transfer-dependent mezzogiorno economy for the foreseeable future is significant. It will take considerable political effort to phase out industrial support programs, and any reduction in transfers to households will be even more difficult politically, since any reform in that area touches on the economic interests of West German households, too. There is, perhaps, some hope in the prospect of endogenous institutional change towards market deregulation in East Germany (von Hagen 1997). The rapid decline in the coverage of union contracts in the East German labor market and the recent striving for more liberal shop closing hours might be a first indication of such a development.

References

Akerlof, George A., Andrew Rose, Janet L. Yellen, and Helga Hessenius. 1991. East Germany in from the cold: The economic aftermath of currency union. *Brookings Papers for Economic Activity*, 1–101.

Autorengemeinschaft. 1998. Der Arbeitsmarkt in der Bundesrepublik Deutschland in den Jahren 1997–1998. In *Mitteilungen aus der Arbeitsmarkt- und Berufsforschung* 31: 5–58.

Berthold, Norbert, and Rainer Fehn. 1997. Aktive Arbeitsmarktpolitik- wirksames Instrument der Beschäftiungspolitik oder politische Beruhigungspille. *ORDO* 48: 412–35.

Bizer, Kilian, and Rainer Scholl. 1998. *Finanzprobleme der Gemeinden in den neuen Bundesländern*. Berlin: Analytica.

Bohley, Peter. 1995. Der kommunale Finanzausgaleich in den neuen Bundesländern nach der Wiedervereinigung Deutschlands. In *Finanzierungsprobleme der deutschen Einheit* III, ed. Alois Oberhauser, 189–245. Schriften des Vereins für Sozialpolitik Band 229/III. Berlin: Duncker & Humblot.

Boss, Alfred. 1998. How Germany shouldered the fiscal burden of the unification. Working paper no. 851, Kiel Institute of World Economics, Kiel.

Council of Economic Advisors (SVR). various issues. *Jahresgutachten*. Stuttgart: Metzler-Poeschel.

Czada, Roland. 1995. Der Kampf um die Finanzierung der deutschen Einheit. Discussion paper 95/1, Max Planck Institut für Gesellschaftswessenschaften (MPIFG), Cologne.

Deutsche Bundesbank. various issues. Monthly report. Frankfurt am Main: Deutsche Bundesbank.

Deutsches Institut für Wirtschaftsforschung, Institut für Wirtschaftsforschung, and Institut für Wirtschaftsforschung Halle (DIW, IfW, and IWH). 1999. Gesamtwirtschaftliche und unternehmerische Anpassungsfortschritte in Ostdeutschland. Joint report. Berlin: DIW.

Dietrich, Vera, Joachim Ragnitz, and Jacqueline Rothfels 1998. *Wechselbeziehungen zwischen Transfers, Wirtschaftsstruktur und Wachstum in den neuen Bundesländern.* Sonderheft 1/98. Halle: IWH.

Driffill, John, and Marcus Miller. 1998. *No credit for transition: The Maastricht Treaty and German unemployment.* Discussion paper no. 1929, Center for Economic Policy Research (CEPR), London.

Federal Ministry of Labour and Social Affairs (BMA). 1998. *Übersicht über das Sozialrecht,* 5th ed. Bonn: Author.

Federal Ministry of Finance (BMF). various issues. *Finanzbericht.* Bonn: Author.

Federal Statistical Office. various issues. *Rechnungsergebnisse der kommunalen Haushalte.* Fachserie 14. Reihe 03.03. Wiesbaden: Statistisches Bundesamt.

Federal Statistical Office. various issues. *Finanzen und Steuern: Personal des öffentlichen Dienstes.* Fachserie 14. Reihe 06. Wiesbaden: Statistisches Bundesamt.

Groebel, Annegret. 1996. *Strukturelle Entwicklungsmuster in Markt- und Planwirtschaften.* Heidelberg: Physica.

Hübler, Olaf. 1997. Evaluation beschäftigungspolitischer Maßnahmen in Ostdeutschland. *Jahrbücher für Nationalökonomie und Statistik* 216, no. 1: 22–44.

Nickell, Stephen. 1997. Unemployment and labor market rigidities: Europe versus North America. *Journal of Economic Perspectives,* 11, no. 3: 55–74.

Ragnitz, Joachim, Ingrid Haschke, Gerald Müller, Jacqueline Rothfels, and Udo Ludwig. 1998. *Transfers, Exportleistungen und Produktivität.* Sonderheft 2/98. Halle: Institut für Wirtschaftsforschung (IWH).

Rensch, Wolfgang. 1997. Budgetäre Anpassung statt institutionellen Wandels. Zur finanziellen Bewältigung der Lasten des Beitritts der DDR zur Bundesrepublik. In *Transformation der politisch-administrativen Strukturen in Ostdeutschland,* ed. Hellmut Wollman, Hans-Ulrich Derlien, Klaus König, Wolfgang Renzsch, and Wolfgang Seibel, 49–118. Opladen: Leske & Budrich.

Rose, Richard, Wolfgang Zapf, Wolfgang Seifert, and Edward Page. 1993. *Germans in comparative perspective.* Studies in Public Policy No. 218. Glasgow: University of Strathclyde.

Schneider, Herbert. 1993. Der Aufbau der Kommunalverwaltung und der kommunalen Selbstverwaltung in den neuen Bundesländern. *Aus Politik und Zeitgeschichte,* 36: 18–26.

Schneider, Hilmar. 1998. Der Arbeitsmarkt in den neuen Bundesländern- Probleme und Perspektiven. Mimeo. Institut für Wirtschaftsforschung, Halle.

Schwinn, O. 1997. *Die Finanzierung der deutschen Einheit.* Opladen: Leske & Budrich.

Seitz, Helmut. 1999. Fiscal policy, deficits, and politics of subnational governments: The case of the German Länder. In *Public choice* (forthcoming).

Seitz, Helmut, and Wolfgang Peters. 1999. Der finanzpolitische Anpassungsbedarf im Land Brandenburg und in den anderen neuen Ländern. Mimeo. Viadrina University, Frankfurt (Oder).

Sinn, Gerlinde, and Hans-Werner Sinn. 1991. *Kaltstart*. Tübingen: J.C.B. Mohr (Paul Siebeck).

Sinn, Hans-Werner. 1995. Factor price distortions and public subsidies in East Germany. Discussion paper no. 1155, CEPR, London.

Stamm, Eugen. 1990. Die Länder der DDR. In *DDR Almanach 90*, ed. Günter Fischbach. Bonn: Bonn Aktuell.

Steffen, Johannes. 1995. *Die wesentlichen Änderungen in den Bereichen Arbeitslostenversicherung, Rentenversicherung, Krankenversicherung und Sozialhilfe (HLU) in den vergangenen Jahren.* Mimeo.

von Hagen, Jürgen. 1993. Money demand, money supply, and monetary union. *European Economic Review* 37: 803–36.

von Hagen, Jürgen. 1997. East Germany. In *Going global: Transition from plan to market in the world economy*, ed. Padma Desai, 173–207. Cambridge: MIT Press.

von Hagen, Jürgen, and Rolf R. Strauch. 1999. Tumbling giant: Germany's experience with the Maastricht fiscal criteria. Discussion paper B99, Zentrune für Euoapäische Integoatiousforschung (ZEI).

Wollmann, Hellmut. 1996. Institutionenbildung in Ostdeutschland: Neubau, Umbau und "schöpferische Zerstörung." In *Politisches System*, ed. Max Kaase, Andreas Eisen, Oskar W. Gabriel, Oskar Niedermayer, and Hellmut Wollmann, 47–153. Opladen: Leske & Budrich.

Wollmann, Hellmut. 1997. Transformation der ostdeutschen Kommunalstrukturen: Rezeption, Eigenentwicklung, Innovation. In *Transformation der politisch-administrativen Strukturen in Ostdeutschland*, ed. Hellmut Wollman, Hans-Ulrich Derlien, Klaus König, Wolfgang Renzsch, Wolfgang Seibel, 259–327. Opladen: Leske & Budrich.

5   Ten Years of Polish Economic Transition, 1989–1999

Marek Dabrowski

Introduction

Poland was the first postcommunist country to begin the transition to a market economy. This transition was launched at the end of 1989, when Poland's first democratic government, under Tadeusz Mazowiecki, announced its comprehensive and radical economic program aimed at fighting near-hyperinflation and transforming Poland's socialist economic system into a capitalist one. Having experienced the smallest output decline in transition among postcommunist countries and having been the first to experience posttransition economic growth at an impressive rate, Poland has become a symbol of transition success. International financial institutions and many world-known experts often refer to the Polish experience as a positive example for other postcommunist countries.

Looking back over the last decade, it is necessary, however, to note that the pace of economic change in Poland during transition was uneven. Although the first two years of transition (1990–1991) can be characterized as a period of very fast and comprehensive reforms, this reform process gradually slowed in later years as political will and energy declined and various special-interest groups rebuilt their strength. The final two years of the decade (1998–1999) brought an attempt to accelerate the reform process again, particularly in the institutional, social, and fiscal spheres.

The purpose of this chapter is to make a brief assessment of the 1990s in Poland, its main accomplishments and the problems left unsolved, and also to specify main challenges facing the economic policy of Poland in the next few years. The author who has been personally involved in the Polish transition process and in giving policy advice to other transition countries, has a natural bias toward analyzing Poland's developments from a broader comparative perspective.

The structure of the chapter is as follows: In the next section, I will give a historical overview of the pretransition period, which created a very dramatic starting point to Poland's transformation in 1989. The third section is devoted to the initial stabilization cum liberalization package in the early years of Poland's transition. In the fourth section I will try to answer the question of why an impressive growth record coexisted in Poland with a slow disinflation trend. The fifth section contains a short overview of the liberalization measures taken after 1991 and drawbacks in this process. The sixth section describes the privatization process in Poland and development of the country's new private sector, and the seventh section discusses the reconstruction of Poland's banking sector and development of other segments of the country's financial market. The eighth section gives an overview of four recent social reforms, implemented at the beginning of 1999. The ninth section discusses the political economy of Poland's transition, with special attention given to domestic and external factors that helped push the reform process forward and keep it on track. The final section offers concluding remarks and a brief overview of the remaining agenda of market-oriented reforms in Poland.

Historical Background of Poland's Transition

Generally, the Polish economy in the late 1980s belonged to the same category of reformed planned economies as the former Yugoslavia and Hungary, though Poland was less advanced in economic liberalization than those two countries. Its economic system was partly centrally planned and partly market governed, with a very ineffective macroeconomic control and with enterprises not interested in profit maximization. The foundations of this nonplan and nonmarket system (using Tamas Bauer's terminology) were created mainly in 1981–1982 as a result of the big economic reform debate in 1980–1981. The concrete institutional and regulatory framework solutions were a product of political bargaining and compromises between advocates of different reform proposals.[1] The specific political conditions of martial law imposed in December 1981 to curb the activities of trade unions also affected the eventual shape of Poland's

1982 economic reform. The most important elements of this reform included

• limited autonomy of state-owned enterprises (SOEs), maintained through the institution of employee self-management and partial elimination of intermediate organs and organizations.

• abolishing the traditional central plan targets and replacing them with so-called operational programs and government orders for selected groups of products; central allocation of selected basic raw materials, semiproducts, and foreign currencies were maintained.

• partial liberalization of domestic prices.

• partial demonopolization of foreign trade; a system of retention quotas for part of foreign exchange earnings from exports was introduced.

• limited and controlled openings for domestic private-sector and small-scale foreign investments.

• some liberalization of the state enterprise financial system and individual wage setting.

Although many minor modifications were adopted in the next five years, the general logic of the economic system envisioned in the 1982 reform remained unchanged until 1987.

Macroeconomic equilibrium and discipline was another area in which Poland's situation differed significantly from that of Hungary and the former Yugoslavia. Inflationary processes combined with shortages of goods were a normal phenomenon in Poland in the 1980s. Serious macroeconomic imbalances in Poland had their origins in early 1970s when First Secretary of the Polish United Workers Party Edward Gierek and Prime Minister Piotr Jaroszewicz forced a very intensive modernization of Polish industry and a consumption boom. Both were financed, to a significant extent, through large-scale foreign borrowing that led to a dramatic balance-of-payment crisis at the end of the 1970s.[2] This period also brought the creation of basic elements of a very extensive and expensive system of social protection in Poland. Wage explosion after the August 1980 strikes (which gave a foundation for the "Solidarity" movement) combined with continued price control devastated the state budget and consumer market. The Polish economy in the summer and autumn of 1981 was in a state of the repressed hyperinflation. Authorities had

to resort to wide-scale rationing of basic food and industrial consumer products.

Under the martial law imposed in February 1982 a large-scale administrative price adjustment took place that decreased the real size
of monetary overhang and market shortages but did not eliminate
them completely. Substantial market shortages, a coupon system (especially for meat products), and open inflation of 15–20 percent per
year became the standard picture in this decade. Unfortunately, the
process of creating excessive social obligations for the state continued
during this period, especially in relation to the pension system.

Inflationary processes accelerated in Poland in the fall of 1987
when the government of Zbigniew Messner announced the so-called
Second Stage of Economic Reform, including a "price-income operation" that was an attempt at a typical administrative price adjustment that was finally implemented at the beginning of 1988. The
long political discussion of this operation as well as the referendum
on economic reforms in November 1987 contributed to a big market
panic. A strong wage pressure (two waves of strikes, in April–May
and August 1988) additionally undermined the macroeconomic effect of the operation.

Messner's government started some institutional and structural
reforms in 1988, such as deconcentration of many SOEs, transforming Poland's monobank system into a two-tier banking system, and
merging numerous branch industrial ministries into the single
Ministry of Industry. The last predemocratic government, that of
Mieczyslaw Rakowski, had some important achievements in the
liberalization and institutional sphere. Among other things, it contributed to a significant liberalization of founding new companies,
including private ones (the Law on Economic Activity of December
23, 1988), to the liberalization of foreign trade and the foreign exchange market, and to the limited liberalization of foreign direct
investments. Rakowski's government finally liquidated the intermediate organizations grouping SOEs (trust and associations). It also
introduced an equal corporate income tax in all the ownership sectors and tried to start the process of privatization. Unfortunately, this
last attempt was unsuccessful, because unclear rules and techniques
preferring the so-called nomenklatura prevailed (Blaszczyk and
Dabrowski 1993).

Despite the above achievements, the lack of macroeconomic stability became the weakest point of the policy of Rakowski's govern-

ment. The Program for Consolidation of the National Economy, an essential policy document of Rakowski's cabinet, neglected from the start the role of monetary and fiscal discipline. The state budget for 1989 was accepted by the parliament despite its containing a big deficit. During the next few months, the country's macroeconomic situation further deteriorated because of a number of factors: an extremely accommodating monetary policy with unlimited financing of fiscal deficit, populist tendencies brought to the fore during round-table negotiations on economic policy from February to April 1989, instability affected by the electoral campaign, an administrative increase in the minimum procurement prices for agricultural products in April 1989, a price and wage increase in July 1989, and an across-the-board indexation of wages forced through by Solidarity Independent Trade Union and the National Council of Trade Unions (OPZZ). Earlier, in January 1989, the Polish parliament had passed the Law on Wages in the State Budgetary Sphere, which guaranteed a rising level of parity indexation of wages, starting from 97 percent in 1989 to the targeted 106 percent of wages in the enterprise sector at the end of 1992.[3] Again, a huge monetary overhang combined with an administrative price control led to a significant deficit of many goods on the domestic market.

In this situation the Rakowski government's decision August 1, 1989, to free food prices from state control and eliminate the rationing system on caused a near-hyperinflation (monthly rates of 39.5 percent in August and 54.8 percent in October 1989). Though absolutely necessary, this decision came few months too late and was accompanied by proinflationary monetary, fiscal, and wage policies.

In trying to characterize the initial conditions of Poland's transformation, one can find both relative advantages and disadvantages in comparison with those in other transition countries. Among the positive elements, one can stress the presence of many more market institutions and regulations than in other former communist countries (except Hungary and the former Yugoslavia). These include, among other things, limited autonomy of state enterprises, and the above-mentioned late-1980s reforms liberalizing market entry for small business, demonopolizing and deconcentrating traditional enterprise structures, opening the Polish economy for foreign investments, and moving from the monobank structure to a two-tier banking sector. Additionally, the political regime was a bit more liberal than in some other communist countries, allowing, for example, for more freedom in economic discussions or private contacts with the West. In some respects Poland managed to retain pre–World War II institutional solutions in economic relations: for example, predominantly private agriculture, nominally private ownership of part of nonagriculture real estates (though heavily restricted in effectiveness in regard to exerting real property rights), and part of the legal system (the commercial code or bankruptcy law). Among the negative factors, one must mention the above-described domestic and external macroeconomic imbalances and widespread populism of both late communist authorities and Solidarity opposition. Poland's role as pioneer in postcommunist transition sometimes did not help it make proper policy choices and implementation new solutions rapidly (especially in the sphere of privatization), as the relevant experience of other countries was not yet available.

Choice of Transition Strategy and Initial Reform Package

The government of Tadeusz Mazowiecki, the first postcommunist government in Poland, appointed on September 12, 1989, inherited an economy in a state of near-hyperinflation and regulatory chaos. A month after its appointment, it publicly presented a comprehensive program of economic transformation. The choice of fast and radical reform strategy was determined both by the gravity of the economic situation at the time and by the accumulated experience (mostly negative) of the previous partial reform attempts both in Poland and in other East European countries.

In the last quarter of 1989, preparations were made for the introduction of a macroeconomic stabilization and liberalization package, which was enacted on January 1, 1990. In the meantime, some transitory emergency measures were taken. Beginning October 1, 1989, most of the subsidies to food products and to some intermediate inputs were eliminated. Starting in September 1989, the National Bank of Poland (NBP) began to tighten the country's money supply, to increase its nominal interest rate, and to depreciate the official exchange rate of the zloty against the U.S. dollar both in nominal and real terms. This policy enabled the huge gap between the official and the free-market exchange rate to be closed almost completely by the end of 1989. In October 1989, the wage indexation in the enterprise sphere was limited and full indexation was not allowed.

The basic package introduced on January 1, 1990, and drawn up in consultation with the International Monetary Fund (IMF) consisted of five major components:

1. Restrictive monetary policy, most clearly expressed by a drastic reduction in the money supply as well as the establishment of a high interest rate (exceeding inflation in real terms as of March 1990). This move was accompanied by a law regulating credit operations by introducing interest rate adjustments in all credit agreements made in the past. The law also restricted so-called preferential credit (i.e., credit extended under nonmarket conditions).

2. Elimination of the budget deficit, predominantly through further drastic reduction in subsidies for food, raw materials, production inputs, and energy carriers as well as the elimination of most tax exemptions. A substantial budget surplus was achieved in the first three quarters of 1990.

3. Further liberalization of prices (after January 1990, about 90 percent of prices were determined by the market) as well as a significant increase in those prices still under administrative control, for example, fuels and energy, transportation tariffs, housing rents, and pharmaceuticals. Some other price deregulation steps were taken during 1990 (e.g., liberalization of coal prices beginning July 1, 1990). Housing rents were partly deregulated in 1994 and gasoline prices only in 1997.

4. Introduction of current account convertibility of the Polish currency, linked with its considerable devaluation and the emergence of a single exchange rate,[4] which was stabilized at the level 9,500 zloty per U.S. dollar as a nominal anchor.[5] The exchange rate policy was accompanied by liberalization of foreign trade (elimination of all import quotas and most export quotas, unification of exchange rate relative to developed countries, and decreasing of tariffs). Despite these significant steps, the relative level of tariffs was still rather high in the first half of 1990. Some export quotas and export taxes, especially in the raw materials and energy industry as well as in agriculture, were also preserved. Further import tariff liberalization as well as the removal of most export barriers came in the third quarter of 1990. Most tariffs became temporary and were either totally suspended or radically decreased. Beginning at the end of 1990, strong political pressure to return to trade protectionism was exerted first by the agricultural lobby, and later also by the industrial lobby. In

spring 1991, several import tariff rates for agriculture products were increased. On August 1, 1991, all custom tariffs were doubled. After the Polish government signed an association agreement with European Economic Community (EEC) in December 1991 (followed by a free trade agreement with European Free Trade Area (EFTA) and creation of Central European Free Trade Area (CEFTA)), import tariff policy became more stable.

5. Restrictive income policy, manifested mainly in the elimination, at the end of 1989, of the general wage indexation in the enterprise sector introduced in July 1989 and the introduction of severe taxation penalties on wage increases (so-called *popiwek*),[6] a policy that allowed only a modest growth in wages with respect to price increases (the index ratio was as follows: 0.3 in January 1990, 0.2 from February through April, 0.6 in May and June, 1.0 in July, and 0.6 in August and after). During subsequent years, taxation of excess wages (i.e., wages above average) was gradually relaxed[7] (especially after December 1992), and the tax was finally abandoned at the end of 1994.

The objectives of this reform program were to stifle high inflation and eliminate shortages, to open the economy to domestic and foreign competition, to deregulate the majority of commodity markets, to liberalize the structure of prices and to bring it closer to that of the free market, to break down the wage indexation policy, and to balance and stabilize the state budget. In general the program was meant to create a macroeconomic basis for subsequent microeconomic restructuring. Simultaneously, several microeconomic reforms were started. Among the most important:

1. Creation of a uniform tax policy for all ownership sectors of the economy; removal of a significant number of allowances, exemptions, and special benefits from the tax system; and reduction of top bracket tax rates for direct taxes. The second stage of tax reform included the introduction of the personal income tax, beginning January 1, 1992, a new law on corporate income tax in March 1992, and the value-added tax on July 5, 1993.

2. Introduction of a customs law corresponding to EEC standards (from 1990).

3. Extensive public finance reform, including the abolition of almost all extrabudgetary funds and introduction of a new budgetary law (in 1991).

4. Acceptance of new antimonopoly legislation (March 1990), creation of an antimonopoly office (April 1990), and the breakup of SOEs into a number of industries.

5. Updating of the civil code, civil process code, and legislation governing land use (autumn 1990). Among other things, the changes made sped up the formation of a real estate market, helped develop collateral lending, improved the execution of civil contracts, and eliminated inequitable treatment of state and private contractors. Together with an updated state enterprise law, they allowed SOEs to sell out or rent redundant assets, which contributed both to speeding up small privatization (i.e., the privatization of small enterprises) and to restructuring many SOEs.

6. Speeding up the reorganization of the banking sector and updating the banking law. This was accomplished in several steps. The most significant changes to the banking law, introducing the Western European norms of bank behavior and accounting, started in March 1992. Many new privately owned banks were formed in 1989–1991, including some with foreign investment.

7. Strengthening the independent position of the NBP. The same legislative initiative that changed the banking law also changed the law governing the NBP, giving the governor of the NBP personal independence. Unfortunately, the legislation did not make the NBP fully independent of Sejm, which had to approve the monetary program each year and set either an upper or a lower limit on fiscal deficit financing by the central bank in each year's budget. Only in 1998 was this situation finally changed (see "Poland's Macroeconomic Situation in the 1990s" for details).

8. Speeding up of small privatization, especially in retail and wholesale trade, and in road transport, construction, and services. Practically, this process was not finished until the end of 1991.

9. Creation of a legal and institutional basis for large privatization (i.e., the privatization of large enterprises) (1990).

10. Acceptance by the parliament of the Law on the Securities Market and Mutual Funds (March 1991); opening the Warsaw Stock Exchange in April 1991.

11. Acceptance of the new Foreign Investment Law eliminating most licenses and allowing free repatriation of profit and invested capital (July 1991).

12. Implementation of a system of local self-government and reintroduction of municipal ownership, abolished in 1950 (May 1990).

13. A new employment law (December 1989) creating a network of employment offices and introducing unemployment benefits.

14. Introduction of a decentralized system of social aid for poor people in January 1991.

15. Partial deregulation of the real estate (1990) and housing (1994) markets.

After 1991, the pace of institutional reforms became much slower and less regular.

Poland's Macroeconomic Situation in the 1990s: Fast Growth and Slow Disinflation

The macroeconomic results of ten years of Polish transition have been uneven. On the one hand, Poland has established the best cumulative GDP record among transition countries (see table 5.1). The decline in GDP lasted only two years after the start of transition (1990–1991), and its cumulative effect did not exceed 20 percent, according to official statistics.[8] Since 1992, or more specifically since the last quarter of 1991, Poland has experienced output recovery at a very high rate. Only the second half of 1998 and first half of 1999 brought some deceleration in growth, mainly as a result of the Russian financial crisis, but this seemed to be a transitory phenomenon.

On the other hand, in spite of having been the first postcommunist country to implement a stabilization program (on January 1, 1990[9]), Poland is obviously not a leader in the disinflation process. Although the annual rate of inflation has decreased every year since the stabilization program was implemented, the end-of-year result recorded in 1998 (8.6 percent) gives Poland only fourteenth position among transition countries behind Azerbaijan (−7.8 percent), Armenia (−1.1 percent), FYR Macedonia (−0.8 percent), Bulgaria (0.9 percent), Kazakhstan (1.9 percent), Lithuania (2.4 percent), Tajikistan (2.7 percent), Latvia (2.8 percent), Estonia (4.5 percent), Croatia (5.6 percent), Slovakia (5.6 percent), Slovenia (5.7 percent), and the Czech Republic (6.8 percent). Albania (8.7 percent) achieved a result very similar to the Polish one.

If we take into consideration the pace of disinflation in Poland, it looks quite favorable compared to that of the two other Central

Table 5.1
Poland: Basic macroeconomic indicators, 1993–1998 (percentage of GDP, unless otherwise indicated)

Indicator	1993	1994	1995	1996	1997	1998
Real GDP (percentage change)	3.8	5.2	7.0	6.1	6.9	4.8
CPI (end of year) (percentage change)	37.6	29.5	21.6	18.5	13.2	8.6
Money and quasi-money (M2) (percentage change)	36.0	33.8	39.4	29.2	31.0	25.0
Exchange rate depreciation (−) against U.S. Dollar (period average) (percentage change)	−24.9	−20.2	−6.3	−10.1	−17.8	−6.2
State budget revenues	29.0	29.2	28.1	26.4	25.4	24.3
State budget expenditure	32.9	32.8	32.0	30.2	28.2	27.2
State budget balance	−3.9	−3.6	−3.9	−3.8	−2.8	−2.9
General government balance	−3.4	−3.2	−3.3	−3.6	−3.3	−3.0
General government expenditure	—	50.4	49.1	48.5	47.7	45.8
Public-sector debt	—	69.5	55.7	49.4	46.2	42.7
External	—	45.8	35.0	29.2	26.4	23.6
Current account, including unclassified transactions	−0.1	2.3	3.3	−1.0	−3.1	−4.5

Source: IMF 1999, tables 1, 3, and 5.
Note: Dashes indicate negative value.

European countries, the Czech Republic and Hungary,[10] but far less favorable compared to many countries of the former Soviet Union and former Yugoslavia, such as Estonia, Latvia, Moldova, Lithuania, Georgia, Kazakhstan, Armenia, Azerbaijan, Slovenia, Croatia, and Macedonia. An IMF analysis of twenty-five transition countries (IMF, 1998, table 2) compares the period each country needed, from the beginning of its stabilization program, to cross disinflation thresholds set at the levels of 60, 30, 15, and 7.5 percent of twelve-month inflation.[11] It took Poland eighteen months from the start of its stabilization program to cross the highest (60 percent) threshold.[12] Reaching subsequent thresholds took much more time for Poland than for other countries: thirty-three months to cross the 30-percent threshold and twenty-one months to cross the 15-percent threshold.

The above developments might suggest the existence of a trade-off between a stronger disinflation trend and growth. Such a suggestion, however, would contradict the results of all contemporary empirical research related to this issue (see, e.g., Ghosh and Phillips 1998), at least in respect to the level of inflation that prevailed in Poland during most of this decade (i.e., two-digit, moderate level). Sources of fast economic growth of Poland can rather be identified in the microeconomic sphere. Although I know of no formal quantitative analyses related to factors of economic growth in Poland, some descriptive hypotheses may be seen as worthy of further investigation. First, a deep initial liberalization boosted rapid development of the new private sector, which remained the main vehicle of restructuring and economic recovery. Second, SOEs received a great deal of autonomy combined with fairly hard budget constraints, which pushed most of them toward real restructuring and long-range adaptations to the new market environment.[13] Restructuring of SOEs helped additionally in the development of a new private sector, freeing redundant human and material resources and accelerating their market-oriented reallocation. Third, Polish agriculture, already predominantly privately owned before transition began, did not need as deep a restructuring and reorganization as that of other transition countries. Therefore, the impact of recession in the agriculture sector, so powerful in other transition countries, was almost nonexistent in Poland.

Some additional structural factors, such as the relatively young demographic structure of the Polish population, the relative availability of labor resources, and geographic location, probably also played an important role. Concerning this last factor, a very high rate of growth in registered and unregistered exports to Russia, Ukraine, and other Commonwealth of Independent States (CIS) countries in 1995–1997 evidently added to the growth rate of the Polish GDP.

To answer the question of why disinflation in Poland progressed relatively slowly, one must look at the main components of macroeconomic policy, that is, monetary and exchange rate policy and fiscal policy. With respect to Poland's fiscal policy stance, apart from 1990, the general government budget balance was negative throughout all the transition period (a particularly high negative balance was recorded in 1989, 1991, and 1992). Of course, at that time the country's fiscal deficit was financed predominantly from the NBP's credit pushing up the money supply (see below). Since 1993, the general government deficit has decreased as a result of output recovery, the completion of comprehensive tax reform, and limited adjustments on the expenditure side (Dabrowski 1996). The adjustment process was stopped in 1995 and 1996, however, and even slightly reversed, despite fast GDP growth and improved tax collection. Only 1997 and the first half of 1998 brought a new phase of moderate fiscal adjustment. In 1999, some fiscal deterioration was observed again as a result of the country's lower growth rate (see above) and the implementation of four big social reforms (see "Four Social Reforms of 1999," below).

The fiscal adjustment effort of 1997–1998 was enhanced by some institutional measures: setting of the maximum level of public debt at 60 percent of GDP (in the country's new constitution, which entered into force on October 17, 1997) and a new law governing the public finance system (adopted by the Polish parliament in 1998). However, a newly introduced set of institutional reforms related to public-sector services, government decentralization, and the pension system (see "Four Social Reforms of 1999") created a serious challenge for fiscal management in subsequent years.

Poland's total public debt and, in particular, its total external debt decreased to a significant extent, as a result of debt reduction decisions made by the Paris and London clubs in 1991 and 1994. The real appreciation of the zloty starting in 1995 also contributed to this trend. Both factors also influenced the change of composition of the total public debt in favor of its domestic component (see Siwinska 1999).

The size of Poland's 1997 fiscal deficit puts Poland in the middle rank of Central and Eastern European countries (IMF 1998). In this respect, Poland is doing better than Romania, Albania, Hungary, and most countries of the former Soviet Union but worse than Estonia, the Czech Republic, Slovenia, and Croatia. Poland's continuous budget deficit, despite very high GDP growth rate and improving tax collection, is not the only fiscal problem the country is experiencing. As in other Central European countries, the size of government in Poland is excessive and threatens the long-term fundamentals of economic growth (Dabrowski and Kosterna 1996). This is particularly true with respect to social expenditures, where pension benefits play an absolutely dominant role (see Golinowska 1996).

Although far from the desired pattern and missing some historical opportunities during a high-growth period, fiscal policy cannot be blamed alone for slow pace of disinflation. Compared to that of other transition economies Poland's fiscal balance during the 1990s was not so bad. The second part of the story, beyond the effects of fiscal policy, is connected with unstable, inconsequent, and accommodative monetary policy.

First, up to 1997, the NBP was directly involved in direct financing of a significant part of Poland's fiscal deficit, an effect of the NBP's weak political position in relation to the Polish parliament and government, despite some legal guarantees of its independence. Poland's new constitution, which took effect in 1997, prohibited deficit financing by the NBP and finally put an end to the practice.

Second, the NBP had huge problems with absorption and sterilization of capital inflow because it did not want to allow the zloty to appreciate in real terms and did want to continue crawling-peg devaluation at any cost (see below). Thus the actual orientation toward balance-of-payment targeting and export promotion did not help in the effective control of this part of the money supply. Although the NBP conducted large-scale sterilization operations, their effectiveness in controlling money supply were also rather limited. They involved substantial fiscal costs[14] and led to the build up of a huge structural surplus position in the banking system: the net foreign assets of the NBP are equal to approximately 190 percent of the monetary base, and net domestic assets of the NBP must therefore be strongly negative.

Third, maintaining a crawling-peg/-band mechanism created a strong inflationary inertia, probably much stronger than that resulting from the consequences of relative price adjustment (the role of this factor significantly diminished after 1992—see Wozniak 1997) and the in fact nonexistent wage-price spiral (see Walewski 1998).[15] International experience shows that a country's exchange rate mechanism can serve as a good anti-inflationary device, anchoring domestic prices to the international level and reducing inflationary expectations.[16] Exchange rate arrangements can also work in the opposite direction, however, inducing an inflationary inertia, if they are subordinated to targets other than disinflation. This is particularly true of crawling-peg devaluation. Invented originally in developing countries with chronic high inflation as a mechanism for smoothing unavoidable currency depreciation and calming inflationary and devaluation expectations, crawling-peg devaluation becomes an autonomous factor, building an inflationary inertia. Additionally, as with any other indexation mechanism, political economy factors come into play, making it politically difficult to abandon this device under new circumstances (for example, much lower inflation). Usually a country's exporters lobby tries to maintain crawling peg as long as possible, raising all possible arguments about competitiveness, the role of export-led growth, the danger of a balance-of-payment crisis, and the like. Continuing crawling peg in a moderate-inflation environment means perpetuating our subordinating monetary policy to the balance-of-payment or growth targets instead of disinflation targets. In fact, most defenders of the crawling-peg/-band arrangement (see, e.g., Sachs 1996; Gomulka 1998) explicitly or implicitly accept the priority of balance-of-payment targets over disinflation targets. This can mean in practice, however, that monetary policy should accommodate weakness of fiscal policy and structural reform, which in turn will not stimulate progress in these spheres. Hence a crawling-peg/-band regime is rather inconsistent with the consequent anti-inflationary orientation of the country's central bank. Apart from inducing inflationary expectations, it can create a lot of problems with controlling money supply when the exchange rate target must be defended against appreciation pressure needs in intensive interventions. Converting a crawling peg into a crawling band (which occurred in Poland in May 1995) gives more room for current monetary management but does not eliminate the above-mentioned problems.

Fourth, during most of the transition period, interest rates in Poland were relatively low, frequently negative in real terms (as concerns mainly deposits). This in fact stopped the remonetization process: Broad money velocity remained stable from 1991 until 1996 (see Jarocinski 1998). Only 1997 and 1998 brought an increasing trend in demand for money, particularly for its zloty component. This change in trend was possible because of a radical change in Poland's interest rate policy: Interest rates reach their maximum nominal and real level at the end of 1997.

Fifth, the coexistence of many mutually inconsistent targets, some officially declared but not really implemented (controlling money aggregates) and others nondeclared but in fact followed by the NBP (balance-of-payment target, export promotion), and their frequent changes damaged the transparency and credibility of monetary policy.

Sixth, the credibility of monetary and, more generally, all macroeconomic policy was additionally undermined by regular failures in inflation forecasting (until 1996) and by public conflicts between the Ministry of Finance and the NBP (particularly in 1994–1996).

The pattern of Poland's monetary policy started to change in 1998 as result of bold institutional changes in the NBP's legal position and

structure. Apart from regulation, mentioned earlier, the 1997 constitution significantly strengthened the central bank, granting it sole
responsibility for conducting Poland's monetary policy. All previous
parliament prerogatives were transferred to the Monetary Policy
Council (MPC), the new collective body in charge of all essential
monetary policy decisions. Nine members of the MPC enjoy the
same degree of independence from the government and daily political decisions and personal independence as the NBP governor (the ex
officio chairman of the MPC).

In February 1998, the MPC started to move toward a floating exchange rate regime, thus abandoning implicit export promotion/
balance-of-payment targets and crawling-peg devaluation. In September 1998, the MPC declared its adoption of direct inflation targeting (DIT) strategy, making Poland the second transition country
(after the Czech Republic) to do so.

Further Liberalization and Deregulation Process

The initial dynamics of liberalization and deregulation was stopped
in the second half of 1991 as some powerful lobbies rebuilt their
political positions. The list of smaller or bigger reversions included,
among others, agriculture protectionism and interventionism, supporting some loss-making enterprises and sectors (for example, the
coal industry), creation of a sugar cartel, the administrative concentration of cooperative banks, strengthening of the state monopoly
in telecommunication, and reintroduction of many kind of licensing.
Other factors, however, such as international trade agreements, the
association agreement with the EEC, pressure from international
financial institutions, accession to the Organisation for Economic
Cooperation and Development (OECD), and recently, accession negotiations with the European Union, forced the continuation of liberalization of product and capital markets and further institutional
developments. As a result, the effective protection level for imports
of industrial goods from EU, EFTA, and CEFTA countries (most of
the Polish trade partners) is close to zero. Agriculture and food products have higher levels of import protection,[17] but here also import barriers must be gradually reduced as the EU accession process
progresses.

Poland was also forced gradually to open its telecommunication,
banking, and insurance markets. Formal barriers related to foreign-

ers' purchase of land and real estate for investment and housing purposes were significantly reduced in late 1995 in connection with Poland's OECD application. Some remaining formal limitations related to foreign-owned corporations, were also removed at the same time.

The Polish Foreign Exchange Law has been liberalized several times: The most important changes were adopted in late 1994 and in 1998. As result, Poland has partially liberalized its capital account, though capital account liberalization this process is less advanced than in the case of the Czech Republic or Baltic countries.

At the end of 1997, the new Polish government declared a return to the process of removing domestic barriers to entrepreneurship. A special joint committee representing government and business organizations was formed with the mission to identify the main regulatory and bureaucratic obstacles to entrepreneurship in Poland and draft the relevant legislation to eliminate them.

Along the same lines, two dramatic attempts by Deputy Prime Minister and Minister of Finance Leszek Balcerowicz (in 1998 and 1999) to lower and simplify Poland's personal income tax (PIT) to stimulate economic growth and private entrepreneurship also met strong resistance from both the left and right side of the political spectrum. Balcerowicz's first initiative proposed a proportional (flat) PIT with one rate, following the Estonian and Swedish experience but it failed. The second one is less radical offering two PIT rates at the level of 18 and 28 percent and significant cuts in commercial income tax rates in exchange for the elimination of many tax exemptions.

It is also worth remembering that the expected harmonization of Polish business law with European involves some danger of importing many bureaucratic regulations existing in the EU countries that can harm freedom of economic activity.

Contrary to the product and capital markets, the Polish labor market presents much more rigidity inherited from the command system. The new labor code approved by the Polish parliament in 1996 only added new restrictions to the existing ones. These restrictions are particularly detrimental to small and medium-sized businesses, together with the very high social costs of official employment (the payroll tax for the Social Insurance Fund and Employment Fund is equal to 48 percent of an enterprise's wage bill). Polish labor market rigidity is reflected in the high rate of unemployment, which did not fall below 10 percent of the total labor force even in the period of very high economic growth in the country.

Privatization and the Growth of the New Private Sector

Poland started its privatization process with some enclaves of the private sector already in existence—in agriculture, trade, services, construction, handicrafts, and small-scale manufacturing. In 1989, the public sector contributed only 72 percent of Poland's GDP, and another 10 percent came from the cooperative sector. Poland also retained throughout the entire communist period some legal and institutional foundations connected with a private-market economy: a commercial code and bankruptcy law (both originated in 1934), a land and real estate register, some protection of private property rights in the civil code, and so on. On the other hand, lack of international experience in large-scale privatization caused long-lasting professional and political discussion of what privatization methods would be the best ones for Poland. This fascinating debate, which contributed very much to elaborating privatization strategies in other transition countries (particularly in the Czech Republic and Russia) cost Poland at least a one-year delay in starting large privatization. This means that the first political window of opportunity for fast privatization through radical reforms (in 1989–1990) was partly lost.

As result of the above-mentioned debate over privatization methods, Poland adopted a multitrack privatization strategy involving several methods simultaneously. This strategy was reflected in the basic laws of the early 1990s regulating the privatization process.[18]

The Law on Privatization of State Enterprises (of July 13, 1990) constituted a compromise between a number of different concepts and allowed for various privatization methods. Two main privatization methods, however, were established:

1. capital (equity) privatization, designed for large SOEs and consisting of two stages: (i) corporatization, and (ii) privatization of shares through public offerings, tenders, or negotiations following a public invitation

2. liquidation (direct) privatization, involving transfer of enterprise assets to private investors through (i) sale, (ii) in-kind contribution to a newly founded company, and (iii) leasing

The latter method was used extensively for many privatization transactions involving buyouts by management and employees. Although the Law on Privatization of State Enterprises was later replaced by the Law on Commercialization and Privatization of State Enterprises (of August 30, 1996, amended on February 21, 1997) the essential methods of Polish privatization established in 1990 have not changed, apart from granting bigger preferences for employees.

The Law on Financial Restructuring of Enterprises and Banks (of February 3, 1993), among other regulations (see next section) enabled another privatization track: through debt-to-equity conversion. This method was used by a number of large and medium-sized enterprises experiencing serious financial troubles at the beginning of transition, such as shipyards or businesses in the automobile industry.

Some sectors were treated in a specific way with respect to privatization. The first instance relates to agriculture. The Law on Management of Agriculture Property of the State Treasury (of October 19, 1991) established a separate procedure to be used for privatization of state agriculture farms. Under the provisions of the Law on Ownership Transformations of Certain State Enterprises with Special Importance for the National Economy (of February 5, 1993), 155 enterprises from the coal, power generation, and defense industries were also exempted from the standard procedure of privatization. Subsequent legislation added to this "special" list a lot of other activities: telecommunication; production, transmission, and distribution of natural gas; production, transmission, and distribution of oil and oil products; harbors; the shipbuilding industry; air and sea transport; steel plants and other metallurgy; large chemical plants; sulfur and basalt mines; the spirits industry; fishing and fish processing companies; all banks that had not yet been privatized; the largest insurance company, Powszechny Zaktad Ubezpieczeis (PZU); and individual enterprises from other sectors. In fact, in most of the so-called strategic sectors, privatization was either stopped completely, or seriously delayed, by legislation exempting enterprises in those sectors from the privatization process.

Finally, in April 1993, the Law on National Investment Funds (NIFs), the Polish variant of mass privatization, was adopted after two and half years of hot political and professional debate. Another two years were necessary to start this program on the company level and almost six years to privatize NIFs. Finally, 512 enterprises were selected for the program, and 15 NIFs were formed. The NIF program was supposed to accelerate the pace of privatization, at the same time providing for restructuring of enterprises before their privatization, facilitated by the expertise of the professional management companies employed by the NIFs. To the present, at least part of these expectations have not been fulfilled, probably because of the very long and heavily politicized process of program implementation and some of the program's deficiencies in the sphere of corporate governance.

Poland is the only Central European country that has not solved the problem of restitution of property rights to former owners whose property was expropriated by the communist regime yet. All the legislative proposals prepared during the last decade were rejected by the subsequent parliaments.

At the end of 1998, 6,129 or 72.6 percent of all SOEs (8,441) existing in 1990, that is, at the beginning of the privatization process, were subject to ownership transformation. Excluding the 1,654 enterprises taken over by the Agency of Agriculture Property of the State Treasury, the number of remaining enterprises was 4,475. Out of those, privatization was complete in 2,454 enterprises and ongoing in the remaining 2,021 enterprises.

The share of different privatization tracks in the process as a whole was as follows (all data are as of the end of 1998): Corporatization involved 1,343 large companies. Of this group, 240 large companies have been entirely privatized through initial public offerings (IPOs), public tenders, or negotiations following public invitations. Another 512 corporatized companies were allocated to the NIF program. Direct privatization involved 1,551 enterprises. Among these, 1,515 completed the process, of which 1,021 enterprises were leased through employee management buyout (EMBO) schemes, 312 were sold for cash, 127 were contributed in kind to new companies, and the remaining were privatized through mixed methods. Direct privatization is the most popular in Poland, and its time efficiency is remarkable. The so-called liquidation privatization, conducted under the state enterprise law, involved 1,581 state enterprises in weak financial condition. Of these, 699 had been liquidated as of December 1998 through the sale of their assets to private owners (sometimes also employees) for cash.

Additionally, 363 state enterprises were transferred to municipal ownership. As of the end of 1997, 278 bankruptcy procedures involving SOEs had been completed and 203 bank conciliation procedures (under the Law on Financial Restructuring of Enterprises and Banks) had been implemented; in 135 of those, the terms of the debt-to-equity swap had been determined.

At the end of 1998, 2,906 SOEs remained registered, of which 1,818 were at that time conducting full-scale economic activity. The majority of this group consists of small and medium-sized enterprises that are in worse economic condition than the privatized ones. It also includes more than 400 large corporatized companies, owned by the state treasury, in varying financial and economic shape. Among them are the "giants": some 50 of the largest Polish enterprises belonging to the public sector. Some of them may play the role of "locomotives" of privatization, but others need serious restructuring.

Apart from this large privatization, small privatization of the country's trade and services network took place in 1990–1991. It overlapped with the spontaneous creation of many new private firms as result of very radical liberalization of both the domestic and foreign market (see above). These two factors, that is, small privatization and the formation and fast development of a "new" private sector, were the dominant factors changing the ownership structure of the Polish economy, at least in the first half of 1990s.

Table 5.2 shows the share of the private sector in Poland's GDP, employment, fixed assets, and investments at the end of 1997. There are striking differences between the dominant position of the private sector in total employment and GDP and its much smaller share in total fixed assets and investments. These differents reflect the fact that the most capital-intensive sectors of the economy, such as mining, heavy industry; telecommunications; railways; energy generation, transmission, and distribution; and natural gas and oil production, transportation, and distribution, remain in public hands. Private ownership dominates agriculture, trade, services, and labor-intensive manufacturing. Privatization is almost finished in some (particularly consumer goods producing and service branches), is fairly advanced in others (for example, the banking sector) and has not really started in some large sectors (the so-called strategic sectors).

According to European Bank for Reconstruction and Development (EBRD) (1998, 26) estimations, Poland is behind many other transition countries in terms of the private-sector share in GDP (65 percent

Table 5.2
Private-sector share in employment, gross value added, fixed assets, and investment, December 1997 (in percent)

	Private-sector share			
Specification	Employment	Gross value added	Fixed assets	Investment outlays
Total economy	68.2	67.2	42.3	53.4
Section				
Agriculture and forestry	97.9	90.1	82.4	85.4
Construction	87.7	94.8	64.0	52.1
Trade and repair	96.1	97.1	86.6	94.1
Hotels and restaurants	84.5	77.7	53.8	66.3
Transport, storage, and communication	32.9	38.9	3.7	25.3
Financial intermediation	42.0	84.9	59.2	70.2
Real estate	69.8	88.0	81.2	85.4
Industry	63.7	60.0	27.8	52.6
Mining and quarrying	4.5	3.8	3.1	5.5
Manufacturing	74.5	77.6	54.9	76.3
Electricity, gas, and water supply	5.4	3.0	2.0	7.8

Source: Blaszczyk 1999.

in mid-1998): Hungary (80 percent), Albania, the Czech Republic, and Slovakia (75 percent), Estonia, Lithuania, and Russia (70 percent). Although the quality of the privatization completed in Poland (in terms of corporate governance, protection of property rights, and progress in restructuring) is probably better than in many countries that relied, in the first instance, on voucher schemes, the above statistics nonetheless reveal a significant delay in Polish privatization.

The center-right government of Jerzy Buzek formed in October 1997 in Poland made some effort toward accelerating the privatization of the country's banks, starting privatization of Polish Telecom and the country's energy-generating companies, and preparing for the privatization of the PZU, Polish Airlines, and some other "strategic" sectors. On the other hand, privatization of the remaining small and medium-sized companies is almost nonexistent. So-called popular enfranchisement, that is, another kind of voucher privatization, imposed by part of the ruling coalition, does not help in the design and implementation of a consistent privatization strategy.

The Reconstruction of the Banking Sector and Building Other Segments of the Financial Sector

The liberal Polish banking law of 1989 allowed for the rapid creation of new banks, both with state capital and private. As in other transition countries, many of these banks proved too small to survive and had to go through a painful restructuring process (involving, for example, mergers with other banks or liquidation) in the subsequent years. On the other hand, most "traditional" state-owned banks existing before 1989 or formed in the process of separation from the NBP in 1988–1989 continued soft lending to SOEs, building up a substantial bad debt portfolio in 1990–1992 (amounting to 34.8 percent of the total credit portfolio at the end of 1991). Therefore, restructuring and rehabilitation of the Polish banking system became unavoidable at some point.

The above-mentioned Law on Financial Restructuring of Enterprises and Banks (of February 1993) provided a unique decentralized scheme for bank restructuring that minimized the fiscal costs of this operation and the danger of the moral hazard effect. The law provided for the following financial restructuring procedures: debt renegotiations and banking conciliation agreements, public sale of bank debts, debt-to-equity conversion, liquidation, and bankruptcy.

Commercial banks participating in the restructuring operation could get a limited up-front recapitalization if they met some conditions, such as preparing the diagnostic study (by external auditors), analyzing the quality of the bank's loan portfolio, forming a separate organizational unit in charge of managing low-quality loans, and preparing loan portfolio restructuring plans. Recapitalized banks could no longer grant loans to bad debtors, excluding cases where the new funds resulted from the bank conciliation agreement.

Recapitalization was carried out by transferring fifteen-year state treasury bonds to the banks. The state treasury initially services these bonds, but once a bank is privatized, the Fund for Privatization of Polish Banks takes over the burden of servicing bonds transferred to that bank. The total value of bonds distributed among ten state-owned banks amounted to about U.S. $1,600 million. More than half of this amount went to BGZ (Agriculture Bank) and to regional cooperative banks associated with this bank. The case of BGZ differed significantly from those of all other banks, as it represented, in fact, a clear example of political bailing out.

Poland's bank restructuring exercise was followed by a program of privatization of the banking sector with participation of strategic foreign investors. Although a bit delayed in comparison with the initial schedule, the privatization of Poland's banks has become one of the region's biggest success stories. At the end of 1998, out of a total of eighty-three banks in Poland, the state treasury controlled (directly or indirectly) thirteen banks, foreign owners controlled thirty-one, and domestic private owners thirty-nine. Of the equity in Polish commercial banks equity, 49.65 percent belonged to foreign owners (mainly to first-class Western banks), 18.84 percent to the state treasury, 4.45 percent to other state entities, 0.11 percent to the NBP, and 9.63 percent to other (private) domestic owners; 17.33 percent had a diluted character (mainly traded at Warsaw Stock Exchange). However, 48.1 percent of net assets of commercial banks still belonged to the banks, with dominant state ownership that reflects a dominant market position of the State Saving Bank and Agriculture Bank.

EBRD (1998, 26) gives Poland one of the highest scores among transition countries for banking reform: 3+, together with Estonia and behind Hungary (4) only. It also grants the highest score (3+, together with Hungary) for Poland's securities market and nonbank financial institutions. In particular, Poland's security law, regulatory standards worked out by its Security and Exchange Commission, and the organization of the Warsaw Stock Exchange can serve as a good example for other transition countries. The commercial and life insurance sector, on the other hand, are relatively less developed.

Four Social Reforms of 1999

The government of Jerzy Buzek declared four big social reforms in early 1998: further territorial decentralization (introduction of the second and third level of territorial self-government), pension reform, health care reform, and education reform. After very intensive political debate and legislation work through all of 1998, implementation of these reforms began on January 1, 1999. The reform effort tried to address the country's real needs, as the spheres it involved had been put aside in the market-oriented reform process or necessary changes in them had been significantly delayed.

Pension Reform

The reform of the Polish pension system started formally in 1990. The Law on Pension Revalorization of October 1991 was the most important early step. Unfortunately, the final outcome of the 1991 pension reform was not consistent with the country's fiscal constraints and created an enormous financial burden for the expenditure side of the budget. Automatic indexation of pension benefits in relation to wages in the enterprise sector was one fundamental mistake of the 1991 law. Additionally, despite the government's intention, the Polish parliament maintained relatively easy entry criteria to the country's pension system, especially for disability pensions and farmer pensions (traditionally financed at around 95 percent by the state budget) and this made the situation even worse. Several drastic and politically unpopular adjustment steps were thus necessary in 1992 and 1993 to slow the pace of the indexation process and limit pension expenditures. Beginning in 1996, the indexation formula was finally changed from a wage-based one to a mixed formula reflecting both price and wage growth. Eligibility criteria for disability pensions were formally tightened at the same time. The share of disability pensions in the total expenditure of the public pension system is still extremely high, however, one of the highest in the world (see Gomulka 1999).

Conceptual effort to design and then implement comprehensive pension reform in Poland started in 1996. The new pension system is envisaged to consist of three pillars: a reduced pay-as-you-go (PAYG) system, a mandatory funded system operated by private pension funds, and additional, voluntary private pension funds (fully funded). Pension reform is expected to reduce the country's unfunded pension liabilities over next fifty years, but in the meantime, it will bring the additional fiscal costs connected with the transition process (Gomulka and Styczeń 1999). The proceeds from privatization of the "strategic" sectors will be channeled to cover these additional costs, which should soften the political resistance to fast privatization. Creation of private pension funds should also increase market demand for government and corporate securities and stimulate a further development of the Polish capital market.

Territorial Self-Government Reform

After successful introduction of the first stage of local self-government in Poland in 1990, the next steps in this direction were effectively stopped, mainly by strong political resistance of the Polish Peasants Party (PSL), which was part of the government coalition between 1993 and 1997. Only the next parliamentary election in 1997 provided an opportunity to return to this idea.

The new reform introduced the second and third stages of territorial self-government. However, it necessitated a radical change in the administrative map of Poland, which created very serious political resistance on the part of many regional and subregional lobbies. The second, subregional level (*powiat*) had to be completely reestablished, having been eliminated in 1975. The third, regional level (*wojewodztwo*) had to be redesigned: forty-nine small units were merged into sixteen big ones.

Territorial reform was connected with the serious devolution of power from the central government to regions and subregions that should be connected with further fiscal decentralization. However, this last element is still in the process of discussion and correction, as regions and subregions present strongly differentiated fiscal potential.

Health Care Reform

The traditional budgetary system of financing health care in Poland remained almost unchanged until the end of 1998. It was characterized by increasing financial mismanagement, decreasing quality of the services offered, and spontaneous elements of illegal or semilegal privatization, in fact very close to corruption. The health care reform package was initially prepared and adopted by the Polish parliament in 1996–1997 but was later significantly corrected in 1998. Its implementation began on January 1, 1999.

The new system of health care financing is basing on compulsory contributions to regional public health insurance funds (HIFs) automatically deducted from personal income tax liabilities. Beginning in 2001, private HIFs can be also created. HIFs are in charge of contracting medical services on behalf of their members. Services can be provided both by autonomous public hospitals and ambulatories (transferred in the meantime to the ownership of territorial self-governments) and by private practitioners and enterprises. However, the privatization of the supply side of Polish health care is in the initial stage only.

Polish health care reform is very similar to the Hungarian and Czech reforms implemented earlier that have brought a huge cost explosion (especially the Czech one). There is a danger that Poland will also experience such an explosion in health care costs, especially taking into account the country's very weak health administration and its powerful trade unions of medical personnel.

Education Reform

So far, education reform in Poland has involved mainly changes in school organization (moving from a two- to a three-tiered school system) and in education programs. The future system of education financing is as yet unclear, apart from attempts to introduce partial tuition in university education and a system of special loans for university students.

Political Economy of Poland's Transition

What have been the driving forces of the Polish transition? What enabled the country to undertake a very difficult reform program at the end of 1989 and implement it quite successfully? Why, despite frequent changes of government (once a year on average), relative political instability in the first years of transition, and unique, very strong political position of trade unions, has the country been able to sustain the course of reform over a decade and not abandon it?

In the first and most important stage of Polish transition (until 1991), authorities enjoyed the special political window of opportunity created in 1989 by the collapse of the communist regime (the period of "extraordinary" politics, according to Balcerowicz's [1994] terminology). Radical change of the political regime and regaining the full independence of the country gave the first noncommunist government a substantial political credit. The country's dramatic economic situation and incipient hyperinflation convinced many people that partial reforms and half measures were hopeless and that only radical, comprehensive therapy could yield positive results. Additionally, the political changes paralyzed many traditional lobbies operating under the previous regime.

As mentioned before, the Polish economy inherited from the 1980s relatively strong employee self-management institutions in the SOEs backed by the Solidarity trade union on the enterprise level. Many liberal-minded economists and politicians considered this factor a potentially serious obstacle to the planned transformation, particularly in relation to its privatization component. They were right to a certain extent: The presence of strong trade unions and an employee self-management movement complicated and delayed the privatization debate in late 1989 and 1990 and adoption of the first privatization laws. It also led to relatively significant privileges for employees in the privatization process (though smaller than those in some other countries, such as Russia). On the other hand, however, employee self-management in SOEs brought some positive and rather unexpected effects. First, it contributed to decentralization of trade union pressure and bargaining at the enterprise level, which was less dangerous for macroeconomic policy. Second, giving more power and responsibility to employee self-management organs on the enterprise level helped impose hard budget constraints and oriented the political energy of trade unions and worker councils toward restructuring/privatization actions rather than bargaining with government. Third and most important, worker councils started a spontaneous process of verifying managers, which contributed to fast changes of the top management of SOEs and their relatively fast restructuring. As result, Poland never had problems with a "red" directors lobby like those that have plagued many other transition countries.

After the initial two years of transition, the period of extraordinary political opportunity was definitely over.[19] Many people by then considered radical economic reforms to be connected with substantial social costs (in fact, these were mostly cumulative costs of the previous system's inefficiency and its spontaneous decomposition at the end of 1980s). This turn in public opinion reactivated economic populism in the country and rebuilt the strength of special-interest groups. Proreform enthusiasm definitely evaporated. Because of the political decomposition of the Solidarity movement and some mistakes in the election law (following the principle of a pure proportionality), the parliament elected in Poland in October 1991 became very fragmented. Therefore, governments during next two years were short lived and lacking in sufficient political support. This led to earlier parliamentary elections in September 1993 and the victory in those elections of political parties with roots in the communist system. They came to power with rather antireformatory and populist slogans.

Despite all the above-mentioned political difficulties, promarket economic reforms continued, although slowed down and less consequent. The domestic political consensus and determination of the first two years of transition were replaced, however, by external factors. Until the end of 1994, the perspective of debt reduction, conditional on progress in the transition process and implementation of IMF programs, played the crucial role in forcing Polish politicians to follow a responsible macroeconomic policy and continue systemic transformation. In 1995, when Poland completed successfully the last stand-by agreement and debt reduction negotiations were over, other external factors became important. Poland started to apply for OECD membership and just after for the membership in NATO and the European Union. Particularly, the EU accession process involves carrying out complex institutional reforms in many spheres of economic and noneconomic life comparable to the big transition effort in the early 1990s. This single factor will determine the agenda and speed of the economic and political transformation in the coming few years.

In the meantime, as a result of steady economic growth and an improving quality of life in the country, social support for transition results has returned in Poland. Hence, all main political parties now express their general backing for continuation of market-oriented reforms, stable macroeconomic policy, and prospective EU membership.

Some Concluding Remarks

The above analysis shows that the history of the Polish transition has been more complicated than has usually been perceived by the international public. Although it has generally been successful and effective, the same cannot be said in relation to all of its individual components, for example, attempts of pension reforms in the early 1990s. The fast and radical pace of the first two years of transition was later replaced by a more gradual and less consequent approach. However, basic foundations created by the initial transition package proved so strong and irreversible that they determined the continuation of the reform process in the next couple of years, even when individual political parties declared a different approach during subsequent election campaigns. The domestic political environment, although not always very supportive, particularly in the middle of the decade, could not do too much damage because of the role of external factors. Poland also simply had a bit of luck, with very good and strong professionals in charge of economic policy in the successive governments.

Analyzing the individual components of the transition process, it is hard to declare Poland as a leader in some respects, such as speed of disinflation or privatization. However, the reform process in Poland kept its comprehensiveness and internal consistency, making its transitional economic system pretty effective. One must also remember that Poland started its transition earlier and inherited relatively better institutions from the previous regime than in the case of many other countries (particularly the post-Soviet ones). Despite the uneven speed of reforms and numerous mistakes, successive governments through the decade avoided major reversals in reform process or macroeconomic crises.

Building a modern market economy in Poland is not a finished task, however. The remaining economic agenda involves reducing inflation to the EU level, continuing fiscal consolidation, and reducing the size of government, mainly through reduction of some social entitlements, completing the privatization process, continuation of social reforms, labor market reform, reducing the excessive role of trade unions, and preserving the liberal character of the economic system. Most of the reforms carried out in the coming years will be dictated by the harmonization requirements connected with the country's future EU membership.

References

Antczak, Malgorzata, and Urban Górski. 1998. The influence of the exchange rate stability on inflation: A comparative analysis. Studies and Analyses no. 137, CASE—Center for Social and Economic Research, Warsaw.

Balcerowicz, Leszek. 1994. Understanding postcommunist transitions. *Journal of Democracy* 5, no. 4 (October).

Balcerowicz, L., H. Bak, B. Blaszczyk, M. Dabrowski, J. Eysymontt, W. Kaminski, S. Kasiewicz, A. Lipowski, R. Michalski, A. Parkola, and P. Pysz. 1981. Reforma gospodarcza: glowne kierunki i sposob realizacji (Economic reform: Main directions and the method of realization). In *Reforma gospodarcza—propozycje, tendencje, kierunki dyskusji* (Economic reform—Proposals, tendencies, directions of discussion), ed. R. Krawczyk. Warszawa: PWE.

Belka, Marek, Saul Estrin, Mark E. Schaffer, and Inderjit J. Singh. 1994. Enterprise adjustment in Poland: Evidence from a survey of 200 private, privatized, and state-owned firms. Paper presented at the World Bank Workshop on Enterprise Adjustment in Eastern Europe, Washington, D.C., September.

Blaszczyk, Barbara. 1999. Privatization and residual state property in Poland. Report prepared within ACE PHARE research project (no. P 96-6040-R) "Privatization and Management of Residual State Property," conducted under direction of Andreja Bohm at the Central and Eastern European Privatization Network (CEEPN) in Ljubljana, Slovenia, March.

Blaszczyk, Barbara, and Marek Dabrowski. 1993. The privatization process in Poland 1989–1992: Expectations, results and remaining dilemmas. Working paper, Centre for Research into Post-Communist Economics (CRCE), London.

Bratkowski, Andrzej S. 1993. The shock of transformation or the transformation of the shock, *Communist Economies and Economic Transformation* 5, no. 1.

Cukrowski, Jacek, and Jaroslaw Janecki. 1998. Financing budget deficits by seigniorage revenues: The case of Poland 1990–1997. Studies and Analyses no. 155, CASE—Center for Social and Economic Research, Warsaw.

Dabrowski, Marek. 1996. Fiscal crisis in the transformation period: Trends, stylized facts and some conceptual problems. Studies and Analyses no. 72, CASE—Center for Social and Economic Research, Warsaw.

Dabrowski, Marek, and Urszula Kosterna. 1996. Fiscal policy issues in Central and Eastern Europe. Paper presented at CEPR/IEWS conference "Economic Policy Initiative Forum," Budapest, November 15–17.

European Bank for Reconstruction and Development (EBRD). 1998. *Transition Report.*

Ghosh, Atish, and Steven Phillips. 1998. Warning: Inflation May Be Harmful to Your Growth, *IMF Staff Papers* 45, no. 4 (December).

Golinowska, Stanislawa. 1996. State social policy and social expenditure in Central and Eastern Europe. Studies and Analyses no. 81, CASE—Center for Social and Economic Research, Warsaw.

Gomulka, Stanisław. 1998. Managing capital flows in Poland, 1995–1998. Working papers series no. 7, CASE-CEU, Warsaw.

Gomulka, Stanislaw. 1999. Comparative notes on pension developments and reforms in the Czech Republic, Hungary, Poland and Romania. Studies and Analyses no. 182, CASE—Center for Social and Economic Research, Warsaw.

Gomulka, Stanislaw, and Marek Styczeń. 1999. Estimating the impact of the 1999 pension reform in Poland, 2000–2050. Working papers series no. 27, CASE-CEU, Warsaw.

International Monetary Fund (IMF). 1998. Disinflation in transition: 1993–1997. Working paper, International Monetary Fund, European I Department (in consultation with European II Department), Washington, D.C.

International Monetary Fund (IMF). 1999. Republic of Poland. Staff report for the 1998 Article IV consultation, International Monetary Fund, Washington, D.C.

Jarocinski, Marek. 1998. Money demand and monetization in transition economies. Working papers series no. 13, CASE-CEU, Warsaw.

Sachs, Jeffrey D. 1996. Economic transition and exchange rate regime. *American Economic Review* 86, no. 2.

Siwinska, Joanna. 1999. Public debt dynamics and structure in selected transition economies. Studies and Analyses no. 162, CASE—Center for Social and Economic Research, Warsaw.

Tomczynska, Magdalena. 1998. Exchange rate regimes in transition economies. Studies and Analyses no. 128, CASE—Center for Social and Economic Research, Warsaw.

Walewski, Mateusz. 1998. Wage-price spiral in Poland and other postcommunist countries. Working papers series no. 22, CASE-CEU, Warsaw.

Wozniak, Przemysław. 1997. Relative prices and inflation in Poland 1989–1997. Studies and Analyses no. 121, CASE—Center for Social and Economic Research, Warsaw.

6

Fiscal Foundations of Convergence to the European Union: The Hungarian Economy toward EU Accession

László Halpern and Judit Neményi

Introduction

The advanced Associated Countries (ACs), those with which EU membership negotiations started in 1998,[1] more or less completed the most painful phase of economic transformation by 1999 and have now entered the period of convergence leading to accession to the EU. Although there are common features among them, the ACs present quite different pictures in terms of the stage of their market economies (microrestructuring) and their macroeconomic indicators, both of which reflect the capability of the candidates to meet the requirements for early EMU membership. Whereas the so-called transition period in the 1990s was intended to create market conditions by restructuring the centrally planned economies, the convergence period, overlapping the date of Euro-zone entry, is aimed at closing the gap between the level of development of EU and transition economies.

This chapter focuses on the new challenges that the advanced ACs, having completed the task of transition, now face in the final phase leading up to EU accession, taking Hungary as a case for illustration. Two features of Hungary's transition, however, have had an impact on its transition and may limit the relevance of its experience for other transition countries. On the one hand, the fact that some partial market reforms had already been introduced in Hungary since the 1970s represented a net advantage for Hungary over other transition countries. On the other hand, Hungary started transition in the 1990s as a heavily indebted country, and its debt burden was the most difficult financial constraint it faced, exacerbating the effects of other external shocks—primarily the collapse of the CMEA (Council for Mutual Economic Assistance)—that contributed to a serious output loss in the early 1990s. Hungary's critical debt situation made radical steps—such as bankruptcy law, bank consolidation, rapid privatization, reform in the general government budget and the elimination of relative price distortions)—unavoidable already in the early transition period.

First, this chapter briefly summarizes the most important lessons of Hungarian transition, which may be instructive for countries in which the early phase of transition to a market economy is still a current issue. Then the crucial points of medium-term economic programs in the convergence period are discussed, focusing on the sources of tensions stemming from contradictions between real and nominal aspects of convergence. Anticipated trade-offs among different policy choices in real and nominal convergence are then presented. Finally, the chapter concludes with an overview of policy options.

Brief Lessons of Hungarian Transition

Hungary's economic transition offers quite a rich history of the development of macrolevel and microlevel policy issues. It is beyond the scope of the chapter to present policy discussions of the early period, between 1990 and 1994, including the potential threat of an excessive increase in Hungary's debt-to-GDP ratio.[2] We have also chosen to forego an assessment of the factors leading to the introduction in Hungary of austerity measures in March 1995 and their role in the subsequent development of the Hungarian economy.[3] Only a few general lessons from the ten years of Hungarian transition are offered here:

Coordinated Macropolicies

The March 1995 adjustment package—based mostly on radical improvement of the fiscal stance—restored macroeconomic equilibrium to Hungary and created the conditions necessary for economic recovery. The general government borrowing requirement was cut, as budget deficit declined from above 9 percent of GDP in 1994 to lower than 5 percent by 1996, and brought in to line with the financing ability of the market, a precondition for reducing Hungary's current account deficit to a sustainable level. Strengthening growth in the country was led by outstanding export dynamics and a strong investment boom. All of these factors supported to make disinflation in Hungary continuous in the second half of the 1990s.

Creating a Private Sector

Macroeconomic stabilisation in Hungary was supported by micro-economic restructuring, which had already started well before March 1995 in the form of privatization, institutional and infrastructure development of the money and capital markets, and similar measures. Microeconomic policy concentrated on facilitating the structural adjustments necessary to enhance the competitiveness of the Hungarian economy in the single market of the European Union. Macroeconomic adjustment created favourable conditions for further privatisation and deregulation. Since 1996, efforts made by the Hungarian governments to achieve a stable, predictable legal and tax environment obviously played a crucial role in this respect as well as schemes to encourage research and development and investment by multinationals, on the one hand, and domestic small and medium size enterprises, on the other. Restructuring of the social security system has been a longer-term project. Whereas the basic pay-as-you-go pension system was complemented quite easily with a competitive system based on capital markets, the transformation of the health care system remains a difficult issue left for the future. As high social security contributions add to wage costs and thereby erode the competitiveness of Hungarian corporations, health care finances should obviously be in the focus of structural policy, and various insurance schemes are under consideration.

Creation and Regulation of Financial Markets

As a result of certain restructuring programs undertaken in the 1990s,[4] the indicators (the capital adequacy ratio, the rate of earnings, and return on assets) characterizing the Hungarian banking sector activity have improved significantly. The government securities market experienced spectacular development, especially since 1995, as the public-sector borrowing requirement was set according to macroconsistency. Thanks to coordinated borrowing and issue policies, in the second half of the 1990s, it was possible to extend the market yield curve up to a ten-year horizon.[5] Liberalization promoted deepening of the secondary market in government bonds. The development of the government securities market supported the evolution of the wider securities markets as well.[6] Of course, there are still several imperfections in capital market operation due to market segmentation, collusion, and the lack of transparency of over-the-counter (OTC) markets. As compared with Anglo-Saxon markets, domestic institutional investors in the Hungarian market are still weak, accounting for approximately 3 percent of stock market capitalization in 1998. Nevertheless, the amounts invested in mutual funds, insurance bills, and pensions funds have been steadily growing. Derivative markets can play a very beneficial role in improving efficiency of money and capital markets operation by providing market participants with facilities for pricing and redistributing risk. The Budapest Stock Exchange and the Commodity Exchange have derivative sections for index, individual stock price, interest rate, and exchange rate futures.

Capital control was eased gradually during the 1990s, and only protection against short-term inflow has been maintained, since foreigners are not allowed to invest debt instruments with original maturity of less than one year, and short-term Forint (HUF) loans and futures contracts are unavailable to nonresidents. Obviously, composite OTC market products can easily evade these restrictions, but the higher costs and risks (transaction, settlement, and counterparty) involved as well as prudent regulation and supervision may somewhat limit the volatility of short-term capital flows.

Quick Performance Check at the Commencement of the Convergence Period

Convergence primarily means high growth. In this sense "high" means higher than the growth rate of the country's main trading partners, higher than the growth rate of neighboring countries, and higher than the growth rate of the more developed world. It is quite often forgotten that there is another way of catching up to the level of development of EMU countries: until the candidate countries have their own currency, hence the exchange rate policy, at their disposal, the real appreciation of the domestic currencies of ACs against the more developed countries is equivalent to higher GDP growth.[7] Real appreciation, however, can be achieved in ACs through inflation rates that are higher than those abroad or by nominal appreciation of the exchange rate. This creates a true dilemma of policy choice for the monetary policy makers in the convergence period, which will be analyzed later in the chapter. Let us now consider Hungary's most important performance criteria in an international comparison: growth, inflation, real exchange rate, and fiscal stance.

Growth

Hungary entered its third consecutive year of relatively high growth in 1999. Radical structural changes, speeded by the bankruptcy law, bank restructuring programs, and relative price corrections, made transformation in Hungary deeper, but also more painful than in other ACs, as reflected by the relatively slow resumption of growth after the transitional shocks in Hungary in the second half of the 1990s. Nevertheless, the restoration and expansion of growth potential can be assumed to be lasting in Hungary, precisely because of the aforementioned radical reforms. These reforms were carried out in both the private and public sectors, strengthening financial institutions and promoting the evolution of the country's money and capital markets.

Hungary's growth potential was reinforced by the foreign direct investment (FDI) that the country has received since the end of 1980s (see table 6.1 and figure 6.1). Increasing the growth potential in the ACs in of primary importance in the convergence period in order to accelerate the process of closing the gap between the income levels of new candidates and Euro-land. A particular country's potential for growth is determined by the level of microrestructuring it has achieved, its integration with the world and EU economies, and its past and future FDI.

Table 6.1
Foreign Direct Investment in ACs (in millions of U.S. dollars)

	1990	1991	1992	1993	1994	1995	1996	1997	1998
Czech Republic	132	513	1,004	654	878	2,568	1,435	1,268	1,617
Estonia	—	—	82	162	214	201	150	266	485
Hungary	311	1,462	1,479	2,339	1,144	4,519	1,983	2,085	1,935
Poland	10	291	678	1,715	1,875	3,659	2,768	3,077	6,326
Slovenia	4	65	111	113	128	176	185	321	165

Note: 1998 figures for Czech Republic and Estonia are extrapolated from January–September data for that year. Dashes indicate nonavailability of data.

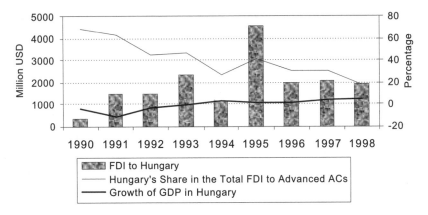

Figure 6.1
Foreign direct investment and potential growth in Hungary, 1990–1998

Though the "growth race" is far from over, Hungary, after a slow start, seems to be catching up to the other ACs in late 1990s (see appendix table 6A.1). Hungary was more successful than other transition countries, however, in withstanding the negative impacts of the Russian crisis in 1998 and flagging EU demand for their goods. EU countries purchase 80 percent of Hungarian exports, with 60 percent of this flow consisting of manufactured goods. This shows that the Hungarian economy's vulnerability to external shocks might originate mostly from the main EU trading partners, if their demand for the products of ACs falls and from Hungary's immediate region in the form of war and serious financial crises. Moreover, until accession to the EU, tensions in emerging markets will always have an impact on the Hungarian economy through contagion effects. This may result in a higher risk premium for the region or in capital outflow. Both of these phenomena—the excess risk premium required for the emerging market status and volatility of capital flows—might slow down the catching up to EU by increasing the costs of investments, thus constraining the increase in potential growth.

Inflation

Being a small, open, and largely liberalized economy, Hungary's economic performance has always depended much on external conditions, and equilibrium indicators with respect to the current account and general government deficits have been continuously monitored by market players. This is why the exchange rate played an outstanding role in Hungarian stabilization over the whole transition period. The central bank has relied on exchange rate targeting regimes, using the exchange rate as intermediate target for the reduction of inflation. It started with a fixed exchange rate regime with adjustments to parity on an irregular basis in the first half of the 1990s.[8] With the aim of promoting stabilization and gaining credibility, the adjustable peg was replaced, in 1995, by a crawling peg exchange rate regime with a ± 2.25 percent wide band. In this so-called narrow band, crawling exchange rate regime, central parity has been devalued on daily basis according to a preannounced rate of monthly devaluation.

The ultimate target of Hungarian monetary policy after March 1995 was clearly to achieve continuous decline in the rate of inflation, with the aim of promoting the resumption of economic growth. In setting target inflation and the rate of preannounced crawl, the so-called sustainable disinflation policy pursued by Hungary attempted to take several factors (expectations, competitiveness, etc.) into account.[9] The preannounced monthly rate of the crawl has been gradually reduced from the 1.9 percent in 1995 to 0.3 percent in 2000, and the consumer price inflation decreased from its peak of 32 percent in 1995 to the high single-digit range by the end of 1990s (see figure 6.2).

Sustainablity of disinflation meant that Hungarian authorities have never overstrained the trade-off between disinflation and competitiveness in favor of the former. In 1997, for instance, when Hungary benefited from large FDI inflows, reflecting the growing credibility of the economic policy introduced in 1995, the nominal appreciation of the Forint was limited by the narrow band, though its slope was reduced from 1.2 percent to 1.0 percent per month. Due to the strong capital inflow, the National Bank of Hungary (NBH) was compelled to intervene at the strong edge of the band. A smaller depreciation of the central parity or a large appreciation of the market exchange rate allowed by widening the band would have carried two types of risk:

As an immediate reaction, only the relative prices of tradable to nontradable goods would have been changed. This could have led to a deterioration in the current account, which should be avoided in a country like Hungary where the potential threat of any reversal in the external debt would cause problems with creditworthiness.

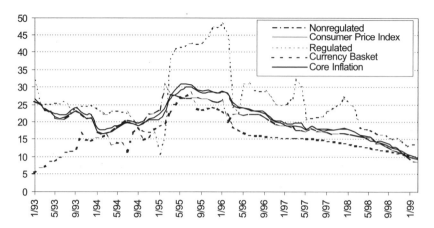

Figure 6.2
Components of CPI inflation in Hungary

Even if we assume that the multinational sector, which benefited first and foremost from the capital inflow, has a less vulnerable profit margin and more favorable access to external borrowing, it can be supposed that the growth just beginning in more traditional branches of the economy would have probably been hit harder by unexpected appreciation.

Hence, Hungary's disinflation policy has aimed at achieving a "soft lending" in disinflation and at avoiding turning points possibly stemming from suppressed inflation. The transitional structural-inflationary pressures, however, such as energy prices, utilities prices, and regulated prices, may have an impact on disinflation in spite of efforts to make them transparent. The policy has never targeted a rate of disinflation of more than four or five percentage points, quite a remarkable achievement according to international standards, especially as disinflation in Hungary has not required large sacrifices in terms of growth.

In the first quarter of 1999, the consumer price index (CPI) in Hungary fell to the single-digit range for the first time since 1987 and, though worldwide deflation played a significant role in this result, a detailed analysis shows that domestic factors—primarily the quick adjustment of Hungarian corporate sector to the fall in external demand after the Russian crisis—were more important than imported disinflation in causing the 8 percentage point drop in the inflation rate recorded in 1998. Wage agreements in the tradable sector were observed to be following the disinflation trend, reflecting the increase in credibility of the preannounced exchange rate regime. As a result, nominal wage increases started to decline in 1998; they nevertheless exceeded the rate targeted in the economic program somewhat, but the adjustment toward slower wage increases shows that both employers and employees have been convinced of the merits of disinflation and have accepted that the same real wage increase can be achieved with lower nominal wage increases. This has made it possible to slow the wage-price spiral while GDP growth has remained relatively high.

The preannounced crawling peg has increasingly played the role of a nominal anchor in the pricing behaviour of tradable sectors in the Hungarian economy. Depreciation within the band due to international financial crises (Asian and Russian) has hardly had any effect, showing that market players have accepted the preannounced peg as a benchmark for pricing and fluctuations of the exchange rate were taken as temporary. The success of disinflation in Hungary can be foreseen by the market players' steadily declining inflationary expectations, closely related to the strengthening credibility of the crawling exchange rate regime as well as that of the underlying economic policy. This was reflected by the subsequent capital inflows and the lowering of required interest premium on Forint-denominated assets. Actually, this occurred surprisingly quickly following the implementation of the March 1995 adjustment package: starting from early 1996, the risk premium on assets denominated in domestic currency was consistently much lower in Hungary than in Poland or in the Czech Republic, where disinflation was based more on monetary restrictions and / or more volatile exchange rates (see figure 6.3).

The NBH has followed the policy of sterilized intervention since 1995: the bank bought foreign exchange whenever the exchange rate touched the strong edge of the band and issued sterilization instruments to absorb the excess liquidity. One can argue that this policy may induce "extra" costs showing up in high interest payments on public debt in terms of GDP. No doubt sterilization pushes up (or decelerates the fall of) interest rates in domestic capital markets and may increase the interest burden of public debt. As a matter of fact, however, this was not the case in Hungary in the 1990s. The average costs of sterilization were estimated at approximately 0.16 percent of

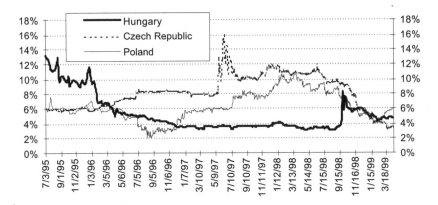

Figure 6.3
Interest premium in Hungary, the Czech Republic, and Poland, July 3, 1995–April 13, 1999
Note: Interest premium calculated on the basis of domestic three-month interbank rates, three-month forward-looking announced crawling depreciation (= zero in the Czech Republic) and LIBOR rates (70 percent DEM—30 percent U.S. dollar).

GDP,[10] and the percentage of interest payments in the central government budget expenditure shrank from 9 percent in 1995 to 6.4 percent in 1999.

Disinflation factors in transition economies are analyzed in detail in Cottarelli and Szapáry 1998. The Hungarian experience in 1990s demonstrates that a country's fiscal stance is of crucial importance in disinflation; however, under transition conditions it is extremely difficult to keep the fiscal policy on the right track. As the first-best policy mix—tight fiscal policy with not too tight monetary policy (see Begg 1998)—is almost always impossible to put into practice, the fiscal conditions (the size of the deficit, the level of taxes, and the composition of expenditures) predetermine the scope and efficiency of monetary policy in achieving the inflation target.

Real Exchange Rates

In respect to fast growing, catching up economies, the equilibrium real exchange rate (on a CPI basis) can be expected to appreciate in the medium terms. This comes from the permanently higher productivity of the tradable sector vis-à-vis both the nontradable (services) sector and Hungary's main trading partners (the so-called Balassa-Samuelson effect). Indeed, price-based real exchange rates in

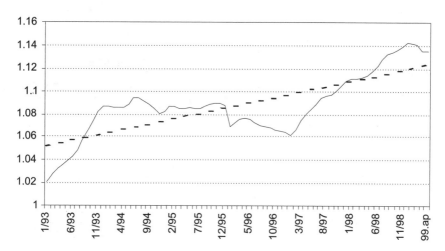

Figure 6.4
Nontradable/tradable inflation in Hungary (1991 = 1)

Hungary follow an explicit trend of real appreciation (figures 6.4 and 6.5). The Hungarian authorities, however, have intentionally constrained the exchange rate appreciation by reducing the rate of pre-announced devaluation gradually. On the other hand, the unit labor cost based real exchange rate depreciated significantly, thanks to the increase in productivity of export-oriented firms, which compensated for the wage increases exceeding inflation. Thus the relative profitability of the Hungarian tradable sector to the country's main trading partners has been improving a great deal since early 1990s. In this respect, one should also factor in the decreasing share of labor costs, as compared with the capital costs enhanced by FDI. The high downward flexibility of real wages in Hungary, when the March 1995 adjustment package surprised the public with a surge in inflation, also contributed to the restoration of profitability observed in 1995–1996 (figure 6.5). It should, however, be mentioned, that these after-crisis low-level wages could not be sustained and required correction later on, when the stabilization yielded higher growth.

In light of the principles of disinflation policy discussed previously, policymakers in Hungary agreed that the risk of output loss stemming from a more ambitious nominal and real appreciation was too high to take. It was commonly believed that unexpected appreciation might repress inflation without convincing the public of the sustainability of further disinflation. Thus, a policy based on more appré-

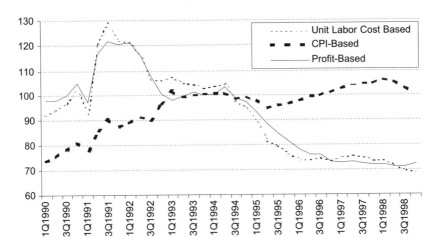

Figure 6.5
Real effective exchange rate of the forint (1994 = 100)
Note: Higher value indicates real appreciation. Unit labor cost and profit-based indices
are calculated from value-added figures.

ciating Hungarian currency would have not solved the problem of
moderate inflation in the long run. Later on, in 1998–1999, it turned
out that the adjustment capability of the privatized tradable sector
to different (real and nominal) shocks had probably been underestimated when the stabilization program was launched: wage adjustment proved to be smoother than expected, wages followed more
closely than before the target inflation and the exchange rate path,
and wage setting has increasingly been affected by productivity development and profitability considerations.

Over the more than six-year history of the crawling exchange rate
regime in Hungary, monetary policy has almost permanently faced
an intensive nominal appreciation pressure induced by strong capital
inflows. Therefore, it has been a real policy dilemma whether it is
more advantageous to insist on keeping the narrow band exchange
rate regime for the benefit of predictability or to reduce exposure to
the speculative capital flows and to increase the flexibility of the exchange rate regime by widening the fluctuation band.

Fiscal Stance

Fiscal policy and its efficiency are the major issues a country faces
during stabilization and convergence to the EU. How to measure

them is a rich source of issues to be clarified. Deficit and debt indicators cannot be compared easily for transition countries, nor for the advanced ACs. Lack of transparency in fiscal statistics is one of the major obstacles to comparison of fiscal policies in EU candidate countries, especially if the analysis covers the general government, including extrabudgetary funds, social security funds, and local governments as well. Comparison of central government budgets is also hindered by methodological differences.

Even if we disregard the fact that one or several parts of the general government are missing from official statistics for some countries, it remains a crucial question whether transformation in the different countries has already arrived at a stage where the contingent liabilities have already been accounted for in the budget and sources of off-budget obligations have been eliminated. Because the ACs are very different in terms of the structure of their general governments as well as their debt service obligations and the composition of their debt according to the ownership and denomination, not to mention the inflation differentials compared to the rest of the world, the well-known, published headline budget deficit and public debt figures might be very misleading when evaluating the fiscal stance.

Hungary has been running a positive primary balance since 1995, which has been enforced by the debt situation and by the worsening financial conditions of debt finance (table 6.2 and figure 6.6).[11] This was the major factor behind Hungarian debt consolidation: both gross and net debt-to-GDP ratios in Hungary have declined rather quickly in the second half of 1990s. In respect to the other components that reduced Hungary's net public debt to GDP ratio in this period, privatization revenues[12] spent on retirement of old debt with unfavorable conditions also played also an important role, while the effect of GDP growth was less significant. What is clear from this breakdown of the public debt to GDP ratio (table 6.2) is that Hungary, though indebtedness of the country has significantly been reduced by the end of 1990s, has to account for a large, almost constant 3–4 percent annual increase in debt ratio due to the effect of the real interest rates. Since the real interest rates on the outstanding stock of government's liabilities were higher than the rate of GDP growth, the combined effect of interest rates and growth rate was positive, contributing to the increase of the indebtedness over the 1990s. Real exchange rate has had only a negligible effect on the debt ratio, since the size of real appreciation has been intentionally constrained by the

Table 6.2
Factors influencing change in debt[a]-to-GDP ratio in Hungary (in percent)

	1991	1992	1993	1994	1995	1996	1997	1998
Gross public debt-to-GDP ratio	79.0	74.9	95.7	96.2	100.3	83.6	74.3	72.8
Change in gross debt-to-GDP ratio	8.6	−4.1	20.8	0.5	4.1	−16.7	−9.3	−1.5
Net public debt-to-GDP ratio	38.9	40.6	55.3	60.2	57.8	50.1	45.1	45.0
Change in net public debt-to-GDP ratio (1 − 2 − 3 + 4 + 5 + 6)	2.1	1.7	14.7	4.9	−2.4	−7.7	−4.9	−0.1
1. Primary deficit	−1.0	2.6	2.9	2.7	−1.6	−4.3	−3.1	−1.6
2. Seigniorage[b]	5.3	2.7	0.0	0.2	1.6	0.9	1.0	1.2
3. Privatization revenues	0.0	0.8	0.3	0.8	6.6	1.1	3.0	0.5
4. Impact of growth and real interest rate (a + b)	10.2	4.2	2.1	1.1	2.9	3.2	1.6	1.3
a. Growth effect	5.0	1.2	0.2	−1.6	−0.9	−0.7	−2.2	−2.2
b. Real interest rate effect	5.2	3.0	1.9	2.7	3.8	3.9	3.8	3.5
5. Impact of Change in real effective exchange rate	−2.1	−2.3	−3.9	−0.2	4.4	−0.6	−0.7	0.2
6. Change in nondeficit financing debt[c]	0.3	0.7	13.9	2.4	0.2	−4.0	1.2	1.7
Memorandum items								
Change in real effective exchange rate[d]	96.4	94.4	88.5	99.5	110.6	98.0	96.0	101.6
Real interest rate	12.5	7.4	4.6	4.9	6.3	6.8	8.0	8.2
GDP growth rate	−11.9	−3.1	−0.6	2.9	1.5	1.3	4.6	5.1
GDP deflator	125.4	121.6	121.3	119.5	125.5	121.2	113.5	113.7

[a] Consolidated public debt computed from the asset-liability balance sheet of the general government and the central bank.
[b] Change in M0 less interest paid on mandatory reserves.
[c] Government bonds issued to cover off-budget expenditures (bank restructuring).
[d] Computed with GDP deflator; values below 100 indicate real appreciation.

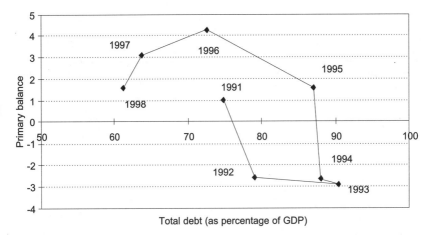

Figure 6.6
Hungary's debt situation

policy of sustainable disinflation. As a consequence, the path of the real exchange rate, between 1996 and 1998, seemed to be very close to its equilibrium long-term trend. The other factors influencing the debt ratio, such as the bank consolidation program in 1993, have not shown a clear time trend, contributing to an increase in off-budget obligations and public debt.

Contrary to common belief, seigniorage has not been a significant source of income for the Hungarian budget in the 1990s, amounting to about 1.5–2 percent of GDP (see table 6.3).[13] It can be seen from the table that the inflation tax component of seigniorage has been declining in line with the decline in inflation, but the other two components (the development of the real monetary base and the interest paid on mandatory reserves) have counteracted the movement of inflation tax, and neither gross nor net seigniorage[14] showed a clear trend in the 1990s.

Foundations of Convergence

The turmoil in emerging markets in 1997–1998 was a test for the strength of the new status of converging economies. Hungary emerged from this crisis with enhanced credibility, and its fundamentals were hurt no more than those of any other European economy. Partly due to these external developments and other factors

Table 6.3
Components of seigniorage in Hungary (as percentage of GDP)

	1991	1992	1993	1994	1995	1996	1997	1998
1. Seigniorage gross (a + b)	6.2	3.4	0.1	0.5	2.3	1.6	1.6	1.6
a. Change in monetary base	1.6	−0.2	−3.1	−2.2	−0.8	−0.5	−0.2	0.6
b. Inflation tax	4.6	3.6	3.2	2.7	3.1	2.1	1.8	1.0
2. Interest paid on mandatory reserves	0.9	0.6	0.1	0.2	0.7	0.7	0.6	0.4
3. Seigniorage net (1 − 2)	5.3	2.7	0.0	0.2	1.6	0.9	1.0	1.2

related to domestic economic and political conditions, the upward pressure on the Hungarian currency has vanished. The collapse of the Russian market and the Yugoslav war have had some impact on external demand, but the Hungarian business cycle is now more driven by demand from EU countries.

Quick Convergence Check of Euro-Land

Inflation and exchange rate convergence has been achieved quite smoothly among member nations of the European Union. Nevertheless, the fiscal foundation of nominal convergence in the Euro-zone, as set forth in the Stability and Growth Pact, has required substantial, very rapid fiscal adjustment on the part of these nations (see figure 6.7). Whether this adjustment is sustainable, especially in more indebted countries, for example, Belgium or Italy, is an open issue; it may induce politically unsustainable strain in the future.

Convergence in Five ACs

Just as in case of EMU countries, inflation and exchange rate criteria are likely to be met by the ACs within the horizon of EU membership, but the countries differ significantly in terms of relative price adjustment. By the time they become EU members, these countries will have long-term interest rates reflecting the expected real interest rate and inflation. When and how they will meet the Maastricht convergence criteria is an open issue (see table 6.4), which is closely related to the fiscal stance of each country. The major problem facing

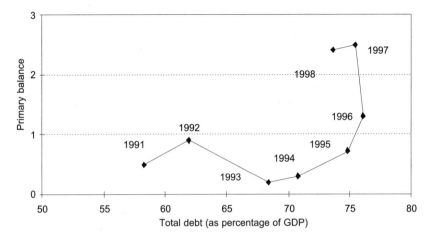

Figure 6.7
Euro-area

Table 6.4
Convergence indicators of five associated countries (1997–1998)

	Consumer price inflation (year/year, percent)		General government balance/ GDP (percent)		Gross central government debt/GDP (percent)		Long-term interest rates[a] (percent)	
	1997	1998	1997	1998	1997	1998	1997	1998
Czech Republic	8.5	10.7	−1.2	−2.4	12.6	—	—	—
Estonia	11.1	10.6	2.3	2.6	—	—	—	—
Hungary	18.3	14.2	−4.8	−4.7	63.7	61.2	—	9.8[b]
Poland	15.0	11.8	−3.8	−3.7	50.8	—	—	—
Slovenia	8.4	8.0	−1.1	−1.0	—	—	—	—
Reference value	2.6	2.0	−3.0	−3.0	60.0	60.0	6.0	4.7

Sources: IMF World Economic Outlook, ECB, national data.
Note: Dashes indicate nonavailability of data.
[a] Ten-year government bond yield.
[b] First issue in January 1999.

each country is not only the ability meet the double fiscal (budget deficit and public debt) criteria, but also providing sufficient and necessary transparency conditions to be able to assess whether the criteria have been met.

Fiscal Convergence in Hungary

The debt ratio in Hungary has recently been substantially reduced, the gross public debt to GDP ratio fell by almost thirty percentage points between 1995 and 1998, and approached 70 percent in 1998. Hungary's current indebtedness is still, however, too high for its present level of development, and a further decrease in it is necessary for convergence to be sustainable. When the developed industrial economies were at Hungary's present level of development, their debt-to-GDP ratio was significantly lower than that of Hungary today.[15] As the analysis above suggests, Hungary can reduce its debt-to-GDP ratio substantially only by running sizable surplus in its primary budget balance, taking into account the fact that other factors' contribution to the decline in debt ratio can be expected to be rather limited. Privatization in Hungary has more or less been completed, and seigniorage cannot provide the government with a significant source of financing, as disinflation continues. The effect of seigniorage in reducing the debt ratio can be estimated at around 1 percent for the future, because the inflation tax will further decline as the inflation goes down, which might be compensated for by the increase in transaction money demand.

Moreover, the GDP growth rate can only occasionally be expected to be higher than the real interest rate paid on government debt; therefore, the combined effect of growth and interest rate on the debt ratio will at best be neutral in the long run. Hence, in the case of Hungary, the debt sustainability requirement for the primary surplus might be relatively large, and the possibility of deviation from the long-run, cyclically neutral equilibrium is highly constrained.

A falling debt-to-GDP ratio during periods of fast growth cannot be used as an argument for deviating from the long-run cyclically neutral budget equilibrium in Hungary. Any fiscal expansion may jeopardize the country's disinflation process and macroeconomic equilibrium. Maintaining a low budget deficit is important for avoiding an increase in the country's debt-to-GDP ratio and for keeping economic growth on a sustainable path. In this regard, the country's budget balance must be considered as part of domestic savings, and since at an increasing level of domestic savings the country's economy can grow on a higher equilibrium path, a rise in the primary surplus—paradoxically—may result in a higher economic growth rate in the medium run. Since the real interest rates are likely to be around their present level, in spite of relatively high growth rate and trend real appreciation, the primary balance requirement should be 2–4 percent, in order to obtain a sustainable—declining—debt ratio.

Conclusions: Policy Options in the Convergence Period

The first period of nominal convergence for a country ends when a credible commitment to peg the exchange rate for the country's currency to the Euro becomes a real option.[16] After that has been accomplished, a new policy dilemma emerges, namely, what is the most efficient form of trend real appreciation characterizing the ACs in the catching-up period,[17] by higher inflation or by nominal appreciation? If we assume that the trend real appreciation is 2–3 percent per year[18] and EU inflation is lower than 2 percent, then a pegged exchange rate regime is compatible with a 4–5 percent inflation rate. If price stability—as in Economic and Monetary Union—is to be preferred, then 2–3 percent annual nominal appreciation must be allowed.

If the ACs are to meet the Maastricht inflation criterion, then nominal appreciation is the only way to comply with the real appreciation of equlibrium real exchange rate in their countries. Nominal appreciation does affect the corporate sector according to the foreign trade exposure, which varies across sectors. If the corporations are not able to compensate on the cost side for the loss on the revenue side, say, by constantly improving unit factor costs, then the constant loss of profitability may undermine a country's foreign competitiveness. This sort of adjustment requires nominal flexibility, which has been in short supply until now in the ACs. Nontradable prices in these countries have been growing faster than tradables, therefore inflation convergence toward price stability would suppose prices of tradables to decrease. Is this really feasible? If not, then the price stability requirement as determined in the EMU should be reconsidered for the ACs.

Hence, the combination of price stability and nominal appreciation is an option for the economic and monetary policy in converging countries only if prices and wages in a country are sufficiently flexible downward. For the time being this is not the case in the ACs. In this respect it is important to study the experience of fast growing Euro-countries (Ireland, Spain, Portugal). They are now confronted with the same type of policy dilemma the ACs will probably face in the accession period. There is no way to let their currency appreciate in these countries, so all the adjustment must be made on the fiscal side in order to approach price stability as required in the Euro-area. The best example is that of Ireland, the most quickly growing country in the Euro-zone, where the general government—not only the primary—balance is in surplus.[19]

The whole story of convergence is largely determined by the appropriate choice of fiscal and monetary policy mix. Long-run economic stabilization requires fulfillment of very strict fiscal constraints that could be exacerbated by a fast disinflation policy. This is another argument in favor of gradual disinflation, especially in the single-digit region.

Today it is difficult to evaluate the fiscal stance (deficit and debt to GDP ratios) in the ACs. The content of fiscal indicators for the ACs' general government balances and debt, which will be used in the qualification process for EU membership, must be defined precisely. This is a precondition for monitoring sustainability of ACs' performance.[20] As an example, the introduction in a country the elements of a fully funded pension system increases the general government deficit in that country by making explicit the liabilities that have been implicit in a pay-as-you-go system. This "excess" deficit is, however, automatically financed by increased household savings in pension funds, so it has no fiscal impact. Pension reform in Hungary in 1999, for example, introducing a two-pillar regime, added between 0.5 and 1 percent to the budget deficit in terms of GDP each year.

An additional problem arises as to how the policymakers in ACs should react to faster-than-expected disinflation and slower-than-planned growth, as it happened in 1998. Both phenomena may have a negative impact on a country's budget balance, through reducing the primary surplus. To cope with such unexpected shocks, in good years targeting a budget and primary balance that is a bit higher than that required by a cyclically neutral position can be advantageous in ACs, allowing somewhat of a softening in fiscal constraint when business cycle goes down. But implementing such a policy seems very difficult, even in the developed world.[21]

Appendix

Table 6A.1
Selected economic indicators of Central and Eastern European Countries (in percent)

	Year	Bulgaria	Czech Republic	Estonia	Hungary	Poland	Romania	Slovakia	Slovenia
GDP	1997	-6.9	1.0	8.4	4.6	6.9	-6.6	6.5	3.8
(year/year)	1998	3.0	-2.3	4.4	5.1	4.8	-5.0	5.0	4.0
Inflation	1997	1,185.0	8.5	11.1	18.3	15.0	154.0	6.1	8.4
(year/year)	1998	22.2	10.0	10.6	14.3	11.8	60.0	6.7	8.0
Inflation	1997	580.0	10.0	12.3	18.4	13.3	151.0	6.4	8.8
(end year)	1998	1.0	6.8	6.8	10.3	9.2	43.0	5.5	6.5
Unemployment	1997	13.7	5.2	4.6	8.7	10.3	8.8	13.0	14.5
(percent)	1998	12.0	7.5	5.1	7.8	9.7	10.3	15.6	14.4
General	1997	-2.1	-1.2	2.3	-4.8	-3.8	-3.6	-3.8	-1.1
government[a]	1998	-2.0	-2.4	2.6	-4.7	-3.7	-5.5	-5.3	-1.0
Current account[b]	1997	0.3	-3.2	-0.6	-1.0	-4.3	-2.4	-1.3	0.04
	1998	-0.1	-1.0	-0.4	-2.3	-4.5	-3.4	-2.0	0.0
Current account[a]	1997	4.2	-6.2	-12.1	-2.1	-3.2[c]	-7.1	-6.6	0.2
	1998	-0.8	-1.9	-9.6	-4.8	-3.8[c]	-7.0	-10.0	0.0
Gross external	1997	9.8	21.4	2.6	21.7	48.9	10.9	9.9	4.2
debt[b]	1998	10.0	24.5	2.9	23.2	56.8	11.7	13.1	5.0
Gross external	1997	96.8	41.0	55.3	47.5	36.0	29.2	50.9	23.1
debt[a]	1998	78.9	44.4	55.6	48.9	36.2	29.0	63.0	25.3

Source: EBRD Transition Report, 1998.
[a] As percentage of GDP.
[b] Billions of U.S. dollars.
[c] Surplus of nonregistered trade is included.

References

Barabás, G., I. Hamecz, and J. Neményi. 1998. Fiscal consolidation, public debt containment and disinflation (Hungary's experience in transition). Working paper 1998/5, National Bank of Hungary, Budapest.

Begg, D. 1998. Solvency, price level determination and competitiveness: Fiscal foundation for exchange rate management in transition economies. Paper produced as a part of Centre for Economic Policy Research (CEPR) project funded by EU PHARE for the National Bank of Hungary. Manuscript, CEPR, London.

Bokros, L., and J.-J. Dethier. 1998. *Public Finance Reform during the Transition: The Experience of Hungary.* Washington, D.C.: World Bank.

Buiter, W. H. 1992. Should we worry about the fiscal numerology of Maastricht? Discussion papers no. 668, Centre for Economic Policy Research, London.

Buiter, W. H., G. Corsetti, and N. Roubini. 1992. "Excessive deficits": Sense and nonsense in the Treaty of Maastricht. Discussion papers no. 750, Centre for Economic Policy Research, London.

Buti, M., D. Franco, and H. Ongena. 1998. Fiscal disipline and flexibility in EMU: The implementation of the stability and growth pact. *Oxford Review of Economic Policy* 14, no. 3: 81–97.

Cottarelli, C., and G. Szapáry. 1998. *Moderate Inflation: The Experience of Transition Economies, the International Monetary Fund and the National Bank of Hungary.* Washington, D.C.

Csajbók, A., and J. Neményi. 1998. The contribution of the government securities market to the development of wider securities markets in Hungary. In *Capital market development in transition economies: Country experiences and policies for the future OECD,* ed. Ms. E. Thiel Blommestein, 57–81. Paris: OECD.

Easterly, W. 1999. When is fiscal adjustment an illusion? *Economic Policy* 28: 57–86.

Halpern, L., and C. Wyplosz. 1997. Equilibrium exchange rates in transition economies. *International Monetary Fund Staff Papers* 44, no. 4: 430–61.

Halpern, L., and C. Wyplosz. 1998. The hidden Hungarian miracle. In *Hungary: Towards a Market Economy,* ed. L. Halpern and C. Wyplosz, 1–19. London: Cambridge University Press and Centre for Economic Policy Research.

Jakab, Z., and G. Szapáry. 1998. Exchange rate policy in transition economies: The case of Hungary. *Journal of Comparative Economics* 26, no. 4: 691–717.

Kopits, G. 1999. Implications of EMU for exchange rate policy in Central and Eastern Europe. Working paper no. 9, International Monetary Fund, Washington, D.C.

Kovács, M., and A. Simon. 1998. The components of the real exchange rate in Hungary. Working paper 1998/3, National Bank of Hungary, Budapest.

Surányi, G., and J. Vincze. 1998. Inflation in Hungary 1990–97. In *Moderate Inflation: The Experience of Transition Economies, the International Monetary Fund, and the National Bank of Hungary,* ed. C. Cottarelli and G. Szapáry, 57–81. Washington, D.C.: International Monetary Fund and National Bank of Hungary.

7   The Czech Republic: Ten Years of Transition

Vladimír Dlouhý

Introduction

At the end of the 1980s, the Czech Republic, as a part of the former Czechoslovakia, was a standard socialist country, albeit with several specific features. Compared to Hungary and Poland, the country passed through virtually no period of perestroika-type reforms, its private sector was virtually nonexistent, almost no systemic changes took place at all, and most of the decision makers, both in the state administration and inside the Communist Party, had been in their seats since the normalization years after the end of Prague Spring in 1968. At the same time, the Czech economy suffered from extreme hypertrophy of heavy industry, most of whose products could have been allocated only in the soft markets of the Council for Mutual Economic Cooperation (COMECON) and other socialist countries. This hypertrophy was accompanied by comparatively high energy and material intensities, an extremely high labor participation rate, and a distorted trade structure, again to a larger extent than in the neighboring socialist countries (Jonáš 1997). On the other hand, Czechoslovakia was a country with its macroeconomic fundamentals under control (Portes 1989). Hidden inflation and foreign debt were comparatively lower than in other countries and, along with Hungary, Czechoslovakia had the best supply in the consumer goods market, which had important consequences for the country's political limbo.

The Initial Reform: A Success

Czechoslovakia, and later the Czech Republic, quickly turned out to be a favorite reform country in the eyes of politicians, potential foreign investors, and many scholars. The reasons seemed rather straightforward:

1. The Czech economic reform, firmly rooted in the economic policy of the Czechoslovak government after December 1989, was based on three main pillars:
• quick systemic changes (price liberalization, dismantling of the state monopoly on foreign trade, substantial change in the legal framework, tax reform, and many others)
• macroeconomic stabilization (anti-inflationary policies, change in the exchange rate regime, etc.)
• privatization

2. The Czech government was determined to follow these reform steps quickly, from both the economic and legal points of view.

3. The country was politically and socially stable, and the government enjoyed rather strong support of the population, even with regard to unpopular policy steps.

4. The Czech Republic was considered by outside observers to be a country with a strong industrial and cultural tradition and with a skilled and highly educated population. The hypertrophy of its heavy industry, which turned out to be an important hindrance to microeconomic restructuring, was to much extent disregarded by both politicians and economists.

Today, Czech economic reform is believed to have been based upon adoption of the so-called Washington consensus policies (Williamson 1990, 1997), and consequently the Czech decision makers of that time are considered the prime example of those policies' failure. This is misleading. First, there was never any explicit consensus, either inside or outside Washington (Stiglitz 1998), concerning a unique set of policy prescriptions for the former socialist economies in transition. Second, the set of policies labeled today as the "Washington consensus," namely quick structural reforms together with macroeconomic stabilization, was an inevitable condition for success at the initial phase of the Czech reform (see also chapter 15). I argue later in this chapter that the successful Czech economic development in 1990–1993 is just one more proof of this fact. Third, no explicit policy was adopted by the Czech government that would formalize the "famous negatives of the Washington consensus" (Stiglitz 1998), namely, neglecting to build strong institutions and to improve the country's legal and regulatory environment quickly. The fact that the Czech policymakers indeed failed in this area was much more the consequence of worsening political relations inside the governing coalition, combined with the fact that the country and its policymakers were much less prepared for the change its legal and institutional framework than for the quick adoption of stabilization and liberalization policies in the initial stage of the reform.[1]

Like that of all other countries in Central Europe, the Czech economy suffered several external shocks during the transition period. Apart from the collapse of the COMECON markets and the emergence of the Russian economic crisis, the Czech economy had to overcome the consequences of the separation of Czechoslovakia into two independent nations. The domestic market shrank by one third virtually overnight, and new exports to Slovakia were hit rather soon after separation by the emergence of Slovak protectionism, both open and hidden.[2]

Despite these external shocks, after the quick initial systemic changes and crucial liberalization of prices and foreign trade, the Czech economic policy achieved quick success both in macroeconomic stabilization and in privatization (Aghevli, Borzensztein, and van der Willingen 1992):

1. *Macroeconomic stabilization policy.* In the open Czech economy, the fixed exchange rate regime adopted under the Czechoslovak government on January 1, 1991, played the most important role during the initial reform period. The fixed exchange rate served as a decisive anchor to macroeconomic stabilization, and undervalued currency was the best single export-promoting mechanism.

Monetary policy had to face strong inflationary pressures after price liberalization took place at the beginning of 1991. The monetary restriction was drastic (in the first quarter, the total enterprise credits nominally increased by 6.0 percent, but producer prices increased by 47.6 percent), but quick price stabilization allowed for subsequent release of the restriction, and at the end of 1991 M2 fell by 17 percent, which is approximately equal to the fall of GDP, reflecting the decrease of transaction demand for money. Cautious monetary policy continued during the first half of 1992, but after the elections in June of that year, monetary policy faced new a problem: potential destabilization, given the separation of Czechoslovakia. This continued during all of 1993, and the fact that the separation was accompanied

neither by inflationary pressures nor by an increase in foreign indebtedness can be considered as evidence of an essential success.

In the first years after the start of transformation, fiscal policy in
Czechoslovakia succeeded in fulfilling two main tasks (Tanzi 1993):
(1) lowering the share of public expenditures on GDP to a level comparable to the standard in the developed market economies and (2)
supporting macroeconomic stability, which—given the fact that at the
beginning of transformation, it was almost impossible to finance
budget deficits on the international markets—led to the adoption of
balanced budget policies. Both tasks were fulfilled in Czechoslovakia
and by the Czech Republic in the initial stages of reform.

2. *Privatization.* It is widely believed that the Czechoslovak government adopted voucher scheme privatization as the main privatization procedure. This is not exactly correct: Out of the total privatized
assets, with an approximate book value of 760–780 billion Czech
crowns, some 350 billion crowns were privatized by the voucher
method. Other standard methods were used as well, but there is no
doubt that the voucher method played a crucial role in privatization
and ensured political support for the government's privatization
program among the population. The reasons for and goals of the
program were clear:

• Given the highly distorted price structure, lack of domestic capital,
and almost absolute nationalization of the Czech economy, the use
of vouchers represented the most straightforward and fastest way of
privatization and—at least at that time—also the most transparent
one.

• The goal was to privatize the bulk of the Czech economy as
quickly as possible. The application of voucher scheme privatization
in Czechoslovakia is linked to the famous discussion about the
sequencing between privatization and restructuring of firms. Application of the vouchers favored privatization over restructuring; nevertheless, when other privatization methods were applied, a lot of
restructuring of government occurred.[3]

The subsequent years, 1993 and 1994, seemed to confirm the conventional wisdom that the Czech Republic was a country at the
forefront of the economic transformation in Central Europe. After a
strong initial decrease in economic activity (between 1989 and 1993,
the Czech GDP fell by more than 20 percent) and initial inflationary

pressures, the Czech economy reached a turning point in 1993 (growth was still negative by 0.9 percent, but this was probably due to the effects of the dissolution of Czechoslovakia and the accompanying turmoil) and achieved rather favorable growth rates in both 1994 and 1995 (2.6 and 4.8 percent, respectively). Inflation was steadily decreasing (from 18.2 percent in 1993 to 7.9 percent in 1995). The budget was revealing a slight surplus every year, foreign exchange reserves were increasing rather sharply (which was considered a substantial achievement given the uncertainties linked to the separation of the former Czechoslovak currency), and unemployment remained low (a very palatable fact for even a conservative politician). Exports, which lost important markets in the former COMECON (and especially in the former Soviet Union, whose share of total Czech exports fell from almost 40 percent in 1989 to 8.3 percent in 1993), quickly found a new allocation in the markets of the European Union and elsewhere.[4] The number of imports was low, because of suppressed aggregate demand, and the trade balance was positive (with the exception of the last quarter of 1992) during the entire period from 1989 through May 1994.

Given the favorable development, during 1994 the Czech Republic emerged as a country that seemed to be behind the main transformation steps, macroeconomically stabilized, with a decisive GDP share of private sector and a new trade structure and attractive to foreign investors. The country's economic growth, after a deep fall at the initial period of the transformation (and after the negative effect of the separation of Czechoslovakia), returned to attractive rates. The country started negotiations for entry into the Organisation for Economic Cooperation and Development (OECD) and in some areas has even been cited as a model for the EU economies. The comparative graphs in figure 7.1 demonstrate this situation.

Recently, in discussions of the Czech economy, a new approach has been taken to explaining the development of inflation during the first years of transformation. Czech inflation has always been impressively lower than that in other former socialist economies in the region. Considered a major achievement until recently, this is sometimes now declared to have been an important reason for payment arrears among Czech firms and for the current crises of the Czech banking sector. Those who make this assertion argue that in the Polish and Hungarian cases it was inflation that to a great extent wiped out the debts firms had accumulated in the past, allowing the

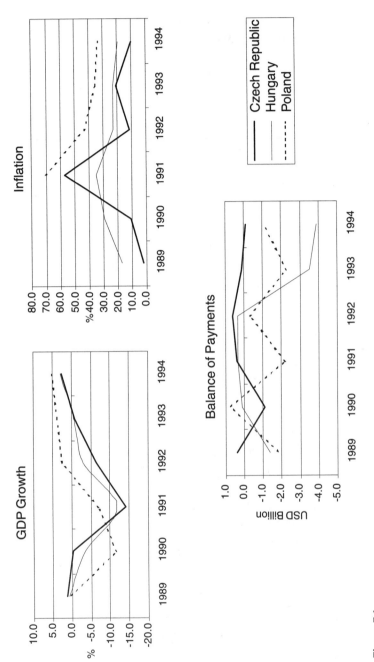

Figure 7.1
Comparative performance of the Czech economy, 1989–1994

industries to have a much healthier restart after privatization. This chapter does not follow this line of argumentation; at a minimum, I consider it too academic to be useful here. As high inflation wipes out not only debts and intracompany arrears, but personal savings as well, there was no political space in Czechoslovakia in the initial years of transformation, much less any support from international institutions, for purposely allowing inflation, to remain at higher levels.

The Completion of Transformation: A Delay

The first signs of a slowdown in the Czech transformation appeared in the second half of 1994. Economic growth in the Czech Republic has been accompanied by extremely low unemployment, which some analysts have linked to the country's slow (or almost nonexistent) microeconomic restructuring; this view has been supported by the very low number of bankruptcies, especially in the industrial sector.[5] At the same time, since mid-1994, growth has also been accompanied by an increasing trade deficit.

After its excellent start, the Czech administration has almost halted its transformation effort since the end of 1994. This has been manifested in all crucial areas of the economic policies.[6]

Privatization and Postprivatization

As has been mentioned above, voucher scheme privatization was just one of the methods adopted by the Czechoslovak (and later Czech) government, and all other standard methods of privatization were applied in the Czech Republic as well. As in all other Central European economies, any privatization approach necessarily generates advantages and shortfalls of its own. Speed, initial transparency, and public support were positives of the voucher privatization scheme, whereas the negatives were rather linked to procedures subsequent to the adoption of the method.

After 1993, however, the Czech government did not continue its scheme of quick privatization. The government was much engaged in the privatization of virtually thousands of state shareholdings remaining from the voucher schemes but made few strategic decisions regarding privatization of the majority state shareholdings in the large industrial companies and specifically in the banks. Instead, with few exceptions, state shares in these enterprises were controlled by the state officials from the National Property Fund (and in selected cases from the governmental ministries), and the entire process of corporate governance was weak.

The decision not to privatize the country's banks appears likely to have been a major mistake of the Czech government in that period. Nevertheless, the critical points, leading to the economic recession later, are to be linked rather with the postprivatization period than with discussions about "proper" privatization techniques. These critical points can summarized in two blocks:

1. Strong relationship between banks, investment funds controlled by the banks, and firms. Close links between banks and the enterprise sector are a characteristic feature of many European economies and have a strong historical tradition, especially in Germany and in Central Europe. In the Czech republic, this link emerged as an immediate consequence of privatization. Soon after the two privatization waves, the structure of the new ownership collapsed in a situation in which many medium- and large-scale enterprises were owned by a rather small number of investment funds, which were directly controlled by the banks. Each of these agents on the market (i.e., banks, funds, and firms) had its own goals and preferences, but the interplay of the different interests did not lead to restructuring, but rather to maintaining the status quo, continuing excessive wage growth and, consequently, low unemployment. Expectations on the part of the new owners about the quick restructuring effort were not fulfilled.[7]

2. Inefficient financial markets and lack of regulation of the capital markets in particular. The beginning of the 1990s was a period of huge changes in world financial and capital markets, and even the most developed market economies learned their lessons about proper regulatory procedures rather painfully through experience. Obviously, reform economies of Central and Eastern Europe passed through such experiences much more painfully, and voucher privatization was probably more vulnerable to this danger of ineffective regulation. In the Czech case, protection of minority shareholders was inadequate, transparency suffered, and disclosure procedures were unclear, which led to disruption of the business ethic, and consequently, political credit for privatization diminished substantially.

There is no doubt today that a combination of the effects described in the list above was the main reason for the critical downturn in the Czech economy in 1997–1999. Many other problems, discussed below, were to a great extent also derived from this major shortcoming of the Czech transformation.

Exchange Rate Policy

The Czech fixed exchange rate, as the nominal anchor for macro-economic stabilization and as an economic policy tool, supporting exports, played an important role in the initial success of the economic transformation. Since 1994, however, with the fixed exchange rate, a high degree of openness of the economy, and inflation still relatively high, both the central bank and the Czech government were less and less able to control aggregate domestic demand and both internal and external equilibrium. As the efficiency of the monetary policy of the central bank was limited in this period by the only partial efficiency of sterilization (see below) and the fiscal policy did not offer a tool flexible enough to regulate aggregate domestic demand, it became clear that a change in the exchange rate regime should occur. In February 1996, the Czech central bank introduced a rather wide fluctuation band (increased from ± 0.5 percent to ± 7.5 percent), but the positive effects on the efficiency of the monetary policy were again only limited (Tůma and Kreidl 1996; Dědek and Derviz 1996). As an immediate reaction, there was a massive outflow of speculative capital from the country (about 600 million Czech crowns) just after the band introduction, but the exchange rate subsequently stabilized rather close to the upper limit of the band, allowing the crown to continue its real appreciation and cutting further the competitiveness of Czech exports. Neither the central bank nor the government were prepared for the introduction of a more profound change in the exchange rate (floating, managed floating, crawling band or peg).

Monetary Policy

After a very restrictive monetary policy in Czechoslovakia and the Czech Republic between 1990 and 1992 (see above), an monetary expansion took place. At the end of 1992, M2 represented some 12 percent of the Czech Republic's GDP, and credits from the entire financial system to the private sector were about 21 percent of GDP. By the end of 1996, the same figures were 82 percent and 62 percent, respectively. There is no doubt that the share of monetary aggregates in GDP had grown substantially, given the need for remonetization of the economy and the real growth of the economy between 1994 and 1996. Part of these credits, however, were allocated through the links described above, and another part of the increase in the monetary aggregates was swallowed up by firms surviving because of the country's inefficient bankruptcy procedures.

With the increasing openness of the Czech economy, with macroeconomic stabilization, and with the country's improved investment rating, the inflow of foreign capital increased substantially after 1993, generating pressure on the money supply in the country. The Czech central bank reacted by instituting sterilization operations, which were costly and only partially efficient.[8] Increasing inflationary pressure, real appreciation of the currency, and the lack of real adjustment on the microeconomic level forced the bank to take a decisive step with far-reaching consequences: It cut the money supply drastically during 1996. This was undoubtedly a step in the right direction; however, the magnitude of the cut (the growth of M2 in 1996 was just one-third of what it was in 1995) is controversial even today. I consider the cut to have been strong overshooting, realized as a single step, without taking into consideration the Czech reality at that time, namely, the fixed exchange rate. The size of the cut was not a primary reason for the crisis in 1997–1999, but it triggered its start, definitely.

Fiscal Policy

After its very successful contribution to the country's macroeconomic stabilization, the balanced budget policy encountered several problems as well. The different components of the consolidated government always revealed larger deficits than state budget did.[9] Local administrations were always suffering from an excess of expenditure over revenues (despite the fact that their revenues grew in certain periods faster than the revenues of the state budget), extra-budgetary funds were always in surplus but tending toward decline, the social security system was moving deeper into deficit, and state financial assets revealed a deficit of almost six billion Czech crowns in 1996. The wages of the state administration had to increase to keep pace at least partially with the wage growth in the private sector in order to maintain a reasonable number of skilled and experienced people in the administration. Since 1994, the budget expenditure for state administration (excluding wages) has increased faster than inflation. Before the parliamentary elections in 1996, a slight fiscal expansion took place.

The Relation between Investment and Savings

Gross domestic investment, which represented some 30 percent of Czech GDP in 1991, fell to less then 20 percent in 1993 and rose again to 32 percent of GDP in 1996. Whereas gross national savings always exceeded gross investment in 1991–1993, the opposite was (and still is) true after that. The decline in private savings dominated that of public savings. The structure of investment in the country was unfavorable for the future economic growth: Infrastructure and ecological investment dominated, without much direct effect on productivity and with little increase in competitiveness. Additional negative effects were generated by the fact that a substantial part of this investment was imported[10] and that the amount of "productive investment"— that is, investment with a positive impact on the increase of productivity—was relatively low.

Income Policy of Firms

In 1990–1996, unit labor costs in Czechoslovakia and the Czech Republic were increasing faster than the average real wage, which, at least since 1994, has been increasing faster than labor productivity. After the price liberalization instituted at the beginning of the reform period, domestic prices increased much faster than wages, and enterprises benefited in the domestic market even when, in some cases, their productivity growth never matched the growth in real wages. At the same time, labor productivity could have experienced a one-time improvement from the removal of the most striking inefficiencies of central planning. Consequently, the link between real wage and labor productivity growth, although followed closely by economists, was not at the center of attention of firms in domestic markets, and in foreign markets exporters enjoyed positive effects from the undervalued Czech currency, so that lack of competitiveness was not as visible before 1995.

"Legal" Inefficiency

The country had to adopt a new commercial code after transformation, and this process turned out to be as painful as, say, seeking an adequate regulatory framework for the capital market; in this, the legislators were as successful (or unsuccessful) as the economists. This resulted in an extremely small number of bankruptcies, perpetuated overemployment, and in combination with the above-mentioned link between the banks and the owners, only multiplied the pressure ultimately leading to excessive growth in aggregate domestic demand.

Antitrust Policies and Regulation of Natural Monopolies

The first serious antitrust legislation in the Czech Republic was introduced during 1994, the law on public procurement one year later. The competition policies instituted, despite some criticism, met the standard of other Central European economies. The regulation of natural monopolies, however, namely those in the energy sector, proceeded rather slowly. The government failed to speed up the deregulation of energy prices for households, maintaining the cross-subsidies from prices for the industrial sector. Slow progress was made on the privatization of the regional utilities, and despite a governmental effort to introduce a third-party access model, the main electric utility was kept as a state monopoly, including the control of the high-voltage national transmission grid. In telecommunications, better progress toward privatization was achieved, but the monopolistic position of the main fixed-line operator was maintained until 2001. Efforts to establish an independent regulatory body to govern the Czech electricity market were unsuccessful.

The Crisis and Stabilization Again

Summarizing the facts described above, four main conclusions about the Czech economic transformation can be drawn:

1. Under the fixed exchange rate, large capital flows occurred, complicated macroeconomic management, and stimulated domestic de-

mand, which accelerated imports, with strong effects on the balance of payments.[11] To offset the resulting inflationary pressures, the Czech central bank massively sterilized the inflow of hot money, but the country's fixed exchange rate was maintained, leading to a slowdown of exports.

2. Weak corporate governance fueled wage growth well above productivity growth. This was truth both for the "semistate" companies (banks and large industrial companies, controlled by the National Property Fund) and for companies in the private sector.

3. The investment ratio was relatively high, but this was to a large extent dictated by the infrastructural and environmental investment (very often of a mandatory nature).

4. Rapid growth of real wages eroded enterprise savings and encouraged consumer spending, and the overall saving ratio declined.

At the beginning of 1997, the current account deficit grew sharply (up to 7.5 percent of GDP), and inflation persisted at levels higher than those in the country's main trading partners. Consequently, after March 1997, the market perceived the Czech current account deficit as unsustainable, which resulted in a foreign exchange crisis in May of that year, with a speculative effect triggered by the contagion effects from other emerging markets. Both the government and the central bank reacted promptly. A floating exchange rate regime was adopted, leading to the depreciation of the Czech crown by almost 20 percent. Budget expenditures were cut by almost 15 percent over two months, and the country's monetary policy remained neutral. At the same time, the government adopted several short-term systemic measures to alleviate at least the most pressing problems.

Stabilization after this crisis was quick and successful. The main macroeconomic indicators were fully under control by the end of the decade: The current account deficit improved to less then 2 percent of GDP by the end of 1998; inflation began to decrease again, and the currency was stabilized. Figure 7.2, which also provides comparisons with Hungary and Poland, clearly demonstrates this improvement in the macroeconomic indicators.

Conclusions: Beyond the Crisis

The price that the Czech Republic had to pay for stabilization after the crisis of 1997 was not negligible. Economic growth was negative

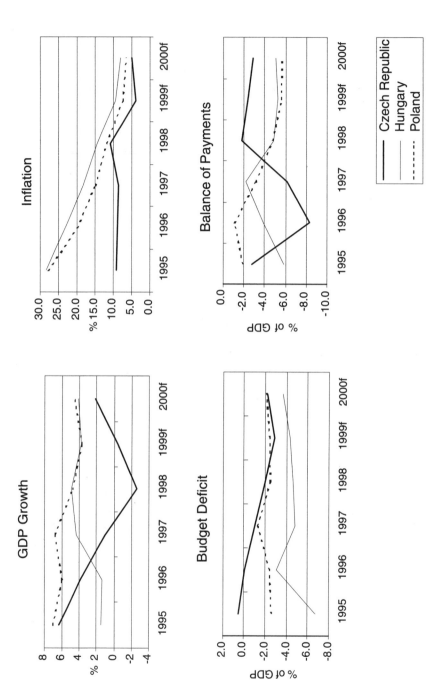

Figure 7.2
Comparative performance of the Czech economy, 1995–2000

in 1998 (−2.2 percent) and in 1999 (−0.8 percent) and resumed in 2000 only (3.1 percent). As can be observed from figure 7.2, the Czech economic recession came at a time when neighboring former socialist economies were enjoying healthy growth rates. At the same time, the country's quick stabilization was achieved by macroeconomic measures only, which cut aggregate domestic demand and slowed imports while exports enjoyed the benefit of the depreciation of the Czech crown.[12] The systemic and structural changes and microeconomic adjustment that have taken place in response to the crisis have so far not been sufficient for real microeconomic changes, and any substantial increase in domestic aggregate demand might bring the current account deficit to critical levels again.[13]

The Czech experience during the first decade of transition can be readily divided to three periods:

• 1990–1994, when the country successfully realized its initial steps toward reform.

• 1994–1997, when the reform effort slowed down, then almost stopped, with transformation remaining incomplete.

• 1997–1999, when, in reaction to a crisis in the country's currency in May 1997, quick stabilization took place, with negative consequences to growth; by the end of the decade, the position of the Czech banking sector was very difficult, negative growth prevailed during most of 1998–1999, and political forces finally began to agree and to realize the remaining reform steps and measures.

The principal reason for the crisis in 1997–1999 was the country's lack of microeconomic adjustment, caused by the factors described above. The country's problems with macroeconomic management either can be considered merely a series of wrong decisions made under the pressure of the deteriorating and more complicated economic situation or were indeed autonomous single mistakes (like the overshooting of the cut in money supply in 1996) that could not, however, have led to the deep crisis of 1997 had it not been for the country's lack of adjustment on the microeconomic level. The privatization method selected should not be considered the source of the problems; as has already been mentioned, even in the Czech Republic the privatization process was based on a combination of all possible approaches and not on voucher schemes only. Rather, the absence of strong private financial institutions, the lack of adjustment and restructuring in the enterprises (which led to the excessive wage growth), the absence of regulation of the capital markets and the long-lasting monopolistic position of some producers caused the recession of the late 1990s. Given the strong hypertrophy of Czech heavy industry at the beginning of transformation, painful microeconomic restructuring would have come in any case. Governmental policies caused a delay in this restructuring, with two negative consequences: (1) stabilization after the crisis came at a higher price. (2) Microeconomic restructuring faced a much more hostile political and social environment when it was finally undertaken than it would have four or five years previously.

Maintaining state control in the country's main commercial banks is a problem that has a strong impact on the Czech economic situation even today. The financial position of the banks has been deteriorating continuously since 1995, and central bank policies that strengthened the rules for capital adequacy and provisions have intensified the deterioration.[14] Since 1998 Czech banks have restricted their credit policies substantially, which coincided with the recession period as a result of the stabilization after the 1997 crisis and made the recession even deeper and longer lasting. The central bank, given the situation and political pressure, has decreased interest rates continuously, but the Czech economy is in a kind of liquidity trap: The banks are not lending money and will not be lending money under any interest rates until they are privatized and their bad assets are cleaned. The government's positive steps toward transformation are taking place slowly, and their positive effects will manifest themselves only with a substantial time delay.

In the second half of 1999, however, signs of recovery appeared, and it is clear that the Czech economic recession will not last forever. The country has strong potential and still has several important long-term comparative advantages. The country's process of learning from its own mistakes is definitely under way. Returning, however, to the criticisms of the so-called Washington consensus (which never existed anyway) the main conclusion should be well remembered: Markets do not fail, only policymakers do.

References

Aghevli, B., E. Borensztein, and T. van der Willigen. 1992. Stabilization and structural reform in the Czech and Slovak Federal Republic: First stage. Occasional paper 92, International Monetary Fund, Washington, D.C.

Blanchard, O. 1996. Theoretical aspects of transition. *The American Economic Review, Papers and Proceedings, May.*

Calvo, G. A., R. Sahay, and C. A. Végh. 1995. Capital flows in Central and Eastern Europe: Evidence and policy options. Working paper 95/57, International Monetary Fund, Washington, D.C.

Dědek, O., and A. Derviz. 1996. Kursová politika rozšířeného fluktuačního pásma (Exchange-Rate Policy of the Fluctuating Band. Economic Institute, Research Publication, no. 63). ČNB, Institut ekonomie, VP č.63, Praha.

Jonáš, J. 1995. Měnový kurs a platební bilance (Exchange Rate and Balance of Payments. *Finance and Credit* 4–5). Finance a úvěr 4–5.

Jonáš, J. 1997. Ekonomická transformace v České Republice (Economic Transformation in the Czech Republic). Prague: Management Press.

Portes, R. 1989. The theory and measurement of macroeconomic disequilibrium in centrally planned economies. In *Models of disequilibrium and shortage in centrally planned economies*, ed. Christopher Davis and Wojciech Charemza, 27–47. London: Chapman and Hall.

Stiglitz, J. E. 1998. Economic science, economic policy, and economic advice. Paper presented at annual Conference on Development Economics (Knowledge of Development), World Bank. Washington, D.C., May.

Tanzi, V. 1993. Fiscal policy and the economic restructuring of economies in transition. Working paper 93/22, International Monetary Fund, Washington, D.C.

Tůma, Z., and V. Kreidl. 1996. Stará kotva opuštěna: kde hledat novou? (Old Anchor Abandoned: In the Search of a New One). Ekonom 17: 345–46.

Williamson, J. 1990. What Washington means by policy reform. In *Latin American adjustment: How much has happened?* ed. John Williamson. Washington, D.C.: Institute for International Economics.

Williamson, J. 1997. The Washington consensus revisited. In *Economic and social development into the XXI century*, ed. Louis Emmerij. Washington, D.C.: Inter-American Development Bank.

Winiecki, J. 1995. The applicability of standard reform packages to Eastern Europe. *Journal of Comparative Economies* 19: 323–29.

8   Croatia in the Second Stage of Transition, 1994–1999

Velimir Šonje and Boris Vujčić

Introduction

The year 1999 witnessed a number of conferences on the "decade of transition." The syntagma of the "decade of transition" is an attempt to summarize the experiences of various countries moving from planned economies to market economies. We attempt in this chapter to summarize the important aspects of the transition experience in Croatia, focusing on the second stage of transition, 1994–1999.

There are four main reasons for such an approach. First, in some fields (e.g., the labor market and price liberalization), "transition" started many years ago, while Croatia was still a part of the former Yugoslavia. Second, although Croatia won its independence in 1991, the war and the occupation of a third of Croatian territory[1] during the initial years of "transition" overshadowed economic issues. Third, the main economic events in that period (Croatia's ability to shoulder the burdens of the war and provide for the refugees on its territory, together with the successful exchange rate–based stabilization program in late 1993) have already been described in the literature (e.g., Anušić et al. 1995; Šonje and Škreb 1995) but there is a dearth of literature on the second half of the 1990s. Finally, in the second stage of "transition" (starting in 1994), Croatia increasingly resembled some of the other advanced countries in transition, especially after 1995, when Croatia liberated its previously occupied territories. Throughout the transition period, however, in some respects Croatia was more similar to countries other than transition countries, notably Latin American countries, regarding currency substitution.

The Croatian experience is presented here in terms of international comparisons. The presentation is not historical but links similar problems using international data comparisons and cross-section econometrics.

The first section of the chapter presents stylized facts about the two stages of transition in Croatia using six macroeconomic indicators.

The cross-section econometrics presented in the chapter's second section are based on a data set for forty-four developing countries (including the eight transition countries). Regression analyses shows that low inflation in Croatia cannot be explained by money and exchange rate.

In the third section, the lower-than-expected inflation rate for Croatia is partially explained by currency substitution. In the same section, it is shown that a drop in the velocity of broad money containing foreign exchange (FX) deposits does not necessarily mean reverse currency substitution after stabilization. Such a drop may have occurred in Croatia because of the new foreign exchange deposits that flowed into the banking system as a result of an overall increase in confidence and credibility following successful disinflation.

In the fourth section, it is shown that the interest rate policy of the Croatian banks was the reason for these strong capital inflows (FX deposits). Distressed domestic banks were attracting FX deposits by offering high interest rates on deposits in foreign currency.

The chapter's fifth section discusses the relation between banking supervision, central bank credibility, and the exchange rate regime. The second banking crisis in Croatia in 1998 seriously undermined the hard-earned credibility of the Croatian National Bank, which is responsible for banking supervision in that country. Although bank failures and crises are inevitable in transition, an important issue for central bankers in transition economies is to monitor whether macroeconomic policies are having an adverse systemic impact on the country's banks. Among macroeconomic policies, the exchange rate was a natural candidate for investigation in this regard. We conclude that the presence of currency substitution shifts optimum exchange rate flexibility toward a lower level for a given quality of the banking system in general and banking supervision in particular. Hence the Croatian experience points to important links: Greater exchange rate flexibility is required as long as banking supervision and general financial stability are too weak to support a credible exchange rate peg. On the other hand, the social costs of exchange rate flexibility are likely to increase with currency substitution.

The sixth section discusses the problem of arrears. We discuss the underlying reason for the emergence of arrears in the Croatian economy, that is, poor enforcement of contracts by the government. In the absence of contract enforcement, the resulting Nash equilibrium is necessarily a bad one. We therefore propose some intervention to shift the economy toward a good equilibrium. The Croatian example suggests that arrears or "financial indiscipline" can also be viewed as the asymmetric enforcement of rules between residents and non-residents, with important implications for determining the exchange rate regime.

The seventh section discusses the relationship between monetary and fiscal policies in Croatia. It shows that the Croatian government was involved in a dangerous game of announcing its expected GDP growth rate at the time of parliamentary budget discussions, which had an impact on public perception of the policy regime and introduced a permanent strain in fiscal policy decision making.

The eighth section discusses the reasons for the poor export performance and high external imbalance in Croatia. The main reasons behind the lagging export performance of Croatia, in comparison to other advanced transition economies, are the war's impact (in the region, not only in Croatia) on the economy, particularly tourism, the exclusion of Croatia from trade associations, particularly the European Union and the Central European Free Trade Area (CEFTA), and the lack of foreign direct investments (FDIs) (particularly greenfield FDIs) in comparison to other advanced transition economies.

The chapter's final section demonstrates that labor market developments in Croatia have mostly mirrored developments in the country's real sector, since the demand for labor is directly derived from the demand for the goods and services that it helps to produce. The comparable (based on International Labor Organization [ILO] figures) unemployment rate in Croatia is approximately at the average level for transition economies in Central and Eastern Europe, but the trend is upward because the country recently experienced a recession in 1998–1999. Much of the unemployment problem is of a structural nature and will be difficult to resolve in the near future.

The Two Stages in the First Decade of Transition: Stylized Facts

The first decade of transition can be roughly divided into two stages. The first stage was characterized by declining output, price liberalization, high inflation, and the initial designing of market economy institutions. During the second stage, output recovery began, inflation declined, important institutions of the market economy began to function, and the transition countries became increasingly integrated into the world financial markets and gained access to financing, which widened current account deficits.

The distinction between the two stages is provisional. Judgment about the exact year or a period when a particular country passed from the first to the second depends on the set of macroeconomic indicators used to distinguish the stages. In this chapter, we used a set of six indicators: the ratio of fiscal deficit to GDP; the ratio of the balance-of-payments (BOP) current account deficit to GDP; openness, that is, the ratio of imports of goods to GDP; inflation in the consumer price index; real output growth; and money (M1 per unit of output) growth. Data for the eight transition countries (Bulgaria, Croatia, the Czech Republic, Hungary, Poland, Romania, Slovakia, and Slovenia) are presented in table 8.1. The demarcation between the two stages is 1993–1994 (1994 is assumed to be the first year of the second stage), because output generally began to recover and inflation declined around that time. Despite the war, Croatia fits into this average experience.

Six stylized facts emerge from studying the annual data for the transition countries:

1. Seven out of the eight countries had passed from the first to the second stage of transition as of 1999. Inflation and output varied considerably in Romania, and it is therefore impossible to determine where that country was in the process in 1999. Bulgaria's year of passage to the second stage was 1998, whereas for all the other countries it was 1994 or earlier.

2. By definition, average inflation is lower and average output growth has been higher in the second stage, although there have been noticeable differences in the behavior of the averages for the remaining four indicators.

3. In five out of the seven countries that have passed on to the second stage, the average fiscal deficit has been lower in the second stage. This has not been the case in Slovakia and Slovenia.[2]

4. Money growth per unit of output has halved on average during the second stage of transition. Only Bulgaria and the Czech Republic have had higher growth rates in the second stage than in the first.

5. In six out of the eight countries, average openness (imports of goods to GDP) has been higher in the second stage (with the exceptions of Slovakia and Bulgaria). The largest increases in openness have

Table 8.1a
CPI inflation in selected Central and Southeast European transition countries (in percent)

	Average, 1991–1998	Standard deviation, 1991–1998	Average in first stage of transition, 1991–1993	Standard deviation in first stage of transition, 1991–1993	Average in second stage of transition, 1994–1998	Standard deviation in second stage of transition, 1994–1998
Bulgaria	236.0	355.0	167.5	148.4	277.2	451.6
Croatia	293.8	474.0	779.1	470.4	2.7	3.3
Czech Republic	17.0	16.5	29.5	24.0	9.4	0.9
Hungary	22.9	6.6	26.8	7.1	20.5	5.6
Poland	32.4	18.6	50.0	17.8	21.8	8.6
Romania	132.3	82.4	212.2	43.0	84.3	57.3
Slovakia	17.2	18.6	31.5	26.6	8.6	3.1
Slovenia	51.3	70.9	117.1	84.5	11.8	4.8
Average	100.4	130.3	176.7	102.7	54.5	66.9

Table 8.1b
Real output growth in selected Central and Southeast European transition countries (in percent)

	Average, 1991–1998	Standard deviation, 1991–1998	Average in first stage of transition, 1991–1993	Standard deviation in first stage of transition, 1991–1993	Average in second stage of transition, 1994–1998	Standard deviation in second stage of transition, 1994–1998
Bulgaria	-3.9	5.9	-7.0	5.1	-2.0	6.0
Croatia	-1.6	10.6	-13.6	6.8	5.6	1.7
Czech Republic	-1.1	6.6	-6.9	7.4	2.3	3.1
Hungary	-0.2	5.6	-5.7	5.7	3.0	1.7
Poland	3.5	4.9	-0.8	6.1	6.1	0.9
Romania	-3.1	8.5	-9.2	9.3	0.6	6.2
Slovakia	0.5	8.5	-8.9	6.4	6.1	1.0
Slovenia	1.1	5.3	-3.9	6.0	4.1	0.7
Average	-0.6	7.0	-7.0	6.6	3.2	2.6

Table 8.1c
Fiscal Deficit to GDP Ratio in selected Central and Southeast European transition countries (in percent)

	Average, 1991–1998	Standard deviation, 1991–1998	Average in first stage of transition, 1991–1993	Standard deviation in first stage of transition, 1991–1993	Average in second stage of transition, 1994–1998	Standard deviation in second stage of transition, 1994–1998
Bulgaria	-5.6	3.4	-6.4	3.9	-5.2	3.5
Croatia	-0.7	2.0	-1.9	3.1	0.0	0.8
Czech Republic	-0.6	1.2	-1.5	1.4	-0.1	1.0
Hungary	-6.0	1.9	-6.3	1.8	-5.7	2.1
Poland	-3.0	1.4	-4.2	1.6	-2.3	0.6
Romania	-3.6	1.2	-2.7	1.5	-4.1	0.4
Slovakia	-4.6	1.8	-4.3	1.7	-4.8	2.0
Slovenia	0.2	1.2	1.2	1.2	-0.4	0.6
Average	-3.0	1.8	-3.2	2.0	-2.8	1.4

Table 8.1d
Money growth per unit of output in Selected Central and Southeast European transition countries (in percent)

	Average, 1991–1998	Standard deviation, 1991–1998	Average in first stage of transition, 1991–1993	Standard deviation in first stage of transition, 1991–1993	Average in second stage of transition, 1994–1998	Standard deviation in second stage of transition, 1994–1998
Bulgaria	172.7	311.7	47.4	319.1	222.8	366.9
Croatia	198.5	290.2	611.6	114.3	33.2	42.7
Czech Republic	6.5	21.3	5.8	24.1	6.7	23.2
Hungary	15.1	11.0	24.4	17.2	11.4	6.9
Poland	25.5	13.7	32.4	6.9	22.7	15.3
Romania	66.0	26.1	75.3	25.8	62.3	28.2
Slovakia	2.0	14.1	8.5	20.5	-0.6	12.8
Slovenia	42.3	43.9	88.9	71.1	23.7	10.3
Average	66.1	91.5	111.8	40.8	47.8	63.3

Table 8.1e
Merchandise imports to GDP (openness) in selected Central and Southeast European transition countries (in percent)

	Average, 1991–1998	Standard deviation, 1991–1998	Average in first stage of transition, 1991–1993	Standard deviation in first stage of transition, 1991–1993	Average in second stage of transition, 1994–1998	Standard deviation in second stage of transition, 1994–1998
Bulgaria	43	8	43	9	42	8
Croatia	39	8	36	13	41	4
Czech Republic	47	7	39	3	51	5
Hungary	38	8	32	2	42	8
Poland	25	5	20	2	28	5
Romania	26	4	24	5	27	3
Slovakia	54	5	57	7	53	4
Slovenia	48	5	44	8	50	1
Average	40	6	37	6	42	5

Table 8.1f
Current account deficit to GDP ratio in selected Central and Southeast European transition countries (in percent)

	Average, 1991–1998	Standard deviation 1991–1998	Average in first stage of transition, 1991–1993	Standard deviation in first stage of transition, 1991–1993	Average in second stage of transition, 1994–1998	Standard deviation in second stage of transition, 1994–1998
Bulgaria	-1.5	4.1	-5.1	4.7	0.7	1.7
Croatia	-2.6	6.7	1.8	4.5	-5.2	6.6
Czech Republic	-2.2	3.9	1.2	3.1	-4.3	2.8
Hungary	-3.6	4.2	-2.4	5.7	-4.2	3.6
Poland	-2.1	1.4	-1.6	1.2	-2.3	1.5
Romania	-4.4	2.7	-5.3	2.4	-3.9	3.1
Slovakia	-4.1	6.3	-5.0	n.a.	-3.9	7.0
Slovenia	1.8	2.7	3.4	3.6	0.9	1.8
Average	-2.3	4.0	-1.6	n.a.	-2.8	3.5

Source: International Financial Statistics, *Central European Quarterly.*

occurred in the Czech Republic (twelve percentage points of GDP),[3] Hungary (ten percentage points of GDP) and Poland (eight percentage points of GDP). The experiences of Slovenia (six-percentage-point increase) and Croatia (five-percentage-point increase) confirm that an increase in openness marks the second stage of transition.[4]

6. In five out of the eight countries, the average ratio of BOP current account balance to GDP has been lower in the second stage. Croatia and the Czech Republic shifted from a surplus in the first stage to a deficit in the second stage. Slovenia has had a lower surplus in the second stage, whereas Poland and Hungary have had larger deficits. Slovakia had surpluses in 1994 and 1995, making it an outlier for that subperiod, although in the second stage of development it has been similar to Poland and Hungary (due to the large Slovakian deficits in 1996–1998). Romania moved to a surplus in 1997–1998, and Bulgaria moved to a surplus from 1996 onward (after deficits in 1991–1995). Romania and Bulgaria again exhibit significantly different dynamics in comparison to the other six countries from the sample.

Three interesting features of the Croatian economy emerge from comparison with that of selected transition economies:

1. Croatia had the highest average inflation rate in the first stage and has had the lowest average inflation rate in the second stage.

2. As expected, Croatia had the highest money growth rate (per unit of output) in the first stage. This can be explained by the high fiscal deficit and sharp real contraction during the war in the initial stage of transition. However, Croatia has continued to have one of the highest money growth rates per unit of output in the second stage, when both its inflation and fiscal deficit were the lowest in the sample. Only Bulgaria and Romania, both high-inflation countries, have had higher money growth in the second stage.

3. A possible explanation for this "money puzzle" can be found in external indicators. Croatian data show the largest shift among transition countries of the BOP current account toward deficit between the first and second stages. The increase in openness between the two stages has also been strong (five percentage points of GDP), and the level of openness has been high.

In the next section, we investigate whether and to what extent openness has allowed for higher money growth. The concept is that a

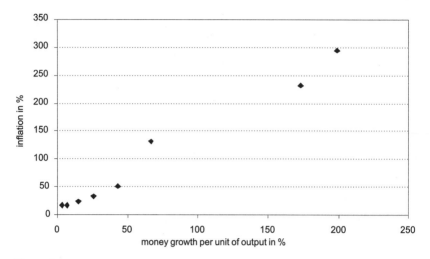

Figure 8.1a
Money growth per unit of output and inflation for eight selected transition countries,
1992–1998

rise in imports can absorb the domestic inflationary pressure in a
small and open economy.

Money, Prices, and Openness

The growth of money stock per unit of output is the most relevant
explanation of inflation in the long run (Schwartz 1973; Duck 1993).
On the other hand, robust empirical indications show that greater
openness is associated with lower inflation (Romer 1993). Therefore,
departure from unit elasticity in the money-price equation can occur
through a failure to exert control in order to obtain the effects associated with openness.

   Figure 8.1a shows that the average inflation for the eight selected
transitional economies from 1992 to 1998 exceeded the average money
growth per unit of output during the same period. This is understandable given what we know about the initial period of transition.
Transition started with an initial monetary overhang, distorted relative prices, and undervalued exchange rates. Price liberalization was
coupled with austerity programs in the first stage, leading to appreciation in the real exchange rate due to inflation and a decrease in
real money (Begg 1996). Figure 8.1b, which presents the same data
for the second stage of transition, when the initial distortions had

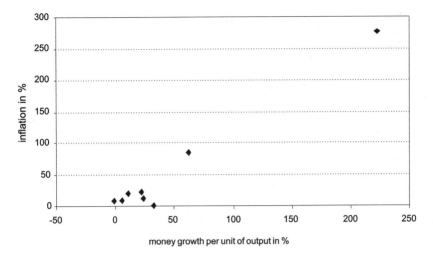

Figure 8.1b
Money growth per unit of output and inflation for eight selected transition countries, 1994–1998

been mostly eliminated, shows a closer grouping of countries around the unit slope (i.e., the unit elasticity of prices to money per unit of output).

The econometric evidence presented in table 8.2 confirms that there have been no significant departures from unit elasticity in the second stage of transition when some effects of openness are properly accounted for. However, the ratio of imports to GDP does not explain the lower inflation for the given money growth. Exchange rate variability is a significant explanatory variable.

The sample includes the thirty-six developing and eight transition countries considered in the first section of the chapter (see table 8.2 for a list of the countries). Developed countries were excluded from the sample on the basis of Romer's (1993) evidence showing that the openness-inflation relation is not relevant for developed countries with mature institutions, which have more or less resolved the time inconsistency problem of monetary policy (Kydland and Prescott 1977; Barro and Gordon 1983). All the variables in the equations whose results are presented in table 8.2 are annual averages for 1991–1997. Exchange rate variability is measured by the coefficient of the variance of the annual nominal exchange rates versus the U.S. dollar during 1993–1997.

Table 8.2
Econometric results: Determinants (t-tests) of average inflation, 1993–1997, for a sample of forty-four developing countries (including eight transition countries)

Independent variables	Equation 1	Equation 2	Equation 3	Equation 4	Equation 5	Equation 6	Equation 7	Equation 8
MPU	1.1422	1.1578	0.9849	1.0308	0.9809	1.0284	0.9703	1.0147
	(29.86)	(34.62)	(10.63)	(12.61)	(10.53)	(12.41)	(11.12)	(12.96)
CRO		−35.7393		−34.0413		−33.5380		−30.7126
		(−3.88)		(−3.76)		(−3.62)		(−3.50)
VAREX			16.9097	13.5842	18.5851	14.3417	20.8409	17.0196
			(1.85)	(1.70)	(1.98)	(1.72)	(2.39)	(2.18)
OPEN					−3.2555	−1.3765		
					(−0.80)	(−0.38)		
OUTPUT							−0.7749	−0.6131
							(−2.55)	(2.24)
R^2	0.942	0.957	0.947	0.960	0.947	0.960	0.954	0.965

Sources: *International Financial Statistics* for transition countries combined with Vienna Institute *Monthly Report*.
Note: MPU—average growth of money per unit of output 1993–1997; CRO—dummy for Croatia; VAREX—coefficient of variation of the nominal exchange rate (local currency vs. USD), 1992–1997; OPEN—imports/GDP (average 1992–1997); OUTPUT—average real output growth 1993–1997. Countries included in the sample: Argentina, Belize, Chile, Costa Rica, Cote d'Ivoire, Ecuador, Egypt, Greece, Guatemala, Honduras, Indonesia, Israel, Jordan, Kenya, Korea, Kuwait, Malaysia, Malta, Mexico, Morocco, Nepal, Pakistan, Peru, Philippines, Portugal, Saudi Arabia, Singapore, South Africa, Sri Lanka, Tanzania, Thailand, Tunisia, Turkey, Uruguay, Venezuela, Yemen, Bulgaria, Croatia, the Czech Republic, Hungary, Poland, Romania, Slovakia, Slovenia.

In the first two equations whose results are presented in table 8.2, the growth of money per unit of output is transmitted onto higher inflation than expected (the coefficient is greater than one). When a transition country's dummy is included in this regression (not shown here), the dummy parameter is not significantly different from zero. When the dummy for Croatia is included, the significant and negative coefficient for Croatia shows that inflation in Croatia was lower than expected for the given money growth. This is also the case in other equations: The coefficient of the transition dummy (not shown) was insignificant in all the equations, but the dummy coefficient for Croatia was significant and highly negative in all the equations.

Equations 3–8 in the table include additional explanatory variables. The coefficient with money per unit of output growth comes close to the expected unit value after the inclusion of these new explanatory variables. The variability of the nominal exchange rate is the most significant among the new explanatory candidates. Higher exchange rate variability implies higher inflation, which is consistent with other empirical findings (e.g., Ghosh et al. 1997). Openness (measured here as the ratio of imports to GDP) has a negative impact on inflation, but that impact is statistically insignificant, similar to Romer's findings for developed countries.

Output growth is negatively and significantly related to inflation. Of course, this relationship does not imply causation, because output and inflation can be related in a number of complex ways. This result merely registers the idea that lower inflation is associated with higher real output growth, which means that supply shocks may have dominated over demand shocks in developing economies during the 1990s. When the four outliers in the sample (Venezuela, Yemen, Bulgaria and Croatia) are controlled for by dummies, however, the coefficient of output growth becomes insignificantly different from zero (not shown in table 8.2). Hence the importance of output growth is influenced by outliers, which may occur because of some other (omitted) explanatory variables. (We discuss these variables in the next section.)

In conclusion, money was the most relevant explanation for prices in the second stage of transition over the long run. Openness was not a significant determinant of inflation, but the variability of the nominal exchange rate was. The same is true for output growth, although this result was influenced by outliers. The low inflation in Croatia remains largely unexplained by this model, which predicts an average inflation rate for Croatia that is more than 30 percent higher than the actual rate. In the next section, we attempt to find an explanation for the low inflation rate in Croatia during the second stage of transition.

External Shocks, Currency Substitution, Velocity of Money, and Financial Deepening

In the econometric work undertaken for this chapter, we used a number of external indicators that did not exhibit any influence on the inflation in our sample (ratio of net capital inflows to GDP, variability of net capital inflows, variability of openness, ratio of current account deficit to GDP, ratio of variability of the current account deficit to GDP). However, indicators of external performance can have an indirect impact on inflation. For example, net capital inflows can help keep the exchange rate stable, and a stable exchange rate might help keep prices stable in a small and open economy. Hence higher money growth can be associated with lower inflation when net capital inflows are strong. In addition, any swing in net capital inflows can destabilize prices via the floating exchange rate.

External financial shocks can be huge, reaching an order of magnitude of several percentage points of GDP annually. In other words, the current account of the BOP and imports can exhibit significant changes as long as (net) capital inflows do the same. Not only short-run speculative inflows can create volatility. In transition, all types of inflows can change rapidly. In Croatia, where the population holds around 80 percent of its savings in foreign exchange deposits (and foreign exchange deposits make up almost 70 percent of broad money), changes in expectations and confidence in the banking system can cause large swings in foreign exchange flows that are almost impossible to control.

Table 8.3 shows the magnitude of the net capital inflows from 1992 to 1997 for developing countries and from 1993 to 1997 for transition countries (1992 data for some of the transition countries are either not available or very unreliable).[5] Inflows are expressed as a percentage of GDP and compared to nontransition developing economies. (Countries from the sample are used in the regression in the previous section.) Three conclusions are derived from the data in the table:

Table 8.3
Cumulative net capital inflows (minus current account balance minus reserves)[a] to GDP (in percent)

	Inflows/GDP	Variability of inflows[b]
Developing countries (without transition countries; $n = 36$), 1992–1997	29.0	3.9
Transition countries ($n = 8$), 1993–1997[c]	29.9	4.9
Croatia	28.4	6.4

Source: International Financial Statistics.
[a] This is equal to financial account, exclusive of reserve assets, plus net errors and omissions.
[b] Standard deviation of annual net capital inflows to GDP ratios.
[c] Time period for transition countries was shortened by one year because in some cases there are no reliable BOP data for 1992. Besides, inflows were modest in 1992 and do not have a significant influence on the conclusions.

1. The average cumulative capital inflows were of remarkably similar size (around 29 percent of GDP) for the two groups of countries (the thirty-six developing countries and the eight transition countries).

2. Net capital inflows to Croatia were around the average for the group as a whole as well as around the average for the transition countries. Hungary and the Czech Republic experienced much stronger inflows.

3. The volatility of inflows (measured by the standard deviation of the ratio of net capital inflows to GDP for five annual observations) was higher in the transition countries than in other developing countries. In Croatia, it was much higher than the average for transition economies.

However, the volatility of inflows could not explain the large difference between money growth and inflation in Croatia, nor could the size of the inflows. We therefore focused on one component of inflows that is reflected in currency substitution as the most important explanatory candidate: the degree of "currency substitution," which actually made the difference between Croatia (with a 60 to 70 percent share of FX deposits in broad money) and other countries.

Currency substitution is a good explanatory candidate for explaining the difference between inflation and money per unit of output growth because this actually means trying to explain changes in money velocity. Clearly, there is no reason to expect that openness

Table 8.4
Econometric results (*t*-tests) with Currency Substitution (CURSUB)

Independent variables	Eq. 1	Eq. 2	Eq. 3 (Venezuela 40%)	Eq. 4 (Venezuela 40%)
MPU	1.0039	1.0336	1.0212	1.0438
	(11.79)	(13.04)	(13.15)	(14.27)
CRO		−27.1276		−22.9143
		(−2.85)		(−3.37)
VAREX	21.5872	17.2298	23.4386	19.7177
	(2.54)	(2.15)	(3.02)	(2.67)
CURSUB	−21.0731	−13.3816	−28.6188	−22.9143
	(−2.99)	(−1.90)	(−4.40)	(−2.62)
R^2	0.956	0.963	0.964	0.969

and/or variations in inflows should necessarily have a direct impact on velocity. Nevertheless, there is a reason to expect that exchange rate variability has something to do with financial deepening and the velocity of money (Hausmann et al. 1999). An effect of this type can be expected in cases where the nominal exchange rate plays the role of the opportunity cost of money in the demand-for-money function. In this case, exchange rate fluctuations can induce large portfolio shifts.

There are great difficulties associated with measuring currency substitution. A proxy that does not include cash—the ratio of foreign currency deposits to broad money—is available (Balino et al. 1999). Data for this proxy (Balino and others used data for 1995) cover twenty-two countries, that is, 50 percent of our sample. For the other twenty-two countries in the regression, we initially assumed that currency substitution was zero. (We later relaxed this assumption.)

The econometric evidence presented in table 8.4 shows the explanatory power of currency substitution. The first two equations show that currency substitution was associated with lower inflation in the 1990s, Croatia still being a significant outlier and an important determinant of the link between the substitution and inflation in the sample. Currency substitution was associated with lower inflation because in the 1990s we saw stabilization and surges of capital inflows around the developing world. In countries with currency substitution, which stabilized successfully, domestic money demand and financial depth rose quite rapidly. (Reverse) currency substitution helped countries maintain relatively stable exchange rates during times of strong capital inflows and monetary expansion.

In equations 3 and 4 in the table, we took into account that half of the sample have zero entries for currency substitution because of the lack of data, which seriously undermines the relevance of the results (and clearly points to new directions of research). Therefore, we performed an experiment in the case of Venezuela, for which we have a zero entry. We assumed that the ratio of foreign currency deposits to broad money was 40 percent for this country and reran regressions. The results point to higher (negative) parameters with currency substitution and a lower (negative) value of the coefficient with the Croatian dummy. This suggests that if the measurement of currency substitution were improved, it might turn out to be the most important factor (together with the variability in nominal exchange rate) in explaining the differences in inflation performance among the developing countries.

In the case of Croatia, credible stabilization as of late 1993 led to reverse currency substitution, a drop in velocity, and an increase in financial depth. It is not completely clear, however, why and how this happened. One should not go beyond the conclusion that there is a link among the variables. Causality and the mechanisms of influence are not at all clear. If we are measuring the velocity of broad money, which includes foreign exchange deposits, the currency portfolio shifts should not influence financial depth and velocity unless the shifts are so large that they deepen the banking system through the multiplier effect and unless additional inflows of deposits to the banking system occur at the same time.

To clarify this issue, in table 8.5 we compare the indicator of money velocity, that is, inverse financial depth, with an indicator of currency substitution for the eight selected transition countries. The link between volatility in the velocity (measured by the standard deviation of five annual observations of the velocity from 1993 to 1997) and currency substitution (the share of foreign exchange deposits in broad money, FXD/M) is confirmed by a significant and positive coefficient in the regression of velocity volatility on currency substitution (0.2 with a t-statistic of 3.1). Again, this regression does not describe the causality mechanism; it is merely an indication of the link between the two phenomena. A higher volatility of the velocity of broad money is associated with higher currency substitution in transitional economies.

Labeling a share of the foreign exchange deposits in broad money as "currency substitution" can be misleading, however, data in table

Table 8.5
Financial depth (broad money to GDP, 1993–1997, in percent) and currency substitution in selected transition countries

	1993	1994	1995	1996	1997	Average depth, 1993–1997	Standard deviation, 1993–1997	Currency substitution (FXD/M), 1995
Croatia	25.9	20.0	25.0	33.9	41.0	29.2	8.3	57.4
Bulgaria	77.5	78.0	64.9	71.2	33.6	65.0	18.4	28.4
Czech Republic	70.0	73.1	84.0	79.4	76.2	76.5	5.4	5.9
Hungary	56.8	52.2	50.0					
Poland	35.9	36.7	36.1	37.6	39.7	37.2	1.5	20.4
Romania	22.3	21.4	25.1	28.0	25.0	24.4	2.6	21.7
Slovakia	68.8	67.7	68.3	71.2	68.2	68.8	1.4	11.1
Slovenia	35.0	40.3	42.2	43.8	47.7	41.8	4.7	31.7

Sources: International financial statistics, *Central European Quarterly*, bulletins of national banks, Balino et al. 1999.

Table 8.6
Velocity of broad money and its components (domestic and foreign) in Croatia, 1994–1998

	1994	1995	1996	1997	1998
Velocity of M4	5.0	4.0	3.0	2.4	2.4
Percentage change in V(M4)		−20.0	−25.0	−20.0	0.0
Velocity of FXD	10.0	7.0	5.0	4.0	3.6
Percentage change in V(FXD)		−30.0	−28.6	−20.0	−10.0
Velocity of M2	10.0	9.3	7.5	6.0	7.2
Percentage change in V(M2)		−7.0	−19.3	−20.0	20.0

Source: Croatian National Bank *Bulletin.*
Note: M2 encompasses the domestic currency component of M4, that is, M1 + time and savings deposits in kuna + bonds, so that M4 = M2 + FXD.

8.6 were constructed to isolate the effects of currency substitution from the effects of new foreign exchange deposit inflows to Croatian banks. The data show that reverse currency substitution was a secondary effect. The primary effect was a continuous increase in foreign exchange deposits in domestic Croatian commercial banks.

The data in table 8.6 show that 1997 was the only year (from 1994 to 1998) when both components (domestic and foreign) of broad money made equal contributions to the drop in velocity in Croatia. From 1994 to 1997, reverse currency substitution was reflected in the declining velocity of domestic M2, but from 1994 to 1996 the growth of FX deposits made an even larger contribution to the drop in the velocity of broad money. In 1998, the velocity of the domestic component actually increased, and therefore the velocity of broad money remained stable because of the continuing growth of foreign exchange deposits in domestic banks. Consequently, during the entire poststabilization period, Croatia experienced growth in the share of FX deposits in broad money, whereas the velocity of the domestic money supply was very volatile: rapidly slowing down in the aftermath of stabilization (1994–1997) and rapidly speeding up later during transition (1998–1999).

The impossibility of reducing the share of FX deposits in broad money after stabilization has been called the "irreversibility" of currency substitution (Balino et al. 1999; Sahay and Vegh 1995; Guidotti and Rodriguez 1992). This term appears, however, to be somewhat misleading in the case of Croatia because it is impossible to prove that currency substitution in Croatia was largely "irreversible."

Instead, the share of foreign exchange deposits in broad money increased because of capital inflows, that is, the repatriation of foreign exchange holdings from abroad and from "mattresses." New inflows were not exchanged for kuna. In this sense, the substitution was "irreversible." All that happened, however, was that the capital that flowed in remained in the original currency, because the interest differential (in Croatia, between the kuna and the foreign currency deposits) was too low to compensate for the local currency risk. The velocity of the domestic money component (M2) stopped dropping in 1998 for the same reason. As an introduction to the next section, we may note that the banks promoted these flows by offering interest rates on foreign exchange deposits that were higher than the interest rates offered abroad.

Banks and Capital Flows

Before stabilization (prior to late 1993), banks in Croatia were of little importance to the economy. Real deposit interest rates in the country were negative because of high inflation (the average monthly inflation rate from January to October 1993 was 28 percent). Nominal interest spreads were extremely large; the economy was in a state of financial repression and rapid disintermediation. Croatia had practically no international reserves at the time. The current account surplus occurred largely because of unrecorded capital outflows (Anušić et al. 1995).

According to Jankov (1999), the Croatian banking system was deeply insolvent in 1989, when bad loans reached the banks' capital on two occasions. This problem continued, and in 1991, thirteen out of twenty-eight banks were insolvent (CNB 1991). The war and high inflation further exacerbated the problem. The government made two bond issues to recapitalize the banks (cf. Šonje, Kraft, and Dorsey 1999; Babić, Jurković, and Šonje 1999). Technically, these operations increased solvency (according to Jankov, capital adequacy was raised to 14 percent through bond issues and accounting tricks) but did not change the banks' ownership and incentive structure.[6]

Problems with the banking industry continued from 1992 to 1995, while Croatia was still partially occupied. After the introduction of the usual accounting practices and provisioning criteria for a market economy, the reform of monetary instruments, and stabilization, four of the six largest banks were found to be insolvent. They were recapitalized and rehabilitated in a transparent way (e.g., Šonje, Kraft, and Dorsey 1999; Babić, Jurković, and Šonje 1999; Lovegrove 1998). This time, the ownership structure and management were changed, coupled with the government's commitment to privatize the top four banks. The largest of these has been privatized and the remaining three were to be privatized in 2000.

This recapitalization and rehabilitation marked the end of the "first Croatian banking crisis, 1989–1996" (Kraft 1999) with a total resolution cost of 22 percent of the 1997 GDP (Babić, Jurković, and Šonje 1999).[7] "The second Croatian banking crisis" (Kraft 1999) began in March 1998, when the fifth largest bank failed (and was subsequently rehabilitated in April 1998). Its failure was followed by those of a number of small and medium-sized bank. The central bank council initiated two bankruptcies of deposit-taking institutions in 1998 and another six in March and April of 1999. The eight institutions together represented 7 percent of the total assets of the banking system. If the fifth largest bank, which was rehabilitated in April 1998, is added, the share of problem banks in total bank assets increases to 12 percent. The general public at that time was aware that there are a few more banks "in the pipeline" toward bankruptcy.

The cost of rehabilitating the fifth largest bank was 2 percent of Croatia's GDP, and preliminary estimates of the costs of repaying the insured deposits in the other failed banks are around 3 percent of GDP.[8] In summary, the aggregate cost of both banking crises (first and second) in 1999 stood at approximately 27 percent of GDP.

That places these among the (fiscally) most expensive banking crises in modern history. For comparison, we used Frydl's (1999) review of the five most influential studies of banking crises (Caprio and Klingebiel 1996; Demirguc-Kunt and Detragiache 1998; Dziobek and Pazarbasioglu 1997; Kaminsky and Reinhart 1996; Lindgren, Garcia, and Saal 1996). In only six cases across all five studies did the costs of crisis resolution exceed 20 percent of GDP:[9] Argentina, 1980–1982 (55.3 percent); the Ivory Coast, 1988–1991 (25 percent); Chile, 1981–1983 (41.2 percent); Israel, 1977–1983 (30 percent); Kuwait, 1992 (42 percent); and Uruguay, 1981–1984 (31.2 percent). We see that the case of Croatia is unexceptional in that high costs of banking crises are associated with wars or debt crises. It is a fair approximation to assume that the first Croatian banking crisis resulted mainly from the war and the legacy of the past in the banking sector, whereas the second banking crisis (costs of resolution up to now

Table 8.7
Number of banks in Croatia by size of assets, 1993–1998

	Number of banks	Value of assets		
		Less than 1 billion HRK	1–10 billion HRK	More than 10 billion HRK
1993	43	35	6	2
1994	50	40	8	2
1995	53	42	9	2
1996	57	42	13	2
1997	60	41	17	2
1998	60	37	21	2

Source: Croatian National Bank *Bulletin.*
Note: HRK 1 billion ≈ USD 140 million.

being estimated at around 5 percent of GDP) was incurred as a consequence of typical market and regulation failures seen elsewhere around the world (including developed countries). In Croatia, capital inflows intermediated via banks were major contributors to the crises, a scenario quite common around the world (for a theoretical consideration, cf. McKinnon and Pill 1995).

In tables 8.7–8.9, we present data that may clarify the reasons for the Croatian banking crises. It should first be noted that the total number of banks in Croatia grew rapidly until 1996 (table 8.7). The number of large and small banks (by Croatian standards) did not change significantly, although the number of medium-sized banks (total assets from U.S. $140 million to U.S. $1.4 billion, that is, from 0.7 percent to 6.7 percent of GDP) increased significantly (from six in 1993 to twenty-one in 1998). These banks grew on the basis of foreign exchange deposit inflows attracted by high interest rates (tables 8.8 and 8.9). Both the repatriation of foreign exchange and the increase in foreign exchange deposits with domestic banks represented more than 10 percent of Croatian exports from 1995 to 1998, when Croatia recorded a large current account deficit. In table 8.8, it is also evident that the motive for reverse currency substitution was weak: The average interest rate on domestic currency deposits corrected for expected depreciation was dropping. In 1998, the deposit interest rate dropped below the expected depreciation. Hence reverse currency substitution, measured by the (dropping) velocity of the domestic M2, stopped at that time.

Table 8.8
Capital inflows and monetary indicators, 1993–1998 (in percent)

	1993	1994	1995	1996	1997	1998
Net capital inflows/exports[a]	−2.4	0.0	24.5	16.0	32.4	21.4
Repatriation[b]/exports[a]	4.5	5.1	12.1	17.0	6.4	12.3
Growth rate of FX deposits[c]	—	62.1	60.7	54.6	42.5	20.5
Increase in FX deposits[b]/exports	—	7.8	13.5	17.7	18.4	11.7
Growth of real M2	—	90.7	16.9	37.5	25.8	−5.9
Lending interest rate[c]	59.0	15.4	22.3	18.5	14.1	16.1
Deposit interest rate[c]	27.4	5.0	6.1	4.2	4.4	4.1
CPI inflation[c]	1149.3	−3.0	3.7	3.4	3.8	5.4
Rate of obligatory reserve requirement[c]	25.9	28.9	41.4	35.9	32.0	30.0

Source: Croatian National Bank *Bulletin.*
[a] Exports of goods and services.
[b] Repatriation is reflected in BOP as a decrease of foreign exchange holdings of other sectors. It does not correspond to an increase in foreign exchange deposits with domestic banks. Foreign exchange deposits can also grow because of current transactions (transfers or income from abroad or unrecorded exports of goods and services).
[c] End of year.
Note: Dashes indicate data are not available.

The data in table 8.9 provide more information on interest rates in Croatia:

1. The money market interest rate was predominantly supply-side driven (dropping during and after the successful bank rehabilitation operations in 1996, rising after the second banking crises started in early 1998, and insensitive to the expected changes in the exchange rate).

2. The uncovered interest differential (measured by the linear difference between the average interest rate on time deposits in domestic and foreign currency) dropped in 1997–1998, which meant that the incentives for reverse currency substitution on the higher end of broad money vanished and became the opposite: a motive for currency substitution (especially given the fact that the expected depreciation became largely positive in 1998).

3. The nominal interest rate on foreign exchange time deposits was extremely high by European standards, more than 6 percent per year until late 1998, when aggressive banks exited the market.

The level of interest rates on foreign exchange time deposits in Croatian banks explains the continuous inflows of foreign exchange

Table 8.9
Banks' interest rates, expected depreciation[a] and distribution of foreign exchange deposits among "good" and "bad" banks[b], 1995:Q1–1999:Q1

	I(mm)	I(tkd)	I(tfxd)	I(dif)	E(e)	I(dif) − E(e)	I(good)	I(bad)	Share(good)	Share(bad)
Q1/95	17.2	9.9	—	—	-1.5	—	—	—	—	—
Q2/95	19.1	10.8	—	—	-3.8	—	—	—	—	—
Q3/95	23.0	11.4	6.6	4.8	4.2	0.6	—	—	—	—
Q4/95	25.2	13.0	6.5	6.5	9.1	-2.6	—	—	—	—
Q1/96	29.7	15.0	6.8	8.2	-2.9	11.1	—	—	—	—
Q2/96	26.3	14.6	6.5	8.1	-8.9	17.0	—	—	—	—
Q3/96	11.4	12.7	6.5	6.2	-5.8	12.0	—	—	—	—
Q4/96	10.0	10.3	7.6	2.7	1.2	3.9	—	—	—	—
Q1/97	11.4	9.9	6.4	3.5	1.4	4.9	—	—	74.9	25.1
Q2/97	11.3	9.9	6.1	3.8	-0.9	4.7	—	—	74.3	25.7
Q3/97	9.3	9.4	5.9	3.5	-1.9	5.4	—	—	73.7	26.3
Q4/97	8.9	8.9	6.1	2.8	-2.5	5.3	—	—	71.0	29.0
Q1/98	10.1	9.0	7.2	1.8	0.2	1.6	4.7	8.3	70.4	29.6
Q2/98	16.0	9.7	7.4	2.3	12.6	-10.3	5.0	8.1	73.1	26.9
Q3/98	16.0	9.7	6.6	3.1	-3.8	6.9	5.2	8.2	74.7	25.3
Q4/98	15.8	8.7	5.4	3.3	16.0	-12.7	4.8	8.2	75.9	24.1
Q1/99	15.7	8.8	5.3	3.5	16.1	-12.6	4.7	8.2	77.2	22.8

Sources: Croatian National Bank *Bulletin*, special calculations by Croatian National Bank Research & Statistics Department.

Note: Dashes indicate that numbers not calculated for previous years. I(mm)—money market interest rate (monthly data are averages of daily observations); I(tkd)—weighted average interest rate on time kuna deposits (deposit inflows used as weights, so interest rates are marginal); I(tfxd)—weighted average interest rate on time foreign exchange deposits (same method of calculation as for I(tkd)); I(dif)—interest differential: I(tkd) − I(tfxd); E(e)—expected depreciation;[a] I(good)—unweighted interest rate paid on foreign exchange time deposits in good banks;[b] I(bad)—unweighted interest rate paid on foreign exchange time deposits in bad banks;[b] Share (good)—share of good banks in total foreign exchange deposits with domestic banks;[b] Share (bad)—share of bad banks in total foreign exchange deposits with domestic banks.[b]

[a] Expected depreciation is calculated as the annualized end-quarterly change of the expected nominal HRK/DM exchange rate, whereas the expected level of the exchange rate is assumed to be produced by an AR (2) process.

[b] "Bad" banks used for the calculation of foreign exchange deposit interest rates (column no. 8) are classified as "bad" either because they already failed or because they exhibit striking similarity regarding liquidity and interest rate policies to the banks that have failed already. "Good" banks (column 7) are banks with strikingly different liquidity positions and interest rate policies. These two groups of banks need not correspond to "good" and "bad" banks which are used for the calculation of group shares in the total FX deposits, although overlapping between the two classification schemes is significant. All the banks that are "bad" in the classification for interest data (column 8) are also bad in the classification for deposit data, but the classification for deposit data additionally includes a number of banks (additional 7) that are using central bank short-run liquidity loans. The "good" ones are the others.

deposits (as well as the continuous decline in the velocity of broad money) and the lack of incentives for a flight back to currency (the "irreversibility" of currency substitution). The interest rate on kuna deposits was low in comparison to the interest rate on FX deposits. It was especially low after the expected depreciation became positive (1998 and 1999). The data in table 8.9 point to the fact that in 1998 the banks stopped compensating for expected depreciation by offering higher interest rates on domestic currency time deposits, because such a policy would have required extremely high interest rates on deposits in domestic currency. Croatian banks probably avoided a sharp increase in domestic interest rates because of fears of adverse selection (prudential reason), because they did not expect a surge in inflation (credibility reason), or simply because they knew that domestic currency deposits had a low interest rate elasticity (Kraft 1999). Hence, reverse currency substitution vanished in 1998 and 1999; in fact, the velocity of domestic broad money began to rise (cf. table 8.6). The last four columns on the right in table 8.9 show that medium-sized, aggressively growing banks based their business development on extremely high deposit interest rates that served as the main vehicle for attracting foreign exchange inflows. While good banks were paying a reasonable premium over the foreign interest rate on foreign exchange deposits (approximately 100 basis points), bad banks stubbornly offered interest rates on FX deposits that were almost twice as high as those of the good banks. This led to a rapidly growing share of bad banks in the FX deposit base (on top of the fact that the base itself was growing rapidly: recall data in table 8.8). The share of bad banks reached a high of 30 percent in early 1998, when the fifth-largest bank failed in a politicoeconomic scandal. Subsequently, this share started to diminish rapidly. Depositors lost confidence in some of the small and medium-sized banks and began to transfer their deposits to banks with a more established reputation.[10]

In conclusion, the capital inflows into Croatian banks were partially an unhealthy process, since they involved moral hazards and imprudent banking practices. Attracting FX deposits from residents and nonresidents with high interest rates represents a type of inflow that has no disciplining effects (which occur when a foreign lender perceives risks, such as in case of FDI and/or portfolio investment), especially when most of the foreign exchange is held by residents and there is no history of bank bankruptcies. The Croatian case is one more instance that confirms previous findings that (1) newly emerging private banks may cause more harm than good in transitional banking markets (Begg 1996; Šonje, Kraft, and Dorsey 1996) and (2) banks and banks' (non)regulation do play a crucial role in building a systemic "overborrowing syndrome" (McKinnon and Pill 1995).

Credibility, Bank Supervision, and the Exchange Rate Regime

A number of failing banks in Croatia in the 1990s were financing equally nonviable, rapidly growing, and badly managed private business groups that emerged as "winners" from the privatization process, most likely with strong support from politically influential groups in Croatia. Thus in a sense, the second banking crisis was a cumulative expression of wrong decisions (by both the public and private sectors) about the allocation of resources made during the first few years of transition.

For Croatia's central bank, which is responsible for banking supervision, the experience was frustrating in two respects. First, everybody was accusing the central bank of failing to control banks, even though the root causes of the failures were to be found in the chosen model of privatization and in political interference, neither of which had anything to do with the central bank.[11] Public allegations coming from all sides (government, politicians, media, depositors who lost money, owners who lost their stakes) eroded the central bank's credibility, which as a by-product of poor supervision, could have had a negative impact on currency stability. In a sense, all of the accomplishments of the earlier period of transition (an independent central bank that is accountable only to the parliament, low inflation) were forgotten, at least for a few months. Wagner (1998) referred to this type of situation, in which too much responsibility is assigned to the central bank, as typical. Wagner concluded that such a situation might lead to a loss of central bank credibility.

Second, Babić, Jurković, and Šonje (1999) point out that the Croatian National Bank (CNB), in a report entitled *Banks at the Crossroads* (CNB 1997), clearly identified the association between moral hazards, high interest rates, and foreign exchange inflows in aggressively growing banks. Hence, the CNB "knew" what was happening almost a year before the largest fifth bank failed, which raised frustrations even higher. People outside the bank thought that knowing about early signals should have been enough to enable the central bank to act and concluded it was too politically weak to act. This eroded the central bank's credibility. Insiders and experts recognized, of course, that knowledge of problems may be necessary but is not sufficient for successful supervision. Educating people, developing procedures, and building a firm legal basis for supervision are very demanding jobs, and it can be quite frustrating when one sees banks running into trouble before the whole institutional setup for preventing it is in place.

Banks were not, however, running into trouble because of ignorance. It would have been to no avail for supervisors to preach optimal banking practices, because the owners and managers in the failed banks were intentionally running into trouble. They paid twice as much for money than the rest of the market and also lent it at a much higher price than the rest of the market.

Another concern for central bankers in transition is the possible correlation between macroeconomic variables that they control and the problems in the banking sector. Monetary policy, including the choice of the exchange regime, should not be formulated independently from the considerations of the banking sector in transition. In the Croatian case, the crucial issue in this respect is whether the choice of the exchange rate regime contributed to perpetuating the problems of the banking sector.

Column 5 of table 8.9 (expected depreciation) closely resembles the actual changes in the exchange rate in Croatia, which were minor by international standards[12] (see also figure 8.2). The CNB always emphasized the importance of exchange rate stability (and built credibility on it) for an economy with currency substitution. On the other hand, it also emphasized that it did not want a fixed exchange rate. Hence it allowed some movement of the nominal exchange rate (ex post facto we know that it was an interval of ±6 percent; see figure 8.2) to show agents where the market was (signaling effect). The CNB believed that this would help the markets learn about managing exchange rate risks and prevent the speculations that might have occurred if the exchange rate had been pegged.

If the exchange rate had been more flexible, Croatian authorities could have targeted the money supply and allowed the exchange rate to appreciate more during the period of strong capital inflows (Anušić 1994; Šonje 1994). Presumably after a period of strong appreciation, agents would change their expectations and begin to expect depreciation. After some time, the expectation-driven changes

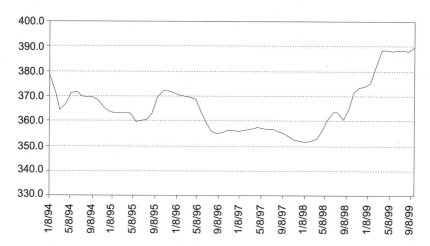

Figure 8.2
Nominal exchange rate of kuna versus DM 100 after stabilization
Source: Croatian National Bank *Bulletin.*

would (hopefully) diminish. Higher exchange rate flexibility would (1) lead to better internalization of the currency risks of the agents investing in domestic currency instruments, (2) leave more room for domestic stabilization policies, and (3) enable the central bank to target money and credit more precisely, so that perhaps the aggressive banks would never have been able to grow as big and as fast as they actually did. However, this thesis cannot be verified, because economic experiments are not repeatable.

On the other hand, Croatia could have adopted some form of crawling-peg or crawling-band regime that could have led to lower inflows and been beneficial for exporters. This thesis, however, has four problems:

1. Successful crawling pegs/bands are forward looking, designed to deal with inflation inertia, a problem that disappeared from Croatia at the very beginning of successful stabilization, in 1993.

2. Crawling pegs/bands are successful in keeping the real exchange rate stable (Hausmann et al. 1999), but the existing regime of a dirty float (unannounced band) was equally successful at doing this in Croatia.

3. The size of inflows is in no way related to the exchange rate regime.[13]

4. Weaker currency would have led to a looser monetary policy, that is, more money and credit with a greater proliferation of bad banks, which would have consequently led to a greater misallocation of resources and an even more expensive second banking crisis.

Although banking supervision and regulation could have provided some protection from the banking problems and recession in Croatia in the late 1990s, banking supervision alone could not have prevented the banking crises. Although higher exchange rate flexibility is desirable in many respects, it can lead either to bank losses (if the banks and/or other sectors have no resources to deal with currency risk) or to the rapid development of unsound banks. The lesson to be learned from the Croatian case, once again, is that policymakers should weigh exchange rate flexibility against the abilities of bank supervisors and the stability of the country's financial system in general. Supervisors must be able to support greater exchange rate stability, because exchange rate stability means strong money demand, faster financial deepening, higher vulnerability to speculations, and higher volatility of money and credit (because of the volatility of capital flows). If supervisors are immature, authorities should aim at the higher exchange rate flexibility provided by monetary or inflation targeting (Mishkin 1999). This trade-off is general. As demonstrated below, it is more complicated in the case of Croatia because of currency substitution.

The RR line in figure 8.3 represents a choice between (1) higher-quality supervision (and greater financial stability in general) and less exchange rate flexibility and (2) a lower quality of banking supervision (and financial stability in general) and greater flexibility of the exchange rate. It may seem that Croatia had "too much" exchange rate stability given the relatively low quality of its banking supervision and fragile banking system. On the other hand, currency substitution[14] means that "too much" exchange rate flexibility can easily induce a costly exit from the currency (flight into foreign assets) instead of increasing the power of domestic countercyclical macroeconomic policy. This fact is reflected in the shift of the RR line in figure 8.3. A country with a medium quality of banking supervision should choose medium exchange rate flexibility unless there is currency substitution. Currency substitution shifts the RR line to the left (higher currency substitution implies a stronger shift to $R'R'$). With currency substitution ($R'R'$), the same quality of banking supervision implies lower optimal flexibility of the exchange rate.

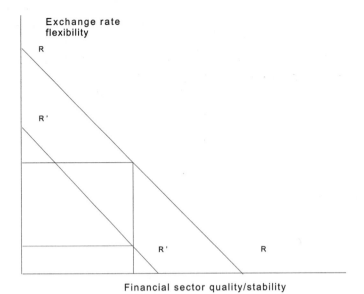

Figure 8.3
Tradeoff between financial stability and exchange rate flexibility

Arrears, Ethics, and Exchange Rate Policy

One of the most serious (transition) problems in Croatia has been the general lack of financial discipline. It is present in all intersector relationships: the private sector versus the state sector (tax evasion), the state sector versus the private sector (government arrears), the state sector versus the state sector (intergovernment arrears) and the private sector versus the private sector (interenterprise arrears). These phenomena have also been labeled "soft budget constraints," "financial indiscipline," and "financial delinquency."

All of these problems are normally present in emerging[15] economies, although the extent of the (lack of) financial discipline varies substantially among countries. In Croatia, financial delinquency became almost endemic in the late 1990s. This can be said even though it is very difficult to quantify many aspects of the problem, and we do not intend to dwell on the details of interenterprise arrears or the extent of tax evasion, as these are rather complicated issues to quantify. To illustrate the extent of the problem, however, it is enough to browse through a few figures, however imperfect they may be. First, using various methods, it has been estimated (Institute for Public

Finance 1997) that the unofficial economy in Croatia amounts to approximately 25 percent of the country's GDP.[16] Second, the extent of government arrears (central government and health fund) at the end of 1998 amounted to approximately 4 billion kunas or 3 percent of GDP. Third, arrears reported to the payments institute[17] rose from 6.2 percent of GDP at the end of 1994 to 11.6 percent at the end of 1998.[18]

At the heart of the problem is poor contract enforcement. Contract enforcement is perhaps the most important task that the government has to perform in order for a market economy to function. In its absence, it is possible to set up the following game:

	A	B
A	5.5	0.7
B	7.0	2.2

The player choosing between the rows is taxpayer/entrepreneur 1, and the player choosing between the columns is taxpayer/entrepreneur 2. If neither of the players knows what strategy the other will choose, we have a common prisoner's dilemma in which each player stands to gain by not paying his taxes/bills (to the government or other entrepreneurs). Both are better off, however, if neither chooses to cheat. Since the cooperative strategy (A, A) is the preferred solution, the role of the government, knowing the payoffs, is to enforce the cooperative (A, A) strategy among all the players and thus bring the economy to a superior Nash equilibrium. If the government is unable to do so, however (if it does so inefficiently), then the players will choose (B, B) and the economy will end up in a bad equilibrium. This exercise is nevertheless different from the common prisoner's dilemma to the extent that the players are, in fact, informed that the others are cheating. There are two main channels for obtaining information about the others' behavior. The first is personal experience. In an environment in which an arrears problem has already set in, entrepreneurs constantly face the problem of collecting payments from other entrepreneurs. Second, tax evasion is so widespread that they regularly read about it in newspapers, hear about it from the government, and share their experiences with other entrepreneurs. Such a situation pretty well describes the state of affairs in Croatia in the late 1990s.

The problem can be couched in the framework of conditional morality. Most individuals do adhere to some basic norms and morality, but as Basu (1999) points out, in reality we often express our morals in a form along the lines of "I believe in paying taxes because it is every citizen's duty to do so; however, I believe that this ceases to be a duty on my part if others do not, and indeed I would not pay taxes if others did not." This is a utilitarian moral system but one based on conditionality. Such conditional morality stems from two urges, as basic as (or even basic than, as Basu points out) the propensity to maximize utility: the urge to adhere to some morality and the urge not to be a sucker. In some cases, this problem can also be described as a "tit for tat" strategy, with the first cooperative move as, for example, in Axelrod 1984, which proved that this strategy maximizes the probability of survival.

The above situation can then be described as a "development trap," in which each agent, given the (assumed) actions of others, acts rationally, and yet the social outcome, the Nash equilibrium, is inefficient. There is now a relatively well-developed literature on how to model such development traps (see Stiglitz and Hoff 1999). They are characterized by multiple (Nash) equilibria, which may be Pareto ranked, and each may be Pareto inefficient in the sense that there exist some interventions that, in principle at least, could make some individuals better off without making anyone else worse off.

The situation in which an increasing number of agents do not pay their bills has its own dynamics, because an ever rising number of cheaters, under conditional morality (although conditional morality is not a necessary condition) produces increasingly more cheaters. The question, of course, is how to get out of a bad equilibrium and into a good one.

Multiple-equilibrium models imply interventions that may affect the equilibrium that is "chosen." Several might be appropriate in this situation:

1. To start with, the government leads by example (it does not cheat). It is very important that the government settle its bills on time. Otherwise (a) it creates a string of arrears and (b) it is very difficult on moral grounds for the government to act as a contract enforcer if it does not obey contracts itself. We return to this issue below.

2. The government vastly improves contract enforcement. Its ability to do so largely depends on the overall efficiency and level of corruption in the government and legal system. To the degree that

contract enforcement is poor, it helps create arrears, depresses lending, and thus depresses growth.

3. The introduction of foreign players may help greatly. Large and reputable foreign companies pay on time and create large networks of domestic companies, which become accustomed to fair and honest business. Gradually, a new culture of behavior spreads around the business sector. It works the same way as negative contagion, but with a different and positive sign. Here, however, the country might be faced with a chicken-and-egg problem: foreign direct investors might not want to enter unless the game is fair, and the game needs foreign players to become fair.

4. To a significant extent, the behavior of economic agents is also influenced by the battle of positive versus bad news spillovers. As Stiglitz once pointed out, in Silicon Valley, for example, people talk about how to earn money by innovating. That induces entrepreneurs to put all their efforts into that activity. It is no wonder then that there are lots of innovations. In Croatia, a large number of "entrepreneurs" set an example by evading taxes, getting good deals through political connections, corruption, and illegal activities. There is news coverage of this. It is no wonder then that the different role model produces a different outcome (an increase in tax evasion). Therefore, it is very important that the government be ready to exploit the "windows of opportunity" to tilt the bad equilibrium and start to produce positive information/spillovers.

Poor contract enforcement and lack of adverse consequences to reputations (which usually accompany endemic cases of weak financial discipline) are the main reasons behind arrears, although various incentives might remedy them as well. One such incentive is the borrowing costs in the market. If interest rates are high, as in Croatia in the late 1990s, arrears become an attractive source of short-term finance. "Lack of financial discipline" might also be viewed as an asymmetry between the incentives for paying domestic and foreign creditors (asymmetric enforcement of rules between residents and nonresidents, which in some cases hurts nonresidents, as in Russia, but in Croatia hurts residents).

Moreover, soft budget constraints might be relevant for the choice of the exchange rate regime. In the absence of the (formal or informal) enforcement of rules, domestic payments due can wait, if such behavior pays off for the debtor. For example, it pays for a net debtor to buy foreign exchange now and run domestic arrears, if there is no enforcement or there are no serious adverse consequences to his reputation from doing so. Everybody delays payments: importers, debtors, and even exporters, who have incentives to run domestic arrears as long as they expect depreciation (because later they will get more units of domestic currency for a unit of foreign currency). Consequently, even small changes in the expected value of the currency can lead to large disruptions in domestic payments, if the foreign and domestic currencies are close substitutes.

In terms of figure 8.3, a lack of financial discipline or serious reputational consequences of delayed payments shift the RR line even more strongly inward, so that for a given quality of banking supervision and degree of currency substitution, the optimum exchange rate flexibility is lower for a country with poor contract enforcement. Large exchange rate swings can have adverse consequences on domestic payments. On the other hand, however, a fixed exchange rate is more difficult to sustain in a country with soft budget constraints because arrears are an easy and cheap credit line for a domestic speculative attack on a currency. It is very hard to know whether a country suffers from financial delinquency of the type that calls for more exchange rate flexibility or for less. In any case, financial delinquency makes the choice of the monetary regime more difficult.

Fiscal Policy: Back to Some Unpleasant Monetarist Arithmetic?

Croatian financial (banking) fragility has shown that sound fiscal policy is neither a necessary nor a sufficient condition for the prevention of financial turmoil. This is an established finding (Diaz-Alejandro 1985). In fact, private sector (i.e., banking sector) successes and failures (not governmental ones) have been the prime drivers behind economic development in Croatia in the second stage of transition. Private capital inflows were the primary source of financing domestic demand growth and the current account deficit, which emerged during 1995–1999. The ratio of increase in public-sector foreign debt to BOP current account deficit (as a measure of the direct role the government sector plays in opening the current account gap) was at a maximum of 22.4 percent in 1997. This ratio was only 11.1 percent in 1995, the first year when the BOP current account deficit emerged, which points to private-sector behavior as a main reason behind the absorption of "foreign savings."[19]

Croatia's fiscal deficit was low in the second stage of transition (table 8.10), so the ratio of public debt to GDP remained more or less

Table 8.10
Fiscal indicators, 1994–1998

	1994	1995	1996	1997	1998
Revenues (consolidated central government, in millions of kuna)	36,882.3	43,283.1	48,396.6	53,345.3	65,110.6
Revenues as percentage of GDP	42.2	44.0	44.8	43.4	48.0
Expenditures (consolidated central government, in millions of kuna)	35,469.3	44,166.1	48,874.0	54,931.9	64,228.5
Expenditures as percentage of GDP	40.6	44.9	45.3	44.7	47.3
Balance (in millions of kuna)	1,413.0	−883.0	−477.4	−1,586.7	882.1
Balance as percentage of GDP	1.6	−0.9	−0.4	−1.3	0.7
Foreign financing	−13.0	755.2	931.1	3,111.7	86.8
Foreign financing as percentage of GDP	0.0	0.8	0.9	2.5	0.1
Foreign financing as percentage of BOP current account balance[a]	−1.6	11.1	20.1	22.4	0.9
Domestic financing	−1,400.0	127.9	−453.7	−1,525.1	−968.9
Domestic financing as percentage of GDP	−1.6	0.1	−0.4	−1.2	−0.7
Banks' claims on government as percentage of banks' total assets (end year)	32.9	27.6	24.9	18.0	16.1
Expenditures /M4 (in percent)	203.0	180.0	133.6	109.1	113.6
Real rate of growth of expenditures		22.1	6.9	8.5	10.6
Real rate of growth of GDP	5.9	6.8	6.0	6.5	2.7
Budgetary central government expenditures – budget plan[b]		28,956.8	31,621.7	33,854.7	37,477.4 (42,754.6)
Outcome		28,476.6	30,972.8	34,395.2	41,473.2
[Outcome – budget plan]/GDP (in percent)		−0.5	−0.6	0.4	3.0 (−1.0)
Balance of budgetary central government (in millions of kuna)	2,410.3	1,791.5	3,775.6	4,436.7	9,683.2
Balance as percentage of GDP	2.8	1.8	3.5	3.6	7.1
Balance of extrabudgetary funds	−997.3	−2,674.6	−4,253.0	−6,023.4	−8,801.1
Balance as percentage of GDP	−1.1	−2.7	−3.9	−4.9	−6.5

Source: Monthly *Statistical Review* of the Ministry of Finance, various issues; Croatian National Bank *Bulletin*, May 1999; Croatian Bureau of Statistics.

[a] This indicator shows the direct role of the central government in financing the current account deficit. Note that in 1994, the current account was in surplus and foreign debt was net repaid, so the indicator turned out to be negative. In the other four years, the current account was in deficit whereas foreign debt was on the rise, so the indicator was positive by definition.

[b] By mid-1998, the budget plan had been revised. The originally planned figure is in the first row and the revised figure is in parentheses below.

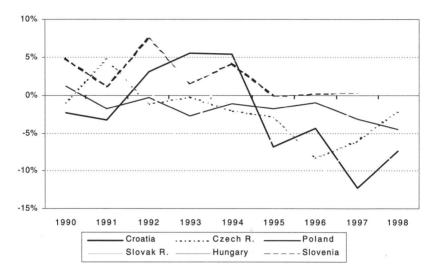

Figure 8.4
Current account deficit in the transition countries (as a percentage of GDP)
Sources: WIIW 1998 and Croatian Bureau of Statistics.

constant. In 1994 and 1998, there were fiscal (consolidated central government) surpluses of 1.6 percent and 0.7 percent of GDP, respectively, whereas during 1995–1997, the fiscal deficit averaged 0.9 percent of GDP per year (see figure 8.4). Domestic public debt arose mainly in the context of bank rehabilitation. Despite these circumstances, domestic public debt was on the decline after 1994. The annual average value of the net repayment of the domestic public debt in terms of GDP was 0.8 percentage points. The only exception was 1995, because the domestic debt in that year was growing at the modest rate of 0.1 percentage points of GDP, but that was the year when Croatia was almost entirely liberated.

A main reason for the rapid decline in the domestic indebtedness of the Croatian government was the interest rate differential. The government raised its level of debt abroad because the interest rate was much lower. Domestic interest rates were higher among other reasons because of expected depreciation. The government perceived foreign interest costs to be lower than those at home because it did not share the same exchange rate expectations with the domestic private sector (the government expected a stronger currency). Therefore, domestic public debt was dropping while foreign public debt was on the rise. The annual average growth of new public debt held by nonresidents during 1994–1998 in terms of GDP was 0.9 percent. Data in table 8.10 point to the fact that 1997 marked the highest increase in the government's net foreign indebtedness, in an amount of 2.5 percent of GDP (22.4 percent of the current account deficit). That was the year when Croatia received an investment grade from leading credit rating agencies, which, of course, made access to foreign financing much easier.

As a consequence, by the end of the 1990s, Croatian financial instruments were held primarily by foreign investors, whereas the domestic market for public debt remained largely underdeveloped. Nevertheless, some good came out of this. The changing structure of financing in favor of foreign sources led to a crowding-in of domestic investment. The share of claims on the government in Croatian banks' total assets decreased from 42.2 percent at the end of 1993 to 16.1 percent at the end of 1998.

Thus fiscal policymakers acted to control the public debt, which yielded fruits in terms of the crowding-in of the private-sector investment. They did not act in the same manner, however, regarding fiscal policy in general. Actually, although it was very efficient in the microeconomic sphere (in relation to the elimination of tax distortions—for example, the introduction of a flat-rate value-added tax [VAT] instead of a multirate sales tax or improved tax collection), the country's fiscal policy failed to adjust to the trends in the real sector.

A closer look at revenues and expenditures points to a high fiscal burden on the economy, which characterizes almost all advanced transition economies (Faulend and Šošić 1999). Moreover, the data in table 8.10 point to the particular problem of a growing fiscal burden. The years 1995 and 1998 were critical in this respect. The real rate of the growth of expenditures was clearly out of line with the growth of real output in those two years. Public expenditures to the GDP ratio were growing rapidly (4.3 percentage points of GDP in 1995 and 2.6 percentage points of GDP in 1998). The growing fiscal burden was associated with a move from a surplus of 1.6 percent of GDP in 1994 to a deficit of 0.9 percent of GDP in 1995. This means that Croatian fiscal expansion was reflected not only in a growing share of public expenditures in GDP but also in a worsening of the fiscal balance by 2.5 percentage points of GDP from 1994 to 1995. The main reasons for this change in fiscal policy were the successful military campaigns that liberated territory in 1995.

The change that occurred in 1998 was substantially different from that which occurred in 1995, because it happened during peacetime and was not associated with a widening deficit. On the contrary, a shift of +2 percentage points occurred in the GDP between 1997 and 1998 (from a deficit of 1.3 percent in 1997 to a surplus of 0.7 percent in 1998). The ratio of expenditures to GDP increased by 2.6 percentage points, but the ratio of revenues to GDP increased much more, by 4.7 percentage points, in comparison to 1997. This large shift was associated with the introduction, as of January 1, 1998, of the VAT, which has brought revenues far in excess of the original budget plan, so that the final outcome of public expenditures for 1998 was four billion kuna (3 percent of GDP) higher than expected before the introduction of the new tax system.[20] Higher VAT revenues than expected were the prime reason for the revision of the country's budget plan in mid-1998. Instead of using the opportunity to lower the country's high payroll taxes, however, the revision increased expenditures.

The budget planning errors in Croatia were not made exclusively within the Ministry of Finance itself. The main reasons for these errors were related to the following: (1) confusion between the growth of value added and the liquidity effect of the introduction of the VAT among politicians, who immediately saw the opportunity to realize ambitious expenditure plans, and (2) failure to adjust fiscal policy for the growth slowdown in the second half of 1998, which is, again, linked to (1).

Confusion between the growth of value added and the liquidity effect of the introduction of the VAT resulted when, immediately after the implementation of the new tax system, public revenues recorded nominal growth rates 40 percent higher than compared to the previous year. Most people knew that the VAT system would diminish tax evasion and increase tax discipline and that there would be some positive initial liquidity effect, but nobody was able to calculate the numbers and assign them to specific causes. Moreover, the Croatian Ministry of Finance traditionally involved itself in a dangerous game of political economy by announcing its growth projections together with its budget plan for each year. Hence, in November of each year, the government submitted its budget plan to the Croatian parliament, initiating public debate about the level and growth of GDP, usually with the purpose of enabling the government to say that the real growth of planned revenues was lower than the expected real growth of output. This was political dynamite. Mishkin (1999, 37) speaks about the problem in general: "Such an announcement is highly problematic because estimates of potential GDP growth are far from precise and change over time. Announcing a specific number for potential GDP growth may thus indicate a certainty that policymakers may not have and may also cause the public to mistakenly believe that this estimate is actually a fixed target for potential GDP growth."

An ex post facto look at the data shows that the ratio of revenues to GDP has a record of remarkable stability in Croatia, given the GDP measurement problems and the fact that Croatia is a postwar country. It was not realistic to expect a rapid decline in the fiscal shares in the GDP during the rebuilding, reconstruction, and consolidation of the fiscal administration under peacetime conditions. Decreases in military and police expenditures (which still left them with high relative shares) could compensate neither for the costs of a much needed stable and efficient public administration during peacetime nor for rising wage demands based on earners' desires to catch up to prewar consumption levels.

Public demands mainly took the form of wage demands by public servants as well as demands for pension increases. Moreover, the number of civil servants was growing constantly. These demands were strongly fueled by extraordinary VAT revenues at the outset of implementation, as well as by announcements of high expected GDP by the Ministry of Finance. Two extrabudgetary funds, the pension and health funds, started to increase deficits (which increased for all the extrabudgetary funds from 1.1 percent of GDP in 1994 to 6.5 percent of GDP in 1998). These deficits were covered by the higher surpluses of the budgetary central government (which increased from 2.8 percent of GDP in 1994 to 7.1 percent of GDP in 1998). Although it became increasingly popular in Croatia to criticize government officials for luxury, it was very unpopular to point to extrabudgetary funds as the main sources of fiscal problems, because that would mean asking tough questions: Can we afford the present level of public health services? Can we afford such pensions for such a large number of people and specifically for some groups with high pensions?[21] The questions were equally embarrassing for the leading party and the opposition.

The 1998 increase in the deficit of extrabudgetary funds was a byproduct of the successful introduction of the VAT, which brought a

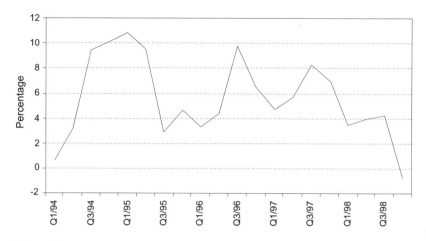

Figure 8.5
Quarterly estimate of GDP (relative to same quarter in previous year)
Source: Croatian Bureau of Statistics.

general feeling in Croatia that there were huge sums of money at the government's disposal. This amounted to a call for a race on funds by the various ministries, lobbies, and public-sector unions.

Hence the introduction of the VAT has been by far the most important event in the recent fiscal history of Croatia. No political power in Croatia could have prevented the strong upsurge in government consumption when revenues started to grow above expectations after the introduction of the new tax system. Unrealistic wage and pension demands permanently reduced the scope for public investment and widened the already wide gap between the budgetary central government surplus and extrabudgetary deficit of funds. Fiscal revenues and expenditures' share in GDP increased in 1998, and the government lost the ability to adjust fiscal policy for the cycle. A great opportunity was missed to reduce the high direct taxes on wages instead of raising government consumption.

As GDP growth slowed in early 1998 and the GDP later (in the last quarter of 1998) started to drop (figure 8.5), the Croatian government had no space in which to maneuver to compensate for the lower revenues. High hopes continued during the budgetary planning process for 1999, since the government was basing its budget plan on a real output growth of 5 percent. This soon turned out to be unrealistic, especially after the NATO military campaign in Yugoslavia began in March 1999. Expenditures, however, continued to be real-

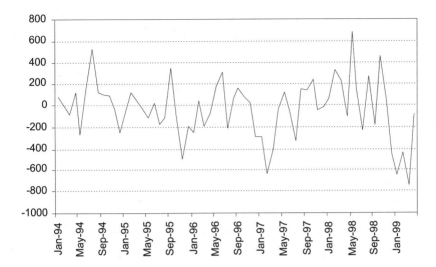

Figure 8.6
Budgetary central government monthly balances (in millions of kuna)
Source: Ministry of Finance *Monthly Bulletin.*

ized as projected, so a large deficit opened in the last quarter of 1998 and the first quarter of 1999 (figure 8.6). Currency depreciated and real output continued to drop, indicating that in the short run there was no possibility for expansionary fiscal policy to act as a stabilization tool. This is consistent with other empirical findings for developing countries (Agenor, McDermott, and Prasad 1999) as well as with the indications that the fiscal deficit in recessions can behave in a procyclical fashion[22] because of a crowding-out in countries with narrow and shallow financial markets: "An alternative possibility is that a tightening in government finances could lead to increases in future output growth by, for instance, 'crowding in' private investment and by signaling the future stability of domestic macroeconomic policy, thereby stimulating foreign investment" (Agenor, McDermott, and Prasad 1999, 12). Other reasons for such effects of fiscal policy in Croatia have been discussed extensively in this chapter: arrears and a lack of credibility. Experience in Croatia shows that they might[23] have a very significant impact on transition.

It has been shown that, given poor contract enforcement, expected exchange rate depreciation might lead to an accumulation of arrears. One possible channel for expansionary fiscal policy to work in this manner when the economy is already in a recession is that expansionary policy leads to exchange rate depreciation, the growth of arrears, and consequently, a loss of credibility, investment, and output. A necessary condition for fiscal expansion to have such adverse consequences is for the deficit to be at least partly financed domestically (otherwise, the FX inflow finances the deficit, and there is no direct reason for currency depreciation). Another more direct channel of influence is via government arrears. A government that is not able to adjust expenditures downward and meet its borrowing requirements by issuing debt on domestic or foreign markets has only two options: increase its debt with the central bank or accumulate arrears. The accumulation of government arrears leads to a loss of fiscal credibility and a decline in confidence in the government, with a likely adverse impact on expectations, investment, and growth. Increasing its debt with the central bank without a limit leads to a loss of general (both fiscal and monetary) credibility and inflation, again with a likely adverse impact on expectations, investment, and growth. Probably the only difference between the two scenarios is that credibility is entirely lost by all parties in the second scenario, whereas the central bank still retains some credibility in the first scenario with arrears. Preserving some credibility for at least one institution can help recovery later, when fiscal policy adjusts. Government arrears in this sense can be interpreted as a sign of a strong central bank, which is a prerequisite for fiscal policy adjustment.

In the case of Croatia, it is not possible to say much more about fiscal policy in the second stage of transition because of the lack of precise fiscal data on an accrual basis (fiscal accounts are compiled on a cash basis). The following occurred simultaneously in Croatia, however, events in late 1998 and early 1999:

1. Output dropped, currency lost value, and the fiscal surplus after the introduction of the VAT turned into a deficit by late 1998.

2. Anecdotal evidence indicates that both government arrears and arrears in general grew during the second half of 1998.[24]

3. The government was fueling overly optimistic expectations and postponing downward adjustment by announcing high output growth targets.[25]

In Croatia, government arrears emerged because the strength of the central bank was partly rooted in the Central National Bank Act, which defines the value of the currency as a prime target for the central bank and sets a limit on credit extended by the central bank to the government at 5 percent of the annual fiscal expenditures. If the institutional position of the central bank were weaker, that is, if fiscal policy were clearly dominant over monetary policy, then inflationary financing would be an optimal solution (Sargent and Wallace 1981). Collective preferences, however, as expressed by the Central National Bank Act make monetary policy powerful in setting limits on the free use of money by fiscal policy. In fact, this legal choice might have some long-run collective rationality, since currency substitution makes money demand in Croatia extremely sensitive to both inflation and currency depreciation. Very high inflation is therefore needed for the ratio of seigniorage to GDP to increase substantially, which probably means that the fiscal benefits from the moderate inflation tax are much lower than the moderate inflation costs for the society as a whole.[26]

Interestingly, Croatia has never had a classic clash between fiscal and monetary policy in a political arena. In the early days of stabilization (1993–1994), a sound fiscal policy actually enlarged the maneuvering space for monetary policy, and fiscal policy should be given credit for that. From 1994 to 1997, the CNB kept its net credit to the government negative. Then came 1998–1999, however, which brought the need for fiscal adjustment once the recession started. The government tried expansionary fiscal policy as a stabilization tool, but it failed because the drop in activity was supply side driven, induced by large-scale failures of companies and related banks in which ownership was typically not separated from control. This points to fiscal tightening (to induce crowding-in) as a proper policy response in a transition-type recession. Croatia has to learn it; economists have to prove it and then share this knowledge with policymakers. After times of a happy fiscal and monetary mix based on a common understanding of the benefits of low inflation has now come a time of searching for a new common understanding, this time about the speed and signs of proper fiscal policy responses in a complex macroeconomic environment of transition.

International Trade, FDIs, and Isolation

Together with GDP and wages (see figure 8.7), imports were subdued in Croatia during the war because of extremely low domestic

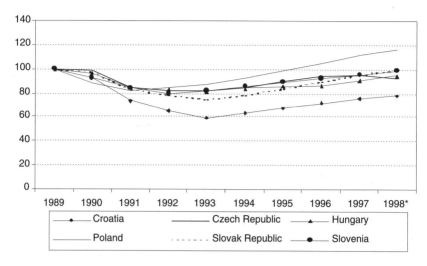

Figure 8.7
GDP in Central and Eastern Europe (1989 = 100)
Source: EBRD *Transition Report Update*, April 1999.
*EBRD estimates.

demand. This resulted in a current account surplus during most of the war period. Once the war ended and incomes increased, imports exploded. The revival of domestic demand buoyed by the postwar consumer catchup, optimism, and increased wages was followed in 1997 by the opening of the banks to the household sector. Loans to the household sector in that year more than doubled (from a relatively low base), which additionally boosted domestic demand and helped create a large current account deficit of 12.2 percent of GDP. Additionally, two one-off effects spurred huge import growth: expectation of the introduction of the VAT and the tariff exemptions granted to veterans and other members of the population affected by the war (see Vujčić and Presečan 1997). Once the one-off effects expired and monetary policy was tightened, the trend was reversed, and the current account deficit was substantially adjusted downward, although it remained relatively high until 2000.[27] All transition countries except Slovenia financed their development in the 1990s by running current account deficits, which is a desirable way of solving the intertemporal problems of emerging economies. In a comparative perspective, however, Croatia along with Slovakia, recorded the highest external deficit of all the advanced transition countries in the late 1990s and should therefore be careful about future financing

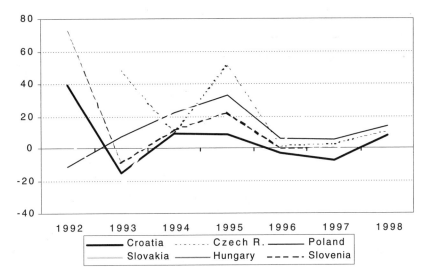

Figure 8.8
Export growth in the transition countries (yearly, in percent)
Sources: Vienna Institute and Croatian Bureau of Statistics.

sustainability. In 2000 deficit declined substantially, so that this warning now sounds outdated.

More worrisome than the current account deficit, however, has been Croatia's flat export performance in the late 1990s (see figure 8.8). Even when the war effect is factored in, Croatian trade performance has been quite disappointing. When they are compared to those of other advanced transition countries, it becomes particularly obvious how Croatian exports underperform. Even when the war ended and the country's GDP started to recover, no growth of exports materialized that would be comparable to the achievements in other advanced Central and Eastern European countries. The remarkable GDP recovery of Croatia's GDP in the postwar period was, in other words, based on an expansion in domestic demand.

The breakup of Yugoslavia, which coincided with the beginning of the transition period in Croatia, had two opposite consequences for Croatian openness and trade. On the one hand, by definition, it made Croatia a more open economy, as more of its GDP (which was previously traded with the former Yugoslav republics) became part of international trade (which explains the large export growth presented in figure 8.8 for both Croatia and the Czech Republic, which had become divorced from Slovakia at the same time). On the other hand, the war immediately started to influence Croatian trade negatively, because most of the links were broken with the eastern parts of the former common country, which was a natural export market for domestic producers (as opposed to the case of the velvet divorce of Czechoslovakia, whereby these links were preserved), and because the economy slumped into a much worse recession than it would have without the war.

Some pieces of evidence on Croatian export competitiveness point to the decrease in the relative Croatian export potential. Vujčić and Presečan 1997 uses the Gruber-Lloyd index, and Kumar and Zajc 1999 uses the Gruber-Lloyd index as well as the Revealed Comparative Advantage (RCA) indices on a more recent set of data. Both articles demonstrate that the intraindustry integration of the Croatian economy with the EU is substantially lower than in other advanced CEFTA countries. To the extent that a lower level of intraindustry integration is an indicator of the trade potential of an economy, the Croatian export industry does not look good. The RCA results also suggest a relatively strong bias of Croatian exports toward labor-intensive sectors, whereas resource-based industry is underrepresented. The largest negative gap between the RCA value and export share is recorded in the capital-intensive sector, which in addition shows a clearly negative tendency.

It should be pointed out that Croatia has always been a trade deficit country, but it has been able to make up for much of its trade deficit through a service (mainly tourism) surplus. A better indicator of its relative export performance is therefore the export of goods and services.

Figure 8.9 compares the export of goods and services per capita in various transition countries in 1997. Here, the relative position of Croatia looks better, although only better than the Baltic States, Bulgaria and Macedonia, since Poland and Romania (which are in any case performing poorly on the export front) are not comparably small and open economies. One can expect that further recovery of tourism in Croatia will increase export performance. It is quite dangerous, however, for the country to rely heavily on a tourism as a dominant export industry, since it is a relatively low value–added sector and in addition, one that is sensitive to bad news, which has proven to be quite a disadvantage in this region. The share of tourism in the current account revenues in Croatia is comparable only to

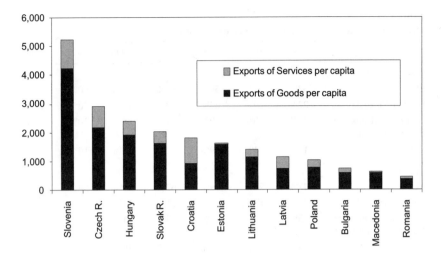

Figure 8.9
Exports of goods and services per capita, 1997 (in U.S. dollars)
Sources: WIIW 1998 and Croatian Bureau of Statistics.

that of Greece among the EU countries, which is not very encouraging, given that Greece is lagging behind the EU core.

There are several reasons for such a relatively disappointing export performance in Croatia, of which we would like to point out the most important in our judgment:

• *Tourism has been a hostage to the war and the subsequent regional instability.* It is straightforward to conclude that the war and instability in the region since the beginning of the transition process have had an enormous impact on the main Croatian export industry. The potential for the recovery and further development of the tourism industry is huge, but such recovery and development will not happen quickly.

• *Exports were hostage to the lack of trade associations.* Croatian trade is oriented toward the EU as its most important trading partner (table 8.11). Much less trade is with the markets of the former Yugoslavia (including Slovenia), and even less with other Central and Eastern European countries (excluding Slovenia). The 1998 increase in exports to "other" countries shown in table 8.11 is due to exports of ships to Liberia.

In contrast to the Central and Eastern European countries that have signed association agreements with the EU, the share of Croatian

Table 8.11
Merchandise trade by destination (as percentage of total)

	1992	1993	1994	1995	1996	1997	1998
Exports, f.o.b.							
EU	53%	57%	59%	58%	51%	50%	48%
Former Yugoslavia	22%	29%	23%	23%	27%	30%	26%
Central and Eastern European countries[a]	14%	0%	9%	9%	8%	10%	10%
Other	12%	14%	9%	10%	14%	10%	17%
Imports, c.i.f.							
EU	47%	56%	59%	62%	59%	59%	59%
Former Yugoslavia	23%	17%	11%	11%	11%	10%	11%
Central and Eastern European countries[a]	5%	4%	11%	9%	11%	12%	12%
Other	25%	23%	19%	17%	19%	18%	18%

Source: Croatian Bureau of Statistics.
[a] Excluding former YU.

trade with the EU is gradually declining (table 8.12). The extent of Croatian exclusion from trade agreements is well illustrated in table 8.13. The lack of the trade association agreements hurts Croatian exports through various channels:

1. The tariffs that Croatian exporters face are generally higher than those for exporters from other Central and Eastern European countries, and the difference is growing larger over time.

2. The rule of origin in the EU and CEFTA countries works against Croatian exporters: Many have lost their partners because of the rule or have been unable to find partners.

3. Foreign investors are reluctant to invest in Croatia as long as it has no association agreement that provides a clear schedule of the trade relations with the absolutely dominant market in the region: that of the EU.

In addition, export access to other markets among Central and Eastern European countries has also been hampered by the lack of a CEFTA trade agreement for Croatia (which is itself dependent on the EU association agreement).

• *Missing FDIs.* It is well documented in the literature that there is a positive correlation among FDIs, export performance, and growth in emerging markets, particularly those of transition countries (see, for example, Stankovsky 1996; Hoekman and Djankov 1996; and

Table 8.12
Trade with EU (as percentage of total trade)

	1990	1992	1993	1994	1995	1996	1997
Exports							
Bulgaria	5.6	31.5	30.0	37.6	37.7	39.1	43.3
Czech Republic	38.4	61.6	49.4	54.1	60.9	58.2	59.9
Croatia	59.9	52.5	57.5	59.4	57.7	51.0	49.8
Hungary	54.1	62.3	58.1	72.0	69.3	69.8	77.5
Poland	52.7	65.7	69.2	69.2	70.0	66.2	64.0
Romania	44.1	35.2	41.3	56.0	61.7	62.2	64.8
Slovak Republic	45.6	50.1	29.5	39.3	40.9	44.8	42.0
Slovenia	64.8	78.6	63.2	65.6	67.0	64.6	63.3
Imports							
Bulgaria	11.5	35.5	32.8	37.5	37.2	35.1	37.3
Czech Republic	40.5	58.9	52.3	55.7	61.1	62.4	61.5
Croatia	54.9	47.5	56.4	59.2	62.1	59.4	59.5
Hungary	43.1	60.0	54.4	61.1	61.5	59.8	62.8
Poland	51.1	62.0	64.7	65.3	64.7	63.9	63.8
Romania	44.1	35.2	41.4	56.0	61.6	62.2	64.8
Slovak Republic	44.8	46.4	27.9	33.4	34.8	37.3	39.5
Slovenia	69.0	74.3	65.6	69.2	76.9	67.5	67.4

Source: The Vienna Institute for International Economic Studies, *Handbook of Statistics: Countries in Transition,* Vienna, 1998.

Borensztein, DeGregorio, and Wha-Lee 1994). The most obvious and most often cited example is Hungary, which has received the most FDI of all the transition countries (figure 8.10) and has recorded very good export performance since. Approximately 80 percent of Hungary's exports have their origin in FDIs. The positive impact of FDIs on exports is characteristic not only of emerging economies but also of the OECD countries. The EU examples of Ireland or Portugal are well known (see, for example, Walsh 1996).

Compared to other advanced Central and Eastern European countries, Croatia has received relatively little FDI, mainly because of the war and the overall political situation in the region, the lack of trade associations with EU/CEFTA, and protection of the vested interests within the country.

In addition, labor costs increased substantially in the second stage of transition. As with unemployment/employment, wages also chiefly mirrored the main real-sector trends during the transition

Table 8.13
Central and Eastern Europe: Trade arrangements

	WTO	CEFTA	PHARE	OBNOVA	Bilateral agreement with EFTA	Other bilateral agreements
Bulgaria	Yes	No	Yes	No	Yes	Czech Republic, Slovak Republic
Croatia	No	No	No	Yes	No	Slovenia, Macedonia
Czech Republic[c]	Yes	Yes	Yes	No	Yes	Bulgaria, Romania
Estonia	Yes	No	Yes	No	Yes	Slovak Republic, Slovenia
Hungary	Yes	Yes	Yes	No	Yes	Israel
Latvia	Yes	Yes	Yes	No	Yes	Slovak Republic, Slovenia
Lithuania	Yes	No	Yes	No	Yes	Slovenia
Poland	Yes	Yes	Yes	No	Yes	—
Romania	Yes	No	Yes	No	Yes	Czech Republic, Slovak Republic
Slovak Republic[c]	Yes	Yes	Yes	No	Yes	Bulgaria, Estonia, Israel
Slovenia	Yes	Yes	Yes	No	Yes	Bulgaria, Croatia, Estonia, Latvia, Lithuania, Macedonia

Source: International Monetary Fund.

[a] Date agreement came into force.

[b] A negative opinion implies that the European Commission's assessment of the country in question is that it is not ready to start accession discussions.

[c] The Czech Republic and the Slovak Republic have a customs union agreement. The Czech and Slovak Federal Republic (CSFR) signed a trade and cooperation agreement in May 1990 and an association agreement in December 1991. Following the dissolution of the CSFR, separate association agreements and supplementary protocols to the interim agreement were signed with each of the successor republics.

[d] An association agreement was signed in June 1996, but it is still in the process of ratification.

EU trade cooperation agreement[a]	EU autonomous preferential trade regime	EU interim agreement[a]	EU association agreement[a]	EU membership application	EU commission opinion[b]
November 1990	No	December 1993	February 1995	December 1995	Negative
November 1990	Yes	No	No	No	No
November 1990	No	March 1992	February 1995	January 1996	Positive
March 1993	No	No	February 1998	November 1995	Positive
December 1988	No	March 1992	February 1994	March 1994	Positive
February 1993	No	No	February 1998	October 1995	Negative
February 1994	No	No	February 1994	December 1995	Negative
December 1989	No	March 1992	February 1995	April 1994	Positive
May 1991	No	May 1993	February 1995	June 1995	Negative
November 1990	No	March 1992	February 1995	June 1995	Negative
September 1993	No	January 1997	June 1996[d]	June 1996	Positive

process (see figure 8.11): First, there was a huge slump at the beginning of the 1990s, with real wages bottoming out in the first quarter of 1993 at only 28 percent of their prewar level. This has been more a consequence of the war than of transition. Only war can cause and bring people to accept such a dramatic decline in the standard of living. The recovery picked up after the successful launch of a stabilization program in October 1993. The quick catchup stage lasted until mid-1995. Currently, only Slovenia has higher gross dollar wages than Croatia, which makes Croatian labor relatively expensive compared to that in other Central and Eastern European countries, which in itself is a partial reason for the lack of FDIs in Croatia, although certainly not the primary one.

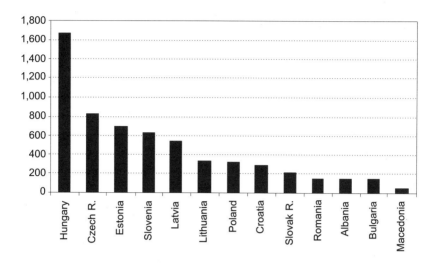

Figure 8.10
Cumulative foreign direct investment inflows, 1989–1997, per capita (in U.S. dollars)
Source: EBRD.

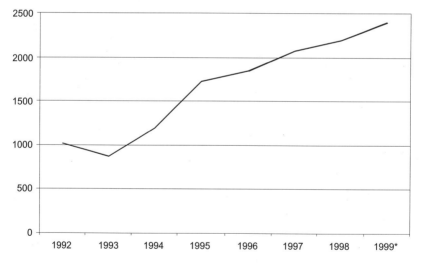

Figure 8.11
Real average net wage (HRK-constant prices, January 1994)
Source: Croatian Bureau of Statistics.
*January–October.

Employment, Unemployment, and Structural Change

This concluding section is devoted to what transition is really about: the reallocation of resources.

The Croatian output transition story is similar to the typical U-pattern observed in other countries (see figure 8.7). The important difference is that the Croatian inflexion point was lower than in other transition countries (except for Bulgaria), because in Croatia transition coincided with a war. That makes Croatia, together with, to an even greater extent, Bosnia and Herzegovina, a Central and Eastern European example of a country that went through a war during the first stage of transition.

The employment/unemployment picture in Croatia accurately mirrors output developments, as was the case with other Central and Eastern European transition countries,[28] with the exception of the Czech Republic.[29]

As in other transition countries, unemployment shot up very quickly in Croatia once the transition process started. The Croatian case has two specific features, however, generally not found in other transition countries. First, unlike the other transition countries (except the former Yugoslavia), open unemployment existed in Croatia long before the transition process started. In other words, only part of the country's unemployment was hidden; the rest was already an open unemployment problem at the beginning of transition. In 1990, immediately before transition started, the unemployment rate in Croatia was already 9 percent. To the extent that not all unemployment was disguised, initial transition had a smaller effect on the unemployment rate in Croatia than in other countries.

Second, unlike in other Central and Eastern European transition countries (except Bosnia and Herzegovina), Croatia went through a war in its first years of transition, which resulted in a deeper recession than it would have otherwise undergone. To the extent that the war contributed to the slump in the early 1990s, the unemployment increase was higher than if it were due solely to the beginning of the transition process.

Because these two specific features cancel each other out to some extent, the expected unemployment increase occurred in Croatia during the first years of transition. It was higher than that in other Central and Eastern European countries, however, mainly because of the war (see figure 8.12).

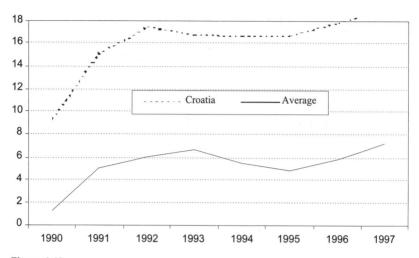

Figure 8.12
Unemployment rate in Croatia, 1990–1997 (employment office figures) (in percent)
Sources: WIIW 1998 and Croatian Bureau of Statistics.

Lack of reliable data prevents us from drawing a precise conclusion
on the level and trend of unemployment in Croatia. An ILO-based
labor force survey was first conducted in Croatia in 1996. Before that,
there was no reliable source of information on labor market statistics
in the country, partly because until 1995, almost a third of the territory was effectively under military occupation, and partly because
although the Croatian Bureau of Statistics accurately recorded the
demise of the old socialist sector, it was much less efficient in recording the emergence of many small and medium-sized companies
and the employment therein. Moreover, the Croatian unemployment
registry has been assigned many of the welfare state's functions. As
a result, employment statistics for Croatia have been biased downward and unemployment statistics upward.

This is well demonstrated by comparing the rate of unemployment
registered through employment offices with that obtained through
the internationally comparable International Labor Organization
(ILO) labor force survey. The two sources paint very different pictures of the unemployment situation in Croatia. The unemployment
rate registered through Croatian employment offices is much higher[30]
in comparison to the average for Central and Eastern European
countries than the rate based on ILO methodology.[31] Whatever the
source of the data used, however, it shows the unemployment prob-

lem in Croatia is serious, and more importantly, that unemployment in the country is on the rise. Dealing with this problem is not going to be easy. Much of the unemployment in Croatia has structural roots, although labor market regulation does not prevent flexibility to the extent that it does in the EU, so too much blame cannot be placed on that usual suspect. It will be important, however, not to allow new labor market rigidities to be introduced in the future, especially once the association process with the EU picks up.

The structural characteristics of much of the unemployment problem in Croatia are not surprising, given the rapid pace of the structural change in the first stage of transition. Structural change in the Croatian labor market has been characterized by a relatively rapid change in the structure of employment in a desirable direction. As shown by Vujčić (1998), Croatia was the most successful among the transition countries in terms of the speed and direction of its structural change[32] during the early years of the transition process. The process of labor market restructuring in Croatia, however, has mainly been a consequence of job destruction in sectors with high hidden unemployment rather than job creation in sectors with growth potential. The Croatian labor market has mostly mirrored developments in the real sector. Of course, this could have been expected, since the demand for labor is simply derived from the demand for the goods and services that it helps to produce.

The sectors in the Croatian economy that experienced the largest job losses (in terms of percentage of jobs lost) were manufacturing, in which employment was nearly halved, and agriculture, in which it decreased to a somewhat lesser extent. As overall employment fell dramatically, however (partly due to the war-related loss of population), the share of agriculture in total employment fell only slightly, whereas that of manufacturing fell somewhat more (see figures 8.13–8.16). Some additional job destruction would still be welcomed in Croatia, because the current level of employment is also reflected in the extent of arrears (soft budget constraints) and open subsidies, whose share in the budget has been constantly increasing.

Some workers who lost jobs in the Croatian manufacturing sector returned to agriculture as a primary activity, which then contributed to the less than desirable decline in the share of agriculture in total employment. Interestingly, it seems that in some countries—Romania, Poland, and Bulgaria—the same phenomenon has resulted in an actual rise in the share of agriculture in total employment.

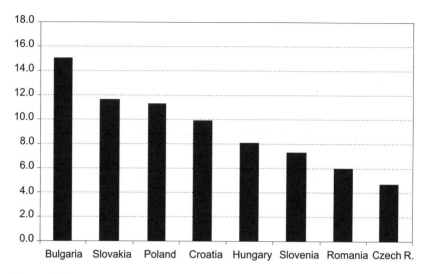

Figure 8.13
Unemployment rate (ILO figures), 1997 (in percent)
Sources: WIIW 1998 and Croatian Bureau of Statistics.

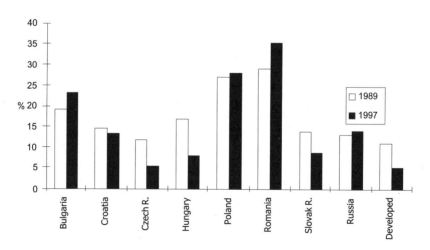

Figure 8.14
Employment in the primary sector
Sources: Commander and Tolstopiatenko 1995 and WIIW 1997.

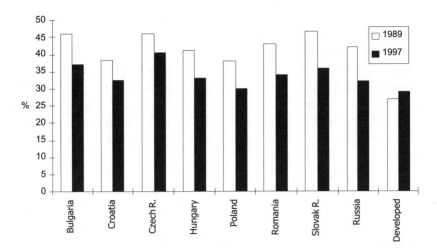

Figure 8.15
Employment in the secondary sector
Sources: Commander and Tolstopiatenko 1995 and WIIW 1997.

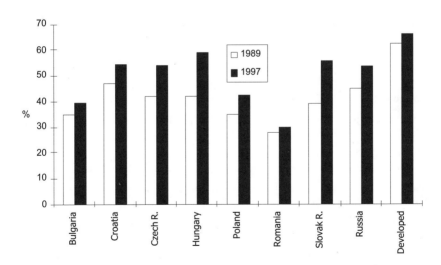

Figure 8.16
Employment in the tertiary sector
Sources: Commander and Tolstopiatenko 1995 and WIIW 1997.

Services, on the other hand, which were traditionally well developed in Croatia, increased their share of total employment even more. The two sectors of the economy that have recorded the highest job gains in Croatia since transition started are trade and finance. Nevertheless, these two sectors also remain potentially the highest job gainers in the future, since their share in overall employment is still much lower than in a typical OECD economy. There is considerable reallocation of resources yet to be done, and this is what transition is all about. In the next stage of transition, however, if the unemployment rate is to be lowered, most of the structural change should come in form of the job creation, rather than job destruction, which has characterized the first two stages of transition.

References

Agenor, P.-R., J. C. McDermott, and E. Prasad. 1999. Macroeconomic fluctuations in developing countries: Some stylized facts. Working paper 99/35, International Monetary Fund, Washington, D.C.

Anušić, Z. 1994. Ekonometrijska ocjena osnovnog ravnotežnog tečaja hrvatske kune (Econometric estimate of the fundamental equilibrium exchange rate of Croatian kuna). *Privredna kretanja i ekonomska politika* 33: 20–38.

Anušić, Z., Ž. Rohatinski, and V. Šonje, eds. 1995. *Road to low inflation: Croatia 1993–1994*. Zagreb: Government of the Republic of Croatia.

Axelrod, R. M. 1984. *The evolution of cooperation*. New York: Basic.

Babić, M., P. Jurković, and V. Šonje. 1999. Banking system development in Croatia. *Zagreb Journal of Economics* 3, no. 3: 75–113.

Balino, T. J. T., A. Bennett, E. Borensztein, eds. 1999. Monetary policy in dollarized economies. Occasional paper no. 171, International Monetary Fund, Washington, D.C.

Barro, R. J., and D. B. Gordon. 1983. A positive theory of monetary policy in a natural rate model. *Journal of Political Economy* 91, no. 4: 589–610.

Basu, K. 1999. On the goals of development. Paper presented at conference "Future of Development Economics in Perspective," Dubrovnik, Croatia, May.

Begg, D. H. 1996. Monetary policy in Central and Eastern Europe: Lessons after half a decade of transition. Working paper 108/96, International Monetary Fund, Washington, D.C.

Borensztein, E., J. DeGregorio, and Jong Wha-Lee. 1994. How does foreign direct investment affect growth? Working paper 110/94, International Monetary Fund, Washington, D.C.

Caprio, G., Jr., and D. Klingebiel. 1996. Bank insolvencies: Cross country experience. Working paper no. 1620, World Bank, Washington, D.C.

Commander, S., and Tolstopiatenko, A. 1995. *Unemployment, restructuring and the pace of the transition.* World Bank, Washington, D.C., and Moscow State University, Moscow.

Croatian National Bank (CNB). 1991. *Annual report.* Zagreb: CNB.

Croatian National Bank (CNB). 1997. Banks at the crossroads. Croatian National Bank Surveys no. 5, Zagreb.

Demirguc-Kunt, A., and E. Detragiache. 1998. The determinants of banking crises in developing and developed countries. *IMF Staff Papers* 45, no. 1: 77–124.

Diaz-Alejandro, Carlos. 1985. Good-bye financial repression, hello financial crash. *Journal of Development Economics* 19: 1–24.

Duck, N. 1993. Some international evidence on the quantity theory of money. *Journal of Money, Credit and Banking* 25, no. 1: 1–12.

Dziobek, C., and C. Pazarbasioglu. 1997. Lessons from systemic bank restructuring: A survey of 24 countries. Working paper 97/161, International Monetary Fund, Washington, D.C.

Faulend, M., and V. Šošić. 1999. Uravnoteženost proračuna, inflacija i ekonomski rast u tranzicijskim zemljama (Fiscal equilibrium, inflation, and economic growth in transition countries). Croatian National Bank, Zagreb. Mimeographed.

Frydl, E. J. 1999. The length and cost of banking crises. Working paper 99/30, International Monetary Fund, Washington, D.C.

Ghosh, A. R. 1997. Inflation in transition economies: How much? and why? Working paper 97/80, International Monetary Fund, Washington, D.C.

Ghosh, A. R., A.-M. Gulde, J. D. Ostry, and H. C. Wolf. 1997. Does the nominal exchange rate regime matter? Working paper no. 5874, National Bureau of Economic Research, Cambridge, Mass.

Guidotti, P., and C. Rodriguez. 1992. Dollarization in Latin America: Gresham's law in reverse? *IMF Staff Papers* 39: 518–44.

Hausmann, R., M. Gavin, C. Pagges-Sera, and E. Stein. 1999. Financial turmoil and the choice of the exchange rate regime. Working paper, Inter-American Development Bank, Washington, D.C.

Hellman, T., K. Murdock, and J. Stiglitz. 1998. Liberalization, moral hazard in banking, and prudential regulation: Are capital requirements enough? World Bank, Washington, D.C. Mimeographed.

Hoekman, B., and S. Djankov. 1996. Intra-industry trade, foreign direct investments and the reorientation of East European exports. Discussion paper 1377, Centre for Economic Policy Research, London.

Institute for Public Finance. 1997. Neslužbeno gospodorstvo u Republici Hrvatskoj (Unofficial eocnomy in Croatia). Zagreb. Mimeographed.

Jankov, L. 1999. Problemi banaka: uzroci, načini rješavanja i posljedice. Croatian National Bank, Zagreb, Mimeographed.

Kaminsky, G. L., and C. M. Reinhart. 1996. The twin crises: The causes of banking and balance of payments problems. International finance discussion paper 544, Board of Governors of the Federal Reserve System, Washington, D.C.

Kraft, E. 1999. Croatia's second banking crisis. Paper presented at Third International Conference on Enterprise in Transition, Split, Croatia, May 17–18.

Kumar, A., and K. Zajc. 1999. Selected integration potential indicators for Slovenia and Croatia. Paper presented at conference "Economic System of the EU and Adjustment of the Republic of Croatia," Rijeka, Croatia, April.

Kydland, F. E., and E. C. Prescott. 1977. Rules rather than discretion: The inconsistency of optimal plans. *Journal of Political Economy* 85, no. 6: 473–91.

Lindgren, C.-J., G. Garcia, and M. I. Saal. 1996. Bank soundness and macroeconomic policy. International Monetary Fund, Washington, D.C. Mimeographed.

Lovegrove, A. 1998. *The bank rehabilitation programme in Croatia*. Leatherhead, U.K.: Glendale Consulting.

McKinnnon, R., and H. Pill. 1995. Credible liberalizations and international capital flows: The overborrowing syndrome. Stanford University, Stanford, Calif. Mimeographed.

Menu, D. 1999. Macroeconomic stability in the economy and confidence and trust in the banking system. Paper presented at the third annual conference "Croatian Money Market," Zagreb, May 24–25.

Mishkin, F. S. 1999. International experiences with different monetary policy regimes. Working paper 6965, National Bureau of Economic Research, Cambridge, Mass.

Romer, D. 1993. Openness and inflation: Theory and evidence. *Quarterly Journal of Economics* 108, no. 4: 869–903.

Sahay, R., and C. Vegh. 1995. Dollarization in transition economies: Evidence and policy implications. Working paper 95/96, International Monetary Fund, Washington, D.C.

Sargent, T. J., and N. Wallace. 1981. Some unpleasant monetarist arithmetic. *Federal Reserve Bank of Minneapolis Quarterly Review* 5: 1–17.

Schwartz, A. J. 1973. Secular price change in historical perspective. *Journal of Money, Credit and Banking* 5, no. 1: 243–69.

Šonje, V. 1994. Utjecaj promjenjive rigidnosti cijena na ravnotežni nominalni tečaj hrvatske kune (Impact of changes in price rigidity on equilibrium nominal exchange rate of Croatian kuna). *Privredna kretanja i ekonomska politika* 34: 22–34.

Šonje, V., E. Kraft, and T. Dorsey. 1996. Monetary and exchange rate policy, capital inflows and the structure of the banking system in Croatia. Paper presented at Second Dubrovnik Conference on Economies in Transition, Dubrovnik, Croatia, June. Also in *Financial sector transformation: Lessons from economies in transition*, ed. M. Blejer and M. Škreb, 237–65. Cambridge: Cambridge University Press, 1999.

Šonje, V., and M. Škreb. 1995. Exchange rate and prices in a stabilization program: The case of Croatia. Paper presented at First Dubrovnik Conference on Economies in Transition, Dubrovnik, Croatia, June 7–9. Also in *Macroeconomic stabilization in transition economies*, ed. M. Blejer and M. Škreb, 212–33. Cambridge: Cambridge University Press, 1997.

Stankovsky, J. 1996. The role of FDI in Eastern Europe. *Austrian Economic Quarterly* 2: 109–20.

Stiglitz, J., and K. Hoff. 1999. Modern economic theory and development. Paper presented at conference "Future of Development Economics in Perspective," Dubrovnik, Croatia, May 13–14.

Vegh, C. 1989. The optimal inflation tax in the presence of currency substitution. *Journal of Monetary Economics* 24: 139–46.

Vujčić, B. 1998. Structural change in the Croatian labour market. *Zagreb Journal of Economics and Business* 1, no. 2: 107–25.

Vujčić, B., and T. Presečan. 1999. External deficit, exchange rate, and competitiveness in Croatia: Is there a problem? In *Balance of payments, exchange rates, and competitiveness in transition economies*, ed. M. Blejer and M. Škreb, 285–318. Boston/Dordrecht/London: Kluwer Academic.

Wagner, H. 1998. Central Banking in Transition Countries. Working paper 126/98, International Monetary Fund, Washington, D.C.

Walsh, B. 1996. Stabilization and adjustment in a small open economy: Ireland, 1979–95. *Oxford Review of Economic Policy* 12, no. 3: 74–86.

9 Fiscal Impulse of Transition: The Case of Slovenia

Velimir Bole

Introduction

In transforming government functions, the transition economies have been targeting the government's role in developed economies. Before transition started, many of the government functions normal in market economies (for example, social security) had been carried by enterprises; others had been almost absent or considered unnecessary (for example, creating a regulatory infrastructure for different markets and preventing environmental degradation). So expenditure and revenue functions as well as regulatory activities of the government in transitional economies have had be completely reshuffled to enable the government to be active in the same areas as in developed market economies.

Especially in the years of Kornai's "transformation depression," activities to implement such (long-term) goals in transforming government functions have been subordinated to the urgent transformation of some basic government functions necessary for the real-time support of the transformation process in other segments of the economy. So in the first years of transition, the scale and the dynamics of necessary reform of government activities were tuned to those faced by the business sector.

Among the most urgent changes in government functions in transition economies were building a new social safety net, alleviating the effects of restructuring in some segments of enterprises with a preprivatization phase (to back privatization), reshaping and strengthening tax administration, and establishing a regulatory infrastructure for different (especially financial) markets. In the period of transformation depression and immediately afterward, the transformation of these government functions was necessary to overcome two basic problems in the first phase of restructuring: massive collapse of enterprises and fast-increasing unemployment. In that phase, existing market structure and incentives, the state of the available social safety net, and the capacity of judicial bankruptcy procedures were insufficient to intermediate the restructuring of the economy alone. So the transformation of the above-mentioned government functions was actually the precondition for a sustainable transition of the economy toward a modern market economy.

Government activity supporting the dynamics of the restructuring of the economy obviously "contaminated" the fiscal stance of transition economies: The size and structure of government expenditures and revenues were different from the targeted values for the longer term. To evaluate the longer-term sustainability (controllability)[1] of the fiscal position of economies in transition, it is necessary to estimate such (one-time) changes in the fiscal stance caused by (discretionary) government activities directly supporting the transitional restructuring of the economy.

Analyzing the fiscal position of a country (and the size of fiscal impulse it faces), it is quite common not only to study less aggregated components, but also to adjust government expenditures (and balance) for cyclical component.[2] A similar approach could be used in the case of transition economies. By insulating the impact of transition on a country's fiscal position (a "transitional fiscal impulse") not only could "transition"-adjusted government expenditures (and the balance) be evaluated but also an appraisal of the sustainability (controllability) of the country's fiscal position could be made more easily.

There are several arguments against analyzing the transitional fiscal impulse on aggregate categories of fiscal position. First, there are important measurement and conceptual problems with using a country's budget deficit as a single measure of its fiscal stance, especially in developing economies; the breakdown of expenditures and revenues is important for evaluating fiscal position even for developed economies.[3] Second, governments often attempt to operationalize increased involvement in the economy through other (nonorthodox) instruments, usually quasi-fiscal activities and quasi regulations, if they want to increase their involvement in the economy but cannot (or do not want to) raise the level of taxation.[4] And third, the transitional fiscal impulse would have to encompass government measures targeted to problems created by a rocketing level of unemployment and enterprises in distress. But those measures have been, as a rule, discretionary, not discernable in aggregate categories. So the transitional fiscal impulse has to be evaluated by analyzing detailed components of public-sector revenue and spending, observing orthodox (traditional) and nonorthodox instruments.

The fiscal position in Slovenia did not change significantly until 1996, when the country's GDP attained the level it had had immediately before the beginning of transition. In the period between the start of transition and 1996, according to the values of the general government deficit and primary deficit, the country's fiscal position was stable (both indicators were in surplus). Besides, these indicators do not reveal any clear sign of transition-induced swings during that period. In the same period, especially in the first two years of transition, the Slovenian government launched several measures to mitigate the adverse effects of the accelerated collapse of enterprises and skyrocketing unemployment. Nevertheless, in the aggregate categories of the fiscal position, these government activities are not observable.

This chapter focuses on changes in Slovenia's fiscal position caused by discretionary fiscal measures (instruments) aimed at mitigating the adverse effects of the restructuring of the country's economy during transition. I argue that the period of such measures coincides with the period of transition decline in GDP. The analysis presented in the chapter quantifies fiscal position effects of corresponding traditional-orthodox instruments of government expenditure, the effects of public debt and guarantees instruments, and the fiscal position implications of other-nonorthodox tools of government intervention.

The rest of the chapter has the following structure. Arguments for the chosen period of transition-tuned fiscal policy are given in the next section, as well as a brief overview of transition fiscal policy instruments in Slovenia. The increase in public debt caused by swapping government bonds for transition-induced nonperforming assets in some segments of enterprises and banks is estimated in the third section, which also presents a description of the size and dynamics of those government guarantees, which were channeled to enterprises facing severe restructuring problems. The effects of transition fiscal policy on government expenditures (through orthodox instruments) are analyzed in the fourth section. In the fifth section, the chapter tackles the effects of using some nonorthodox instruments of fiscal policy in the transition period studied. Overall effects of Slovenia's transition fiscal policy are summarized in the final section.

Transition Fiscal Policy

The Period of Transition Fiscal Policy

In the restructuring period, in which existing market mechanisms and incentives, the state of the social safety net, and judicial bankruptcy procedure capacity were not able to cope adequately with increasing unemployment and massive collapse of enterprises, Slovenian fiscal policy explicitly and on a large scale intervened to mitigate the social pressure created by the increase in unemployment and to prevent massive collapse of enterprises. That period will be defined as a period of transition fiscal policy, and corresponding discretionary measures as instruments of transition fiscal policy (or simply, transition instruments). In this chapter, it is supposed that in Slovenia the period of transition fiscal policy lasted from 1991 to 1996. These are some compelling arguments for this choice of the period.[5]

Although the liberalization of the establishment of private firms and several modifications in incentive structure were launched when Slovenia was still a part of Yugoslavia, the policy that supported the country's full-scale transition to a market economy started after 1990 (when Slovenia became an independent state). So 1990 is considered in this analysis to be the last pretransition year.

High inflation, a decline in economic activity, and skyrocketing unemployment followed the collapse of the (Yugoslav) market.[6] A considerable number of enterprises that lost markets in the former Yugoslavia were also exporters to hard-currency markets, so costs would have had to be cut enough (about 70 percent) for them to switch to these markets.[7] Enormous (additional) labor cost pressures, however, and the high costs of getting credits to finance market switching pushed many enterprises to the brink of bankruptcy.[8] Squeezed by the accumulation of losses, enterprises moved to significant cutting of (over) employment and to scaling down. The other (smaller) segment of enterprises, for which markets in the former Yugoslavia were essential (predominantly, steel works), faced even more drastic restructuring.

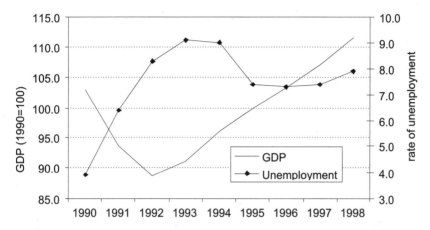

Figure 9.1
Unemployment and GDP in Slovenia

The government (as defined in appendix 9.1) used (mostly discretionary) instruments to mitigate the adverse effects of enterprise restructuring and the drastic increase in unemployment. The bulk of these measures were enacted in the period of Kornai's transformation depression, which lasted in Slovenia until the beginning of 1993; the effects of these discretionary measures slowly vanished afterward.

To corroborate the chosen transition time and profile, real GDP level and unemployment rate in Slovenia (measured according to International Labor Organization [ILO] standards) are illustrated in figure 9.1. After two years of transition depression, the GDP picked up in the third year of transition (1993) and again attained its pretransition level in the sixth year of transition (1996). The unemployment profile was the inverse of that of the economic activity, but the turning dates were similar; unemployment registered its highest value in the third year of transition (9.1 percent) and fell afterward. In the sixth year of transition (1996) it reached its lowest value (7.3 percent) since transition began.

That the Slovenian economy was already on the "normal" track by 1996 is documented also by figures 9.2 and 9.3. Figure 9.2 illustrates the flow of newly incorporated enterprises in Slovenia, and Figure 9.3 gives the average age of the newly retired. Obviously the growth in the number of enterprises stabilized after 1995 at around 2.5 percent yearly. The dynamics of retirement also corroborate the supposition that transition ended in 1996. After dropping for almost two

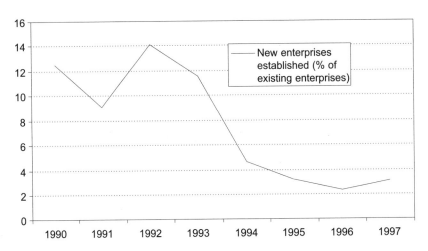

Figure 9.2
New enterprises in Slovenia

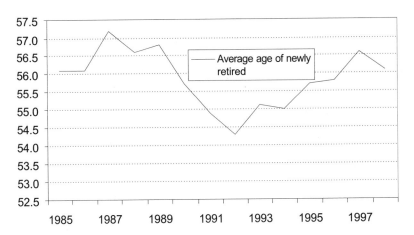

Figure 9.3
Age of the newly retired in Slovenia

years, in 1996, the age of the newly retired also normalized: It returned to pretransition values. In the first years of transition, then, policymakers explicitly stimulated early retirement to mitigate pressures on unemployment.[9]

In the rest of the chapter, I suppose that in 1996 the Slovenian economy took the track of normal restructuring, that is, the phase when market incentives and mechanisms, the established social safety net, and judicial (bankruptcy) procedure capacity became able to intermediate the restructuring. So the sixth year of transition (1996) is considered in this chapter also to have been the final year of transition fiscal policy.

Instruments of the Transition Fiscal Policy: Overview

The social pressures created by fast-increasing unemployment were primarily mitigated in Slovenia through two explicit policy measures: a favorable unemployment scheme and an early retirement scheme. Unemployment cash benefits were high, long term, and pegged to the beneficiary's wage before becoming unemployed, and control of the eligibility of beneficiaries was weak. High unemployment cash benefits pushed fiscal costs up and the seeking of labor down, so later the government reduced cash benefits and made other terms of unemployment less favorable.[10] The early retirement scheme was used for workers of enterprises in restructuring or in bankruptcy and for the long-term unemployed. "Buying years" (the fee paid for entering the early retirement scheme) was cheap in the period of transition fiscal policy.

Government assistance for enterprise sector restructuring in Slovenia used a multitrack approach: It included the rehabilitation of the banking sector and an active approach to loss-making enterprises, as well as assistance and incentive programs for enterprises in financial distress but still reporting a break-even balance-of-income statement.[11]

The main instrument used for rehabilitating the Slovenian banking sector was a swap of nonperforming assets for government bonds. In addition, banks in rehabilitation had access to special central bank credit facilities.

In fostering transition restructuring of enterprises in the real sector, the Slovenian government in principle used swaps for enterprises with adversely affected assets and guarantees (for credits to enterprises) for highly indebted enterprises. Swaps of government bonds for nonperforming assets were used to accelerate the restructuring of enterprises and mitigate exporters' losses attributable to exchange rate appreciation from the very beginning of transition, when Slovenia was still part of the Yugoslav monetary area. Claims against some segments of enterprises from the rest of the world, which became nonperforming after the collapse of Yugoslav market, were also swapped for government bonds.

Government guarantees were offered to highly indebted although otherwise viable enterprises (banking clients of substandard quality, classified in Slovenia as B clients), enabling them to lower the costs of financing. Because of government guarantees and therefore lower risk, real interest rates on such credits were equal to interest rates for the best clients (classified in Slovenia as A clients).

Swaps of nonperforming assets and guarantees were basically used for enterprises still showing a break-even balance on their income statements but facing transition-induced deterioration in the structure of their financing or in the quality of their assets. Cash subsidies and capital transfers (as an instrument of transition fiscal instrument) were mainly used for loss-making enterprises to enable their fast scaling down ("buying years" for early retirement of over-staffed employees) and paying interest (to prevent the withdrawal of bank financing). Cash subsidies were used also for accelerating the growth of small enterprises.

Nonorthodox fiscal tools were also used in transition to mitigate the adverse effects of transition restructuring: extrabudgetary activities, tax arrears, and special credits for banks in rehabilitation were used. Two extrabudgetary funds were active in alleviating the adverse effects of enterprise restructuring. Cash transfers and noncash transfers of assets of the general government were channeled into restructuring severely distressed enterprises through the (extrabudgetary) Development Fund (Razvojni sklad) and the Fund for the Development of Small Enterprises (Sklad RS za razvoj malega gospodarstva).

In the period of transition fiscal policy, tax arrears—tax liabilities accrued but not paid—were mostly enforced by heavily distressed firms. In addition, the bulk of arrears were accumulated in a small number of enterprises, therefore whether the stock of arrears (including) interest would be repaid was highly questionable. So the flow of (new) arrears can be treated as a kind of subsidy.

At the very beginning of bank rehabilitation, nonperforming assets were swapped for government bonds. In the following years, until the end of rehabilitation, banks in rehabilitation had access to special liquidity facilities of the central bank.

Transition-Caused Increase in Debt and Guarantees

Debt Increase

During the period of transition fiscal policy in Slovenia (1991–1996) the balance of general government was in surplus (see table 9.1). So government debt was generated almost exclusively through two channels for issuing noncash debt instruments: first, by issuing noncash debt instruments (of transitional fiscal policy) to swap corresponding nonperforming assets in banking and enterprises sector for government bonds, and second, through swapping government bonds for claims against the government and central bank stemming from the former Yugoslavia. The stock of total government debt and transitional government debt are illustrated in terms of GDP in figure 9.4, and figure 9.5 presents two channels of debt "disburse-[3] ment" in terms of GDP.

The bulk of Slovenia's transition-caused debt was generated in the period of transformation depression. The main characteristics of corresponding (transition) government bonds were long maturity, indexation to the exchange rate, and an actual two-year moratorium on payment of interest; some of them (used for banking rehabilita-

Table 9.1
Consolidated general government expenditure in Slovenia (as percentage of GDP)

	1991	1992	1993	1994	1995	1996	1997	1998
Total expenditure	37.67	41.90	43.65	43.29	43.05	42.32	43.17	43.09
Goods and services	6.20	9.53	9.58	9.24	9.04	8.59	8.36	8.47
Wages and salaries	8.50	8.85	9.14	8.29	8.72	9.17	9.80	9.57
Transfers to households	16.05	16.49	17.20	17.67	17.64	17.38	17.86	17.56
Subsidies and capital transfers	3.40	3.45	3.20	3.41	3.33	2.71	2.82	2.89
Interest payments	0.32	0.49	1.26	1.45	1.15	1.22	1.19	1.28
Fixed capital assets	3.20	3.09	3.27	3.23	3.17	3.25	3.14	3.32
Deficit/surplus	2.60	1.22	0.87	0.01	0.04	0.32	−1.17	−0.78

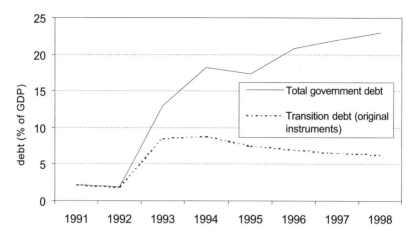

Figure 9.4
Government debt in Slovenia

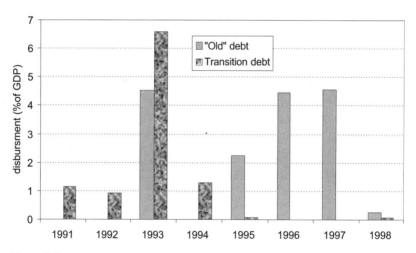

Figure 9.5
Debt "disbursement" in Slovenia

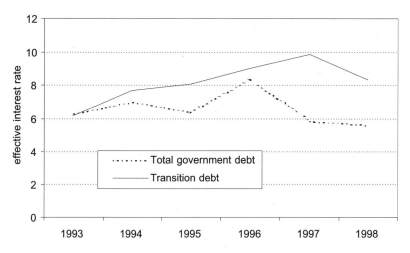

Figure 9.6
Effective interest rates in Slovenia

tion) were also nontransferable. Such characteristics resulted from the highly uncertain future track of the country's fiscal position and government access to (foreign) borrowing as well as its unstable performance of the economy during the time when the largest part of those bonds were disbursed. In that period economic activity was depressed and inflation high, and the scale of collapse of enterprises and the number of unemployed were just attaining their maximum values.

Transition bonds had long maturities, so that the first big "chunk" of principal had to be repaid only after 2000. That is the major reason why the stock of original debt instruments used to support transition was still so high at the end of 1998. In figure 9.4, the stock of original debt instruments of transitional fiscal policy is presented in terms of GDP. The long maturities on the bonds were intended to enable the government to postpone repayment of principal well into the post-transition period, by which time the performance of the economy and fiscal position would be more stable and the borrowing capabilities of the government better. Because of this strategy, however, the transition-caused debt caused an extension of high real interest rates in Slovenia well after the period of stabilizing inflation, that is, the period when government bonds were disbursed.[12] Figure 9.6 shows effective (paid) interest rates for total government debt and for transition debt disbursed in the period of falling economic activity (until 1993) in Slovenia. Because of increasing fiscal costs,[13] the government restructured the nontransferable part of its transition-caused bonds: The maturity periods for new bonds and interest rates were reduced, and transferability was introduced.

Although bonds used for swapping bad assets of enterprises had long maturity and grace periods, they had an immediate redistribution effect. Because of the lack of forex-denominated instruments to close their forex positions, Slovenian banks were ready to buy the government's foreign-exchange-indexed bonds. By the end of 1991, the amount of those bonds in the balances of the banking sector had already reached 0.8 percent of GDP.[14]

Increase in Guarantees

Special government guarantees on loans were used as a discretionary instrument of Slovenian transitional fiscal policy (transitional guarantees). Short-term guarantees (for banking credits with maturities of less than one year) were used to obtain cheaper credit (at the interest rate reserved for the best clients) for highly indebted but non-loss-making firms. Long-term guarantees were given to loss-making (state-owned) firms (for example, steel works) to enable them to restructure their debt (to offer their own bonds but with government guarantees).

Total government guarantees, guarantees used as a transition fiscal instrument, and total payment of government guarantees in Slovenia are illustrated in figure 9.7. The stock of transition guarantees has been growing continuously in the country since 1992, but the major increase in government guarantees came in the first three years of transition, 1992–1994. After 1994, an accelerated decline in real interest rates reduced the demand of firms eligible for guarantees (banking clients with credits classified as A or B).[15] By the end of the period of transition fiscal policy (1996), the stock of transition guarantees had reached slightly less than 2 percent of GDP.

Payments of Guarantees

In the year transition guarantees were launched (1992), the loose eligibility criteria for getting a government guarantee on a loan and the country's low economic activity (GDP reached its bottom level) pushed total payments of guarantees in Slovenia to almost 25 per-

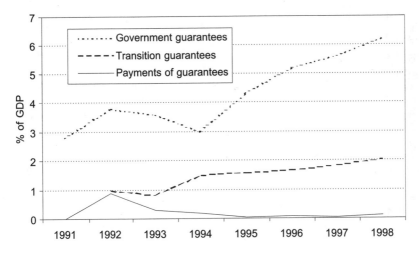

Figure 9.7
Government guarantees in Slovenia

cent of the stock of guarantees. The bulk of these payments were made for transition guarantees.

After 1992, the eligibility criteria for government guarantees were tightened. Payment for guarantees was no longer automatic when a guaranteed loan defaulted: the receiving bank first had to complete a judicial procedure for recovering the (nonperforming) credit, so the moral hazard of banks decreased, and payments of guarantees dropped considerably, to less than 2 percent of the stock of guarantees, by 1996. Because the percentage of guarantees paid became much more stable, the government increased the volume of guarantees it offered substantially; when issuing (transition) guarantees, the government actually started to target given provisions (determined in the budget) necessary for payments of guarantees.

Transition's Impact on Expenditures of the General Government

Transfers to Households

Two transition fiscal instruments were used in Slovenia to mitigate the effects of fast-declining employment: an unemployment scheme and an early retirement scheme. Before transition, unemployment cash benefits in Slovenia had been very attractive, by the standards of developed countries. Benefits were high, long-term, and pegged to

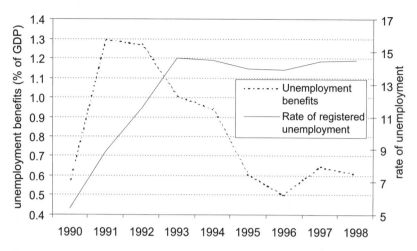

Figure 9.8
Unemployment in Slovenia

the beneficiary's wage before becoming unemployed, and control of beneficiaries' eligibility was weak. In addition, the government made pension system contributions for those registered as unemployed. At the beginning of transition, the benefits of the unemployment scheme were not changed. Such favorable benefits were an important reason the registered number of unemployed remained so high so long after transition started. In addition, the increase in unemployment triggered by transition pushed the costs of unemployment cash benefits even higher.

Recognizing the adverse effects of the favorable unemployment scheme,[16] Slovenian policymakers adjusted the eligibility conditions and the level of unemployment cash benefits. Figure 9.8 presents unemployment cash benefits paid (in terms of GDP) and the rate of registered unemployment in Slovenia. Obviously, not only the height but also the path of registered unemployment and unemployment from the labor force survey (according to ILO standards) were different (compare registered unemployment in figure 9.8 with survey unemployment in figure 9.1). At the same time, the difference in the paths of the graphs in figure 9.8 documents that noncash benefits were important for those registered as unemployed.

In the first four years of transition fiscal policy, expenditures for unemployment cash benefits in Slovenia were considerable. Especially in the first two years, unemployment cash benefits were higher on average by almost 1 percent of GDP than in the final year of the transition period. Unemployment cash benefits became "normal" much sooner than, for example, the number of early retirements, a second channel for reducing unemployment pressure in the period of transition fiscal policy. Already by the fifth year of transition (1995) unemployment cash benefits dropped to normal values.

In the first years of transition, the number of unemployed in Slovenia was increasing very rapidly; nevertheless the reduction in employment was occurring even faster. Thus the reduction of employment resulted not only in increasing levels of unemployment but also in decreasing participation.[17] In Slovenia, economic policy deliberately stimulated mitigating the pressure of unemployment through early retirement. Workers in enterprises in bankruptcy or in restructuring as well as the long-term unemployed could become eligible for early retirement through a scheme that involved "buying years." The price for early retirement was low (much lower than discounted leftover contributions), and in the case of restructuring, enterprises paid the early retirement fee.

Early retirement during transition caused a considerable reduction (by more than two years) in the average age of the newly retired in Slovenia (see figure 9.3). At the end of the transition fiscal period, the average age of the retired again attained trend values. Using the average age of the newly retired as a variable, the impact of transition on general government expenditure on pensions in Slovenia can be estimated (the estimatation equation is presented in appendix 9.1). Figure 9.9 shows total pension expenditures and transition-caused increases in pension expenditures in Slovenia (both in terms of GDP). Transition's impact on expenditures for pensions was the highest in the first three years of the country's transition, falling smoothly afterward. Although the peak values for pension experditures were lower than those for unemployment benefits transition-inflated expenditure for pensions leveled off much more slowly than transition-increased unemployment cash benefits. The cumulative effects on the volume of transfers to households (taking into account a significant swing in GDP) of both instruments were almost the same.

Subsidies and Capital Transfers

During Slovenia's transition years, the fragmentation of types (purposes) of government subsidies offered was enormous.[18] Heuristically,

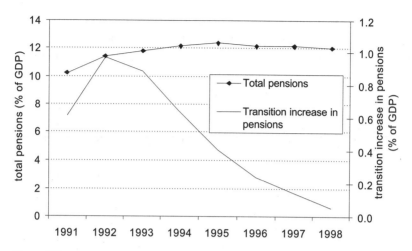

Figure 9.9
Pensions in Slovenia

five types of subsidies can be distinguished: those for retraining and new employment, for big loss-making enterprises, for promoting restructuring of exporters and new small enterprises, for enterprises with regulated prices, and for agricultural producers.

Subsidies for enterprises with regulated prices and for agricultural producers were targeted consumer subsidies inherited from the pre-transition period. They were operationalized through regulating prices of some products (for example, in transportation and agriculture). Actual fiscal expenditures were made when enterprises with regulated prices had to be subsidized. These subsidies are illustrated in figure 9.10. As they were not earmarked for mitigating problems caused by restructuring of enterprises during transition, it is understandable that a significant reduction in these subsidies actually followed the transition process, that is, through liberalization of regulated prices.

To estimate subsidies used to mitigate the adverse effects of transition, the restructuring of consumer targeted subsidies must be excluded (see appendix 9.1). Transition subsidies therefore include, roughly speaking, the first three mentioned types of subsidies. Subsidies to big loss-making enterprises (steel works and truck manufacturers) to enable them to scaled down their size and sales volume without an increase in social pressure (because of large employment in these enterprises), especially in the regions where these enterprises

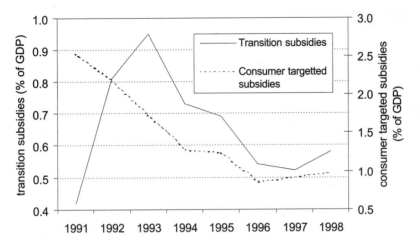

Figure 9.10
Subsidies in Slovenia

were located. These subsidies mostly took the form of payment for retraining, reimbursement of the fee paid for laid-off workers to retire early by buying years, and credits for wages. Refunds of import duties were used to subsidize exporters. The restructuring of smaller enterprises was supported through subsidizing interest rates and refunding import duties paid on investment goods (trucks, for example). The bulk of subsidies were given to other (nonpublic) enterprises. Subsidies to nonfinancial public enterprises mostly included covering losses and offsetting the costs of laying off sufficient workers in railways; both items increased considerably in transition because railway transport plummeted after Yugoslavia fell apart. Capital transfers to other (private) enterprises were small.

Figure 9.10 depicts transition subsidies (subsidies used to alleviate the adverse effects of transition restructuring) and consumer-targeted subsidies in Slovenia. Transition subsidies reached their highest level (slightly over 0.9 percent of GDP) in the third year of Slovenia's transition (1993). Although the amount of total subsidies in Slovenia's business sector was near the minimal values for other, more advanced transition economies at the same point in their transition,[19] transition subsidies in Slovenia were much lower (less than 20 percent of total subsidies). In addition, transition subsidies were cut almost in half by the end of the transition period; such a reduction indicates that transition had a significant impact on the country's fiscal position through subsidies in its first years.

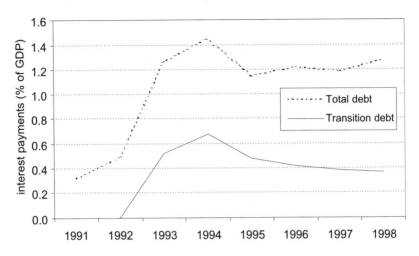

Figure 9.11
Interest payments in Slovenia

Targeted consumer subsidies (inherited from the pretransition period) fell almost uniformly in transition. This was an understandable effect of the gradual liberalization of regulated prices.

Interest Payments

All debt used by Slovenia's government to alleviate the effects of transition restructuring was issued as noncash debt; the corresponding debt instruments had long maturities, as noted above, and those used for swapping bad assets of enterprises (in the real sector) also had a two-year moratorium on interest payments. So transition debt significantly affected the government's interest payments only in the third year of transition, and amortization of its transition-triggered debt was minimal until 1996 (the final year of the fiscal transition period).

Figure 9.11 presents interest payments on transition debt and on total government debt. Interest payments on transition debt obviously reached their maximum level (at 0.5 percent of GDP) in the fourth year of transition. Because inflation was high at the time they were issued, all transition debt instruments were indexed (to the exchange rate or to moving averages of inflation in previous months). The "real part" of interest rates on these instruments was fixed at values prevailing in a period of high real interest rates, which characterized the period of stabilization, when transition debt was issued.[20] Long maturities for these instruments stretched such real interest rates over many years, so the effective interest rates on transition debt became significantly higher than the effective interest rates on total government debt when stabilization came to an end and real interest rates fell (see figure 9.6). The government's subsequent restructuring of part of this transition debt is the main reason the graph of transition-caused interest payments presented in figure 9.11 takes a sharp downward turn after 1994.

Nonorthodox Instruments of Transition Fiscal Policy

Governments often attempt to operationalize increased involvement in the economy through instruments other than those described in the previous section, if they want to increase their involvement in the economy but cannot (or do not want to) raise the level of taxation. The use of these other instruments is an important explanation for the much lower level (by at least 50 percent) of tax revenue and public expenditures (measured in terms of GDP) in developing countries, in comparison with developed countries.[21]

In the period of transition, when the tax system and administration are still in the making and public expenditures hit the ceiling (because of the exploding number of social safety net beneficiaries and enterprises in distress), it is hard to expect that governments would avoid the use of such fiscal instruments as tax arrears, extrabudgetary funds financing, and special credits for banks in rehabilitation. Empirical evidence confirms that more advanced transition economies used at least some such instruments quite substantially.[22] That is to say, the analysis of the fiscal impact of transition on a country must take into account, in principle, not only traditional fiscal instruments but also other, possibly nonorthodox tools.

Tax Arrears

In the period of transition fiscal policy in Slovenia, the enforcement of tax administration for business units from the sector of corporate enterprises was much higher than for business units from the self-employed sector. That is, because of the (inherited) institutional structure of the existing payment system, the Slovenian tax administration was able to block payments of some transactions (since tax

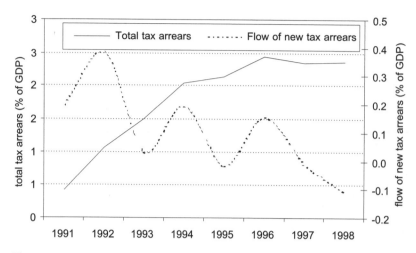

Figure 9.12
Tax arrears in Slovenia

administration claims had higher seniority by law) by firms in the sector of corporate enterprises that had not paid their taxes. They were unable to block such payments by the self-employed, however, because the self-employed were not included in the old payment system but rather in a kind of bank-based clearing system of "small values."[23]

Only after the worst of the pressure from the transition-triggered increase in expenditures of the general government was over did the reform of the tax administration and payment system in Slovenia start. A value-added tax replaced the sales tax in 1999. The strategy was, heuristically speaking, first to get control over long-term (transition-adjusted) government expenditures and then to reform the tax system.[24] This enforcement policy of the tax administration probably enabled Slovenia to have a lower level of tax erosion than other transition economies in the first years of transition.[25]

Nevertheless, tax arrears were increasing in the period of transition fiscal policy. Figure 9.12 presents total tax arrears (including interest) and flow of new tax arrears in Slovenia (sources of data and the method for estimating arrears are presented in appendix 9.1). As with the results of the (orthodox) fiscal instruments launched to alleviate the effects of transition restructuring, so the stock of arrears leveled off in the sixth year of transition (1996). In 1996, arrears leveled off at about 2.4 percent of GDP, far less than in other developed transition countries, where the stock of tax arrears had already significantly exceeded 4 percent GDP by 1993.[26]

The average lag in tax payments due in Slovenia was around two years in 1998. Obviously, only a small portion of the total tax arrears were likely to be recovered in the period of transition, particulary since a significant portion of the arrears were concentrated in a small number of enterprises. Therefore, all new arrears could be sensibly treated as subsidies to firms in distress.[27] The flow of new tax arrears, depicted in figure 9.12, illustrates that through tax arrears firms in Slovenia were subsidized in an amount of about 0.3 percent of GDP at the beginning, and about 0.1 percent of GDP at the end of the period of transition fiscal policy.

Because of very high interest rates (late penalty rates) and long delays in making tax payments that were due, the accumulated stock of interest represented 55 percent of the total stock of tax arrears at the end of Slovenia's transition period. However, the time path of interest stock accumulation was not uniform in the period of transition. At the beginning of the transition period, interest contributed considerably more to the total stock of arrears, because inflation was much higher and enterprises were much more distressed.

Extrabudgetary Funds Financing

Until 1998, the Slovenian government had thirteen extrabudgetary funds at its disposal; their operations are not included in the activities of the general government (as defined in this chapter).[28] Only two of these funds, however, were actively used in mitigating the unfavorable effects of transition restructuring. Instruments of fiscal policy (lending, capital transfers) that were effective through the activities of these extrabudgetary funds are included among nonorthodox measures of transition fiscal policy.

The first of these two funds, the Development Fund restructured highly distressed enterprises and privatized (sold) them.[29] Enterprises looking for the fund's help had to accept conversion into fund-state ownership (and therefore to give up potential claims arising from privatization of the enterprise). The fund used other harsh selection criteria as well, so enterprises looking only for government subsidies and without serious intention to undergo restructuring and privatization were excluded from receiving the fund's assistance, as a practical matter.[30] The second fund, the Fund for the Development

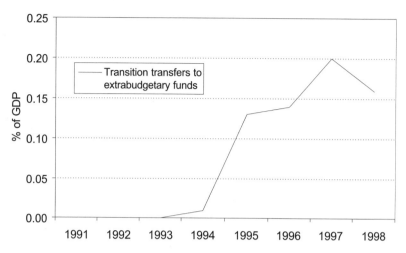

Figure 9.13
Transfers to extrabudgetary funds in Slovenia

of Small Enterprises, engaged in accelerating and promoting the rise of new enterprises and so mitigating the adverse social effects of high unemployment.

Figure 9.13 shows government financing of transition restructuring through these two extrabudgetary funds in terms of GDP. Because the bulk of government funds channeled into extrabudgetary funds were actually privatization receipts, the steep increase in such funds after 1994 is understandable: Only after 1994 did privatization receipts increase to a stable level of around 0.4–0.5 percent of GDP per year.[31]

Interest Rates for Bank in Rehabilitation

When rehabilitation of the banking industry in Slovenia began, non-performing assets were swapped for government bonds. Banks in rehabilitation did not get any fresh money. Their liquidity was instead facilitated through standard credit facilities of the central bank, and special (although highly collaterized) liquidity credits that were made available only to banks in rehabilitation status. Until the end of rehabilitation, banks had to repay all special credit facilities they made use of.

Banking rehabilitation in Slovenia took place during the years of high real interest rates and costly access to the central bank liquidity.

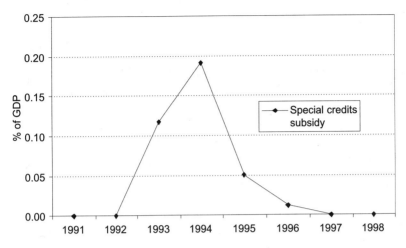

Figure 9.14
Subsidies to Slovenian banks in rehabilitation

So special credit facilities for banks in rehabilitation could amount to a significant subsidy, although the average difference between the effective interest rate on special credit facilities and the money market interest rate was almost negligible: The interbank money market was shallow, and 35 percent of the banking sector was in rehabilitation status.[32] So corresponding interest rates would have been much higher if banks in rehabilitation had not acquired liquidity from the central bank, corresponding interest rates would have been much higher than actual interest rates on the money market. Because such special liquidity facilities, on one hand, decreased the profit of the central bank (earmarked for the budget) and, on the other, subsidized a segment of the banking sector, such a subsidy must be added to the transition-caused change in the country's fiscal position (using indirect fiscal instruments). The scale on which banks in rehabilitation were subsidized by the Slovenian government (through cheaper access to liquidity) is documented in figure 9.14.

Rehabilitation of Slovenia's banks started in 1993. The stock of special credit facilities (for banks in rehabilitation) attained its peak values (in terms of base money) in the first year of rehabilitation; that pushed the subsidy to banks in rehabilitation as high as 0.18 percent of GDP. In the following years, the subsidy fell pretty quickly.

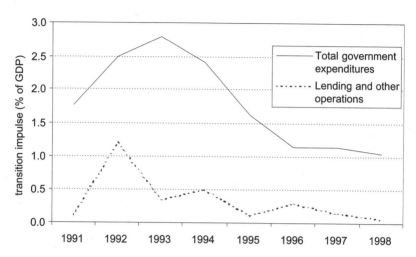

Figure 9.15
Transition fiscal impulse in Slovenia

The Fiscal Impulse of Transition Restructuring

To estimate the overall fiscal impulse of transition restructuring, the fiscal impulse is insulated (as described in appendix 9.1) for every analyzed transition instrument. The estimated effects of transition on fiscal position are then aggregated in two variables: transition impulse to total expenditure and transition impulse to lending and other operations. The first variable includes transition's impact on transfers to the household sector, transition subsidies to the business sector, and interest paid on transition debt. The second variable encompasses payments of transition guarantees, tax arrears, effects of lower interest rates for banks in rehabilitation, and transition's impact on extrabudgetary operations. Both variables are presented (in percentages of GDP) in figure 9.15.

Both graphs in figure 9.15 illustrate the same time profile: an accelerated increase of transition-caused changes in the country's fiscal position in the first three years of transition followed by a slow disappearance of its effects afterward. In the sixth year of transition, transition's impulse to the fiscal position leveled off at around 1 percent of GDP for the total general government expenditure and at around 0 for lending and other operations. The same time profile also characterizes other analyzed instruments of transition fiscal policy. It coincides also with the transition time profile of unemployment and GDP contraction.

Government activities for mitigating the adverse effects of transition restructuring increased the expenditure of the general government, lending, and other operations to more than 3 percent of GDP in the second and third years of transition. After leveling off in the sixth year, the transition impulse to the country's fiscal position still remained slightly over 1 percent of GDP.

The decrease in the transition impulse to general government expenditure as well as the reduction of consumer-targeted subsidies were offset mostly by the increase in other transfers to the household sector and capital transfers to the extrabudgetary fund for building motorways (DARS). So changes in the structure (by economic functions) and the size of the general government expenditure were not significant in the period of transition (see table 9.1).

Summary

In the first phase of transition restructuring in Slovenia, the existing market structure and incentives, the (un)available social safety net, and the capacity of the judicial bankruptcy procedures were insufficient to intermediate the restructuring of the economy without considerable increase in unemployment and massive collapse of enterprises. Government activities significantly alleviated such adverse effects of the transition restructuring. The government's transition fiscal policy was an important precondition for the Slovenian economy's sustainable transition toward a modern market economy.

The Slovenian government's activities in alleviating the adverse effects of transition restructuring were operationalized through discretionary orthodox and nonorthodox fiscal instruments. Among orthodox fiscal instruments used, the most important were instruments of noncash issued debt, guarantees, an early retirement scheme, a modification of the existing unemployment scheme, and subsidies. The most important indirect (nonorthodox) fiscal instruments employed were tax arrears, special credits for banks in rehabilitation, and operations of extrabudgetary funds.

A country's transition time could conceivably be defined by several variables: regaining a pretransition level of GDP, leveling off of the growth of new firms, leveling off of the unemployment rate, and attaining the pretransition average age of the newly retired. All show the same period of transition restructuring for Slovenia: Transition in a narrow sense was over in 1996, when minimal institutional setup had been completed, so that endogenous restructuring could proceed afterward.

The time profile of the transition impulse of analyzed fiscal instruments coincides with that of unemployment and GDP contraction in Slovenia. Overall transition impulse to fiscal position attained its highest values in the second and third year of the transition (over 3 percent of GDP). After leveling off in 1996, the transition impulse to fiscal position still remained at around 1 percent of GDP.

In the later phase of transition, a vanishing transition effect on general government expenditure was completely offset by an increase in other transfers to households and capital transfers to the extrabudgetary fund for building motorways.

The Slovenian government also issued noncash debt to mitigate the adverse effects of transition restructuring. Original instruments of that debt attained their peak value (at over 8 percent of GDP) in the fourth year of transition (1994). Because of their long maturities, the stock of original debt instruments was still higher than 6 percent of GDP by the end of 1998.

The numeric rule (numerical target) for fiscal position cannot be used as a commitment device for countries in transition without making a "transition adjustment" of the fiscal stance before hand. Any comparison of transition with nontransition countries also requires a transition adjustment of the transition countries' fiscal stance, as does any evaluation of the sustainability of their fiscal stance.

Appendix 9.1 Definitions and Sources of Data and Estimation

General Government

In this chapter, "general government" is defined as an aggregate of the Slovenian central government, local governments (146 municipalities), pension and disability insurance fund, and health insurance fund. The main source of data used for analyses of expenditure items of the general government is the Ministry of Finance's *Balances of Public Financing in the Republic of Slovenia in 1992–1998* and some internal data from a database used in preparation of that publication, which follows IMF Government Finance Statistics standards.

Quantification of the Transition Fiscal Impulse

Heuristically speaking, the fiscal impulse of a country's transition would have to quantify the increase (in comparison with the normal, nontransition state) in the intensity of the country's fiscal policy aimed at mitigating the transition-caused adverse effects on unemployment and restructuring of enterprises. Some activities of Slovenia's transition fiscal policy can be identified and quantified explicitly (without estimation), because data on corresponding (discretionary) instruments are available (examples would be transition-caused debt instruments, guarantees, interest payments, and liquidity facilities for banks in rehabilitation). The transition fiscal impulse of other activities of fiscal policy is estimated in the chapter as the difference between the actual value of a particular variable (corresponding to analyzed activity) and its leveling-off (normal) value.

Debts and Guarantees

Five noncash issuances of bonds by Slovenia's government for swapping nonperforming assets in banks and enterprises are classified in the chapter as transition (-triggered) debt. Only bonds swapped for claims against enterprises (domestic and foreign) and disbursed after transition started are included in the transition debt. Data on debts are taken from different volumes of *Report on the Debt of the Republic of Slovenia* (Ministry of Finance). Government guarantees for credits to (or bonds issued by) nonfinancial corporations, except public utilities, are included among transition guarantees. Data on guarantees are collected from different volumes of *Report on Guarantees of the Republic of Slovenia* (Ministry of Finance); quarterly figures are available.

Data on payments for particular guarantee instrument are not available. Therefore, the payments on transition guarantees are estimated by subtracting "normal" values of the guarantee payments from total guarantee payments. It is assumed that the leveling-off value of the bell-shaped curve of the guarantee payments shows "normal" value. If the guarantee payments per unit of GDP (gp_t) are fitted to the nonlinear time trend (*time*),

$$gp_t = 0.794^* \ \exp(-2.783^*(time - 92)^2) + 0.096 + e_t,$$
$$\quad (6.7) \qquad\qquad (-1.6) \qquad\qquad\qquad (2.0)$$

$DW = 1.49, \quad R^2 = 0.90,$

payments for transition guarantees per unit of GDP (gpt_t) are estimated by

$gpt_t = gp_t - 0.096.$

In the estimated function, residuals are marked by e_t.

Transfers to Households

In Slovenia's transition, two effects, increasing unemployment and
decreasing benefits, determined the dynamics of the unemployment
cash benefits variable. This variable is used in the chapter's analysis.
Data on unemployment cash benefits are collected from *Balances of
Public Financing in the Republic of Slovenia in 1992–1998* (Ministry of
Finance) and *Statistical Yearbook* (Statistical Office of the Republic of
Slovenia).

To estimate the transition impulse to unemployment cash benefits,
the "normal" (leveling-off) value has to be subtracted. To quantify
the leveling-off value, unemployment cash benefits per unit of GDP
are fitted to the following bell-shaped trend:

$unb_t = 0.718^* \exp(-0.219^*(time - 92)^2) + 0.575 + e_t,$
$\quad\quad (6.8) \quad\quad\quad (-2.2) \quad\quad\quad\quad\quad (7.9)$

$DW = 2.01, \quad R^2 = 0.90,$

where unb_t denotes unemployment cash benefits, *time* denotes time
trend, and e_t denotes residuals.

The amount of unemployment cash benefits per unit of GDP
($unbt_t$) caused by transition restructuring is estimated by

$unbt_t = unb_t - 0.575.$

Explicit data on early retirements in Slovenia are not available.
Because the country's public pension system is a mature system
burdened with a high and fast-increasing system and population
dependency rate (as well as a high replacement rate),[33] any estimation of the costs of the transition-caused increase in retirement in
Slovenia must take into account the long-term increase in the number
of retired people in the country. Therefore, the transition-caused increase in the costs of the pension system is quantified by estimating,

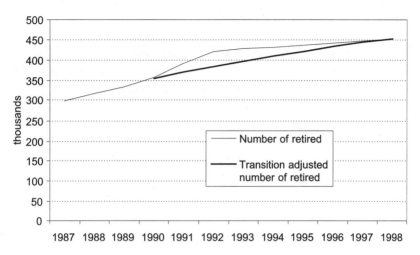

Figure 9.A1
Numbered of retired people in Slovenia

first, the trend in the number of retired, and then second, calculating the number of transition-caused retirements as a deviation from a "trend part" of the regression function. The number of retired (nr_t) is regressed on the quadratic time trend (*time*) and the average age of the newly retired ($nnrage_t$):

$$nr_t = 242.55 + 21.27^* time - 0.45^* time^2 - 14.61^* nnrage_t + e_t,$$
$$\quad\;\; (329.3) \quad\; (9.8) \qquad\quad (-3.3) \qquad\quad\; (-5.6)$$

$$DW = 2.3, \quad R^2 = 0.99, \qquad \text{period: 1985–1998.}$$

The number of retirements caused by transition restructuring (nrt_t) is estimated as

$$nrt_t = nr_t - (242.55 + 21.27^* time - 0.45^* time^2).$$

Figure 9.A1 shows trend (transition-adjusted) and total number of retired people in Slovenia. Transition's impact on the volume of pension transfers is then estimated by multiplying nrt_t by the average pension for year t of the transition period. Data were collected from various issues of the *Statistical Yearbook* (Statistical Office of the Republic of Slovenia) and a 1997 study prepared for the pension system reform known as the *White Book* (Ministry for Labour, Family and Social Security).

Interest and Guarantee Payments

Interest payments on the transition-triggered debt, disbursement, and repayment of the debt are explicitly calculated as a sum of figures for all transition debt instruments. The main source of data is various volumes of the *Report on the Debt of the Republic of Slovenia.* (Ministry of Finance)

No source of separate data for guarantee payments is available, so data on total payments for guarantees are analyzed. The main source of data is *Balances of Public Financing in the Republic of Slovenia in 1992–1998* (Ministry of Finance).

Subsidies

A number of different types of subsidies for a number of different purposes were used by the Slovenian government during transition.[34] Although discretionary instruments were used when subsidies were operationalized, it is impossible to detect targeted segments of enterprises and quantify corresponding benefits for every type of subsidy separately, especially because many subsidies only indirectly mitigated the adverse effects of transition restructuring. Although the breakdown of subsidies is very detailed, and a huge number of instruments was used, analytically consistent data are available only for aggregate items.

"Transition subsidies" are defined in the chapter as the sum of subsidies to nonpublic, nonfinancial corporations, subsidies to public enterprises (encompassing almost exclusively subsidies to railways), and capital transfers to nonpublic, nonfinancial corporations, less targeted consumer subsidies (illustrated in figure 9.10). In estimating transition subsidies, data are used from a number of publications: *Balances of Public Financing in the Republic of Slovenia in 1992–1998* (Ministry of Finance), *General Government Accounts 1991–1994 and Proposed Budgets for 1995* (Ministry of Finance) and *Statistical Yearbook* (Statistical Office of the Republic of Slovenia), *Input-Output Tables for 1992* (Statistical Office of the Republic of Slovenia) and *Input-Output Tables for 1995 and 1997* (Institute of Macroeconomic Analysis and Development); data from the internal database of the Ministry of Finance are also used.

Tax Arrears

The main source for estimating tax arrears is the *Yearly Report* of the Slovenian Tax Administration, which provides data on the stock of tax payments due but not paid (without interest) for corporate enterprises, on the stock of tax arrears (including interest) for the self-employed, and on the volume of unsuccessful attempts to collect taxes.

To evaluate the stock of interest (on the stock of tax arrears of corporate enterprises), the lag distribution is estimated using detailed data on tax payments due but not paid for a sample of important taxpayers. For that purpose, internal data from the Tax Administration are used. Once the lag distribution of tax arrears is estimated, the stock of interest payments is calculated by the using late-penalty rate (from the *Monthly Bulletin* of the Bank of Slovenia).

Operations of Extrabudgetary Funds

Two extrabudgetary funds, the Development Fund (and its successor, the Slovenian Development Fund) and the Fund for the Development of Small Enterprises were active also in accelerating transition restructuring and in alleviating effects of the mass collapse of enterprises. Part of the financing of those two funds came from cash capital transfers from the Slovenian government. The government also channeled to those funds through lending transactions (part of) the privatization receipts. To analyze the transition impact on the country's fiscal position of the activities financed through these two extrabudgetary funds, the sum of corresponding cash (capital) transfers and privatization receipts is estimated. Any debt increase caused by these funds' issuing their own bonds is already included in the transition-triggered debt or guarantees increase.

The main sources of data for quantification of these nonorthodox fiscal activities are Korže 1995, *Balances of Public Financing in the Republic of Slovenia in 1992–1998* (Ministry of Finance), internal data of the Agency for Payment System (APP or Agencija za plačilni promet) (balance sheet and income statement for both funds in the transition years) and audited balance sheets and income statements published for the Development Fund in the daily newspaper *Delo.*

Interests Paid by Banks in Rehabilitation

The potential scale of subsidies to banks in rehabilitation through cheaper access to liquidity is estimated as the difference in the interest rates (for interbank deposits and for special credit facilities of the central bank available only to banks in rehabilitation) multiplied by the volume of (nonstandard) liquidity credits to banks in rehabilitation. Data on standard instruments are obtained from the *Monthly Bulletin* (Bank of Slovenia), and data for credit facilities available only to banks in rehabilitation are from the internal database of the Bank of Slovenia.

References

Alesina, A., and R. Perotti. 1995. Fiscal expansion and adjustments in OECD countries. *Economic Policy* 21: 1170–88.

Alesina, A., and R. Perotti. 1997. Fiscal adjustment in OECD countries: Composition and macroeconomic effects. *IMF Staff Papers* 44: 210–48.

Alesina, A., R. Perotti, and J. Tavares. 1998. The political economy of fiscal adjustments. *Brookings Papers on Economic Activity*: 197–266.

Blanchard, O. 1990. Suggestions for a new set of fiscal indicators. OECD working paper no. 79, Organisation for Economic Cooperation and Development, Paris.

Blanchard, O. 1997. *The economics of post-communist transition.* Oxford: Clarendon.

Blanchard, O., and M. Kremer. 1997. Disorganization. *Quarterly Journal of Economics*: 1091–1126.

Blejer, M. I., and A. Cheasty. 1991. The measurement of fiscal deficits: Analytical and methodological issues. *Journal of Economic Literature* 29: 1644–78.

Bole, V. 1997. Stabilization in Slovenia: From high inflation to excessive inflow of foreign capital. In *Macroeconomic stabilization in transition economies*, ed. M. I. Blejer and M. Škreb, 234–55. Cambridge: Cambridge University Press.

Bole, V. 1998. Financing the transition of the public pension system in Slovenia. Paper presented at World Bank workshop "Second Pillar Issues," Ljubljana, Slovenia, March 23.

Bole, V. 1999. The financial sector and high interest rates: Lessons from Slovenia. In *Financial sector transformation: Lessons from economies in transition*, ed. I. M. Blejer and M. Škreb, 309–32. Cambridge: Cambridge University Press.

International Monetary Fund. (IMF). 1995. Eastern Europe—Factors underlying the weakening performance of tax revenues. *Economic Systems* 19: 101–24.

International Monetary Fund. (IMF). 1997. Slovenia: Report of the government finance statistics mission. International Monetary Fund, Washington, D.C.

Korže, U. 1994. Restructuring of the loss-making enterprises in Slovenia. In *Privatization through restructuring*, ed. A. Bohm and U. Korže, 107–21. Ljubljana, Slovenia: Central and Eastern European Privatization Network (CEEPN).

Lindbeck, A. 1994. Overshooting, reform and retreat of the welfare state. *Economist* 142: 1–19.

Mencinger, J. 1998. Generating employment in economies of transition. EIPF Working Paper, Economic Institute at School of Law, Ljubljana, Slovenia.

Ministry for Labor, Family and Social Security. 1997. *White book*. Ljubljana, Slovenia: Author.

Ministry of Finance. 1999. *Balances of public financing in the Republic of Slovenia in 1992–1998*. Ljubljana, Slovenia.

Organisation for Economic Cooperation and Development (OECD). 1999. *National accounts for the Republic of Slovenia*. OECD Centre for Co-operation with the Non-Members. Paris.

Perotti, R. 1996. Fiscal consolidation in Europe: Composition matters. *American Economic Review, Papers and Proceedings* 86: 105–10.

Perotti, R., R. Strauch, and J. von Hagen. 1997. Sustainability of public finances. Discussion paper series, Centre for Economic Policy Research, London.

Rebrica, N. 1998. Government assets managed by extrabudgetary funds (in Slovene). Unpublished paper, University of Ljubljana, Ljubljana, Slovenia.

Schaffer, M. E. 1995. Tax arrears in transitional economies. In *Tax and benefit reform in Central and Eastern Europe*, ed. M. G. Newbery David, 115–44. London: Centre for Economic Policy Research.

Stanovnik, T. 1998. Social, demographic and fiscal implications of new economic instruments for Social Security" (in Slovene). Institute for Economic Research, Ljubljana, Slovenia. Mimeographed.

Stanovnik, T., and S. Kukar. 1995. The pension system in Slovenia: Past developments and future prospects. *International Social Security Review* 48: 35–44.

Tanzi, V. 1993. The budget deficit in transition. *IMF Staff Papers* 40: 697–707.

Tanzi, V. 1995. Government role and the efficiency of policy instruments. Working paper 100, International Monetary Fund, Washington, D.C.

Tanzi, V., and H. H. Zee. 1997. Fiscal policy and long-run growth. *IMF Staff Papers* 44: 179–209.

Vodopivec, M. 1995. Labour market effects of old-age insurance: Experience from Slovenia. Unpublished paper, Ministry for Labor, Family and Social Security, Ljubljana, Slovenia.

Vodopivec, M. 1996. Unemployment insurance and duration of unemployment: Evidence from Slovenia's transition. Unpublished paper, World Bank, Washington, D.C.

Zee, H. H. 1996. Empirics of crosscountry tax revenue comparison. *World Development* 24: 1659–71.

10

The Legacy of the Socialist Economy: The Macro- and Microeconomic Consequences of Soft Budget Constraints

Yegor Gaidar

The protracted recessions in a number of transition economies are frequently explained with reference to the excessive radicalism of economic reforms, the misapplication of monetarist prescriptions, and a failure to understand the role of the state. In this connection I will attempt to analyze the relationship in a transition economy between the toughness of fiscal policy, the speed of fiscal and monetary stabilization, and the pace of adaptation of the enterprise sector to working in conditions of a market economy.[1]

Almost all postsocialist countries encountered the problem of fiscal crisis during late socialism and were faced with the necessity of getting rid of the monetary overhang that built up during the socialist period and also with an appreciable leap in inflation at the start of the transition.[2] In this connection, it is possible to divide countries into two groups: those that were capable of counteracting fiscal crisis with tight monetary policy and over a short period of time succeeded in cutting inflation down to moderate levels, and those where monetary policy was soft, the rate of nominal money supply growth fluctuated sharply, and the period of high inflation was prolonged. Roughly speaking, the economic policy conducted in the first group of countries can be called "monetarist" and in the second group "populist."[3]

The choice of quantitative criteria for separating the monetarist group of countries from the populist group (the length and scale of disinflation) inevitably involves a subjective element. Bearing in mind, however, that Poland has the firm reputation of a country that implemented "shock therapy," including the area of monetary policy, we will place in the monetarist group those countries that achieved disinflation in a period and on a scale similar to, or faster than, Poland (reducing average monthly inflation rates to 3 percent or less per month within three years following price liberalization), and in the populist group those countries in which disinflation turned out to be a much more protracted process.[4] First I will analyze the situation in countries which implemented a policy of rapid disinflation and its relationship with change in enterprise behavior, and then we will try to compare them with the macro and microeconomy of countries in which monetary stabilization was delayed.

The General Tendency of the Postcommunist Transition

Highly industrialized socialist economies are characterized by the inefficiency and nonviability under market conditions of a substantial section of enterprises. Economic development in the U.S.S.R. and Council for Mutual Economic Assistance (COMECON) countries in the 1970s and 1980s was strongly influenced by the appropriation of sizable oil rents made available by the exploitation of western Siberian oil fields and favorable conditions on the world oil market. The abrupt drop in oil prices in the mid-1980s intensified the crisis in enterprises that had been set up under socialism.[5] In this context, the drop in levels of production in postsocialist countries during the first three to four years following the collapse of socialism was general and extremely weakly linked to the economic policy pursued.

Another feature of the late socialist economy was the existence of monetary overhang—the money mass exceeded the demand for money displayed by economic agents, and this manifested itself in shortages of goods. The socialist economy is an economy of suppressed inflation. In conditions of fixed prices the state can easily increase the money mass. The surplus money supply engendered by financing the budget deficit or by crediting enterprises in the state sector does not translate into higher prices but accumulates in the form of forced savings and unsatisfied demand for goods and services.

An economy of suppressed inflation can function stably if the state determines the volume and structure of enterprise production and distribution of output on the basis of charging specific enterprises with certain tasks, the failure of which leads to harsh sanctions for the managers responsible. The collapse in socialist countries of the hierarchical economy tightly linked to the authoritarian political regime demanded the introduction of market mechanisms of coordination. In turn, liberalization of prices and of economic agents radically changed the environment in which monetary policy was conducted. Now surplus money supply leads to a worsening of the deficit and to an acceleration of inflation. Whereas under socialism the consumer had no choice between saving or purchasing goods at a higher price, after price liberalization the consumer did have such a choice. And it is this choice that reveals the real level of demand for money. The key factors determining this demand are prior monetary history and the level of confidence in the national currency and in the stabilization efforts of the government.

Thus the two major macroeconomic processes that postsocialist countries have encountered are a sharp drop in production and in the real money mass. Moreover, as a rule the drop has been much greater than that expected by the government that initiated the reforms. This is the source of theories that appear in economic and political debates immediately after the start of reforms, linking the fall in production to an excessive money and credit squeeze and proposing to increase the rate of monetary growth to stabilize production.[6] Where governments proved resistant to such proposals and monetary policy was tight, the inflationary wave produced by liquidating the monetary overhang quickly fizzled out, the inflation rate fell, and demand for the national currency and the real money mass started to grow. In those cases where monetary policy softened and the government tried to support production by increasing the money supply, the process of disinflation proved much more protracted.

Serious structural shifts in a country's economy occur in reaction to the start of economic reforms and tight monetary policy. During the transition recession, which lasts three to four years, the share of population employed in industry falls and the share of industrial output in GDP does also, whereas employment in the services sector grows as does the share of the latter in GDP. Serious shifts occur in the structure of industrial production itself. The most dynamic part of the economy, as a rule, is the private sector, which emerges not so much on the basis of privatized state enterprises, but alongside them.

The first macroeconomic indicator revealing an imminent upsurge in a country's economy is the growth of exports in convertible currency, which normally starts immediately after price liberalization and is followed by general growth of exports. From the second year of reform, as a rule, the level of real incomes and real wages stabilizes and starts to grow. Investment dynamics lag behind output dynamics. The growth of capital investment usually starts only after general economic growth begins.[7]

In countries that undertake radical reforms that ensure rapid disinflation, the transition recession is pronouncedly Schumpeterian in character. Resources that were previously tied up in inefficient and nonviable enterprises are quickly redistributed to enterprises and sectors that are capable of competing in harsh market conditions. General growth in production begins when the growth of output in the new private sector, and also in that part of the state sector that is able to adapt to the new conditions, proves capable of more than compensating for the continuing cuts in ineffective enterprises inherited from the socialist period.

The key role for the success of market reforms of structural changes and the emergence of a broad section of enterprises capable of competing in the marketplace demands that special attention be devoted to the mechanisms that underpin them. An important cause of the economic stagnation and crisis of socialism that led to its collapse was the absence of institutions in the socialist economy that ensured the generation and introduction of efficient innovations and the automatic redistribution of resources to economic units capable of using them effectively.

Creating an environment that provides such incentives has been a strategic goal of the postsocialist transition. In a developed market economy the most important mechanism for ensuring this is a hard budget constraint for enterprises.[8] Enterprises that are incapable of using resources efficiently and are not using the most rational production methods become uncompetitive, start to experience liquidity problems, and become loss making, their managers lose their jobs, and owners lose their property. The strong link between effectiveness/financial stability and the maintenance of control over the corresponding resource flows is the most important mechanism giving the market economy the edge over its socialist competitor.

In a socialist economy budget constraints are soft. Whether a manager keeps his job or not depends directly on his loyalty to those above him and on the fulfillment of production tasks they consider important, but not at all on his efficiency of resource use and positive financial results. The amount of financial and credit resources allotted to enterprises is determined by hierarchical bargaining and is extremely weakly linked to financial results. The obvious negative consequences of this state of affairs in providing incentives for effective production led to the development of the concept of "market socialism," in which the fundamental characteristics of the socialist system are preserved (the dominant role of state property and authoritarian political control by the communist party) while giving enterprises considerable autonomy in everday operations and in choosing the structure of production and counterparties and in which financial results become a very important criterion for measuring performance.

Experience in the functioning of the socialist market economy has shown that under these conditions budget constraints remain soft. Even the enterprises that are formally proclaimed to be autonomous remain part of a single sociopolitical structure in socialist society. The managers' careers and the preservation of their positions are to a much greater extent determined by relations with upper levels of the hierarchy than with the results of their work. The enterprise is part of the state. Even poor performance is not grounds for cutting the resources allotted to an enterprise, let alone for closing it down. The production capacity created during socialist industrialization continues to be used, regardless of its efficiency. Enterprises that operate in conditions of market socialism react much better than traditional socialist enterprises to changes in consumer demands and are better able to compete in terms of quality of output on domestic and foreign markets. Incentives to raise efficiency still remain weak, however, and there is no functioning mechanism for the automatic support of innovations. The low level of financial discipline in market socialist enterprises leads to the spread of nonpayments; a situation prevails in which enterprises fail en masse to fulfill financial obligations to one another and fail to fulfill their credit obligations to banks, and yet this leads neither to enterprise bankruptcy nor to change in management.[9]

The immediate reaction of such an enterprise to the challenge presented by radical economic changes (liberalization of prices and of the foreign trade regime, the collapse of COMECON, etc.) is to let mutual nonpayments balloon. These nonpayments serve as a shock absorber, weakening the connection between the changing conditions in enterprises' external environment (free prices, convertible currency, competition from imported goods, etc.) and the slow adaptation of economic units to these conditions. An enterprise that is incapable of producing and selling products that are competitive on the market and therefore do not generate sufficient financial resources not only is able to continue operating but also preserves its access to resource inputs, paying for them through the buildup of debts.

The fact that a state enterprise cannot be closed because it has no money is as abundantly obvious to its manager as it is to the state officials who are in a position to apply tough sanctions. Moreover, the legal and organizational underpinnings that guarantee strong financial discipline in a stable market economy do not exist. There is no experience of using bankruptcy legislation or legislation permitting the seizure of enterprise property in settlement of debts. Relations between enterprises and the state, on account of mutual financial obligations, reproduce the hierarchical bargaining that is characteristic of socialism. It becomes clear that an enterprise can accumulate tax arrears without serious consequences either for the enterprise itself or for the management team. In these conditions, a number of factors of importance in the bargaining process around real tax obligations come to the fore. If nonpayment of taxes by enterprises and the lack of money in their accounts are grounds for lowering real tax demands, then that creates huge incentives for increased nonpayment of taxes and the demonstration of impecuniousness.

The consequences of hierarchical bargaining and soft budget constraints becoming entrenched is of fundamental importance, and not only for the financial position of the state. In conditions of soft budget constraints, mechanisms ensuring the redistribution of resources to economic units that are capable of using them efficiently do not function. The managers and owners of uncompetitive enterprises are able to preserve their control over the corresponding resource flows.

In traditional socialism soft budget constraints and weak financial discipline are compensated for by the strong accountability of managers in the fulfillment of certain plan targets that the upper levels of the hierarchy deem critically important. In market socialism the link between enterprise management, the state, and the ruling party is weaker, but as before the state controls important personnel appointments. After the collapse of socialism, with persisting soft budget constraints, enterprises find themselves in a unique position: Weak administrative accountability is combined with weak financial discipline. An enterprise is not under any obligation to fulfill quantitative production targets and can be chronically loss making and insolvent without harsh sanctions being visited upon the management. The evolution of former state enterprises toward entrenching soft budget constraints occurs organically and is determined by the existing traditions of enterprise-state relations, by managerial experience, and by the condition of the legal infrastructure.

The most important factor counteracting such a turn of events in countries that implemented a policy of forced disinflation has been the harshness of financial constraints acting upon the state itself. A stabilizational monetary policy limits, through emission, the size of any permitted budget deficit and of financing it. Not staying within these limits is tantamount to admitting that the chosen strategy for transition to a market economy and the course of forced convergence with Europe has failed. The overwhelming majority of postsocialist governments have been faced with transitional fiscal crises and budget problems caused by the erosion of sources of state revenue and obstacles inherited from their socialist periods.[10] In this situation refusal to apply tough sanctions to delinquent enterprises, allowing them to accumulate tax arrears, is incompatible with maintaining adequate revenue levels for the state budget. A reformist government has to choose between tough budget constraints on the state (and, accordingly, a hardening of enterprise budget constraints) and the growth of budget imbalances, heralding the collapse of the stabilization policy. The exigencies of the budget that force the state to be tough on their own enterprises, forcing market norms of behavior on them (see figure 10.1).

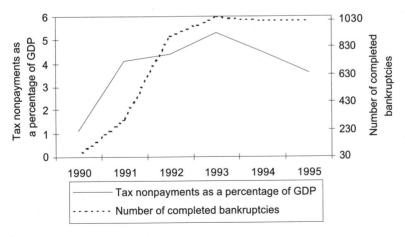

Figure 10.1
Tax nonpayments and bankruptcy in Poland, 1990–1995

The hardening of financial constraints on state enterprises not only changes the enterprises' priorities, but no less importantly, leads to the active redistribution of resources they have freed up to the rapidly growing new private sector. In this sector, in the absence of traditional ties with the managerial hierarchy, traditions of hard budget constraints become entrenched from the very beginning. The low level of financial discipline of former state enterprises, particularly major ones with good political contacts, means that the tax arrears concentrated in them remain a serious political and economic problem for many years after the beginning of market reforms; the size of this sector quickly decreases, however, and it stops playing a dominant role in the economy. Toughening the financial discipline of enterprises has significance that goes well beyond the problems of the state budget. Enterprises are forced to react more rapidly to changes in market conditions and in relative price levels. The inability of enterprise management to ensure the production of competitive products leads to a loss of control over resource flows. There is fast turnover in the economic elite and advancement of those capable of working in market conditions. There is a convergence of the standards of postsocialist enterprises to the standards characteristic of developed market economies. The enterprises that work under hard budget constraints do not have tax arrears and become the main motors of incipient economic growth.[11]

The experience of Czechoslovakia provides a distinctive illustration of the link between budget problems and the dynamics of restructuring enterprises. Czechoslovakia inherited from the socialist period a fiscal system that had minimal imbalances. Its state budgets in 1988–1990 had deficits that did not exceed 1 percent of GDP, and rates of monetary aggregate growth were stable and low. In 1990, on the eve of price liberalization, the new democratic government produced a budget with a primary surplus (0.7 percent of GDP). Reducing extremely high revenues and expenditures that had been characteristic of the socialist period was a conscious policy of the Czechoslovak government. The maintenance of a satisfactorily functioning tax system saved the Czechoslovak authorities from the fiscal crisis that many postsocialist countries suffered. Moreover, after the split of Czechoslovakia, the Czech Republic, which had been a net contributor to the federal budget, effectively acquired additional financial resources.

An important difference between Czechoslovakia and Poland or Hungary, however, was the almost complete absence in Czechoslovakia of a private sector in the prereform period. Under postsocialist new conditions, the Czechoslovak state enterprises encountered serious financial problems. The strong position of the state budget allowed the authorities to combine tough budget and monetary policies at the macro level with tolerance of soft budget constraints in the state enterprise sector. The law on bankruptcy adopted in 1991 was effectively suspended. In 1991–1992 there were no cases of bankruptcy or liquidation of large or medium-sized enterprises. As a result Czechoslovak enterprises responded to the challenges presented by the radically changing environment in a manner typical of enterprises in market socialism: by expansion of mutual nonpayments. Only in April 1993 was it possible to implement bankruptcy legislation to halt further growth of mutual arrears.

The restructuring of enterprises, the freeing up of resources, and the development of the new private sector moved much more slowly in Czechoslovakia than in Poland. A clear indicator of this is the low level of unemployment in the former. The combination of tight budget and monetary policies at the macro level and soft budget constraints at the enterprise level meant that the Czech Republic demonstrated a combination of low inflation (less than 10 percent per year from 1993 on) and low unemployment (less than 3 percent of those employed throughout the whole period), which was unusual for transition economies. The price paid, however, was the long-term preservation of inefficient enterprises, the holding back of structural improvements, and the preservation of a managerial corpus that had not adapted to market conditions. As a result, the growth of GDP that began in 1994 was slow and unstable, and in 1997 turned into a new recession.

To resolve the problem of increasing enterprise efficiency, Czech authorities were the first to focus on rapid, mass privatisation using vouchers. The basic hypothesis behind this privatization scheme was the belief that control by an owner would force former state enterprises to change their operations radically and raise the quality of management. Practice showed that in the absence of hard budget constraints the behaviour of privatised postsocialist enterprises that preserve close ties with the state and can accumulate arrears is similar to the behavior of state enterprises. The major role of insiders in privatisation and the preservation of the previous managerial elite in managing the privatized enterprises, which is characteristic of the overwhelming majority of postsocialist countries, makes it impossible to break the traditional ties of former state enterprises with the state.

Thus an analysis of countries that implemented tough anti-inflationary policies at the start of the transition period shows that the decline in output and in the ratio of money in GDP are unavoidable features of the initial phase of postsocialist transition. Provided that policies of steady, low monetary growth rates and minimal monetary financing of the budget deficit are pursued, the inflationary leap engendered by the liquidation of the inherited monetary overhang can be quickly brought under control. The rapidly growing new private sector, as a rule, provides the motor of economic growth. Furthermore, rapid, major structural shifts in production and employment are characteristic of the transition process. Under these conditions the evolution of enterprise behavior adheres to the following scheme:

1. Soft budget constraints and the reproduction of behavior inherent in market socialism are the norm for former state enterprises at the start of the transition period. The trend of growing mutual nonpayments is one manifestation of this. If the state does not resist by pursuing a policy of toughening financial discipline, this behavior becomes entrenched and is preserved even after privatization.

2. The financial problems of the state and the need to control the budget deficit to hold inflation in check are the most important factors pushing postsocialist governments to ensure that enterprises follow a tough financial regime.

3. Only the entrenchment of hard budget constraints brings norms of postsocialist enterprise behavior into line with those accepted in developed market economies and with those that form the foundation of modern microeconomic theory. The fundamental hypothesis of modern microeconomy concerning enterprises striving to maximize profits does not apply to postsocialist enterprises with soft budget constraints. Instead a fundamentally different system of behavioral norms develops, differing from both traditional socialist and standard market systems.

These processes are most developed in countries with slower implementation of postsocialist reforms and where the period of high inflation is more protracted. I therefore examine them in more detail in the the next section.

Weak Budgetary Policy and Its Effects

A distinguishing feature of those countries that manage to achieve rapid disinflation and create the basis for the revival of economic growth is consensus within the political elite concerning the choice of strategic development course for the country. Despite changes in government these countries have striven for rapid integration and convergence with the European Union. This has made it possible to place a de facto veto on large-scale experiments with economic populism. In the course of election campaigns, populist policies have regularly been endorsed proposing that economic problems be resolved through major monetary financing and increased budget expenditures, but they impinged weakly on economic policy.

In the overwhelming majority of countries of the former Soviet Union and also in Romania and Bulgaria, there was no such consensus. In these countries the choice of economic course was the subject of acute political battles, and fiscal and monetary policies conducted were subject to sharp fluctuations. In some of these countries, the governments from the outset attempted to implement "soft" or gradualist reforms (Romania, Ukraine, et al.). In others, initial radical reforms did not have enough political support and were quickly superseded by soft monetary and budgetary policies (Russia and Bulgaria). The result was that high rates of inflation endured for an extended period and financial stabilisation was delayed. Further developments have demonstrated that sustained high inflation leads to a number of micro- and macroeconomic phenomena that are stable and have a significant influence on the further development of the national economy, holding back economic growth and creating financial instability. As in the countries that pursued a tough stabilization policy, the first visible results of the postsocialist reforms were a drop in production and a fall in the ratio of money to GDP.

If there is weak political support for stabilization, however, state enterprises respond to the challenges of the changing economic environment by building up much greater mutual nonpayments compared with countries in which a policy of rapid disinflation is pursued. The drop in output, along with the sharp reduction in the real monetary mass and the explosive growth of mutual nonpayments, gives rise to the idea that the following cycle exists in the economy: An excessively tough monetary policy conducted out of doctrinaire monetarist considerations leads to a lack of money in the economy, causing enterprise nonpayments and the decline of production.

The standard prescription for what to do stems from this idea: increase the money supply ("saturate the economy with money") and resolve the problem of nonpayments by means of monetary financing and offsets to provide the foundations for economic growth. Usually all this is wrapped up in a discussion of the Keynesian alternative and the experience of pulling out of the Great Depression. A powerful sociopolitical coalition forms in support of this change in economic policy, uniting the management and workers of state enterprises interested in maintaining soft budget constraints and in avoiding radical restructuring and the representatives of various lobby groups interested in increasing budget expenditures financed through monetary emission. As a result, the contradiction between a tough budget policy at the macro level and soft budget constraints for state enterprises is resolved by softening the state's budget and monetary policies.

The consequences of this outcome are fairly predictable and have been observed in dozens of postsocialist countries that have experimented with slow disinflation. The fast growth of the money supply means that for a short period (two to six months) the real money mass also grows. Demand for products increases on the part of the population and enterprises, and the decline in production halts—indeed signs of economic reinvigoration are discernible. Once the brief period necessary for the adaptation of economic agents to the new money supply conditions ends, inflationary expectations grow sharply and demand for cash balances falls. The level of dollarization of the economy rises, the inflation rate overtakes the monetary growth rate, the real money mass starts to decrease, and after the drop in real solvent demand, decline in production once again accelerates.

Such experiments can be repeated several times in a particular country, prolonging the period of high inflation and of production decline. Sooner or later when people get fed up with high inflation and a situation in which demand for national currency is low and real budget revenues are rapidly reduced because of monetary financing, a political coalition comes together that is capable of implementing monetary stabilization by lowering the degree of monetary financing of the budget deficit and monetary aggregate growth rates to a level compatible with a slowing down of inflation. Even after this,

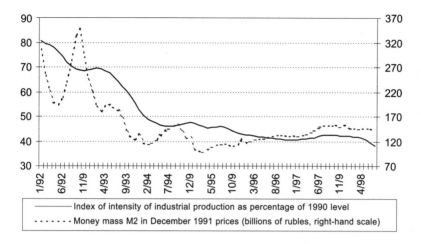

Figure 10.2
Industrial output and money—M2 in Russia
Note: Money mass in unchanged prices calculated by IET; indicators of industrial output calculated by TsEK.

however, countries in which the process of financial stabilization is delayed demonstrate a number of important common characteristics:

1. A long period of high inflation undermines confidence in the national currency and leads to a decline in the monetization of GDP as well as to a high level of dollarization of the economy. These are stable features that can only be overcome slowly over the course of a subsequent period of monetary stability (see figure 10.2).

2. The behavioral norms that are formed in conditions of a soft financial regime (offsets, arrears, nonpayments, and barter) cause a steady fall in the share of budget revenues in GDP to a level considerably lower than in countries that implement shock therapy (see figure 10.3). Correspondingly, reduction in the share of expenditure in GDP at the stage of financial stabilization is much sharper (see tables 10.1, 10.2).

3. High inflation leads to a much more profound stratification of society in terms of income levels and inequality as compared with countries in the first group following rapid disinflationary policy. Combined with a significant reduction in budget expenditures, this leads to a sharp increase in the share of poor people in the population.

4. For a prolonged period soft budget constraints for enterprises combine with weak fiscal constraints. During this time a distinct

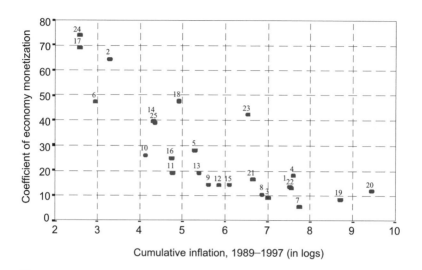

Figure 10.3
Inflation and monetization in transition economies
Note: 1—Azerbaijan; 2—Albania; 3—Armenia; 4—Belarus; 5—Bulgaria; 6—Hungary; 7—Georgia; 8—Kazakhstan; 9—Kyrgyzstan; 10—Latvia; 11—Lithuania; 12—Macedonia; 13—Moldova; 14—Poland; 15—Russia; 16—Romania; 17—Slovakia; 18—Slovenia; 19—Tajikistan; 20—Turkmenistan; 21—Uzbekistan; 22—Ukraine; 23—Croatia; 24—Czech Republic; 25—Estonia.

system of standards and norms of behavior takes root in the former state sector that differs substantially both from those in classical and market socialism and from those in a market economy as described in standard microeconomics. Moreover this system is extremely stable and reproduces itself even following such major changes as privatization and monetary stabilization.

Soft Budgetary Constraints and the Formation of the Nomenklatura Economic Sphere

I now focus in more detail on the problem of changing the system of incentives and norms of behavior in former state enterprises.

The classic socialist enterprise is organically built into the overall socialist hierarchy, which regulates the creation and redistribution of goods flows in the socialist economy. For enterprise managers, maintaining one's position and career advancement depends on fulfillment of a number of formal and informal demands (from demonstrations of political loyalty to the ability to fulfill tasks set by the leadership).

Table 10.1
Revenues, expenditures and budget deficit in countries with rapid disinflation, 1990–1997 (as percentage of GDP)

Country		1990	1991	1992	1993	1994	1995	1996	1997
Albania	Revenues	47.1	30.9	23.7	20.5	18.8	20.5	16.9	14.9
	Expenditures	62.1	61.9	44.0	34.9	31.2	30.8	29.0	27.6
	Deficit	–15	–31.0	–20.3	–14.4	–12.4	–10.3	–12.1	–12.7
Hungary	Revenues	53.9	52.5	52.6	55.1	52.5	47.2	45.2	48.0
	Expenditures	53.5	55.4	59.4	60.6	60.9	53.9	48.3	52.9
	Deficit	0.4	–2.9	–6.8	–5.5	–8.4	–6.7	–3.1	–4.9
Latvia	Revenues	—	—	27.4	35.8	34.1	34.7	36.6	39.6
	Expenditures	—	—	28.2	35.2	38.2	38.2	38.0	38.2
	Deficit	—	—	–0.8	0.6	–4.1	–3.5	–1.4	1.4
Poland	Revenues	42.9	42.3	42.8	47.4	45.8	45.1	44.2	45.0
	Expenditures	39.8	49.0	49.5	50.5	48.9	47.9	47.5	48.1
	Deficit	3.1	–6.7	–6.7	–3.1	–3.1	–2.8	–3.3	–3.1
Czech Republic	Revenues	—	—	—	42.4	42.1	41.0	40.7	39.5
	Expenditures	—	—	—	41.9	43.3	42.8	41.8	41.6
	Deficit	—	–1.9	–3.1	0.5	–1.2	–1.8	–1.2	–2.1
Slovakia	Revenues	—	—	—	44.0	46.7	47.2	47.1	47.2
	Expenditures	—	—	—	51.0	48.0	47.0	49.0	51.0
	Deficit	—	—	—	–7.0	–1.3	0.2	–1.9	–3.8
Estonia	Revenues	—	—	34.6	39.6	40.5	40.1	39.0	39.6
	Expenditures	—	—	34.9	40.3	39.2	41.4	40.5	37.4
	Deficit	—	5.2	–0.3	–0.7	1.3	–1.3	–1.5	2.2

Note: Dashes indicate the nonavailability of data.

Table 10.2
Revenues, expenditures and budget deficit in countries with slow disinflation, 1990–1997 (as percentage of GDP)

Countries		1990	1991	1992	1993	1994	1995	1996	1997
Azerbaijan	Revenues	—	—	—	40.6	33.8	17.5	17.6	19.7
	Expenditures	—	—	—	55.9	45.9	22.4	20.4	21.4
	Deficit	—	—	—	-15.3	-12.1	-4.9	-2.8	-1.7
Armenia	Revenues	—	26.1	32.8	28.2	32.4	15.6	14.4	18.2
	Expenditures	—	28.0	46.7	82.9	42.9	26.6	23.7	24.5
	Deficit	—	-1.9	-13.9	-54.7	-10.5	-11.0	-9.3	-6.3
Belarus	Revenues	—	—	46.0	54.3	47.5	42.7	41.0	44.7
	Expenditures	—	—	46.0	56.2	50.0	44.6	42.6	46.8
	Deficit	—	—	0.0	-1.9	-2.5	-1.9	-1.6	-2.1
Georgia	Revenues	—	30.0	10.3	9.7	16.1	7.1	9.7	10.6
	Expenditures	—	33.0	35.7	35.9	23.5	11.6	14.1	14.4
	Deficit	—	-3.0	-25.4	-26.2	-7.4	-4.5	-4.4	-3.8
Kazakhstan	Revenues	32.8	25.6	24.5	23.8	18.7	17.4	15.5	16.6
	Expenditures	31.4	32.9	31.8	25.2	25.9	19.9	18.6	20.3
	Deficit	1.4	-7.3	-7.3	-1.4	-7.2	-2.5	-3.1	-3.7
Kyrgystan	Revenues	—	—	—	—	—	16.7	15.9	16.9
	Expenditures	—	—	—	—	—	33.7	24.9	26.3
	Deficit	—	—	—	—	—	-17.0	-9.0	-9.4
Lithuania	Revenues	43.7	41.4	32.0	31.8	33.0	32.3	29.6	32.9
	Expenditures	49.1	38.7	31.5	35.1	38.5	36.8	34.1	34.7
	Deficit	-5.4	2.7	0.5	-3.3	-5.5	-4.5	-4.5	-1.8

Moldova	Revenues	—	24.7	30.4	22.0	31.9	34.0	32.0	34.3
	Expenditures	—	24.7	56.6	29.4	40.6	39.7	38.7	41.8
	Deficit	—	0.0	−26.2	−7.4	−8.7	−5.7	−6.7	−7.5
Russia	Revenues	—	—	33.1	33.3	36.9	31.3	31.8	33.3
	Expenditures	—	—	37.2	40.7	45.9	37.0	40.1	40.7
	Deficit	—	—	−4.1	−7.4	−9.0	−5.7	−8.3	−7.4
Romania	Revenues	39.7	42.0	37.4	33.8	32.0	31.9	30.1	30.7
	Expenditures	38.7	38.7	42.0	34.2	33.9	34.5	34.1	34.3
	Deficit	1.0	3.3	−4.6	−0.4	−1.9	−2.6	−4.0	−3.6
Tadjikistan	Revenues	—	33.2	26.6	27.1	40.6	15.3	12.1	13.7
	Expenditures	—	49.6	55.0	50.7	54.8	26.5	17.9	17.0
	Deficit	—	−16.4	−28.4	−23.6	−10.2	−11.2	−5.8	−3.3
Turkmenistan	Revenues	44.8	40.7	55.4	18.7	9.0	10.9	16.7	29.2
	Expenditures	43.6	38.2	42.2	19.2	10.4	12.5	16.9	29.2
	Deficit	1.2	2.5	13.2	−0.5	−1.4	−1.6	−0.2	0.01
Uzbekistan	Revenues	45.0	49.1	25.0	36.0	29.2	34.6	34.3	30.5
	Expenditures	46.1	52.7	43.4	46.4	35.3	38.7	41.6	32.8
	Deficit	−1.1	−3.6	−18.4	−10.4	−6.1	−4.1	−7.3	−2.3
Ukraine	Revenues	—	—	33.0	38.3	36.7	29.9	28.4	29.2
	Expenditures	—	—	58.4	54.5	45.8	37.4	31.6	34.8
	Deficit	—	—	−25.4	−16.2	−9.1	−7.5	−3.2	−5.6

Note: Dashes indicate nonavailability of data.

The most important factors determining enterprise operations emerge in the process of hierarchical bargaining, during which enterprise managers strive to maximize the volume of resources allotted to them and minimize their own obligations. By no means can all aspects of the actual functioning of enterprises be normatively described or fall within existing legislation. The resolution of the most difficult problem for a socialist enterprise—ensuring access to the resources necessary for fulfilling the targets set—demands the building of a ramified system of contacts based on personal connections and the provision of mutual services of a normative and nonnormative character.[12] The flip side of the difficulty of hierarchical coordination of microeconomic links is the inertia of enterprises, the absence of a linkage between the efficient use of resources and the continued functioning of enterprises, and the rejection of innovations that demand the reorganization of existing links.

Under market socialism enterprise autonomy expands sharply. The enterprises themselves start to determine or at least to exercise substantial influence over the structure of production and of links with other economic units. Higher levels of the hierarchy have much weaker control over the enterprise under market socialism, and change of management for reasons of unsatisfactory performance is less frequent and more problematic. Although the ruling party maintains authoritarian political control and the power to remove management, however, the enterprise remains a part of the socialist economy, and the managers remain members of a single managerial elite, united by hierarchical links and common norms of behavior. The redistribution of enterprise property on a moderate scale to companies affiliated with the management falls within these norms, although conspicuous consumption does not. An enterprise director constantly has to prove that he is a loyal member of the nomenklatura and not a private entrepreneur. His position involves a core of contradictions that subsequently come to the surface in the postsocialist period—that is, the combination of limited administrative accountability of the manager with weak financial discipline of the enterprise—but they are not clearly visible.

The collapse of the communist regime radically changed the position of enterprise managers. The united social structure, of which they were more or less loyal members, has disappeared. Their position is strengthened considerably, and the chances of their removal for disloyalty to the new authorities decline. They find themselves in

a unique position in which financial and administrative irresponsi-
bility can be combined. The change in the situation does not become
clear immediately or automatically. In the initial period the inertia of
norms of behavior inherited from classical and market socialism
prevail, but with the consolidation of soft budget constraints in the
period of high inflation there is a gradual transformation, and fundamentally new facets appear.

Already in the period of market socialism it was revealed that the
real hardness of budget constraints differs substantially depending
on the size of the enterprise and the sector of the economy (highest
for small enterprises in low-priority sectors and lowest for major
enterprises in high-priority sectors). Within postsocialism these differences are underscored by the division of the economy into two
sectors that can be referred to as "market" and "nomenklatura."

The market sector is made up first and foremost of new private
enterprises that have no traditional ties to the state sector and also of
former state enterprises that have lost or broken their ties with the
state. The distinguishing feature of this sector is that it operates
under hard budget constraints. Enterprises in this sector cannot (and
have no desire to) run up tax arrears, and their relations with the
state are regulated by acting legislation. They willingly avail themselves of existing loopholes in the tax regime to reduce their tax
obligations, but they remain solvent.

The situation in the nomenklatura sector is fundamentally different; it consists of major enterprises in priority sectors, and as a rule,
they are run by authoritative representatives of the old economic
elite. The distinguishing feature of these enterprises is that even after
the collapse of socialism they still perceive the state as their own and
consider their problems to be the state's problems. The fear of social
conflicts, the threat of a sharp rise in unemployment, and traditional
personal ties—all this forces state bodies to handle these problems
with understanding, refraining from applying tough sanctions even
to those which do not fulfill their budget obligations. The fundamental difference between enterprises in the nomenklatura and market
sectors is that the former can accumulate budget arrears, and thus its
financial relations with the state are based not on legal norms but on
bargaining.

In the fundamentally new conditions, the old system of hierarchical bargaining, characteristic of the socialist period, in which the chief
goal of the enterprise is to limit state bodies' access to information

about its real condition and prospects (in this case financial), reproduces itself. If the volume of resources to be redistributed to the state is the result of hierarchical bargaining, then it is natural that an enterprise is interested in minimizing the flow of information while, of course, adhering to the rules of the game and making sure that proper relations are maintained with state bodies. This explains why the set of parameters on which reduction of real tax obligations depends is of such fundamental importance. An analysis of tax administration in postsocialist economies shows that there are several such parameters:

1. the number of workers employed at an enterprise
2. the volume of overdue debts
3. the existence of wage arrears
4. the existence of money on the enterprise's accounts

If an enterprise's real tax obligations are inversely proportional to the number of employees, the volume of debt, and the volume of wage arrears while being directly proportional to the amount of money in enterprise accounts, it is not hard to figure out what characteristics will be dominant in a nomenklatura enterprise after the establishment of corresponding behavioral norms: It will have a significant quantity of fictitious and surplus employees, major debts for products supplied and services provided, significant wage arrears, and no money in its account. Any other outcome would point to the economic irrationality of the enterprise management.

The most important consequence of the prolonged maintenance of soft budget constraints is the stability of the managerial elite's position and the absence of a link between retaining their jobs and efficiency of production and financial results. An enterprise that uses its resources inefficiently is able to maintain control over its resource flows, compensating for its unsatisfactory financial results by reducing its obligations to the budget. The cost of this financial softness, however is the shakiness of ownership rights and thus of control over resource flows in a given enterprise. While the enterprise management has good relations with state bodies its position is relatively secure, but there are no guarantees that things will always remain that way, and from a formal, legal point of view, the enterprise, which has accumulated major debts to the budget and other creditors, is bankrupt. Even after privatization, during which management succeeded in establishing de facto ownership control over its enterprise, this property remains insecure, and retaining it depends on loyalty to the authorities.

The peculiar incentives of the postsocialist manager-owner working in the nomenklatura sector stem from this. He tries to preserve control over the enterprise for its cash flows, but because of the lack of guaranteed property rights, he is extremely reluctant to invest private financial resources in it. He is also preoccupied with transferring part of the enterprise's resources to private companies that are linked personally to him, that is, in transferring resources from quasi-private to private property. The key instrument for doing this is interenterprise debts. An enterprise can, for example, pay in advance for goods and services ordered and never receive anything, while a certain short-lived company disappears, but not before transferring money to the accounts of a firm belonging to the family of the director or owner of the parent company. Or vice versa, an enterprise can deliver goods or services to an enterprise that never pays to the enterprise's accounts, but instead makes a payment to another account (by previous arrangement); thus the director, in accordance with the accepted rules of the game, complains about a lack of money and the nonpayments that plague everybody. For this reason, the nomenklatura sector enterprises form a number of quasi-private entities around the parent company to service the transfer of revenues generated to the fully private property of the enterprise's managerial team.

All activities concerned with the transfer of enterprise resources are semilegal or illegal. At the very least, these activities are legally vulnerable, and sometimes they are blatantly illegal. Thus when executing the transfer of funds the management team has an interest in minimizing the risk of confiscation of accumulated private property, in the case of tough sanctions being applied for embezzlement of enterprise funds. The likelihood of confiscation is considerably reduced if property is transferred abroad. This explains the organic link between interenterprise nonpayments, nonpayment to the budget, and export of capital.

The behavioral norms of the nomenklatura economy exercise significant influence over the relations between business and the authorities. The opportunity to accumulate tax arrears without tough sanctions being doled out presupposes the maintenance of close and regular contact between the enterprise and the state, which are both involved in bargaining over the real volume of tax obligations. Preserving a cooperative relationship with the authorities provides the greatest security in maintaining control over enterprises and financial flows. This system of relations is predicated on individual, not normatively regulated relations between business and government officials, which traditionally has been considered a breeding ground for corruption in the state administration. The managerial team of the nomenklatura enterprise regularly removes part of the enterprise's funds from under the control of the enterprise and transfers them to the accounts of affiliated enterprises.

At the start of the transition period, when enterprises and authorities were still adapting to the new and radically changing conditions, it was still possible to suppose that government officials participating in bargaining over real tax obligations were in a state of childishly sincere incomprehension about the nature of nonpayments and the logic of nomenklatura enterprise behavior. With the entrenchment of this practice, however, this hypothesis becomes rather hard to support. The tight link between the reduction of real tax obligations and growth of capital flight involves the cooperation of officials in securing the unhindered functioning of the relevant chain of financial transactions. In this connection, widespread corruption is an integral part of the postsocialist economy in which enterprises operate under soft budget constraints.

The symbiosis of property and power in the nomenklatura sector and the differing rules of the game for various market participants create serious obstacles for private-sector development:

• The preservation of inefficient enterprises in the nomenklatura sector limits the flow of resources that could provide the basis for the dynamic development of the private sector.

• The private sector is forced to adapt to conditions of unfair competition in which nomenklatura sector enterprises have obvious advantages because of their special relations with the authorities (e.g., the opportunity to reduce their real tax obligations).

• The symbiosis of property and power characteristic of nomenklatura capitalism makes it possible to limit the market entry of private enterprises that could compete with the nomenklatura enterprises.

• The creation, alongside nomenklatura enterprises, of a network of quasi-private companies that service the transfer of funds obstructs the entrenchment of acceptable norms of business ethics in the private sector and impinges negatively on public perceptions of this sector.

A characteristic feature of the norms and standards of business behavior in the nomenklatura sector is the resistance to major changes in the conditions under which enterprises operate. The standards of behavior of nomenklatura capitalism are formed in conditions of state property being preserved in postsocialist enterprises. Their state character is an important argument in support of the need for an individual approach, for taking the enterprise's interests into account, and for not allowing the full implementation of the bankruptcy mechanism. The preservation of their formal state status does not in any way obstruct the formation of the behavioral norms of nomenklatura capitalism. For example, in Bulgaria the overwhelming majority of large and medium-sized enterprises remained in the state sector until 1997–1998, they acquired real economic autonomy in full, and the managerial elite developed a number of quasi-ownership norms of behavior with all the attendant attributes (mass nonpayments, tax arrears, the transfer of capital from enterprises, close ties between enterprises and the state administrative apparatus, etc.). Moreover, as experience demonstrates, not even privatization leads to a radical change in the functioning of nomenklatura enterprises.

Compromise with the economic elite of the former regime, which is unavoidable in conditions of postsocialism, tends to hinder regulated privatization and leads to insiders, connected with the economic elite of the former state enterprises, preserving key positions even after privatization. The existing informal relations of enterprise management with state officials make it possible for enterprises to accumulate tax arrears and prove resistant to changes in the form of ownership. Serious changes in enterprise behavior are visible only where privatization is attended by a hardening of budget constraints, particularly in the sphere of small enterprises and in low-priority branches of the economy. For major enterprises budget constraints remain soft even after privatization, and the system of norms of nomenklatura capitalism continue to function.

The tight integration of the traditional socialist economic elite, the existing system of informal support and ties of mutual assistance, the identification of themselves as "us" as opposed to "them"—those from the private sector who have no ties with the nomenklatura— these are all important factors in the emergence of nomenklatura capitalism. In the early years of the postsocialist transformation there was an overt link between the social origin of enterprise managers (their membership in the nomenklatura of the ancien regime) and the enterprise's particular relations with the state—for example, as manifested in the right to accumulate tax arrears. State officials divide enterprises into those that they consider "their own" and those that they do not, depending on whether the former director is in charge or someone who has no developed system of contacts with the communist elite. With time, however, as nomenklatura capitalism stabilizes, this link weakens, as the case of the so-called oligarchs in Russia convincingly demonstrates. The majority of these oligarchs were not members of the economic elite of the ancien regime, although some of them were linked to it (pseudoprivate firms handling the transfer of funds, Komsomol businesses, etc.). There was an assumption that the sudden strengthening of the position of this group in 1995–1996, when they gained control of major Russian enterprises, as a result of a shift in the balance of power in the economic and political elites, would lead to substantial changes in the behavior of enterprises under their control. In the majority of cases this did not happen. The characteristic norms of behavior of nomenklatura capitalism (accumulation of tax arrears, nonpayments, transfer of funds to affiliated companies, limited interest in investment and innovation, soft budget constraints, etc.) as a rule have been preserved even after the radical change in the management elite.

Whereas "red directors" formed a privileged group the members of which were allowed to build up tax arrears by virtue of their background, the oligarchs acquired the same privileges by virtue of their influence and contacts in the state apparatus. In the two-sector economy that had emerged, they could not be reconciled with membership in the commercial sector, which was forced to pay taxes on time. If tax privileges exist, the rich and politically influential will acquire them regardless of social background. The norms of behavior of the old economic elite proved to be better entrenched than the position of the elite itself.

The system of nomenklatura capitalism formed in conditions of the weak budget policy of the early years of the postsocialist transition, organically complementing enterprise soft budget constraints. Major monetary financing of budget expenditures allows the state to be soft in its treatment of enterprises: preserving subsidies, preferential credits, import subsidies, tolerance of tax arrears, and the like.

It is in these conditions that the system of state protectionism, individual relations between the state and enterprises, and the bureaucratic bargaining over the volume of funds to be allotted to enterprises and their obligations to the state fits in most organically. With time the possibilities of monetary finance are curtailed and high inflation stimulates flight from the national currency, dollarization of the economy, a decline in the ratio of money to GDP, and as a result, a reduction in the value of real incomes due to seigniorage.

Alongside the traditional factors that have been well explained by economic theory linking high inflation and the fall in demand for the national currency,[13] under postsocialism there is one more nontrivial factor: the link between the volume of tax obligations, nonpayments, and the presence of funds in enterprise accounts creates an incentive for enterprises to reduce their demand for national currency. The standard reaction of a postsocialist nomenklatura enterprise to attempts by the state to increase money supply is to increase financial flows, transferring funds to affiliated companies, including foreign ones. This leads to a further decline in enterprise demand for cash balances in the national currency. With the fall of the ratio of money to GDP, real income from emission is reduced, and together with this the ability to fulfill budget obligations by means of central bank credits. The entrenchment of soft budget constraints and the accumulation tax arrears, along with the standard factors described by V. Tanzi,[14] lead to an erosion of tax receipts. High inflation accompanied by attempts to saturate the economy with money over time undermines confidence in the pseudo-Keynesian prescriptions for resolving the macroeconomic problems of postsocialism. This inevitably leads to the formation of a political coalition that is prepared to reduce monetary financing of the budget and on the basis of this to cut inflation rates to a level characteristic of those countries that from the very outset of transition conducted tough monetary policies.

Delayed financial stabilization, occurring after several years of high inflation and after the formation of a nomenklatura capitalist sector, has a number of specific characteristics. By the beginning of the stabilization attempt, confidence in the national currency has been undermined and the ratio of money to GDP is low. In this situation even limited emissionary finance of the budget deficit leads to rates of monetary growth that are incompatible with successful stabilization. The road to softer disinflation, with gradual reduction of the scale of monetary financing of the deficit (à la Poland 1990–1993), is closed.

The soft budget constraints that become entrenched during the period of high inflation lead to a long-term drop in tax receipts to a level significantly lower than that which is characteristic for countries that implement monetary stabilization at the start of the postsocialist transition. As a result, it is necessary to reduce state expenditures much more sharply than in countries that conduct a monetarist policy.

The erosion of budget expenditures, the low level of monetization of the economy, and the sociopolitical problem of reducing spending obligations sufficiently determine the budget problems typical of delayed stabilization. From this point of view, the following are the components of an optimal strategy for the situation characteristic of delayed stabilization:

• restructuring and reducing the budget obligations to a level which can realistically be covered by budget revenues

• minimizing the budget deficit

• toughening the financial discipline of enterprises

• making active attempts to reduce the size of the nomenklatura sector by increasing financial discipline and stimulating the redistribution of resources to the private sector, which operates under conditions of hard budget constraints.

Only such measures can prepare the way for the resumption of economic growth, which would increase budget revenues and the financing of the state's priority budget obligations.

In the current sociopolitical situation, however, it is difficult to realize such a strategy. Thus a characteristic feature of delayed stabilization has been the gulf between mobilizable budget revenues and budget obligations, which have been partly covered by external and internal financing of the budget deficit, and in part this feature has manifested itself in the state falling behind on its obligations. Tight monetary policy is compatible with a soft budgetary policy only in the short term. The success of such a combination depends on the ability of the state to liquidate fiscal imbalances in the context of falling inflation (raising additional revenues, reducing spending obligations, stimulating economic growth, etc.). Without this prerequisite financing of the budget deficit by government, debt inevitably leads to increased spending on servicing the debt and sooner or later forces a return to monetary financing of the budget deficit, that is, monetary policy falls into line with the soft budget policy. For postsocialist countries with delayed stabilization, the risk of such an outcome is increased by the low ratio of money to GDP, which limits the possibilities of domestic financing of the budget deficit, and by the strong dependence of the budget on external sources for closing the budget deficit (foreign portfolio investment), the dynamics of which are subject to sharp fluctuations. Thus delayed stabilization is inherently unstable and risky.

A distinguishing feature of delayed stabilization is that it is commenced in the context of an entrenched nomenklatura capitalist sector occupying a dominant position in the economy and with strong political support for its own interests. Whereas at the previous stage the state's soft financial policy is organically fused with soft budget constraints for enterprises, the move toward stabilization exacerbates the contradictions between the interests and norms of the nomenklatura sector and stabilization policy conducted at the macro level.

In contrast to the situation characteristic in developed market economies, in which the volume of the state's tax receipts is determined first and foremost by the relevant legislation, in postsocialist countries with a significant nomenklatura sector, tax receipts are the result of bargaining between enterprises and the state. With the loss of monetary sources of financing the budget deficit, the state finds itself in a tough position. Now the ability to fulfill its functions, to support sociopolitical stability, is determined by the mobilizable revenues from taxation of the commercial sector and the household sector and by the results of bargaining with enterprises in the nomenklatura sector. Thus there is an inevitable exacerbation of the conflict between the state, on the one hand, and enterprises in the nomenklatura sector, on the other, over the latter's real tax obligations.

By the start of delayed stabilization, nomenklatura sector enterprises have long surrounded themselves with a number of affiliated, quasi-private enterprises, and they have perfected the technique of milking funds from parent enterprises while demonstrating that the enterprise is strapped for cash. Attempts by state bodies to come to grips with the intricate schemes underpinning these operations have had little success. Thus strengthening the state's position in tax bargaining and increasing the share of tax revenues in GDP can be achieved only by a demonstration of the state's ability to apply harsh and effective sanctions to major tax delinquents by undermining the control of the current managers and owners over an enterprise's financial flows (the use of bankruptcy procedures, etc.). Once the state proves itself capable of energetic action on this front, there will be a partial return of funds from affiliated companies to the parent enterprise, a slowdown in the growth of or an absolute drop in tax arrears, and an increase in the money revenues to the budget. If the state shows itself to be weak and unwilling to use existing sanctions on tax delinquents, the growth rate of nonpayments, the growth rate of tax arrears, and the scale of capital flight will all increase, and tax receipts to the budget will fall. The problem of taxing the nomenklatura capitalist sector at the stage of delayed stabilization is always a political problem and a problem of political will, not of tax administration as traditionally understood in developed market economies.

A characteristic feature of the nomenklatura capitalist sector is its concentration of large enterprises. Thus the battle over tax obligations and the financial discipline of leading enterprises in the sector has a public demonstration effect. A show of political will and the toughening of the financial discipline imposed on even just a few very large enterprises in the nomenklatura sector has a powerful demonstration effect, forcing even those who are not directly affected by the measures to correct their behavior. In just the same way, a show of weakness and indecisiveness on the part of the authorities toward major tax delinquents quickly has a knock-on effect across the nomeklatura sector as a whole.

The intensity of the conflict between the needed tightening of fiscal pressure on the nomenklatura sphere on the forefront of delayed stabilization and, on the other hand, the prevailing norms and principles of behavior in this sphere is determined by the fact that for a significant section of enterprises in the nomenklatura sector, toughening financial discipline does leads not simply to a drop in owners' incomes, but also to the real threat that they could lose control of the parent company. As has been demonstrated, the essence of the phenomenon of nomenklatura capitalism lies in the combination of weak administrative accountability and soft financial discipline, which makes it possible for managers and owners of inefficiently run enterprises to maintain control over resource flows, to minimize the volume of investments, and to transfer funds from the enterprises, compensating for their unsatisfactory financial results by reducing obligations to the budget. Toughening financial discipline presupposes the activation of mechanisms for removing inefficient managers and owners who are unable to operate in a market economy and replacing them with people who are capable of working in market conditions and who will fulfill in full the financial obligations of the parent enterprise. This in turn leads to an erosion of the no-menklatura sector as it is squeezed by the real private sector. This turn of events makes it possible to remove obstacles to efficient structural changes and economic growth that have been put in place by the dominance of the nomenklatura sector in the economy. The issue of relations between the state and largest enterprises of the nomenklatura sector is not a technical accounting problem but one of property and power, of the strategy of economic development and the possibility of stimulating economic growth after the collapse of socialism.

The sharp contradiction between tough financial constraints at the state level and preservation of soft constraints in the nomenklatura sector, characteristic of delayed stabilization, does not allow for delay in resolving it. Either the state succeeds in raising the level of financial discipline of enterprises, stabilizes the budget revenues, and creates preconditions for stable economic growth or it faces a number of indissoluble social and financial problems (growing wage and pension arrears, a decline in the real wages of state sector employees, rapid buildup of state debt and growth of expenditure on servicing it, and loss of foreign investor confidence in the ability of the state to fulfill its obligations), forcing it to abandon stabilization attempts and return to monetary financing of budget expenditures and high levels of inflation in the economy.

The Main Problems of the Postcommunist Transformation in Russia

In the context of what has been set forth above, I will briefly examine the economic and political problems of the postsocialist transformation in Russia as well as the sources of the development of the current crisis.

Economic reforms and macroeconomic stabilization in Russia were slow, and the period of extremely high inflation dragged on for four years. The first two attempts at financial stabilization (winter to spring 1992 and autumn to winter 1993) did not enjoy sufficient political support and were superseded by rapid expansion of the money supply (see figure 10.4).

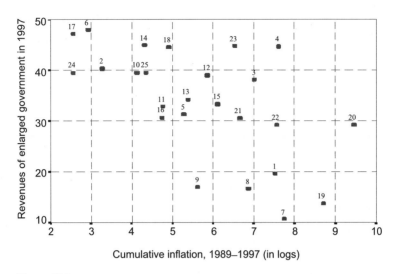

Figure 10.4
Government revenues and inflation in transition economies
Note: 1—Azerbaijan; 2—Albania; 3—Armenia; 4—Belarus; 5—Bulgaria; 6—Hungary;
7—Georgia; 8—Kazakhstan; 9—Kyrgyzstan; 10—Latvia; 11—Lithuania; 12—Mace-
donia; 13—Moldova; 14—Poland; 15—Russia; 16—Romania; 17—Slovakia; 18—
Slovenia; 19—Tajikistan; 20—Turkmenistan; 21—Uzbekistan; 22—Ukraine; 23—
Croatia; 24—Czech Republic; 25—Estonia.

Throughout the whole postsocialist period representatives of the
traditional economic elite in Russia have maintained a strong base of
support in the parliament, regional administrations, and (from summer 1992) the federal government. Control of the economic nomenklatura over the government was consolidated in 1992 when, with
the support of the Congress of People's Deputies, Viktor Cherno-
myrdin, a man whose whole career had been spent working very
closely with the major socialist enterprise sector, was appointed
prime minister.

The Russian law on bankruptcy of enterprises was adopted late
and until 1996–1997 was hardly applied. The legislation on privatization that was adopted by the Supreme Soviet (above all the second
privatization option, offering enterprise workers the possibility of
purchasing 51 percent of shares at book price) strengthened the control of the traditional economic nomenklatura over enterprises after
privatization. In the context of high inflation the nomenklatura capitalist sector of the economy rapidly formed with all its characteristic
features (low levels of financial discipline, bargaining with the state

over tax obligations, the outflow of enterprise resources to affiliated companies).

After an inflationary burst in Russia in the autumn of 1994, the Russian government started to implement its stabilization program, posited on the rejection of monetary financing of the budget deficit and reduction of the deficit. This made it possible to cut inflation to moderate levels by the autumn of 1995 (something that Poland had achieved in 1991). Disinflation was backed up by a considerable reduction of budget expenditures.

The absence of political support for reform made it impossible for the government to reduce the budget deficit in a more resolute fashion and to achieve serious restructuring of budget obligations. Disinflation was attended by the growth of government debt, financed by domestic and external sources, and the chronic problems of arrears. The latter were used by the nomenklatura capitalist sector as an important argument in support of preserving bargaining in its financial relations with the state. Gradually relations between the state and the largest (budget) debtor enterprises were pushed to the forefront of economic policy. Enterprises react sensitively to changes in the government's resolve to toughening the financial discipline it imposes on them.

Overall, if one ignores the short-term fluctuations, the period 1995–1997 in Russia was characterized by an unstable equilibrium in the relations between the state and the nomenklatura capitalist sector. The share of the consolidated government's revenues in GDP was sufficiently stable, and the growth of arrears on payments to the budget and extrabudgetary funds continued, together with inter-enterprise nonpayments. At the end of 1997, the combination of the international financial crisis and the blocking of the reform program proposed by the government of "young reformers" radically changed the direction of capital flows in Russia. A mass dumping of Russian securities by investors sharply exacerbated the budget crisis. Since then, preservation of the fragile equilibrium of 1995–1997 has been impossible. A choice has to be made between radically tightening budget policy (which would require tough and credible sanctions against major delinquent enterprises, a frontal attack on the nomenklatura capitalist sector, and restructuring of budget obligations) and a return to a high inflationary regime. Sergei Kirienko's government attempted to pursue the first path but was blocked by a parliamentary majority. The result was a return to an inflationary regime.[15]

At the same time, the brisk spiraling inflation that followed the ruble devaluation and the massive financial emissions in fall 1998, as well as the reaction to these developments by the public, frightened the newcomer administration of Yevgeni Primakov. This was particularly the case since the new administration operated in a Duma controlled by the communists. Consequently, by December 1998, the new administration had rejected the continuation of massive monetary emissions in budgetary policy. Instead, Primakov began cutting budget spending in the real sector. Starting in 1999, the sudden boom in commodity prices temporarily removed the pressure from budgetary politics and its many problems. Historically speaking, this factor is of a transitional nature. Tied to this transitional process, the maintenance of a significantly sized nomenklatura economic sector in Russia, one that operates under soft budgetary conditions, remains the key political-economic problem in the near future.

After a heavy, protracted three-and-a-half-year battle, the nomenklatura capitalist sector in Russia asserted its right to soft budget constraints and the accumulation of tax arrears. Attempts by the state to strengthen enterprises' financial discipline ended in failure. The government returned to monetary financing of the budget deficit, bringing budget constraints at the macro level into line with the soft budget constraint on the dominant sector of the economy.

To close, I now draw some conclusions from my analysis of attempts at realizing a strategy of slow, gradualist transformation after the collapse of socialism:

1. A prolonged period of high inflation and soft monetary and budgetary policies allows former state enterprises to preserve soft budget constraints and to increase their debts to the budget and to counterparties without a real threat of losing control over enterprises and the corresponding financial flows. As a result a stable combination of low administrative and financial accountability emerges, when neither the socialist hierarchical discipline nor the market discipline of hard budget constraints is functioning. In the economy, a distinct nomenklatura capitalist sector takes shape, the standards and behavioral norms of which differ significantly from those characteristic both of socialist (classical and market) and of private capitalist enterprises.

2. Nomenklatura capitalist enterprises find themselves bargaining with the state over the issue of real tax obligations and are able to

accumulate tax arrears and debts to suppliers without any real threat that the management and owners will be stripped of control over the enterprises and financial flows. The mechanism that in a market economy ensures the redistribution of resources to efficient enterprises does not function. Nomenklatura capitalist enterprises respond weakly to market incentives.

3. The defining feature of a nomenklatura capitalist enterprise is that it can accumulate nonpayments to the budget and can maintain a bargaining style of relations between enterprises and the state over real tax obligations that leads to the tight interweaving of property and power and to the spread of corruption in the postsocialist economy. The depence of nomenklatura capitalist property on the support of the authorities gives it an unstable character. Therefore, the management elite of nomenklatura capitalist enterprises has an interest in preserving control over resource flows and the transfer of funds to affiliated firms, preferably those located abroad. Thus enterprise nonpayments, budget nonpayments, and the export of capital are interconnected.

4. The fall in monetization of the economy and in real revenues from monetary emission that occurs in conditions of high inflation and the erosion of tax receipts forces the postsocialist state to abandon its inflationary policy and to undertake attempts at monetary stabilization. This stabilization occurs at the level of budget revenues after they have been undermined during the period of high inflation and therefore is tough, socially conflictual, and unstable.

5. Tightening fiscal policy at the macro level gives rise to a conflict between the state's need to mobilize additional tax revenues and the existing norms of enterprise behavior in the nomenklatura capitalist sector, which functions under conditions of soft budget constraints. The battle over real tax obligations becomes political, and its outcome exercises definitive influence over the results of the stabilization attempts.

Ensuring durable financial stabilization presupposes the resolute dismantling of the nomenklatura capitalist sector, the freeing up of resources, and the removal of obstacles along the path to private-sector development. If this fails, attempts at financial stabilization prove to be short-lived, and financial and monetary policy at the macro level fall into line with the soft budget constraints under which nomenklatura capitalist enterprises operate. The economy then returns to a regime of stagnation and high inflation.

References

Cagan, P. 1956. The monetary dynamics of hyperinflation. In *Studies in the quantity theory of money*, ed. Milton Friedman. Chicago: University of Chicago Press.

Calvo, G., and F. Coricelli. 1992. *Output collapse in Eastern Europe: The role of credit—The macroeconomic situation in Eastern Europe.* Washington, D.C.: World Bank and International Monetary Fund.

Dombrovsky, Marek. 1996. *Fiskal'nyi krizis v period transformatsii* (Fiscal crisis in the period of transformation). Warsaw: CASE.

Gaidar, Yegor. 1997a. *Anomalii eknomicheskogo rosta* (Anomalies of economic growth). Moscow: Evraziya.

Gaidar, Yegor. 1997b. *Ekonomicheskie reformy i ierarkhicheskie struktury* (Economic reforms and hierarchic structures), vol. 2, 15–278. Moscow: Evraziya.

Gaidar, Yegor. 1997c. Detskie bolenzi postsotsializma (K voprosu o prirode byudzhetnykh protsessov etapa finansovoi stabilizatsii) (Children's illness of postsocialism (to the problem of the essence of budgetary processes at the stage of budgetary stabilization)). *Voprosy economiki* 1997, no. 4: 4–25.

Gedeon, S. 1987. Monetary disequilibrium and bank reform proposals in Yugoslavia. *Soviet Studies* 39, no. 2: 281–91.

Hemming, R., A. Cheasry, and A. Lahiri. 1997. The revenue decline—Policy experiences and issues in the Baltics, Russia, and other countries of the former Soviet Union. *IMF Occasional Paper* 33. Washington: IMF.

IEPPP. 1999. *Rossiyskaya ekonomika v 1998 godu: Tendentsii i perspecktivi* (Russian economy in 1998: Trends and outlooks). Moscow: Institute for the Economy in Transition/Institut Ekonomicheskikh Problem Perekhodnogo Perioda.

Kornai, Janos. 1980. *The economics of shortage.* Amsterdam: North Holland.

Organisation for Economic Cooperation and Development (OECD). 1997. Economic surveys—Poland.

Sargent, T. 1982. The ends of four big inflations. In *Inflation: Causes and effects*, ed. R. Hall. Chicago: University of Chicago Press.

Tanzi, V. 1978. Inflation, real tax revenue, and the case for inflationary finance: Theory with an application to Argentina. *IMF Staff Papers* 25 (September): 417–51.

Tyson, L. 1977. Liquidity crises in the Yugoslav economy: An alternative to bankruptcy? *Soviet Studies* 29 no. 2: 284–95.

11   Belarus: A Command Economy without Central Planning

D. Mario Nuti

Premise

Conventionally since the early 1990s Belarus has generally been considered as a postcommunist country in transition to democracy and markets—admittedly a laggard, but definitely a member of the club. In truth in 1992–1994 the country did make some progress in that direction, with a measure of price liberalization forced by the Russian stabilization program, the introduction of a domestic currency managed by a formally independent central bank, and the issuing of mass privatization vouchers. Since 1994, however, it has become increasingly apparent that Belarus is not, politically or economically, a postcommunist transition country—not any more, at least, than, say, China or Vietnam is.

Politically, Belarus is still characterized by Communist Party monopoly. President Aleksander Lukashenko, democratically elected in 1994, following a 1996 referendum broadened his powers and prolonged his term of office by two years to 2001, dissolved Belarus's parliament, replacing it with a co-opted assembly; he rules by decree. Political parties are subject to reregistration and other hurdles; the country's press is controlled.

Economically, Belarus is a command economy without central planning, like, say, Poland in the second half of the 1980s. State enterprises are still predominant; there are widespread administrative controls on output and employment by large state enterprises, on prices, and on exchange rates, and there are directed subsidized credits. Macroeconomic stabilization has foundered, with the resumption of high inflation, in spite of widespread economic and administrative controls, and with the reappearance of domestic shortages and external imbalances, due to an overvalued currency.

Without privatization and with hardly any foreign direct investment, capacity restructuring in the country has been exceedingly slow, and foreign trade is still largely with Russia.

Yet in some respects the Belarus economy has performed better than Russia's. Belarus has not squandered state capital through debt-for-equity swaps or insider privatization; it has little domestic and foreign indebtedness, respectively 4 percent and 8 percent of GDP; the government collects taxes and pays for its purchases, wages, and pensions; interenterprise arrears are low; and barter is limited to trade with Russia. Criminality—economic and non—has been kept in check, as a by-product of a zero-tolerance approach; corruption—which in 1994 Lukashenko was elected to fight—is much less common than in Russia. Above all, in 1996–1998 Belarus's GDP recovered much faster than that of other former Soviet republics (see table 11.1 for a summary of Belarus economic statistics 1992–1998 and table 11.2 for an update to those statistics).

In all these respects Belarus is an outlier. This chapter reviews Belarus's failure to reform and to stabilize and assesses its economic performance and prospects, including the prospective monetary union with Russia.

The Transition That Never Was

EBRD Scores

Belarus has a very low rating on the European Bank for Reconstruction and Development's (EBRD's) Transition Scoreboard, published yearly in the organization's *Transition Report*, for 1994–1998, and that rating has moreover been falling in the last three years. In addition to showing private-sector share in GDP, table 11.3 provides the EBRD's scores for Belarus, the Russian Federation, and Poland covering various aspects of transition. The EBRD scores range from 1 (little or no change) to 4+ (OECD standards). Those scores are subjective (though "expert"), the scales are arbitrary (for a start, they do not begin from 0 and therefore have an upward bias) and heterogeneous (unless the private-sector share of GDP is also ranked on the same scale), and in any case their aggregation into a single index involves arbitrary weights, whether implicit or explicit. Yet there can be no doubt that on that scoreboard Belarus has the last place, or at best can be placed, with Tajikistan and Turkmenistan, among the last

Table 11.1
Belarus: Summary Statistics, 1992–1999

	1992	1993	1994	1995	1996	1997	Estimate 1998	Projection 1999
Output					(Percentage change)			
GDP at constant prices	-9.6	-7.6	-12.6	-10.4	2.8	10.4	8	-2
Industrial gross output	-9.4	-10.0	-17.1	-11.7	3.5	17.1	11	—
Agricultural gross input	-9	3.7	-14.3	-4.7	2.4	-6.4	-0.4	—
Employment					(Percentage change)			
Labor force (end-year)	-2.9	-0.6	-2.4	-5.7	0.1	-2.5	—	—
Employment	-2.6	-1.3	-2.5	-6.2	-1	-2	—	—
Unemployment (officially registered)	0.5	1.4	2.1	2.7	3.9	2.8	2.3	—
				(In percent of labor force)				
Prices and wages					(Percentage change)			
Consumer prices (annual average)	969	1,188	2,200	709	53	64	77	150
Consumer prices (end-year)	1,559	1,996	1,960	244	39	63	182	246
Producer prices (annual average)	2,330	1,536	2,171	462	34	89	77	—
Producer prices (end-year)	3,275	2,316	1,867	122	31	90	204	—
Gross average monthly wages (annual average)	838	1,107	1,504	669	61	88	154	—
Government sector[a]					(In percent of GDP)			
General government balance	0	-1.9	-2.5	-1.9	-1.6	-0.7	-1	-2
General government expenditure	46	56.2	50	44.6	42.6	46.8	48	—
Monetary sector					(Percentage change)			
Broad money (end-year)	—	—	1,111	158.4	52.4	111.4	276	—
Domestic credit (end-year)	—	—	—	157.4	58.5	115.5	110	—

Table 11.1 (continued)

	1992	1993	1994	1995	1996	1997	Estimate 1998	Projection 1999
	(In percent of GDP)							
Broad money (end-year)	—	58.1	39	15	14.8	16.5	32.8	—
Interest and exchange rates								
	(In percent per annum, end-year)							
Refinancing rate	30	210	300	66	35	42	48	—
Treasury bill rate (three-month maturity)	—	—	320	70	37	38	43.2	—
Deposit rate (one year)	—	65	90	101	32	15	33	—
Lending rate (one year)	—	72	149	175	64	33	52.5	—
	(Belarussian roubles per U.S. dollar)							
Exchange rate (end-year)[b]	15	698	10,600	11,500	15,500	31,230	107,000	—
Exchange rate (annual average)[b]	17	269	3,666	11,533	13,292	26,193	46,400	—
External sector								
	(In millions of U.S. dollars)							
Current account	—	−435	−444	−458	−516	−788	−976	−1,150
Trade balance[c]	377	−569	−556	−761	−1,287	−1,388	−1,438	—
Exports[c]	3,580	1,970	2,510	4,803	5,652	7,301	7,081	—
Imports[c]	3,203	2,539	3,066	5,564	6,939	8,689	8,519	—
Foreign direct investment, net	—	18	11	7	70	190	108	70
Gross reserves (end-year) excluding gold[d]	—	91	101	377	369	394	100	—
External debt stock[e]	570	1,014	1,251	1,513	1,785	2,130	2,250	—
	(In months of imports of goods and services)							
Gross reserves (end-year) excluding gold	—	0.4	0.4	0.8	0.6	0.5	0.1	—

Table 11.1 (continued)

	1992	1993	1994	1995	1996	1997	Estimate 1998	Projection 1999
				(In percent of exports of goods and services)				
Debt service	0	0.4	4.2	3.5	2.5	2	2.2	—
				(Denominations as indicated)				
Memorandum items								
Population (millions, end-year)	10.2	10.2	10.3	10.3	10.3	10.2	10.2	—
GDP (in billions of Belarusian roubles)	92	986	17,815	119,813	184,174	351,043	662,400	1,622,880
GDP per capita (in USD)	524	358	472	1,007	1,346	1,314	1,400	—
Share of industry in GDP	40.4	30.9	30.8	31.4	35.3	36.9	38.4	—
Share of agriculture in GDP	23.8	18.3	15	17.7	15.9	14.1	12.7	—
Current account/GDP (%)	—	-30.4	-13.2	-2.4	-3.6	-5.9	-6.8	-18
External debt minus reserves (USD million)	—	932	1,220	1,246	1,416	1,736	2,000	—
External debt/GDP (%)	—	27.7	25.7	14.6	13.1	15.9	15.8	—
External debt/exports (%)	—	51.5	49.8	31.5	31.6	29.2	32.1	—

Note: Dashes indicate data are not available.

a General government includes the state budget, social funds, and extrabudgetary funds, excluding interbudgetary transfers.
b Official noncash exchange rate. The premium on the parallel market was 30 percent by the end of 1997 but reached 300 percent by December 1998. The 1998 Belarus U.S.-dollar GDP would decline from a projected 14.3 billion at the official noncash rate to 4.9 billion at the parallel market rate.
c Data from the balance of payments.
d Foreign exchange reserves of monetary authorities.
e Medium and long-term public and publicly guaranteed debt. From 1996 the debt stock includes estimates of the short-term public and private external debt.

Table 11.2
Belarus summary statistics update: Second Quarter, 1999

	1991	1992	1993	1994	1995	1996	1997	1998
Population (m)	10.28	10.35	10.37	10.35	10.31	10.28	10.20	10.18
Unemployment rate (percentage of total labor force)	0.1	0.5	1.4	2.1	2.7	3.9	2.8	2.3
National accounts (percentage change at comparable prices)								
GDP	−1.2	−9.6	−7.6	−12.6	−10.4	2.8	10.4	8.3
Total consumption	−6.6	−10.3	−3.7	−10.8	−9.5	3.2	9.4	8.0
Private	−6.1	−7.9	−1.5	−13.4	−12.3	4.5	10.9	9.0
Public	−7.7	−15.3	−10.5	−3.0	−2.9	−0.2	6.0	5.8
Gross fixed investment	4.4	−18.1	−15.4	−17.2	−28.7	7.2	14.7	9.4

Source: Ministry of Statistics and Analysis.

	1994	1995	1996	1997	1998	1Q1999
Prices and wages (percentage change over previous period)						
Industrial producer prices	1,866.7	140.3	29.3	90.9	200.5	76.3
Consumer prices	1,959.9	244.0	39.3	63.1	181.7	48.6
Consumer prices (period average)	2,221.0	709.0	52.7	63.8	73.2	60.5
Monthly wages	1,481.1	258.0	56.0	105.7	144.4	45.9
Money						
Velocity of circulation—M3	8.2	9.6	8.4	8.0	7.4	7.5
Velocity of circulation—M2	—	13.9	11.1	11.1	11.0	17.2
Broad money (percentage change)	1,851.7	164.1	51.5	111.4	276.0	20.7
Nominal refinancing rate (percent per annum)	480.0	66.0	35.0	40.0	48.0	82.0
Interest rate (primary GKO placement, end of period)	320.0	70.1	37.1	35.9	43.2	82.0

General government[a] (percentage of GDP)						
Government balance	-2.6	-1.9	-1.6	-2.1	-1.5	1.7
Total revenues	47.9	42.5	41.8	32.1	36.2	39.9
Total expenditures	50.5	44.4	43.4	34.2	37.7	38.2
Domestic debt (BRB billion)	12	2,290	5,415	9,992	17,464	1,879
Domestic debt (percentage of GDP)	0.1	1.9	2.9	2.8	2.7	0.5
Balance of payments (percentage of GDP)						
Current account	-10.9	-4.5	-3.9	-5.9	-6.6	—
Trade balance	-12.0	-6.5	-8.6	-10.1	-10.1	-2.9
Exports	61.6	45.6	43.6	54.5	49.7	60.4
Imports	75.3	53.2	52.2	65.3	59.8	63.3
External debt outstanding[b] (USD million, end of period)	1,227	1,518	947	958	1,050	953
External debt (percentage of GDP)[c]	25.1	14.6	7.1	7.2	7.4	10.7
External debt (percentage of GDP)[d]	—	14.8	8.4	9.5	14.9	18.5
Gross official reserves (in months of imports)	0.4	0.9	0.7	0.5	0.1	0.3
BRB/USD exchange rate						
Minsk interbank currency exchange	10,600	11,500	15,500	30,740	107,000	237,000
Percentage change over the period	51.6	8.5	34.8	98.3	248.1	121.5
Moscow interbank currency exchange*	—	11,702	26,322	40,790	218,000	300,000
Percentage change over the period	—	—	124.9	55.0	434.4	37.6

Sources: Minstat, MinFin, NBB, and BET staff calculations.

Note: Dashes indicate data are not available.

[a] Including extrabudgetary and social funds, but excluding the presidential fund.

[b] Excluding gas arrears.

[c] GDP in U.S. dollars at BCSE rate.

[d] GDP in U.S. dollars at MICEX rate.

*From March 21, 1998, there is no quotation of BRB/USD at MICEX. From this date BET uses instead the Reuters quoted Parallel Interbank Market (PIM) exchange rate.

Table 11.3
EBRD transition indicators for Belarus, the Russian Federation, and Poland

	Belarus					Russian Federation					Poland				
	1994	1995	1996	1997	1998	1994	1995	1996	1997	1998	1994	1995	1996	1997	1998
Private-sector share of GDP, in percent (midyear EBRD estimate)	15	15	15	20	20	50	55	60	70	70	55	60	60	65	65
1. Enterprises															
Large-scale privatization	2	2	1	1	1	3	3	3	3+	3+	3	3	3	3+	3+
Small-scale privatization	2	2	2	2	2	3	4	4	4	4	4	4+	4+	4+	4+
Enterprise restructuring	2	2	2	1	1	2	2	2	2	2	3	3	3	3	3
2. Markets and trade															
Price liberalization	2	3	3	3	2	3	3	3	3	3–	3	3	3	3	3+
Trade and foreign exchange system	1	2	2	1	1	3	3	4	4	2+	4	4+	4+	4+	4+
Competition policy	2	2	2	2	2	3	2	2	2+	2+	3	3	3	3	3
3. Financial institutions															
Banking reform and interest rate liberalization	1	2	1	1	1	2	2	2	2+	2	3	3	3	3	3+
Securities markets and nonbank financial institutions	—	2	2	2	2	—	2	3	3	2–	—	3	3	3+	3+
(1) + (2) + (3) Average score*	1.7	2.1	1.9	1.6	1.5	2.7	2.6	2.9	3.1	2.6	3.3	3.4	3.4	3.5	3.6
Legal reform															
Extensiveness and effectiveness of legal rules on investment	—	2	1	2	2	—	2	3	3	3	—	4	4	4	4
Extensiveness	—	—	—	2	2	—	—	—	3+	4–	—	—	—	4	4
Effectiveness	—	—	—	2	2	—	—	—	3	2	—	—	—	4+	4

Belarus

Infrastructure indicators										
Telecommunications	—	—	—	1+	—	—	3	—	3+
Railways	—	—	—	1	—	—	2+	—	3+
Electric power	—	—	—	1	—	—	2	—	3

Note: Dashes indicate data are not available. Scores range from 1 to 4+ unless otherwise indicated. Large-scale privatization: 1—Little private ownership; 2—Comprehensive scheme almost ready for implementation; some sales completed; 3—More than 25 percent of large-scale enterprise assets in private hands or in the process of being privatized (with the process having reached a stage at which the state has effectively ceded its ownership rights), possibly with major unresolved issues regarding corporate governance. Small-scale privatization: 2—Substantial share privatized; 3—Nearly comprehensive program implemented; 4—Complete privatization of small companies with tradable ownership rights; 4+—Standards and performance typical of advanced industrial economies: no state ownership of small enterprises; effective tradability of land. Enterprise restructuring: 1—Soft budget constraints (lax credit and subsidy policies weakening financial discipline at the enterprise level); few other reforms to promote corporate governance; 2—Moderately tight credit and subsidy policy but weak enforcement of bankruptcy legislation and little action taken to strengthen competition and corporate governance; 3—Significant and sustained actions to harden budget constraints and to promote corporate governance effectively (e.g., through privatization combined with tight credit and subsidy policies and/or enforcement of bankruptcy legislation). Price liberalization: 2—Price controls for several important product categories; state procurement at nonmarket prices largely phased out. Trade and foreign exchange system: 1—Widespread import and/or export controls or very limited legitimate access to foreign exchange; 2—Some liberalization of import and/or export controls; almost full current account convertibility in principle but with a foreign exchange regime that is not fully transparent (possibly with multiple exchange rates); 3—Removal of almost all quantitative and administrative import and export restrictions; almost full current account convertibility; 4—Removal of all quantitative and administrative import and export restrictions (apart from agriculture) and all significant export tariffs; insignificant direct involvement in exports and imports by ministries and state-owned trading companies; no major nonuniformity of custom duties for nonagricultural goods and services; full current account convertibility; 4+—Standards and performance norms of advanced industrial economies: removal of most tariff barriers; membership in WTO. Competition policy: 2—Competition policy legislation and institutions set up; some reduction of entry restrictions or enforcement action on dominant firms; 3—Some enforcement actions to reduce abuse of market power and to promote a competitive environment, including break-ups of dominant conglomerates; substantial reduction of entry restrictions. Banking reform and interest rate liberalization: 1—Little progress beyond establishment of a two-tier system; 2—Significant liberalization of interest rates and credit allocation; limited use of direct credit or interest rate liberalization ceilings; 3—Substantial progress in establishment of bank solvency and of a framework for prudential supervision and regulation; full interest rate liberalization with little preferential access to cheap refinancing; significant lending to private enterprises and significant presence of private banks. Securities markets and nonbank financial institutions: 2—Formation of securities exchanges, market makers, and brokers; some trading in government paper and/or securities; rudimentary legal and regulatory framework for the issuance and trading of securities; 3—Substantial issuance of securities by private enterprises; establishment of independent share registries, secure clearance and settlement procedures, and some protection of minority shareholders; emergence of nonbank financial institutions (e.g., investment funds, private insurance and pension funds, leasing companies) and associated regulatory framework.

three ex-Soviet republics. Belarus's private-sector share of GDP, at 20 percent, is the lowest throughout the 26 countries of EBRD operations; its average score on the other factors is 1.5, which numerically covers only one-seventh of the distance between the minimum score of 1 and the maximum of 4+ (treated here as equivalent to 4.5).

A more detailed background for this evaluation is provided in table 11.4 (from the 1998 *Transition Report*). Partly the scores reflect an objective deterioration of some of Belarus's indicators over time; partly they show a changing perception of Belarus's achievements as more distant from transition targets than was believed earlier. In many respects the EBRD scores are overly generous to Belarus. For instance, they underestimate the share of administered prices in the consumer price index (CPI) (see below). The data on budgetary subsidies do not include quasi-fiscal items (see below). Belarus's low international standing in the transition league is reflected in the International Monetary Fund's (IMF's) withdrawal of its permanent representative from Minsk in March 1998, the lack of a CCFF (Compensatory and Contingency Financing Facility) loan to Belarus, and the withdrawal of the World Bank permanent representative in September 1998 (though the representative was reinstated in the summer of 1999).

The Target Model

The target model officially adopted by Belarus is the "socially oriented market economy." In the Belarusian policy document "Major Trends in the Social and Economic Development of the Republic of Belarus in 1996–2000," this is defined as a competitive market economy with mixed private and state ownership on equal footing and social welfare policies (high and stable employment, a social safety net, etc.). Commitments to implement such a model have been expressed in various policy documents submitted to the IMF and the World Bank and included in public announcements about its gradual implementation over time.

This notion evokes a German-style social market economy, or the Third Way, sought in the European Union today in thirteen out of fifteen member states that are governed by social democratic parties or left-wing coalitions (Ireland and Spain being the exceptions), like Blair's New Labour in Great Britain or Schroeder's Neue Mitte in Germany. But the new European Third Way recognizes the primacy of markets both domestically and globally; it favors the privatization of state ownership and enterprise; and it is committed to affordable policies, recognizing the importance of hard budget constraints and fiscal and monetary prudence (see Nuti 1999). Belarus's Third Way, on the other hand, is an old-style pretransition attempt at reconciling state ownership and markets, but the country's government has not really gotten around to constructing a market economy or hardening soft budgets. Too many market elements, even some that could be quickly implemented, are missing or are overridden by central controls; the weight of the state is still overwhelming, and there is no sign of progress. One cannot socially orient a market economy that is not there, and its construction takes more than five McDonald's restaurants in Minsk.

Exactly the same label (that is, the "socially oriented market economy") was adopted by President Islam Karimov of Uzbekistan for his own country in 1993, but he characterized it as a model in which the state would maintain its role as a "collective entrepreneur," "production regulator," and "investor in priority sectors of the economy" (see Karimov 1993, 37–60). This is actually the negation of a market economy, where entrepreneurship is diffused among a large number of private and state enterprises, where the state sets the rules of the game (that is, regulates markets, not production), and where there are no priority sectors and the state invests mostly or exclusively in public infrastructure. Karimov's characterization, however, fits precisely the model adopted by Belarus today; both have invoked a gradual, evolutionary process of reform. The difference between the two is that Uzbekistan stated clearly what it intended to achieve and since 1998 has done a U-turn, whereas Belarus targeted the same model, paying lip service to the market economy and never (to date) changing its target.

The Belarusian model—like the early Uzbek approach—does not have the advantages of central planning, and there is no way back in that direction, but it retains some of the advantages of a command economy, such as high employment and a low open inflation. Of course the administrative containment of inflation is a form of financial repression, which in the Soviet system mounted over time and wrecked the system. If persistent, repressed inflation could also ruin the Belarusian economy. High employment is obtained at the expense of efficiency; higher physical output lowers national income, as it piles up as unsaleable inventories or is traded internationally on

Table 11.4
Belarus: Transition Assessments

			1994	1995	1996	1997
Liberalization						
Exchange rate regime	Managed float	Share of administered prices in CPI	60	45	30	27
Current account convertibility	Limited	Administered prices in "EBRD-15" basket	5	5	5	5
Interest rate liberalisation	Limited de facto	Share of trade in GDP	61.7	47.0	45.9	60.1
Wage regulation	Yes	Tariff revenue (as percentage of imports)	4.9	3.4	3.7	1.0
Privatization						
Primary privatisation method	MEBOs	Private-sector share in GDP	15	15	15	20
Secondary privatisation method	Vouchers	Share of firms privatized	11.7	14.3	19.7	25.5
Tradability of land rights	Limited de jure	Privatization revenues (as percentage of GDP)	0.30	0.26	0.00	0.15
Enterprises						
Protection of shareholder rights	Ineffective	Budgetary subsidies (as percentage of GDP)	6.3	3.4	2.9	1.3
Bankruptcy proceedings	Ineffective	Credit to enterprises (as percentage of GDP)	16.3	5.5	10.9	11.7
Competition office	No	Labor productivity in industry (percentage change)	−12.6	−1.5	11.1	20.0
Infrastructure						
Independent telecoms regulator	No	Main telephone lines per 100 inhabitants	18.6	19.0	20.8	22.6
Separation of railway accounts	No	Railway labour productivity (1989 = 100)	33.6	29.9	—	—
Independent electricity regulator	No	Electricity tariff, US¢/kWh (collection ratio, in percent)	—	—	1.5(80)	1.1(87)

		48(—)	42(1)	38(1)	38(2)
Financial institutions					
Deposit insurance	Yes				
Secured transactions law	Restricted				
Insider dealing prohibited	Na				
Securities commission	No				
Number of banks (number foreign owned)		48(—)	42(1)	38(1)	38(2)
Asset share of state-owned banks		69.2	62.3	54.1	55.2
Bad loans (as percentage of total loans)		8.4	11.8	14.2	12.7
Stock market capitalization (as percentage of GDP)		—	—	—	—
Fiscal and social sector					
Private pension funds	No				
Share of population in poverty	23 percent				
Tax revenues (as percentage of GDP)		41.6	34.4	32.0	34.7
Earnings inequality (Gini coefficient)		—	—	—	—

Source: EBRD *Transition Report* 1998.
Note: Dashes indicate data are not available.

unfavorable terms, through disadvantageous barter or even unpaid transactions (see below). Earlier attempts at this kind of Third Way in the Soviet era failed precisely because they did not allow prices to reach market-clearing levels and because of the inertia and lack of incentives associated with state-owned enterprises.

The trouble with this model, as in the old Soviet days, is not only the inconsistency of planned prices and actual achieved quantities, but more generally the adoption of an impossible set of policy targets: noninflationary growth, extensive subsidies, directed credits swelling the nonfiscal deficit, low nominal interest rates that are negative in real terms, multiple official exchange rates administratively fixed at a stable but increasingly overvalued rate (with various freer transactions registering a much higher price for foreign exchange), and exceedingly low savings. These are not consistent policies, and their reconciliation in practice can only be disappointing, inefficient, and costly.

Privatization

The EBRD estimate of Belarus's private-sector size, at 20 percent of GDP and roughly also of employment, is the lowest among post-Soviet and other transition economies but even so is probably an overestimate, as it includes the share of minority private participations in state enterprises. Belarusian official sources give a private share of 12 percent in industrial output and 8 percent in industrial employment in 1997 and a 40 percent private share of agriculture. Comprehensive data on Belarus privatization at both the republican and communal level are provided in table 11.5. Belarusian usage treats corporatization, that is, the transformation of state enterprises into share stock companies, as a form of "ownership transformation" regardless of actual ownership transfer, whereas it is actually simply a precondition or even a facilitating factor. In 1996 only thirty-one corporatized enterprises in Belarus passed into majority private ownership, fourteen in 1997, and none in 1998.

Mass privatization in Belarus has proceeded more slowly than planned, partly because of the need for prior approval by enterprise employees and, for assets valued at more than 10,000 times the minimum monthly wage, by the president of Belarus. There is a voucher overhang, that is, vouchers' nominal value is not matched by that of the shares on offer; 70 percent of privatization vouchers are still unredeemed and, in theory, could be cashed in by their holders at their nominal value plus interest.

The main privatization method in Belarus has been that of direct sale, but revenue from privatization has been truly insignificant (see table 11.4). Preference in the allocation and price of shares is given in privatization to enterprise employees and managers. Decree no. 591 of 1997 opened the possibility of maintaining state control over privatized enterprises through retention of a golden share.

Land ownership rights are far more restricted in Belarus than in Russia; neither residents nor foreigners can buy agricultural land, which can only be leased, though leases cannot be transferred nor used as collateral (and in some cases they are subject to the condition that no additional labor is hired to work the land).

Foreign direct investment (FDI) in Belarus is modest, at a cumulative total of US $237 million at the end of 1998, that is, less than 0.5 percent of the US $50 billion which in 1996 the Belarus government announced was the amount of FDI the country needed (see Charman 1999). Foreign capital has played no significant part in the Belarusian privatization process. There is official hostility toward FDI on the alleged ground that it leads to trade imbalances with investors' countries, although experience shows that in 1998 companies with foreign capital had a share of 1.3 percent of employment but accounted for 8 percent of Belarus's exports (though admittedly 9.5 percent of imports).

Administered Prices

Prices in Belarus are largely administratively controlled, both in their level and structure. Directive no. 249 of December 15, 1994, established a category of "socially significant goods" whose prices are controlled at the republican and regional levels. Goods whose prices are centrally fixed are officially claimed to represent only about 5 percent of the country's total goods, but in addition there are prices fixed by local authorities (about thirty "socially significant goods"), price ceilings, statutory criteria for price formation, obligations to report and justify price increases, and controls over natural monopolies (such as housing and public utilities). In 1998 these covered at least one-third of consumption. There are also controls over supplies to the military.

Table 11.5
Privatization and structural change transformation in Belarus

Indicator	Number of units									
	1991	1992	1993	1994	1995	1996	1997	1998	1Q1999	Total
Republican Property										
Transformed Republican Total	19	32	140	184	53	131	192	140	26	917
By branches										
Industry	12	23	68	58	15	37	74	38	9	334
Agriculture (including Soviet and state farms)	1	0	9	9	27	22	13	11	2	94
Construction	5	4	28	40	3	22	34	32	4	172
Transport and communications	0	0	9	10	1	24	26	7	5	82
Trade	0	0	1	14	3	6	3	15	1	43
Public catering	0	0	0	1	0	0	2	0	0	3
Household services	1	3	1	23	0	0	1	0	0	29
Housing and communal services	0	1	0	1	0	0	1	1	0	4
Health services	0	0	0	0	0	3	0	5	2	10
Culture	0	0	0	0	0	0	1	2	0	3
Other	0	1	24	28	4	16	30	25	2	130
By method of privatization										
Buyout of leased property by leaseholders	9	20	44	28	1	5	1	11	0	119
Buyout of state property by workers	6	8	10	1	0	0	0	0	0	25
Buyout of state property by individuals	0	1	0	0	0	0	0	0	0	1
Corporatization (state or nonstate)	3	3	68	152	52	92	96	40	1	507
Sell at competition	1	0	11	3	0	0	0	0	0	15
Sell at auction	0	0	7	0	0	0	0	0	0	7
Alienation	0	0	0	0	0	34	95	89	25	243
Communal Property										
Transformed Communal Total	42	158	104	457	412	390	380	278	24	2245
By branches										
Industry	11	12	1	5	2	0	5	24	12	72
Agriculture (including Soviet and state farms)	0	0	3	39	191	103	57	14	0	407

Construction	2	5	3	3	2	0	6	1	1	26
Trade	5	49	30	222	128	173	184	115	9	915
Public catering	16	5	7	57	30	31	43	21	1	211
Household services	5	67	26	54	21	41	43	49	1	307
Housing and communal services	0	0	10	59	9	11	6	1	0	96
Culture	0	0	2	0	0	0	0	0	0	2
Public education	0	0	6	0	0	0	0	0	0	6
Other	3	20	16	18	29	28	36	53	0	203
By method of privatization										
Buyout of leased property by leaseholders	25	27	13	124	34	53	75	42	5	398
Buyout of state property by workers	7	79	14	11	1	0	0	0	0	112
Corporatization (state or nonstate)	0	1	3	64	205	129	82	49	15	548
Sell at competition	10	50	40	93	32	42	41	24	1	333
Sell at auction	0	0	34	165	140	166	182	163	3	853

Index of real net indebtedness of state-owned enterprises (December 1993 = 100) and net indebtedness (as percentage of monthly GDP)

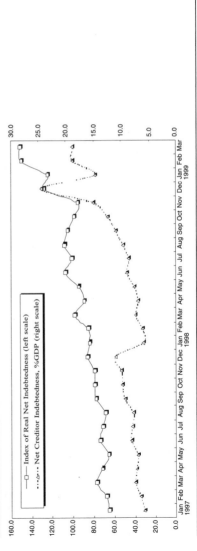

Source: Belarus Economic Trends, May 1999.

Law no. 255–3 of May 10, 1999, "On Price Formation," ruled that prices for products of enterprises holding a dominant position in the market and prices for some socially important goods (set by the president or by the Council of Ministers on presidential instructions) are subject to state control. The very notion of "price formation" rules reveals the nonmarket nature of the economy. Presidential Decree no. 285 of May 19, 1999, "On Measures for Stabilization of Prices (Tariffs) in the Republic of Belarus," prohibits any price increase that is not compensated for by measures of social protection; annual limits for price indices are set by the Council of Ministers and the National Bank of Belarus (NBB).

In addition there are informal controls on prices. There are also presidential decrees fixing the maximum monthly rate of inflation and latent controls that are activated in case that rate is exceeded. Decree no. 590 of December 1996 targeted inflation at a maximum rate of 2 percent per month in retail trade. In August 1997 penalties, including fines and even managerial dismissals from their jobs, were introduced for raising prices above the monthly 2 percent rate. As a result, retail prices have increased much more slowly than producer prices, squeezing profit margins in retail trade. On March 23, 1998, seeing that prices were exceeding the statutory maximum 2 percent per month, the president decreed that they should revert to the level prevailing on March 1. Thus latent price controls cover in practice up to 100 percent of formal transactions.

There is an official view that high inflation is evidence that prices are not controlled in Belarus because there is high inflation. This is plainly a non sequitur: Inflation may be held down by administrative means, maintaining prices below market-clearing levels, but still run fast or even very fast. The counterproof that price controls actually bite is the appearance of shortages (see below), as well as the negative impact of controls on enterprise profitability (defined as the ratio of profits from sales to the cost of products sold; this ratio was small though rising, from 10.6 percent in 1996 to 13.2 percent in 1997, and slightly higher in 1998).

In practice wages are also centrally fixed, rather than being the result of negotiations between employers and trade unions. The stated principle of Belarusian wage policy is a tendency toward the restoration of Soviet real wage levels (see table 11.6). The minimum wage and the so-called first-grade wage (i.e., the entry-level wage) in the budgetary sphere are raised steadily, providing indicative parameters for public and private enterprises. In late 1996 Decree no. 344 required the timely payment of wages, pensions, and benefits, so that, unlike Russia, Belarus has a small level of total wage arrears (0.1 percent of GDP in 1997; see table 11.12).

Other Administrative Controls

Besides controls on prices, wages, and state enterprise output, widespread administrative controls, especially financial controls, are exercised by a variety of state agencies such as the State Control Committee, the Tax Committee, and the State Committee on Financial Investigation. A 1998 World Bank study, based on a questionnaire administered to a sample of Belarusian enterprises, estimates the direct and indirect cost of administrative controls to be on the order of 4–8 percent of GDP.

The number of private enterprises in Belarus was slashed as a result of a reregistration campaign conducted in February 1996–April 1997; enterprises not properly registered could not operate. Only 30 percent of enterprises had reregistered before the deadline; registration was later reopened without a new date, then again halted, and then again reopened. A draft decree of November 1998 limited registrations to three per person. Decrees, unlike laws, can be retroactive; once published, draft decrees, even if never approved or later withdrawn, are often just as effective as those that are approved and can be more damaging because of the underlying uncertainty that accompanies them.

Shortages

Generalized price controls may be ineffective in stemming inflation but are effective enough to bring about shortages. These became visible in March 1998 and were worsened by the Belarusian ruble (BRB) crisis associated with the Russian crisis in August 1998. A Council of Ministers meeting of February 16, 1999, recognized that "[i]n some districts ... there are shortages of foodstuffs, shoes, textiles, etc...." On arrival at Minsk International Airport visitors in 1999 were handed a "Welcome to Minsk" pamphlet that actually informed them that Belarus is an economy without market-clearing prices: "Minsk is a very 'cheap' city. Low prices for most types of food products and public transportation are regulated by the state.

Table 11.6
Prices, wages, and inflation in Belarus

	1994	1995	1996	1997	1998	1Q1999	Apr. 1999
Industrial producer price index (IPPI)	1866.7	140.3	29.3	90.9	200.5	76.3	6.3
Consumer price index (CPI)	1959.9	244.0	39.3	63.4	181.7	48.6	7.4
Food	2108.6	213.0	43.4	66.1	186.8	54.0	7.9
Nonfood	1565.5	258.8	30.3	49.4	197.7	42.5	5.8
Services	2240.9	477.0	29.6	66.3	126.8	23.3	6.7
Monthly wages	1482.1	257.9	56.0	105.7	144.5	45.9	10.0
Minimum wage (thousand BRB)	20	60	100	162	275	500	500
Monthly wages (USD, end of period)[a]	27	88	103	107	75	50	53

[a] Monthly wage in U.S. dollars using the NBB exchange rate.

Monthly change in CPI and nominal wages (in percent)

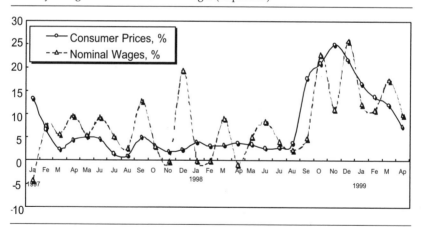

Table 11.6 (continued)

Monthly Inflation (in percent)

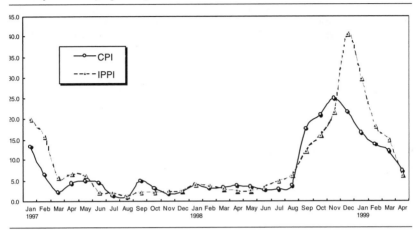

Source: Belarusian Economic Trends, May 1999.

This leads to the limitation and shortage of many cheap products. Do not be surprised if you will not be able to buy a greater quantity of a product than the amount fixed in the store."

Belarus thus actually advertises (or at least it did, as of a few years ago) that it is not a market economy. The combination of domestic price controls and a domestic currency that is greatly overvalued at the official rate but greatly undervalued at the black- or the free-market rate (relatively to purchasing power parity) leads to large-scale informal exports, including cross-border trade. In 1998–1999, in order to avoid this goods drain, supplies of scarce goods were delivered to Minsk shops in the evening, only after the last trains to neighboring capitals have departed. In December 1998, confronted with the depletion of shop supplies before Christmas, the president publicly threatened to punish "those responsible" for shortages.

Stabilization

Fiscal Policy

Unlike Russia, Belarus has been able to continue to collect its taxes and to keep its budget deficit under control and falling as a percentage of GDP (see table 11.7). This favorable trend, however, has been

Table 11.7
The Belarus state budget (cumulative, BRB billion)

	Total revenue	Percent-age of GDP	Total expen-diture	Percent-age of GDP	Total budget balance[a]	Percent-age of GDP
1990	15	35.0	14	32.6	1	2.3
1991	26	30.3	24	27.9	2	2.3
1992	296	32.9	314	34.9	−18	−2.0
1993	3,623	37.0	4,168	42.6	−545	−5.6
1994	6,493	36.8	7,111	40.2	−618	−3.6
1995	35,468	29.9	38,817	32.7	−3,349	−2.8
1996	50,669	27.5	54,315	29.5	−3,646	−2.0
1997	112,837	32.1	120,137	34.2	−7,300	−2.1
1998	239,650	36.2	249,578	37.7	−9,928	−1.5
1Q1997	17,989	30.8	17,509	30.0	480	0.8
2Q	44,076	31.8	43,268	31.2	808	0.6
3Q	75,570	30.6	74,194	30.0	1,376	0.6
4Q	112,837	32.1	120,137	34.2	−7,300	−2.1
1Q1998	41,396	40.2	41,352	40.2	44	0.0
2Q	93,599	41.0	96,824	42.4	−3,225	−1.4
3Q	153,667	37.7	155,989	38.2	−2,322	−0.6
4Q	239,650	36.2	249,578	37.7	−9,928	−1.5
1Q1999	151,899	39.9	145,423	38.2	6,476	1.7
January 1998	12,982	40.2	10,600	32.8	2,382	7.4
February	26,293	40.1	24,395	37.2	1,897	2.9
March	41,396	40.2	41,352	40.2	44	0.0
April	59,042	41.9	60,468	42.9	−1,426	−1.0
May	75,654	42.2	77,569	43.3	−1,915	−1.1
June	93,599	41.0	96,824	42.4	−3,225	−1.4
July	112,451	40.2	115,995	41.4	−3,544	−1.3
August	132,265	38.6	134,649	39.3	−2,384	−0.7
September	153,667	37.7	155,989	38.2	−2,322	−0.6
October	176,816	36.0	180,707	36.8	−3,891	−0.8
November	201,158	35.7	205,245	36.4	−4,087	−0.7
December	239,650	36.2	249,578	37.7	−9,928	−1.5
January 1999	38,177	37.0	32,812	31.8	5,365	5.2
February	88,336	39.4	84,658	37.8	3,678	1.6
March	151,899	39.9	145,423	38.2	6,476	1.7
April	224,914	41.7	216,843	40.2	8,072	1.5

Source: Belarus Economic Trends, May 1999.
[a] Including interest payments on debt servicing.

accompanied by a relatively large and—until recently—rising quasi-fiscal deficit, so that the overall deficit has remained on the order of 3.5–4 percent of GDP (according to IMF estimates, the quasi-fiscal deficit was 2.5 percent of GDP in 1996, 3 percent in 1997, and 4 percent in the first quarter of 1998). The main quasi-fiscal item has been the cost of a large-scale NBB program of directed subsidized credits to agriculture (lent by banks at an interest rate of half the refinance rate) and house construction (at symbolic rates). Among other quasi-fiscal items is the cost of rescheduling loans (especially to agriculture), an increase in the implicit pay-as-you-go (PAYG) pension debt, and a deficit in other extrabudgetary funds. Many assets accumulated by local authorities and in a number of special funds cannot be accessed by the republican budget, so that financing requirements are in excess of the general government deficit. Extensive ad hoc tax (and tariff) exemptions are used to stimulate production.

The size of the Belarusian budget increased significantly, from 46 percent of GDP in 1992 to 56 percent in 1993, then kept falling, down to 42 percent in 1996, before starting to grow again in 1997.

Monetary Policy

In theory Belarus monetary policy is conducted by an independent central bank, which on the basis of a 1994 law is classed in the literature as the ninth most independent bank in the world. In practice the president of Belarus has the power to remove the NBB president and suspend or revoke any NBB decision; directed credits are decided by presidential decree or by the Council of Ministers. In 1994–1999 the NBB has had four presidents: one resigned under pressure, one was imprisoned before dismissal, and another was dismissed and replaced by the former Minister of Finance and First Deputy Premier Piotr Prokopovich, who as a minister had been associated with expansionist budgetary policies, subsidized credit, and inflationary policies. Central bank independence in Belarus is one of the issues under discussion with the IMF.

Monetary expansion in Belarus (see table 11.8) has been due not so much to the requirements of government deficit financing but to a deliberate policy and also to the directed credits mentioned above to agriculture and house construction. As a result inflation has remained higher than the statutory (though relatively high) rate of 2 percent per month decreed in 1996 and flared again after the Russian

Table 11.8
Money and credit in Belarus

	1993	1994	1995	1996	1997	1998	1Q1999	Apr. 1999
Money and credit (percentage change over the period)								
M3	—	1,852	164	52	111	276	21	8
M2	—	1,372	311	67	103	130	19	18
Currency in circulation	—	1,376	412	64	98	120	18	26
NBB loans to the government	—	500	7,450	66	65	305	13	1
NBB claims on banks	—	1,377	79	188	154	201	1	4
Credit to nonfinancial public enterprises	—	—	—	40	100	350	14	6
Claims on private sector	—	—	—	67	146	273	24	7
Bank reserves (end of period)								
M3/Reserve Money	3.91	4.38	2.62	2.25	2.29	3.27	3.27	3.54
Req. reserves/Total deposits	0.05	0.06	0.10	0.14	0.16	0.10	0.12	0.09
Total Reserves/Total deposits	0.13	0.13	0.21	0.27	0.27	0.20	0.20	0.16
Money velocity (M3)								
Over the period[a]	—	8.5	9.2	8.4	8.4	7.4	6.5	—
Last month[b]	8.6	8.2	9.6	8.4	8.0	6.9	7.5	7.0
Money velocity (M2)								
Over the period[a]	—	14.7	14.5	11.3	12.0	11.0	14.9	—
Last month[b]	14.8	14.6	13.9	11.1	11.1	13.2	17.2	15.4
Refinance rate (percentage per annum)	—	480.0	66.0	35.0	40.0	41.3	67.3	90.0
Real refinance rate (percentage per annum)	—	−79.9	7.8	−42.7	6.6	−87.7	−65.7	−19.3
Composition of M3 (percentage, end of period)								
Currency in circulation	14	11	21	23	21	12	12	14
Demand deposits	—	—	35	35	37	25	24	25
Time deposits	—	—	13	18	14	7	7	8
Foreign currency deposits	41	55	31	24	27	56	56	52
Total	100	100	100	100	100	100	100	100

Note: Dashes indicate data are not available.
[a] Annualized GDP divided by M3 averaged over the corresponding period.
[b] Annualized GDP divided by midpoint M3 in the period.

Indices of real money balances (December 1993 = 100)

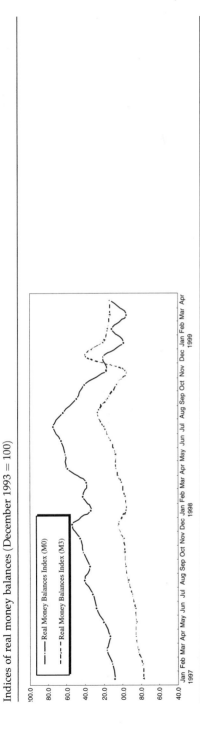

Real interest rates (percent per annum)

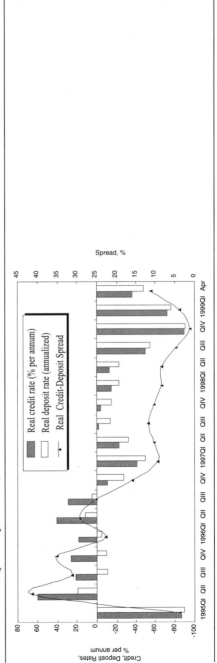

Note: Figure depicts nominal interest rates deflated by monthly annualized inflation rates.
Source: Belarus Economic Trends, May 1999.

crisis of August 1998 (see table 11.6 and the associated figures), of course leading to a rapidly depreciating currency (see below).

Belarus has an extremely low degree of monetization, with an M2-to-GDP ratio that in 1998 has fallen below 10 percent, as in Russia. This is not, as in the Russian case, the result of high interest rates, interenterprise arrears, or budget arrears, for in Belarus real interest rates have been highly negative, interenterprise arrears were only 12 percent of GDP at the end of 1997, and budgetary arrears are non-existent. A considerable proportion of industrial enterprise revenues takes the form of barter, but primarily in foreign trade with Russia. Commercial banks are undercapitalized, often are in difficult financial conditions, and do not enjoy public confidence. Low monetization in Belarus is simply the result of economic agents' rational response to a highly inflationary environment. Dollarization is widespread, with private holdings of U.S. dollars estimated to be on the order of three billion. In 1997–1998 the NBB deliberately sought to raise the degree of monetization through *additional* monetary expansion—a self-defeating, indeed counterproductive, policy.

The NBB has used a number of indirect instruments of monetary policy, including repo operations and foreign exchange swaps, to manage short-term liquidity but could not operate them on the scale that would have been necessary to contain the inflationary implications of credit expansion. Interest rates (see table 11.9 and the last figure of table 11.8) since the last quarter of 1996 have been increasingly negative (improving only slightly since August 1998).

Exchange Rate Policy

Until 1995–1996 there was, effectively, a single legal exchange rate in Belarus, the official one, which appreciated considerably in real terms, plus a black-market rate. Then, at the end of 1996, a parallel, 50-percent-higher rate in BRB for foreign exchange was quoted at the Moscow Interbank Currency Exchange (MICEX); the premium fell as a result of official devaluations, then rose again until March 1998 when, as a result of a currency crisis, MICEX trade in BRB was closed down in cooperation with the Russian authorities (see table 11.10, which after March 21, 1998, shows the Parallel Interbank Market (PIM) rate closest to a market rate).

There is a free over-the-counter (OTC) rate for cash transactions in exchange bureaus where foreign exchange is bought and sold at a premium (30 percent of their receipts must be surrendered to NBB at its average cost); purchases are limited to US $200 per day per person per bureau, but very often they are simply not possible at all for lack of dollar funds.

The official, overvalued exchange rate is adjusted by the NBB on the basis of weekly inflation data and unspecified "social guidelines"; it is the rate at which exporters surrender to the NBB a share of their export earnings, say 40 percent, and at which authorized importers can obtain foreign exchange for the import of essential goods such as energy (although largely this remains unpaid or offset by barter transactions with Russia) and pharmaceuticals. Clearly the compulsory surrender of 40 percent of export earnings at the official rate when the free rate is, say, 60 percent higher is equivalent to a 15 percent (40*.60/1.60) tax on gross export earnings, which is an inefficient and distortionary disincentive to export.

In January 1998 the NBB introduced an afternoon trading session at which it offered to buy (but not resell) foreign exchange in excess of the surrender requirement at a rate initially just under the MICEX rate. When MICEX BRB transactions ended, a purchase rate was offered that was close to the OTC rate.

Until currency redenomination in January 2000, which eliminated four zeros from rouble accounting, the largest banknote (BRB 1,000,000) was worth about three U.S. dollars; wallets had been replaced by briefcases; and the BRB exchange rate had come perilously close to that suggested by the old joke about the appropriate exchange rate between the Soviet ruble, the pound, and the dollar: one dollar = one pound of rubles.

There is a misplaced belief in Belarus that the devaluation experienced by the BRB in any market is due to speculative activities by Russian criminal circles (*mafiya*), as if Belarusian monetary issues had nothing to do with the availability of BRB to Russian operators for speculative transactions. The closing of MICEX BRB trade only moved those transactions to Minsk, Riga, or Tallin and was therefore ineffective and pointless. During the March 1998 financial crisis Belarus monetary authorities actually restricted the use of Belarusian rubles by nonresidents, a counterproductive measure that led to additional BRB sales that depressed the market further. The 1999 "Welcome to Minsk" pamphlet candidly acknowledges that: " 'valyutchiki' " [those who exchange currency illegally] can offer you a more profitable exchange rate.... It is practically impossible to buy foreign currency in

Table 11.9
Interest rates (BRB)

	Average credit interest rate (% per annum)	Real credit interest rate (% per annum)	Average deposit interest rate (% per annum)	Real deposit interest rate (% per annum)	Nominal credit-deposit spread	Real credit-deposit spread	Nominal refinancing rate (% per annum)	Real refinancing rate (% per annum)
1Q1993	23.9	-87.1	18.4	-87.7	5.5	0.6	—	—
2Q	42.4	-88.8	67.0	-86.8	-24.6	-1.9	—	—
3Q	83.8	-90.5	65.3	-91.5	18.5	1.0	—	—
4Q	136.4	-97.1	109.6	-97.4	26.8	0.3	—	—
1Q1994	162.0	-77.2	141.2	-79.0	20.8	1.8	210.0	-73.0
2Q	127.2	-85.2	62.4	-89.4	64.8	4.2	210.0	-79.7
3Q	130.8	-93.5	56.4	-95.6	74.4	2.1	210.0	-91.2
4Q	174.0	-90.5	98.4	-93.1	75.6	2.6	480.0	-79.9
1Q1995	254.4	-85.8	154.8	-89.8	99.6	4.0	180.0	-88.7
2Q	247.2	60.1	157.2	18.6	90.0	41.5	96.0	-9.6
3Q	104.4	21.1	51.6	-10.2	52.8	31.3	66.0	-1.7
4Q	94.0	25.9	39.7	-9.3	54.3	35.2	66.0	7.8
1Q1996	85.8	18.1	49.9	-4.7	35.9	22.8	66.0	5.5
2Q	68.3	41.2	33.2	11.7	35.1	29.4	55.0	30.0
3Q	58.2	29.2	27.3	4.0	30.9	25.2	41.7	15.7
4Q	45.3	-11.2	19.0	-27.2	26.2	16.0	35.0	-17.4
1Q1997	37.7	-40.9	15.8	-50.3	21.9	9.4	39.7	-40.1
2Q	33.8	-22.0	15.9	-32.4	17.9	10.4	42.0	-17.2
3Q	31.4	-1.7	15.7	-13.5	15.7	11.7	40.7	5.2
4Q	28.5	-3.8	14.4	-14.3	14.0	10.5	37.3	2.8

1Q1998	28.4	−14.3	15.5	−22.9	12.9	8.6	46.7	−2.2
2Q	27.8	−13.4	15.2	−21.9	12.6	8.5	41.3	−4.3
3Q	25.9	−49.2	13.8	−54.1	12.1	4.9	38.7	−44.1
4Q	25.9	−89.0	12.8	−90.2	13.2	1.1	41.3	−87.7
1Q1999	36.7	−72.0	17.8	−75.9	19.0	3.9	67.3	−65.7
January 1998	27.9	−19.2	14.8	−27.5	13.1	8.3	40.0	−11.5
February	27.6	−11.5	15.3	−20.1	12.3	8.5	50.0	4.0
March	29.8	−12.1	16.5	−21.1	13.3	9.0	50.0	1.6
April	29.1	−17.5	15.8	−26.0	13.3	8.5	44.0	−8.0
May	27.5	−14.6	15.1	−22.9	12.4	8.3	40.0	−6.3
June	26.9	−7.8	14.8	−16.6	12.1	8.8	40.0	1.7
July	26.7	−9.0	14.5	−17.8	12.2	8.8	40.0	0.5
August	25.8	−19.6	13.9	−27.2	11.9	7.6	38.0	−11.8
September	25.2	−82.1	13.0	−83.8	12.2	1.7	38.0	−80.3
October	25.2	−87.3	13.0	−88.5	12.2	1.2	38.0	−86.0
November	25.2	−91.4	12.3	−92.3	12.9	0.9	38.0	−90.5
December	27.4	−87.9	13.0	−89.3	14.4	1.4	48.0	−86.0
January 1999	30.1	−79.4	14.2	−81.9	15.9	2.5	60.0	−74.7
February	36.7	−70.7	17.7	−74.8	19.0	4.1	60.0	−65.7
March	43.4	−63.6	21.4	−69.2	22.0	5.6	82.0	−53.8
April	50.0	−36.3	23.5	−47.6	26.5	11.3	90.0	−19.3

Source: Belarus Economic Trends, May 1999.
Note: Dashes indicate data are not available.

Table 11.10
Balance of payments and foreign exchange noncash exchange rate (BRB/USD)[a]

	BCSE[b]				PIM[b]				Gap (percent)
	End of period	Percentage change	Average	Percentage change	End of period	Percentage change	Average	Percentage change	
1Q1996	11,500	0.0	11,500	0.0	14,299	22.2	12,374	7.1	7.6
2Q	13,100	13.9	12,750	10.9	14,181	−0.8	14,591	17.9	14.4
3Q	14,650	11.8	15,183	19.1	19,304	36.1	16,825	15.3	10.8
4Q	15,500	5.8	15,433	1.6	26,322	36.4	21,845	29.8	41.5
1Q1997	24,850	60.3	21,615	40.1	30,800	17.0	29,693	35.9	37.4
2Q	26,980	8.6	26,494	22.6	32,100	4.2	33,784	13.8	27.5
3Q	27,830	3.2	27,360	3.3	37,890	18.0	34,970	3.5	27.8
4Q	30,740	10.5	29,450	7.6	40,790	7.7	40,277	15.2	36.8
1Q1998	33,700	9.6	32,247	9.5	53,500	31.2	46,513	15.5	44.2
2Q	37,700	11.9	34,867	8.1	67,000	25.2	63,010	35.5	80.7
3Q	53,300	41.4	45,524	30.6	205,000	206.0	111,773	77.4	145.5
4Q	107,000	100.8	73,228	60.9	218,000	6.3	226,558	102.7	209.4
1Q1999	237,000	121.5	174,720	138.6	300,000	37.6	295,659	30.5	69.2
January 1999	136,000	27.1	123,222	28.1	280,000	28.4	307,813	50.8	149.8
February	229,000	68.4	168,300	36.6	285,000	1.8	280,800	−8.8	66.8
March	237,000	3.5	232,636	38.2	300,000	5.3	298,364	6.3	28.3
April	245,000	3.4	241,000	3.6	310,000	3.3	308,095	3.3	27.8

[a] The noncash exchange rate in Belarus differs from the cash rate. The latter was 298,000/300,000 BRB/USD (Belarusbank exchange offices) at the end of April 1999.
[b] From March 21, 1998, there is no quotation of BRB/USD at MICEX. From April 1998 the recommended rate at the Parallel Interbank Market (PIM), quoted by Reuters, is used as the de facto market rate.
[c] Minsk Interbank Currency Exchange (MICE) before January 1999.

BET real exchange rate indices (December 1993 = 100)

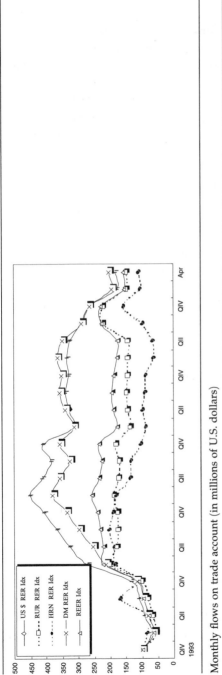

Monthly flows on trade account (in millions of U.S. dollars)

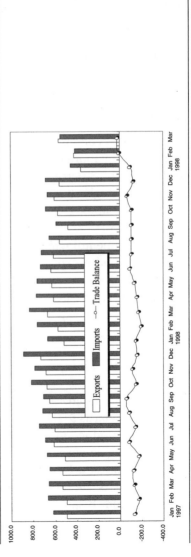

Source: Belarus Economic Trends, May 1999.

the local banks. The only place where you can do it is the 'black' market."

In January 1999, seeing the falling exchange rate of the BRB—both official and unofficial—the president instructed "responsible officials" to restore Belarus's financial position to what it was before August 1998—a tall order, although the Russian crisis, had it not been for the expansionary monetary policy pursued by Belarus in 1998, should have actually strengthened the BRB with respect to the Russian ruble while allowing its much needed devaluation with respect to Western hard currencies.

Belarus's Economic Performance

Economic Recovery

Atypically for a country that had neither significantly reformed nor stabilized its economy, in 1996–1998 Belarus boasted a rapid recovery of its GDP, by more than 20 percent (2.8 percent in 1996, 10.4 percent in 1997, and 8.3 percent in 1998; see tables 11.3 and 11.4), achieving the second highest ratio of 1998 to 1990 GDP (79.4 percent, after Uzbekistan) among Commonwealth of Independent States (CIS) republics. Growth acceleration has been accompanied by a decline in registered unemployment (table 11.11). The main source of GDP growth has been exports, especially to Russia, aided by the implementation of a customs union agreed on in 1995 and the depreciation of the BRB with respect to the Russian ruble as well as direct central "exhortations" to export even on unattractive terms, on credit or for barter.

Reality or Mirage?

Was the Belarusian recovery reality or fiction? To some extent the growth in Belarus's GDP may have been exaggerated by the value of unwanted production without a market outlet, piled up in inventories. Ranging between 40 percent and 55 percent of GDP, inventories in Belarus are much higher than in market economies, but over the recovery years the ratio has been falling, on average. The quality of statistics from Belarusian sources is recognized by Western experts and by independent sample inquiries as being better than those from most countries of the former Soviet Union, so Belarus's differential performance with respect to those countries, rather than its absolute performance, could be exaggerated. A possible source of overestimation is the disposal of current output and inventories through barter or, worse, the buildup of unpaid arrears, mostly in trade with Russia. Also, living standards lagged behind GDP (see figure 11.1); by February 1999 even the president publicly complained that the economic growth recorded in statistical yearbooks was not matched by rising standards of living of the population.

Capital Consumption

A factor that might explain not Belarus GDP recovery but the maintenance of living standards (though these are recovering at a slower rate than GDP owing to the growth of investment) is capital consumption. Investment in Belarusian enterprises—though growing—is still said to be below the level required to maintain current production capacity (see *Belarus Economic Trends*). Belarus is eating away its economic potential built in the past, falling behind its Western neighbors.

The Easier Task of Restructuring

One possible explanation for Belarus's smoother recovery relative to those of more ambitious reformers could be the nature of its part in the division of labor within the former Soviet Union. Specifically, Belarus had not specialized, as part of the Soviet Union, in the vertically integrated production of goods now obsolete or embodying negative value added; it had specialized in assembling finished products from components provided by the rest of the Soviet Union, so much so as to be labeled "the Soviet assembly shop." Therefore restructuring tasks were probably easier for Belarus than for the other Soviet republics, for the equipment and labor involved in the assembly of components must be less specific and easier to redeploy or at any rate smaller than those involved in vertically integrated production.

Another area where Belarus appears to have been able to maintain its export capability is that of armaments. We know, for instance, that it has frequently undertaken substantial barter transactions in this sector with China.

Table 11.11
Employment and labor market in Belarus

	1994	1995	1996	1997	1998	1Q1999	Apr. 1999
Period averages							
Population (thousand)[a]	10,355	10,327	10,246	10,216	10,188	10,172	10,164
Labor force[b]	4,892	4,829	4,751	4,608	4,558	4,626	4,686
(percentage change)	—	-1.3	-1.6	-3.0	-1.1	0.6	2.2
Participation rate (percentage of total population)[c]	47.2	46.8	46.4	45.1	44.7	45.5	46.1
Employees in employment (thousands)[a,d]	4,696	4,405	4,360	4,370	4,258	4,304	4,293
(percentage change)	-2.6	-6.2	-1.0	0.2	-2.6	0.2	-0.3
Total employment[b]	4,802	4,713	4,577	4,453	4,450	4,520	4,583
(percentage change)	1.0	-1.8	-2.9	-2.7	-0.1	0.6	2.3
Unemployed (thousand)[a]	90.1	115.8	174.4	155.7	107.6	106.4	103.1
(percentage change)	—	28.6	50.5	-10.7	-30.9	0.6	-2.3
Unemployment rate[a]	1.8	2.4	3.7	3.4	2.4	2.3	2.2
Vacancies	19.6	18.3	15.8	28.2	41.9	35.2	47.9
Vacancies rate (percentage of labor force)	0.4	0.4	0.3	0.6	0.9	0.8	1.0
End of Period							
Unemployment rate[a]	2.1	2.7	3.9	2.8	2.3	2.3	2.2

Note: Dashes indicate data are not available.
[a] Ministry of Statistics and Analysis data.
[b] BET staff calculations.
[c] Labor force in percentage of total population.
[d] Employees at enterprises, institutions, and organizations: Annual data do not correspond to the average of quarters because Minstat makes a year-over-year correction only on annual data.

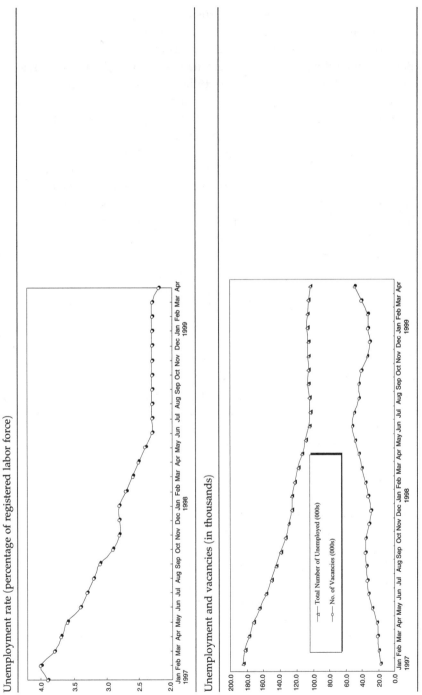

Unemployment rate (percentage of registered labor force)

Unemployment and vacancies (in thousands)

Source: Belarus Economic Trends, May 1999.

But the real cornerstone of Belarusian growth has been its special position and relationship developed with Russia. The dominant position of Russian nationals in Belarus; the strategic position of Belarus, defending Russia's western flank (which is claimed by President Lukashenko to cost U.S. $1 billion per year, a good counter in negotiations with Russia) and allowing a transit route to the West (for the gas pipeline and road transport) more secure than that through Ukraine; the significant popularity of Belarus with Russian electors; and a genuine long-standing complementarity of the two countries' productive structures: All these factors have placed Belarus in an excellent position to export to Russia—as long as Belarus can supply competitively or regardless of cost when Russian producers have no spare capacity. Belarus is totally dependent on energy imports from Russia (apart from producing about 10 percent of its oil consumption), but Gazprom is financing and jointly supervising the trans-European Yamal gas pipeline through Belarus and is active also as barter broker and financial investor.

Sustainability

The real test of an integrated economic policy elevated to a system, as in Belarus, is its sustainability in the medium to long term. Even full communism could be implemented, perhaps for seven days or even seven months, even in one country—contrary to earlier beliefs— especially with a larger neighbor's temporary support; but over a longer period of, say, seven years, it would not be sustainable.

Can the Belarusian system and policy model be sustained into the medium to long run? In general, it can be presumed that recovery to earlier levels and old structures is relatively easy, but after that, higher levels than previously attained and/or new structures require a more flexible, market-oriented mechanism of signals and incentives. For a start, idle capacity margins, first selectively then throughout the economy, will be eroded and absorbed; sustained growth will require new net investment, which at the moment cannot be expected from either domestic or external investors. Different policies toward both must therefore be devised and implemented.

In a system that is so export-driven, the question is whether Belarus can compete internationally in the twenty-first century. The answer will depend on productivity trends, in turn tied to privatization, restructuring, and investment, three areas in which Belarus's record is not at all encouraging; on real-wage trends, which at the moment are bent on recovering earlier Soviet levels regardless of underlying and reduced circumstances; and on an exchange rate policy capable of accommodating an otherwise deteriorating competitiveness, that is, a unified and realistic rate. The outlook on all these grounds must be deemed pessimistic.

Basically Belarus—like all less developed economies, regardless of their transition status—faces the twin gap of domestic savings and current account balance. Unlike the more successful among those economies, Belarus cannot rely—under its present policies and system—on a sustained capital inflow large enough to bridge both gaps. Economic growth has been slowing down, as predicted by all independent forecasters (the World Bank, the EBRD, Planecon, Wharton Economic Forecasts Associates), falling to the rate exactly predicted by the World Bank of 2 percent in 2000.

A Belarus-Russia Monetary Union?

The Schedule

The process of economic integration between Belarus and Russia, begun with the treaties of 1996 and 1997 on their economic union, was taken a stage further on December 25, 1998, when President Lukashenko and Russian President Boris Yeltsin signed in Minsk a declaration of intent to implement a monetary union of the two countries. On February 12, 1999, the chairmen of NBB and of the Russian central bank signed a schedule of concerted actions, including monetary policy unification and coordination of exchange rate policy between the two countries. The NBB then published *The Concept for the Adoption of a Single Currency, the Formation of a Single Central Bank and a Common Banking System of the Belarusian-Russian Union*. On April 28, 1999, in Moscow the two presidents signed eleven documents, including the completion of the Russia-Belarus customs union, the union's budget, and a draft agreement on the unification of the two countries into a Union of Sovereign Republics.

According to the NBB document, the introduction of a single currency in the two countries was planned to take place in 1999 in three swift phases (see *Belarus Economic Trends*, March 1999):

1. In the first stage, in the first quarter of 1999, the monetary policies of Belarus and Russia were supposed to be partially unified; a common capital market for securities would be created; the mutual convertibility of the two countries' currencies would be achieved; and a legal framework for the unification of the currency regulations would be formed.

2. The second phase (April–June 1999) is to deal with the unification of the currency regulations and monetary systems of the two countries, as well as with the adoption of a single currency.

3. In the third phase (in the second half of 1999) a single bank of issue would be created and "the process of adopting a single currency" would be completed. The option preferred by NBB was the establishment of a common noncash currency that would be in circulation alongside the two national currencies and pegged to a convertible currency. This hasty schedule should be contrasted with the long delay expected for the actual introduction of the new currency and the complete replacement of the national currencies, the completion of which is planned for 2008 (*Belarus Economic Trends*, March 1999). There are still many discussions and open questions, however. It is no wonder that these provisions—badly timed shortly after Russia's massive financial crisis of August 1998 and subsequent ruble devaluation—in practice should have remained a dead letter.

The Form

The first question raised by a possible Russia-Belarus monetary union is the actual form that this might take, that is, the nature of the common currency and modalities of its issue and management. It has been suggested that the common currency might resemble the old-style transferable ruble (TR), which was used as a unit of account within the *Council for Mutual Economic Assistance* (CMEA) until its dissolution in 1991. This is out of the question. The TR was neither truly transferable, as TR bilateral balances could not be used automatically in settlement of trade with third-party member countries without their agreement, nor was it even a ruble, as it could not be used even for purchases of Soviet goods and services without Soviet agreement. It was purely an accounting device to record trade imbalances arising in any period for clearance in subsequent periods through planned trade transactions enshrined in bilateral trade agreements between centrally planned economies. A new TR could do absolutely nothing that cannot be done at present with Russian and Belarusian rubles.

Could the Russia-Belarus common currency take the form of the ECU-Euro, that is, a basket of currencies of the two member countries, gradually locked into a permanently fixed exchange rate between themselves and at that point becoming a kind of superruble? In theory, yes, but in practice such a currency basket would not give the Belarusian ruble, under any criterion (such as relative size of population, national income, mutual trade shares), a weight greater than 5 percent or 10 percent and a commensurate weight in the management of the currency and of the new joint monetary institutions. It would hardly seem worth it to undertake such complex transformations in order to set up something virtually indistinguishable from the Russian ruble. At that point it might be infinitely easier for Belarus simply to adopt the Russian ruble. Either way, the question needs to be addressed and resolved of how Belarus could exercise effective control over joint monetary institutions from what necessarily must be a bilateral minority position.

One solution worth considering is the replacement of both the Russian and the Belarusian central banks with a joint currency board. A currency board, such as that introduced in Bulgaria or Estonia, is statutorily bound to issue its own currency only in exchange for hard currencies at an exchange rate permanently fixed with respect to a reference currency or basket of currencies. Initially the board would need enough foreign reserves to cover the joint cash basis at the selected exchange rate; presumably this would have to be provided by G–24 and international financial institutions. This was the solution advocated for Russia by George Soros in *The Financial Times* on August 14, 1998. The cost would be less than 10 percent of GDP for both Belarus and Russia, for such is the order of magnitude of the money-to-income ratio in both countries. One could imagine the two countries adopting a new ruble worth the same amount of foreign exchange in both countries and run in parallel by the two former central banks, each transformed into a currency board, instead of a single currency board; this would facilitate transition to the new system by maintaining national institutions and decoupling the timing of the changeover in the two countries.

The attractions of currency boards are that they have little discretionary power, and therefore there would be virtually no problem of national control by each member, and that budget deficits would not be monetized. Unfortunately currency boards also have significant drawbacks. They leave no room for monetary policy, they cannot act as lender of last resort, and they command no seigniorage (unless they have excess reserves large enough to play that role); furthermore, their credibility may remain difficult to establish, and a run on the currency cannot be ruled out by the fact that cash is covered by foreign exchange. Nevertheless the solution is worth considering, because it may be the only one that does not raise issues of national control and independent monetary management.

Premature Unification

Whatever form the prospective Russia-Belarus monetary union might take, it would be premature, that is, implemented before political unification, which involves much more than the friendship and coordination currently prevailing between the two countries, and before the convergence of their real economic variables (such as real interest rates, labour productivity in real terms, real wages, and unemployment) might bridge their long distance from being an optimum currency area. This may be particularly serious in view of the likely asymmetry of external shocks for the two countries at least with respect to energy prices, with Russia as a net exporter and Belarus as a net importer of energy, respectively, suffering and benefiting from an oil and gas price decline (and vice versa). Such asymmetry is best dealt with by independent monetary and exchange rate policies.

Similar considerations apply to the Euro, but the Russia-Belarus monetary union would also be premature in a much stronger sense than might be the case for the Euro, for several reasons:

1. The two countries are nowhere near fiscal and monetary convergence obtaining in the Euro-zone; indeed, one of them, Russia, has experienced a devastating financial crisis within recent memory (August 1998) with adverse implications on its international credibility and external debt, whereas while Belarus enjoys exceptionally low levels of domestic and international debt.

2. Neither country is a fully monetized economy by the standards of advanced market economies, but Russia has experienced inordinately high degrees of demonetization (with the spread of *wykseli*; interenterprise payment arrears; mounting arrears in tax payments,

wages, and pensions; and endemic barter) of a kind that Belarus has been experiencing only marginally with the development of arrears and barter in its foreign trade (especially with Russia).

3. There are fragile but highly developed financial markets in Russia, which are missing in Belarus.

4. There are different degrees of "marketization" in the two countries, with Russia—for all its faults—approaching a largely private market economy and Belarus having hardly started its own journey toward it.

Therefore it is wrong to believe that the pre-1992 experience of joint membership of the ruble area might make it possible for Russia and Belarus to reestablish a monetary union easily: The pre-1992 division of labor is no longer suited to a different economic system (indeed different systems), to a group of two countries instead of the former fifteen, and to different levels and structures of domestic income and production output. Very little gain would accrue to Belarus from exchange rate certainty with respect to the ruble.

In conclusion, there is no doubt that for the foreseeable future a monetary union between Russia and Belarus is a premature, indeed potentially dangerous diversion. Of course this does not mean that it is not feasible. A purely cosmetic form of monetary union could be set up overnight, for instance, with the union of two issuing some little-used ruble substitute via its modest budget (of just 800 million Russian rubles in 1999).

A premature union could even take a substantial form. German monetary unification in 1991 was also undoubtedly premature, for example, with real wages tending to a single level while productivity in the East was one third of the West German level (though political unification also took place at the same time). It simply was costly in the short to medium run, and it absorbed large-scale resources provided by the German federal budget and international financial market (of a kind which would not available to Belarus and Russia). And even if costly or outright wasteful at least initially, monetary union might have political advantages, though these are not so obvious in the two countries other than in terms of the permanence and continuity of current regimes. In any case the costs and benefits of this project, economic and political, in the short, medium, and long run deserve much closer scrutiny and broader public discussions than they have attracted to date.

In mid-April 1999, in the middle of NATO's attack on the former Yugoslavia, Russia and Belarus offered to include Yugoslavia in a three-way Slavic union (see *Financial Times*, April 13, 1999). This was a purely symbolic move of no practical impact that simply illustrated both the depths of Russia's and Belarus' feelings and their limited options.

Conclusions

Were it not for the almost thirty countries currently undertaking a transition process from a communist-dominated centrally planned economy with state ownership and enterprise toward a democratic, mixed-market economy, it would not occur to anyone to label Belarus—or China, or Vietnam—as a transition economy and/or society, as they are commonly labeled through an undue process of assimilation.

Belarus is still a command economy, with dominant, large state enterprises, central controls on prices and on economic activities in the state and the small private sector, a central bank subordinated to government, large-scale subsidies, monetary overexpansion and associated open and repressed inflation, a multiple exchange rate, and internal and external imbalances. These policies and outcomes are completely at odds with the declared purpose of constructing a socially oriented market economy. Economic stabilization has not been achieved, nor is it in sight. Backwardness in both reform and stabilization has protected Belarus from the worst drawbacks of the Russian transition, but the policies and system that have offered that protection are not sustainable and in any case cannot provide any foundation for sustained recovery and growth.

It would be preferable for Belarus authorities to openly acknowledge their unwillingness to move toward a standard market economy, instead of promising unwanted changes, invoking gradualism and social orientation. This would avoid misunderstandings and recriminations in their relations with international organizations and the unavoidable disappointment deriving from unduly raised expectations. Maintaining a large and dominant state sector, leaving financial markets undeveloped, and keeping out international financial investors is Belarus's sovereign right. Nevertheless, virtually all the other steps that would be necessary to move to a fully fledged market economy are also indispensable to an orderly, efficient, and sustainable monetary economy no longer centrally planned and no longer integrated within a socialist bloc: the elimination of shortages, the pursuit of a sound currency and associated fiscal and quasi-fiscal discipline and monetary restraint, the opening of the economy and therefore the unification and liberalization of exchange rates, the establishment of new governance mechanisms in corporatized state enterprises, and the certainty of law and the elimination of bureaucratic obstacles to the development of small and medium-sized enterprises and to the attraction of foreign direct investment. Even the prospective monetary union with Russia would remain a mirage without such progress in Belarus. Whether this is good news or bad news remains to be seen.

References

Charman, Ken. 1999. *Belarusian Economic Trends, Quarterly Report*, no. 2, TACIS, Minsk.

Karimov, I. 1993. *Building the future: Uzbekistan—Its own model for transition to a market economy*. Tashkent: Uzbekistan Publishers.

Nuti, D. Mario. 1999. Making sense of the Third Way. *Business Strategy Review* 10, no. 3: 57–68.

12   Problems with Economic Transformation in Ukraine

Anders Åslund

Economic transformation in the former Soviet Union has been arduous, with substantial declines in output and welfare. Even in this unfortunate lot, until 1999 Ukraine stood out as one of the least successful countries in its attempts to become a productive market economy. The purpose of this chapter is to try to determine why Ukraine's attempts at economic reform have not been more auspicious.

To clarify Ukraine's position, we first need to look at how Ukraine has fared in comparison with other countries. Considering its preconditions, the most relevant comparison is with other post-Soviet countries, because all these countries had far worse preconditions than those in Central and Eastern Europe. Therefore, I examine some major parameters of economic performance. Next I explore why Ukraine went wrong initially. The curious thing about Ukraine, however, is that until 1999 it does not seem to have moved out of the trap in which it first got stuck. A plausible explanation is the power structure that has arisen, which will be described and then formalized as a four-sector model.

My prime concern in this chapter is how Ukraine possibly can get out of the doldrums. A natural start is an examination of what has not worked in Ukraine. Quite a lot has actually worked, however, and that is the theme of the next section. With these perspectives, I move on to what might work that has not really been tried. Although many of the necessary economic measures are obvious, the key issue is how they can be introduced and implemented politically.

For anybody who has followed the Ukrainian economic reforms, it is evident that the problems of the economic reforms are not in their details or even in their overall design. The problem is rather the politics of economic reforms. Either the political will or the political ability has fallen short. Yet political forces are dependent on economic conditions as well. If one starts on one track, there are natural next steps to take, and it is difficult to change track altogether. The evolution of economic reforms becomes path-dependent.

Ukraine's Poor Economic Performance

The key economic indicator for a country is of course its gross domestic product. Ukraine officially registered a total decline in GDP of about 53 percent from 1989 to 1999. By 1997, no less than seven post-Soviet countries had recorded greater declines, so that does not appear all too disturbing in a comparative context. A greater worry, however, is that Ukraine has not had a single year of growth, but a significant decline in GDP has continued every single year. Ukraine is the only post-Soviet country with such a poor performance. In 2000, though, Ukraine recorded a fundamental breakthrough with a GDP growth of 6 percent likely to continue after impressive structural reforms.

An instant suspicion is that Ukrainian statistics are too poor to register actual growth. It is true that Ukraine's GDP is understated in official statistics, and Ukraine has done less than, for instance, Russia to improve its statistics and measure the unregistered economy. Moreover, the underground economy is undoubtedly large in Ukraine. Simon Johnson, Daniel Kaufmann, and Andrei Shleifer (1997, 183) estimated the underground economy in eleven post-Soviet countries. They found that in Ukraine the underground economy amounted to 49 percent of GDP in 1995. It was larger only in Georgia and Azerbaijan. Moreover, they observed a substantial expansion of the share of the underground economy in GDP every year, whereas this share declined in successful reform countries, such as Poland. Still, even compensating for Ukraine's large underground economy, the country has experienced a considerable decline in output since transition began, in both absolute and relative terms.

Although it took Ukraine several years to get inflation under control, by 1996 inflation fell to 40 percent a year, and it has stayed well below that level. In 1997, inflation was only 10 percent and even in the crisis year 1998, it only doubled. The Ukrainian stabilization policy was augured with a strict monetary policy, but the budget deficit has gradually been brought under control—reaching a budget surplus of 0.5 percent of GDP in 2000 (see table 12.1). The main cause

Table 12.1

	1992	1993	1994	1995	1996	1997	1998	1999	2000 Prediction
Output									
GDP annual growth (percent)	−17.0	−14.2	−22.9	−12.2	−10.0	−3.0	−1.8	−0.4	5.8
GDP (billions of U.S. dollars)	20.8	13.9	24.1	37.0	44.6	50.1	42.7	30.8	5.8
Inflation and budget									
Inflation (percent, end-year)	2730	10155	401	182	40	10	20	19.2	25.8
Budget deficit (percentage of GDP)	−25.4	−16.2	−9.1	−7.1	−3.2	−5.6	−2.7	−1.5	0.5
General government revenues	44.0	43.7	41.9	37.8	36.7	38.0	35.2	35.6	0.5
General government expenditures	73.3	55.5	50.6	43.9	42.8	43.6	37.9	37.1	0.5
External sector (billions of U.S. dollars)									
Current account	−0.6	−0.8	−1.2	−1.2	−1.2	−1.3	−1.3	0.8	1.5
Trade balance	−0.6	−2.5	−2.6	−2.7	−4.3	−4.2	−2.6	−0.5	0.8
Exports	11.3	12.8	13.9	14.2	15.5	15.4	13.7	12.6	15.7
Imports	11.9	15.3	16.5	16.9	19.8	19.6	16.3	12.9	14.9
External debt									
External debt (billions of U.S. dollars)	0.5	3.7	7.7	8.1	9.2	11.8	11.7	11.5	14.9
External debt (percentage of GDP)		11.2	20.5	23.6	21.1	23.8	28.0	37.3	14.9

Sources: IMF Web site; ICPS (2001); EBRD 2000.

of the reduction in the budget deficit has been a lack of financing. Ukraine lingered on the verge of default for most of 1998 until early 2000, but it has avoided actual default, although its international reserves were as low as U.S. $600 million (ten days of imports) in March 1999. Still, Ukraine has proven that it has sufficient treasury controls to avoid default.

Privatization in Ukraine has been slow, and the quality of privatization has been even worse in the sense that it has not promoted new, strong owners who attempt serious enterprise restructuring but an unclear amalgam of dominant insider ownership. Land reform, with the introduction of private ownership of land, has been a persistent aim of the reformers, but the left in the parliament has been too strong and committed to public ownership of land (Lerman 1999). The parliament has intermittently tried to block all kinds of privatization, causing great problems for the government. As a result, enterprise life has been extremely stagnant. In 1996, the average tenure of enterprise managers was ten years, and it was virtually impossible to remove a passive, incompetent, or criminal manager of an enterprise. Many managers had run their companies down close to a standstill, but they did not give up or sell off any assets: They simply demanded more money from the government. Small-scale privatization was completed in 1997, and large-scale privatization has picked up speed. The parliament has effectively vetoed all land reform, and it has blocked thousands of enterprises from privatization, but it has not been the only guilty party. Few large enterprises have been offered in open sales, and the arcane practices of Ukrainian privatization have deterred foreign investors. In 1997, Poland attracted four times more foreign direct investment than the U.S. $2.5 billion Ukraine had accumulated during its whole period of independence (EBRD 1998). The Ukrainian stock market has never taken off, as shareholders' rights have been ignored.

Ukraine's big problem is ubiquitous and arbitrary state intervention. Its deregulation was slow and remains incomplete. Foreign trade was only formally liberalized, and new regulations have been introduced repeatedly, all too obviously to generate more bribes for the foreign trade administration. The same is true of most of the government administration. There are too many government bodies; they are too centralized, and their coordination is minimal, but they allow themselves a great deal of discretion. An extraordinary chaos persists that seems peculiar to Ukraine in its degree. Beneath this administra-

tive disorder, a large number of government officials harass enterprises and enrich themselves in the process. The key public policy
issue is to control the state apparatus to make it possible to run independent enterprises.

Ukraine ranks very low on all liberalization indices. The index of
economic freedom of the Fraser Institute puts Ukraine as number 106
out of 114 countries ranked (with Russia as number 102; Gwartney
and Lawson 1997). The index of economic freedom of the Heritage
Foundation ranks Ukraine as number 124 out of 161 countries ranked
(with Russia as number 106; Holmes, Johnson, and Kirkpatrick 1999).
On the Corruption Perceptions Index of Transparency International
(1998), however, Ukraine is number 69 out of 85 countries, whereas
Russia is number 76, that is, Russia is more corrupt than Ukraine. In
most of these regards, Ukraine appears about as bad as Russia, and
there are after all many countries in the world that are worse than
both. Bribes paid are clearly larger in Russia than in Ukraine. However, Ukraine tops one statistic, that is, senior management time
spent with officials.[1] The problem in Ukraine is less that government
extracts large bribes than that it often seems impossible to get anything done.

Why Ukraine Made a Poor Initial Choice of Economic Course

Initially after independence, the Ukrainian political establishment
was completely preoccupied with nation building for obvious reasons. In several newly independent countries, notably Estonia and
Latvia, market economic reforms were seen as part and parcel of
nation building. In Ukraine, however, nation building was widely
perceived as separate from market economic reform, and many inherent tendencies drove Ukraine in the wrong direction. Key reasons
for Ukraine's choice of economic course was its choice of leader, its
understanding of nation building, its mindset, and the nature of its
political elite.

At the formation of a nation, the leader is of great significance.
On December 1, 1991, Ukrainians elected Leonid Kravchuk the first
president. Kravchuk had been Second Secretary of the Communist
Party of Ukraine, and he was one of the foremost representatives of
the old communist establishment, even if he formally parted with the
communists and stood up for Ukrainian independence. Kravchuk
had been responsible for ideology within the Communist Party with

no understanding of, or interest in, economics. He was a man of consensus, and he was seen as a man who could mediate between the Russified Eastern Ukraine and the nationalistic Western Ukraine as well as between the communist establishment and liberals. His yearning for consensus prevented him from making a clear choice on economic strategy.

The primary concern of the newly independent nation was the building of new national institutions. Although Kyiv had formally been the capital of the Soviet Socialist Republic of Ukraine, it was merely a provincial capital. Some national institutions existed in a rudimentary form, for instance, the Ministry for Foreign Affairs, whereas the central bank and Ministry for Foreign Economic Relations were missing altogether. Naturally the newly independent Ukraine was preoccupied with the establishment of its national symbols, and many Ukrainians wanted national institutions that were as strong as possible, with large staff and extensive powers. Thus it became a national virtue to build up bureaucracy and regulations, as long as they were national. The most disturbing example of this was that Ukraine recreated Soviet-type foreign trade regulations in an attempt to ensure that the Ukrainian state had control over the country's foreign trade. The stage was set for the rule of a massive centralized bureaucracy.

Economics and social sciences had been very weak in Ukraine, because the Soviet authorities had always been particularly afraid of Ukrainian nationalism, subjecting Ukraine to much more control and repression than Russia or the Baltics. As a consequence, Ukraine suffered from an especially great shortage of all nation-building skills. Incredibly, this country of 52 million citizens had only one economic journal, and that was totally dominated by old-style communists. As Ukraine had been rigorously isolated from the outside world, few people in Ukraine spoke English or other foreign languages, which complicated its opening to the West. Ukraine hardly had a critical mass of sufficiently well-educated economists for launching radical economic reforms. Under the Kravchuk administration, various ideas of a special Ukrainian economic model arose. They were not very original and can be described as a mixture of muddled Gorbachevian economic thoughts, that is, the last stage of communist confusion, and surviving statist nationalist economic thinking from the 1930s about the need for a strong regulating state.

Nor did the country's burning economic problems persuade leading Ukrainians to move in the right direction. At the end of 1991, the most apparent economic crisis was massive shortages. Ukraine's shops were virtually empty, because prices were kept regulated by the state at an artificially low level while the central Soviet government issued uncontrolled amounts of credits. Although it was obvious that prices would have to be freed, no leading Ukrainian politician was prepared to take the responsibility for the ensuing inflation. In the end, Ukrainian prices were liberalized to a considerable extent in January 1992, but this action was undertaken in agreement with Russia, which meant that Russia was to blame. The new Ukrainian government took no responsibility, and it displayed no commitment to free prices or free trade.

The devastating financial crisis was another urgent concern. Even before prices were liberalized, Ukraine probably experienced inflation of a couple of hundred percent in 1991, and after prices had been freed they rose by 2,730 percent in 1992. However, inflation was largely perceived as a problem arising from Russia. A prevalent idea was that Ukraine was rich and that the problem was how to escape from Russia's parasitism. Much of the early economic discussion in Ukraine focused on how to isolate Ukraine from Russia's inflation and establish an independent currency. As early as January 1992, Ukraine introduced its own coupon, a parallel Ukrainian currency to the old Soviet ruble, which continued to circulate. Clear thinking about the management of a national currency was missing, however, and Ukraine ended up issuing even larger ruble credits than Russia in relation to its GDP, which in turn led to a Ukrainian inflation of 10,155 percent in 1993, when Russian inflation had fallen to 840 percent.

The fundamental problem was too much continuity in the Ukrainian establishment. The elite was weak, small, and homogenous. The transformation of the Second Secretary of the Communist Party of Ukraine for ideology to the first president of independent Ukraine was emblematic of this harmful continuity and lack of competition. The prime problem was perceived as excessive dependence on Russia, whereas the harm of inheriting a communist system, though universally recognized, was not given sufficient attention. As Ukrainians were anxious to attain consensus around their new state, they were worried about too much competition. In effect, much of the old

Soviet nomenklatura persisted in Ukraine, changing their party cards for national insignia.

The stage was set for extraordinary rent seeking. Radical reforms had been discarded as characteristic Russian rashness, incompatible with Ukrainian peacefulness and moderation. The old establishment largely stayed intact, and it wanted to transform its power into material benefits. A cumbersome bureaucracy and regulatory system were being built as a manifestation of the Ukrainian state. Soon enough, these conditions bred severe corruption and rent seeking. As a natural result, in the winter of 1993–1994, the Ukrainian government was dominated by a group of so-called red directors, enterprise managers from Eastern Ukraine who had joined the government to maximize their personal revenues through cumbersome regulations allowing few but themselves to make money. They intentionally introduced laws and regulations that would generate corruption to their own benefit. The same was true of Pavlo Lazarenko's tenure as prime minister in 1996–1997.

A mixture of state enterprise managers, new entrepreneurs, government officials, commodity traders, bankers, and outright criminals thrived on incomes caused by government subsidies and regulations, that is, rent seeking. There were four dominant forms of rent seeking. The first was to buy metals and chemical in Ukraine, which were cheap because of price regulation, and sell them abroad at the world market price. This required access to these commodities and export permits. About 40 percent of Ukraine's exports were commodities in 1992 (IMF 1993, 113), and their average domestic price was about 10 percent of the world market price. Hence total export rents amounted to some U.S. $4.1 billion or 20 percent of GDP in 1992. The beneficiaries were managers of state metallurgical companies, commodity traders, foreign trade officials, and some politicians.

The second method was to import certain commodities, notably natural gas from Russia, at a low subsidized exchange rate and resell them at a higher price. It was even more profitable if one did not pay for the deliveries but let the government guarantee payments for the gas imports. The main beneficiaries were a small number of gas importers and their government partners.

The third way was subsidized credits. In 1993, Ukraine experienced 10,155-percent inflation, but huge state credits were issued at an interest of 20 percent a year, that is, state credits were sheer gifts, and they were given to a privileged few. In 1992, net credit expansion to enterprises was no less than 65 percent of GDP, and it was 47 percent of GDP in 1993 (calculated from IMF 1993, 109; IMF 1995, 73, 105).

The fourth form of rents was straightforward budget subsidies, which amounted to 8.1 percent of GDP in 1992 and 10.8 percent of GDP in 1993 (IMF 1995, 94). They were concentrated in agriculture and energy, that is, the gas and coal industry, which became totally criminalized by a struggle over these subsidies (IMF 1995, 94).

In comparison with Russia, Ukraine's export rents are lower, its import rents clearly much higher (though not estimated here), its subsidized credit much larger, and its direct enterprise subsidies about the same. In total, rents as a share of GDP were higher in Ukraine than in Russia in both 1992 and 1993 (Åslund 1999). Much of these rents were accumulated abroad in tax havens as capital flight.

In this way, a select group of privileged insiders usurped a huge share of GDP in the early years of transition and grew strong. They have no reason to abandon their enormous power and wealth. It is based not on property, but on arcane financial flows. For society, the result has been sharply rising income differentials. Ukraine has reached a Gini coefficient of 47, about as much as Russia or a Latin American average (Milanovic 1998, 41). In addition, Ukrainian society has gone through hyperinflation, shortages of goods, sharply falling output, and general misery. By June 1996, macroeconomic stabilization was happily taking hold at long last, as monthly inflation reached zero and inflationary rents were largely abolished. The other forms of rents have been maintained, however, Ukraine's dominant problem is that much of the initial rent seeking has been preserved, and it harms economic development, as it is extracted through an overregulation of the country's economy.

Ukraine stands out as one of the most clear-cut examples of gradual reform among postcommunist countries. It illustrates that the choice was not between an early sharp fall in output with radical reform and a protracted but less abrupt decline in production with gradual reform. Ukraine's slow and moderate reforms have brought a lasting degeneration of the economy as a whole. Its experience shows that gradual reforms take a country on a different development path and that gradual reform breeds economic interests that will work for rent seeking rather than profit seeking. Ukraine lacks a middle class of profit-seeking entrepreneurs. Therefore, no strong constituency for economic deregulation has been bred as yet. Ukraine's future evolution is constrained by its unfortunate original path.

Ukraine's Economic-Political Power Structure

To understand Ukraine's economic and political problems, we need to identify the dominant financial-political interest groups. They tell us a lot about the structure of the country's economy, the real political forces, and the constraints on economic policy making. Like Russia, Ukraine has a well-developed oligarchic power structure, but the differences between the two are as interesting as the similarities.

From conversations with leading Ukrainian politicians over the years, I have extracted that the main economic-political groups or clans. The changes have been considerable and fast. The first oligarchic groups were formed around commodity trading, importing natural gas and oil from Russia, while selling metals to the West. Domestic coal oligarchs thrived on government subsidies.

One of the first oligarchic groups was formed by Grigory Surkis and Viktor Medvedchuk, thriving on all kinds of commodity trade primarily in central Ukraine and controlling trade around Kyiv. Surkis owns Dynamo, Kyiv, Ukraine's best football team. While both sit in Parliament, Surkis is primarily a businessman, while Medvedchuk is a leading politician.

Another early group was formed by Ihor Bakai, the head of a series of companies importing gas from Russia. He has made use of a number of political partners, most recently Olexander Volkov who has been a close confident of President Kuchma. Volkov has also been involved in oil imports. Previously, Volkov protected Vadim Rabinovich, who was Ukraine's foremost media tycoon, but he lost out and was expelled from Ukraine after a feud with the then–national security advisor in July 1999.

In Donetsk, an early oligarchic group was formed around the coal industry. Its original leader was Yukhum Zviahilsky, who rose to become acting prime minister in 1993–1994 on the merit of having organized such serious coal miners' strikes that President Kravchuk found no other way out than to let him lead the government. As a leading Kravchuk man, Zaviahilsky, who is also an Israeli citizen, had to flee the country for over a year, because he was publicly accused of having stolen petrol for about $25 million, but his actions were later condoned by the Ukrainian prosecutor general. The

Donetsk group was reconstituted soon afterward under new leadership, but that was purged by Prime Minister Lazarenko in 1996. Recently, however, a new strong Donetsk group has been formed. Its leader is Mykola Azarov, who is the head of the national Tax Service. Other major members are the governor of the Donetsk region, Viktor Yankovich, and the leading regional gangster, Rinat Akhmetov.

Another leading region has all along been Dnepropetrovsk. In 1996–1997, when Pavlo Lazarenko was prime minister, he and his business partner Yulia Timoshenko comprised the dominant oligarchic group in the whole of Ukraine. Timoshenko was CEO of United Energy Systems, which was Ukraine's main gas importer in 1996 and 1997. It was also involved in oil and metal trade. However, Lazarenko was ousted by Kuchma in 1997 after particularly abrasive enrichment, and fled to the United States, where he is being kept in arrest suspected of large-scale money laundering. Timoshenko dwindled in significance without Kuchma's support, and a new group has risen to great importance in Dnepropetrovsk. It is led by Viktor Pinchuk, who became the common-law husband of Kuchma's daughter Elena in 1999. He controls five major steelworks in Dnepropetrovsk, and he remains involved in gas trade.

Groups in the Crimea, Odessa, and Zaporozhe have been important, but they have faded because of less support from the center or local infighting.

The Ukrainian economic-political groups differ from those in Russia in a number of regards:

1. The Russian groups are usually led by one person, the head of a private enterprise group. The Ukrainian groups are often identified by two leaders, one senior government official and one enterprise leader, sometimes of a state enterprise. This shows that there is no real division between government and enterprise in Ukraine as yet, but such a division has already taken place in Russia. This seems to be a merit of the Russian mass privatization.

2. Virtually all the leading Ukrainian businessmen are deputies, for instance, Timoshenko, Lazarenko, and Medvedchuk, whereas few leading Russian businessmen are. The Ukrainian Rada is evidently much more important for corrupt business than the Russian Duma. Moreover, Ukrainian businessmen seem to spend most their time hanging around parliament or government, whereas Russian businessmen devote more time to their enterprises.

3. The leading Ukrainian businessmen are usually commodity traders and outright racketeers. Surkis and Pinchuk have only recently become major producers, while the major oligarchs have bought up most media as a matter of political control rather than business. As late as fall 1998, Ukraine's main gas importer, Igor Bakai, stated in a newspaper interview: "All rich people in Ukraine made their money on Russian gas" (Timoshenko 1998).

4. Unlike the Russian groups, the Ukrainian economic-political groups are primarily regional, which appears to be a reflection of the importance of racketeering for their revenues. Yet relations with the central government are much more important in Ukraine than in Russia.

5. Although the Russian financial-industrial groups are generally perceived as involved in criminal activities, they are not considered to represent outright organized crime. In Ukraine, however, the line between organized crime and the leading economic-political groups is blurred at best.

6. In Russia, the financial-industrial groups provide financing to various parties and to the government. In Ukraine, the economic-political groups rather tend to own political parties. At present, Surkis and Medvedchuk own the United Social Democratic Party, Bakai and Volkov the Democratic Union, Pinchuk Working Ukraine, and Timoshenko Fatherland. These four parties are major forces in the parliament with 30–50 deputies each out of a total of 450. Characteristically, all these oligarchic parties are considered centrist, that is, always prepared to make a deal without any real ideology.

7. The Russian financial-industrial groups have been engaged in vicious and open competition with one another since July 1997. They are sometimes completely opposed to the government but survive. In the elections in March 1998, both Hromada and the United Social Democrats opposed President Kuchma and the government. As a consequence, Lazarenko was forced into exile, while Timoshenko, Surkis, and Medvedchuk switched their allegiance to Kuchma, though Timoshenko only temporarily. Apart from Fatherland, all the oligarchic parties support President Kuchma, which underlines how dependent they are on him.

The Ukrainian Economy as a Four-Sector Model

From this survey of the Ukrainian economic-political elite, we can move on to schematize the main relations in Ukrainian society. The problems of the Ukrainian economy can be seen as a four-sector model. The four sectors are the government, rent-seeking businessmen, the parliament, and the households. Let us scrutinize in turn the objectives and ensuing actions of each of these sectors or actors.

The Ukrainian Government

The Ukrainian government aspires to a monopoly of power to maximize its revenues from bribery. By the Ukrainian government, I mean the presidential administration, the Cabinet of Ministers, all the ministries and state committees, and the regional and local administration. The higher levels of the Ukrainian government seem to live off and for corruption. Several top officials try to act in line with the interests of Ukrainian society, but they usually lose out, as they are in the minority. The predominance of corrupt interests in Ukrainian government has many implications. The government in a broad sense is strongly against any deregulation, because it would reduce its monopoly power and thus its revenues from bribes. A Ukrainian government decision often requires twenty signatures, which is a guarantee that no official sells off government monopoly power. Any attempt to reduce bureaucratization is resisted, as it undermines the government's monopoly on power. Hence, the ministries have little power, which is centralized in the Cabinet of Ministers apparatus and the presidential administration. Conversely, Ukraine has minimal regional autonomy, so the regions cannot undermine the omnipotence of the center.

Until 1997, Ukraine experienced a persistent struggle between the president and the prime minister. Since the president has a stronger position in the new constitution of June 1996, the president now seems to have secured his supremacy over the prime minister (Wise and Pigenko 1999). Arguably, the previous state of affairs suited the objectives of the government. Because of persistent conflicts between president and prime minister, little could be done, which meant that the complicated hierarchical bureaucratic system was preserved and all threats of simplification, autonomy and deregulation were fended off. However, Pavlo Lazarenko, who was prime minister for one year in 1996–1997, upset this status quo. He tried to transform the government monopoly into a personal monopoly, undertaking substantial privatizations to his own benefit and usurping the monopoly rents. As he openly challenged the president and seemed to opt for exclusive personal powers with little return for others, he was ejected from the system.

Rent-Seeking Ukrainian Businessmen

Business in Ukraine is dominated by rent-seeking businessmen, such as those presented above. They focus on elementary monopoly rents, lobbying for regulations that guarantee them some monopoly. Therefore, they favor all kinds of regulations that apply to others but not to themselves. Similarly, they advocate high taxes that others must pay but from which they themselves are exempt in one way or another. They are not much in favor of privatization, as they make their money on the government. Bakai previously ran the private gas-importing company Respublika, but he has now returned to the state sector as CEO of the state company Naftohaz Ukrainy. As management theft is standard procedure and the government is unable to remove state enterprise managers, the advantages of actual ownership of enterprises to these businessmen is dubious. Multiple enterprise inspections of others is in their interest, as it raises the costs for potential competitors and thus limits their competitiveness. The ultimate victory is when inspectors close down competitors. In agriculture, the old agrarians dominate, and their prime interest is to procure products cheaply from the country's farms on the basis of government-imposed low procurement prices and then sell them expensively. The rents can then be divided among agrarian leaders, but they are not dissipated to the actual farmers. This explains why the resistance to the privatization of agricultural land is so great. Thus, the rent-seeking businessmen want a maximum of bureaucracy exactly as the government does.

The Ukrainian Parliament

The Ukrainian parliament (the Supreme Rada) lives largely for bribes, in particular the center that represents the party of power, which essentially supports the government. The level of bribery and wealth in the Supreme Rada is striking. The most common form of bribery seems to be when businessmen contract a parliamentary deputy to block a proposed reform law. The parliament usually has a backlog of about 500 draft laws, showing that this mechanism works well. Sometimes bribes are also paid to get a law through. The amounts of the bribes for passing a law, however, appear to be much larger than those for blocking a law, and several people need to be paid. I heard of one case in which U.S. $700,000 was shared by four deputies who got a law promulgated. The communists and the rest of the left hold about 40 percent of the seats in the Supreme Rada. Although they are not immune to bribery, they have an additional interest in making the situation as bad as possible, as they think they will benefit from popular dissatisfaction. Thus, the parliament is largely interested in making legislation as messy as possible.

Ukrainian Households

The Ukrainian households form the fourth sector. They do suffer from corruption and a dysfunctional economy, but they are also co-opted by the underground economy, as they have to work in it every day to cope. Many are also involved in petty theft and the like. The tragedy of the Ukrainian model, however, is that the households are very weak in all regards. Civil society is so frail that Ukrainians rarely stand up to defend their own interests (O'Loughlin and Bell 1999). One of the rare exceptions has been repeated coal miners' strikes in the East, but these miners have largely been encouraged and exploited by their rent-seeking managers, who have used them to extract more subsidies from the government. The public understands perfectly well that most of the top officials are corrupt, but they do not know what to do about it. As Ukrainian media are very weak, public opinion is poorly informed. Many blame reform, as Ukraine has officially been pursuing reform for years. Still, Ukrainians vote in large number, and they do not like what they see. They regularly protest against the party of power, which is trying to meet their challenge with maximum control of media, though free media still persist. Thus the household sector is simply made to pay for the poor economic policies and rent seeking, and there is no apparent reason to believe that this circumstance will change.

Thus we have in Ukraine an iron triangle of government, business-men, and parliament who all favor a maximum of regulation and state interference to maximize rent-seeking and corruption and a population that is of little consequence and partly co-opted and compromised. This model of self-reinforcing rent seeking looks far too stable and is close to equilibrium. It is reminiscent of the distri-bution of power in a stagnant African country (Collier and Gunning 1999). As the rent seekers rule Ukraine, no level playing field has been allowed to develop. The government does not function expe-diently, because it is not in the interest of the rent-seeking elite. In the spring of 1996, macroeconomic stabilization was apparent, but it was clear that GDP would fall by as much as 10 percent. At the time, I thought this would concern the ruling elite and facilitate reform, but the elite could hardly care less about the decline in output.

Although Russia and Ukraine are similar in many ways, the scheme depicted above differs in important ways from that in Russia. The Ukrainian government is far more cohesive and homogenous than the Russian government, which is deeply divided in openly opposing groups. The Ukrainian regions have none of the autonomy awarded to Russian regions, in particular as Russian governors are popularly elected, whereas the Ukrainian president dismisses and appoints governors at will. It seems more difficult to get a decision out of the Ukrainian government than out of the Russian govern-ment, as more officials have veto power. This lack of ability to make decisions suits the interests of the corruption-seeking officials, how-ever, so it is not to their disadvantage.

Ukrainian businessmen appear more immersed in the state sector and the criminal world than their Russian counterparts. They are largely traders, whereas Ukrainian bankers have never gained much clout, and production provides surprisingly little political clout. Of course, Ukraine does not have the strong oil and gas producers Russia has. Therefore, the Ukrainian oligarchs are more homogenous than their Russian counterparts, and they represent only the first step toward a market economy: elementary trading. They are there-fore more hostile to an open-market economy than Russian busi-nessmen. Whereas the Russian tycoons fight each other openly, the Ukrainian businessmen are much covert in their intrigues.

The Russian State Duma is also deeply corrupt, but its parties are much more important and cohesive than the factions in the Ukrainian Supreme Rada. In the Russian parliament full parties are traded for specific votes in wholesale trade, but the Ukrainian parliament sticks to retail corruption of single deputies, as the parties are so weak and the parliament so fragmented. This makes it more difficult to get any legislation through the Ukrainian Rada than the Russian Duma.

The Russian and Ukrainian populations differ the least of the four sectors. If anything, the Ukrainian population is even more timid than the Russians. In particular, Ukraine lacks Russia's vibrant critical media. If Ukrainian reforms are to succeed, Ukrainians will have to stand up and defend their civil rights. Although reform in Russia may seem sufficiently difficult, these comparisons suggest that it would be even more difficult to undertake reform in Ukraine, as the corrupt establishment is so coherent and dominant. Yet there are several ways in which this consensus of the corrupt can break down. Let us move on to see which approaches to reform have not worked and which ones have.

What Has Not Worked in Ukraine?

Nearly a decade after the end of the Soviet Union we may dare to pass judgment on what has worked and what has not worked in Ukraine, even if some reforms have succeeded quite late, prompting a certain note of caution. Ukraine pursued comprehensive reform only from October 1994 until June 1995. A number of reforms have been attempted, even implemented and revoked, and some reforms seem to have stuck. It is most instructive to start with measures that have not worked and investigate why.

Ukraine has received a large amount of technical assistance, meaning advice from consultants to senior politicians. The reforms that have actually taken place were inspired by this advice. Most of the advice, however, has been ignored. The reason is obvious. The foreign advisors have largely suggested to government officials how they should deprive themselves of power and illicit incomes, and the officials have no interest in that. Similarly, most of the 500 draft laws waiting in the Ukrainian Rada for discussion have been drafted with assistance of foreign advisors, and they are also ignored, because their intention is to reduce government interference and corruption. Clearly, this technical assistance should be reduced and be focused on those few senior officials who appear serious about reform.

Every visitor notices that the Ukrainian state administration is barely functioning. Ukraine suffers from extreme overcentralization and a corresponding dilution of responsibility. A government decision may require more than twenty signatures, and then nobody is perceived as responsible for it. The presidential administration is far too large, with some 1,000 employees, as is the apparatus of the Cabinet of Ministers, with some 700 people. These bodies sit at the top of the government, but they have few useful functions. In effect, they are diluting responsibility from the ministries while breeding intrigues and bureaucracy. Ukraine badly needs a fundamental government reform, which should involve the reduction of these two harmful bodies; the abolition of many useless or even harmful government bodies, such as unjustified control organs; at least a halving of the number of sheer bureaucrats; and a decentralization of decision making and responsibility. In parallel, the quality of civil servants should be certified, and the good ones should be better remunerated. However, the political elite want this concentration of power, and they are not prepared to accept any delegation or any other measure that could reduce monopoly of power or their revenues from corruption. Therefore, multiple attempts to reorganize the government apparatus have resulted in half measures at best and ensuing reversals.

The biggest failure in the Ukrainian economic reforms has been deregulation. Ukraine underwent substantial deregulation twice, in late 1992 and in late 1994 (Kaufmann 1995). Most of the deregulation, however, was swiftly reversed, as both leading businessmen and government officials made most of their money on monopoly rents that were generated by various regulations on trade, prices, and licensing or inspections. Therefore, a number of important sectoral reforms sponsored by the World Bank have come to nothing. They have involved gas, electricity, the coal industry, and agriculture, that is, those industries that have been most imbued with rents. Sometimes the Ukrainian government has followed the letter of an agreement and abolished certain concrete regulations, for instance, in foreign trade, however, a few new, often worse regulations have swiftly emerged, as the political will to regulate has not been weakened.

Licensing is a telling example. Ukraine has suffered from extensive, multiple, tardy, and expensive licensing procedures. After years of discussion, the Ukrainian Supreme Rada promulgated a law on entrepreneurship in 1998. It cut the number of business activities subject to licensing from 112 to 42 and simplified the process of licensing. A new government body was created to handle licensing, and it prohibited other bodies from demanding or issuing licenses. Within half a year, the president had issued three decrees and the Cabinet of Ministers two decrees that extended the demands for licensing to more activities than had been the case before the law on entrepreneurship was adopted (Palianytsia and Segeda 1999). As the government lives off and for licensing, it would not let it go too easily, but as this was an important demand of the whole donor community, a temporary concession could be made.

Similarly, the government tried to limit the number of inspections by decree. Instead, the inspectors undertook longer inspections. During enterprise interviews in 1996, tax inspectors had installed themselves permanently at most large enterprises. In several cases they worked around the clock, while the inspected enterprises were expected to pay all their costs.

Considering the antisocial nature of the ruling forces in Ukraine, we would not expect social expenditures to be too large. However, Ukraine's social expenditures have been persistently sizable, until recently more than 20 percent of GDP. Few countries can afford such large social expenditures, and Ukraine certainly cannot. Yet a strong populist opinion against any cutting back of social expenditures prevails. In particular, the left in the parliament is up in arms any time scaling back of any social benefits is debated. The reason is that "social" expenditures are to an amazing extent concentrated among the richest citizens, as Ukraine has done little to scale back old nomenklatura privileges. In 1995, the poorest fifth of the population received as little as 6 percent of social assistance, none of the unemployment benefits, and only 8 percent of all nonpension cash social transfers (Milanovic 1998, 113). No other transition country has recorded such an antisocial redistribution. Few Ukrainians seem to expect anything good from the state, and many survive on their private agricultural plots, which are comparatively large in Ukraine, encompassing two to three acres of land (Van Atta 1998).

Foreign donors are often blamed for these failures. They could have done more and acted better, but I doubt that would have mattered much. Before 1994, little could be done considering the government philosophy, and after that the rent-seeking community turned out to be too strong. The domestic resistance to reforms has been massive, and as the World Bank rightly concludes, you cannot undertake serious reform on the basis of conditionality for loans only. Relevant constituencies in the receiving country must favor reform, and that has not been the case in Ukraine (World Bank 1998).

What Has Worked in Ukraine?

Still, we should also take note that a lot of reforms have worked in Ukraine, even if most of them have taken hold rather late. Clearly, the proreform forces were too weak to come to the fore at the outset of Ukrainian reforms, and nothing could have succeeded at that time.

The greatest reform success to date in Ukraine is macroeconomic stabilization, which was initiated in late 1994 and completed in the spring of 1996. Since then, inflation has stayed low and predictable, and Ukraine fended off the Russian financial crash with a devaluation of barely 50 percent and a surge in inflation from 10 percent in 1997 to still only 20 percent in 1998 and probably the same in 1999. As is shown in table 12.1, Ukraine undertook a substantial fiscal adjustment to achieve stabilization, cutting the budget deficit from 16 percent of GDP in 1993 to 3.2 percent of GDP in 1996. The ease with which emerging markets could get cheap commercial loans in 1997 tempted the Ukrainians to allow the budget deficit to almost double, but in 1998 the deficit was reined in at 2.7 percent of GDP. Thus since 1996 Ukraine has demonstrated fiscal restraint and control. Whatever the faults of Ukraine's management, the government has repeatedly proven that it can cut expenditures when necessary, and a reasonable treasury control has been established.

Macroeconomic stabilization in Ukraine was preceded by a strict and highly responsible monetary policy initiated in December 1993. The political success of this monetary policy is demonstrated by the continued tenure of Governor Viktor A. Yushchenko from December 1992 to December 1999. Yuschenko could have been ousted by the parliament at any time during his tenure, so his survival was a sign both of his political skills and that it was possible to sell restrictive monetary policies in Ukraine. An important reason that this has been possible is that the proinflationary banking community has been very weak, as the banking sector in Ukraine never developed much, in contrast to that of Russia. Nor did the volume of treasury bills grow all too large as in Russia, and most of those that were issued were bought by the national bank and foreign investors. Therefore, a domestic lobby demanding a large volume of expensive treasury bills never evolved, whereas that was a major destabilizing force in Russia. One underlying reason for the restraint in issuing treasury bills, however, was that foreign portfolio investors were all along more skeptical of Ukraine than Russia and therefore invested comparatively small amounts in Ukraine.

Possibly the most surprising achievement is that Ukraine has undertaken a substantial privatization. By the end of 1997, more than 45,400 small enterprises had been privatized, and by July 1998 more than 7,800 large and medium-sized enterprises had been privatized to at least 70 percent in a mass privatization program. Most of the shares of these enterprises were given to managers and employees, although some were distributed to the public through vouchers (EBRD 1998, 196). Thus more than half of Ukraine's GDP in 1998 came from formally privatized enterprises. Privatization occurred much later in Ukraine than in Russia, however; the insider ownership was even greater; and the stock market in Ukraine did not really develop. Therefore, there has been even less enterprise restructuring in Ukraine than in Russia. This may be why privatization finally occurred: It did not change the pattern of rent seeking and management theft. It might also be a question of attrition. As enterprises had no real owner, the manager eventually assumed formal ownership.

Ukraine was the last post-Soviet country to adopt a new constitution, and doing so was considered virtually impossible until it actually occurred. In the end, the Supreme Rada simply adopted the constitution during a long night in June 1996. A principal outcome of the adoption was the reduction of the power of the prime minister, so that the two centers of power became the president and the parliament. Another important outcome was that the president preserved the right to undertake substantial legislation by decree until July 1999. Up until that date, if the parliament did not explicitly refute a presidential decree within thirty days, it gained legal force (Wise and Pigenko 1999). Although the justification for this stipulation was that the parliament was reluctant to adopt reforms, many presidential decrees under the provision were actually antireform measures.

The Supreme Rada accepted in late 1994 that the country's exorbitant income taxes had to be cut, but then no tax reform was promulgated for years. In the summer of 1998, however, the payroll tax was cut by 12 percent from slightly over 50 percent, as the so-called Chernobyl tax was abolished. Arguably, after tax collection had fallen below a certain level, these taxes did not even make sense for the rent seekers as an impediment to competitors, as literally no Ukrainian enterprise paid them. Therefore, they could just as well be abolished.

Similarly, the government introduced a fixed, lump-sum tax for small entrepreneurs in 1998, which replaced all other taxes. It suddenly led to the emergence of hundreds of thousands of legal entrepreneurs, either new or previously hidden in the underground economy. As the underground economy was thriving in any case and accounted for about half of GDP, it made no sense not to collect any taxes from it. Therefore, these entrepreneurs could just as well be legalized and thus be forced to pay some tax.

From 1995 until 1997, total government expenditures were around 43 percent of GDP, and parliamentarians argued that it was impossible to cut them, for peculiarly Ukrainian reasons. When Ukraine actually faced a financial squeeze in 1998, however, it proved perfectly possible to reduce government expenditures—by no less than 10 percent of GDP from 1997 to 1999. Moreover, the public payroll was reduced by no less than 300,000 people in 1998 and 1999. Thus, the Ukrainian government found it was perfectly capable of cutting expenditures and maintain treasury control when such cost-cutting was necessary.

Contrary to common perceptions, the observed behavior of the Ukrainian decision makers makes good sense, with the four-sector model presented in this chapter as a framework of explanation. The system was more complex and made less sense when the prime minister was an independent player beside the president and the parliament, as was the case until the summer of 1997, when Lazarenko was sacked as prime minister. Prior to that, the president, the prime minister, and the parliament, played a game of mutual blame.

If we accept the four-sector model, in which the rationale for parties' behavior is rent seeking, we can dismiss the model of disorganization that Olivier Blanchard and Michael Kremer (1997) have developed, which has several shortcomings. First, disorganization could make sense if the decline in Ukraine's output had taken place during a brief period. Ukraine has experienced a full decade of steady slump, however, which should be enough to clarify that disorganization cannot be the explanation. Second, Blanchard and Kremer ignore the fact that the decline in output has been greatest where reform has been slow. Third, they fail to distinguish the interests of the manager from the firm. Although Ukrainian enterprises are certainly suffering, their managers are often doing reasonably well because of management theft. Fourth, their empirical proof is a regression showing that more advanced industries have suffered more decline, but those are also the greatest value detractors. Hence, the fall in the country's output is no mystery: It can be explained with the interests of the rent seekers and their strength in decision making. Konings and Walsh (1999) have tested empirically the effects of disorganization on 300 firms in Ukraine, but as they have simply accepted Blanchard and Kremer's dubious premises, their results do not prove that disorganization was the cause of the persistent decline in Ukraine.

The Transformation of 2000

Ukraine had ended up in a very unfortunate position in late 1999, and the question was what could be done to ameliorate its fortunes. The country's main problem could be summarized as a homogenous and hegemonic political and economic elite that aimed at rent seeking. Ukraine remained a relation-based economy, characterized by pervasive corrupt state intervention (Åslund and de Ménil 2000).

Miraculously, Ukraine managed to accomplish most of these things in a profound but rather quiet transformation in 2000, which was preordained by several important changes. The financial crash in Russia of August 1998 had left Ukraine hanging on the verge of financial default, and the risk did not seem to abate. Increasingly, the Ukrainian elite realized that something had to be done. Meanwhile, the Ukrainian population had realized what a real market economy required, and the tolerance of economic populism faded.

Since the main problem is the political and economic elite, the best hope for change is democratic elections, which challenge the elite, possibly divides it, and provides a secure base for opposing groups (Maravall 1994). The breakthrough for reform in October 1994 was conditioned by a temporary interruption in the elite through the presidential election of July 1994, and the reform was surprisingly far-reaching. Unfortunately, the old elite crept back into the government and clawed back the reforms with surprising ease, as the democratic institutions were fledgling. Although the new round of elections did not cause a change of regime, they had a strong positive impact. In October–November 1999, Ukraine held rather unfair presidential elections, in which Kuchma was victorious. However, the elections clarified that no real communist threat persisted, leaving President Kuchma responsible.

The experiences of other postcommunist countries suggest that the parliament must get a reformist majority to promulgate all the necessary reform legislation. The preceding parliamentary elections of March 1998 had introduced partly proportional elections, which had facilitated party formation. The Ukrainian parliament was made up of three blocs, each consisting of several parties. The largest bloc was four to six centrist propresidential oligarchic parties. The communists dominated a leftist bloc, while the national and liberal right formed a third bloc. In December 1999, some ten centrist and right-wing parties formed a reformist coalition. They agreed with President Kuchma to appoint the highly respected reformist governor of the National Bank, Viktor Yushchenko, prime minister. A first condition, a structuring of the parliament, had been accomplished, and a second condition for economic cleansing was that a real reformer was set to lead the process. A third condition was a proper economic understanding, which was largely in place.

The two first tasks of the Yushchenko government were to improve the structure of the government so that it could make decisions, while checking corrupt intentions. This was a matter of elementary organization, which was swiftly accomplished since the will existed. The other task was to tighten up the budget and reinforce treasury controls. As in Russia, monetization had not proceeded, while arrears and barter had proliferated to a similar extent (Gaddy and Ickes 1998; Djankov 1999). To a considerable extent, barter and offsets were means to extract implicit state subsidies. For Russia, a World Bank study has assessed total enterprise subsidies at no less than 16 percent of GDP in 1998 (Pinto, Drebentsov, and Morozov 1999), and the situation was similar in Ukraine. The average cost of a barter deal appears to be about 25 percent of the deal (Djankov 1998, 131). If the tax on a deal is less than 25 percent, it is no longer profitable to opt for barter, which should then decline. Indeed, as the government demanded cash payments of taxes, largely complied with its own payment commitments, and reduced taxes, barter plummeted as in Russia.

The worst problems of nonpayments, offsets, barter, and enterprise subsidies pertained to the energy sector. Yushchenko appointed Yulia Timoshenko deputy prime minister for energy to fight with the other oligarchs, since she knew their tricks. Timoshenko did so with great verve. In the oil sector, Volkov had simply imported oil with an import subsidy, and when Timoshenko abolished this unjustified subsidy, his business disappeared. In the power sector, Surkis and others had bought electricity from state generators but paid for only 7 percent of total deliveries, while selling it for full payment. Timoshenko made sure the state was paid in full. In the gas sector, Bakai had sold gas but not paid Russia for it. In addition, he was accused of stealing a large share of the Russian gas in transit through Ukraine to Europe. Timoshenko had him sacked from Naftohaz Ukrainy, changed the gas supply to Turkmenistan, renegotiated all agreements, stopped the theft from pipeline, and so forth. As most of these changes were promulgated as laws, they are not so easily reversed. In the coal sector, however, Timoshenko and Yushchenko failed to undertake any change before they were both sacked in early 2001 amid furious complaints from the oligarchs. In the end, Volkov and Bakai had at least temporarily been taken out of business, while Surkis had lost a fortune on the changed regulation of the power sector, and both Surkis and Pinchuk lost greatly on the changes in the gas market.[2] Without the assistance of Timoshenko, a dissenting oligarch, this stark reduction in rent seeking had hardly been possible in such a short period.

Since 1998, many of the very large enterprises in Ukraine have been privatized. In 1998 and 1999, most of the privatization benefited the oligarchs that helped Kuchma finance his re-election campaign, notably Surkis who seized seven regional power utilities and Pinchuk who now controls five major metallurgical companies. In 2000, however, major enterprises, for instance, three oil refineries, were bought by big Russian companies. In early 2001, six power utilities were even sold in transparent tenders. The effect of these many privatizations has been that the interests of the oligarchs have been crystallized and their competition has intensified. Undoubtedly, this has helped increase transparency and has driven down rents.

In general, a competitive approach is likely to be helpful in reducing corruption and rent seeking. In their book *Mercantilism as a Rent-Seeking Society*, Robert B. Ekelund and Robert D. Tollison (1981) argued that mercantilism ended in Britain because of a competition between the Royal Court and the parliament over monopoly rents and jurisdiction. In a similar vein, Andrei Shleifer and Robert Vishny (1993) have suggested that corruption should be fought through competition rather than prohibition, which often implies a reinforce-

ment of the monopoly of corruption, something that was characteristic of the Stalinist system. Shleifer and Vishny (1998) and Shleifer
and Daniel Treisman (2000) have tried to devise methods for making deals with the rent seekers for the good of society or to organize
competition among them.

A remaining problem in Ukraine is that state domination remains
so strong, both in terms of employment and public finance. Ukraine
has managed to maintain surprisingly high state revenues at around
35 percent of GDP. Among the CIS countries, only Belarus collects
more in state revenues (Tanzi 1999), and Belarus is no democracy.
Moreover, Ukraine maintains the highest formal tax rates in the CIS,
which means that anybody can be sentenced for inevitable tax vio-
lations. In 1998, Ukraine cut tax rates and simplify the tax system,
because of the dearth of international funding. As state revenues
declined somewhat from 1997 to 1999, badly needed reductions in
public expenditures, the bureaucracy, and the budget deficit turned
out to be possible. Unfortunately, the IMF is persistently pushing for
higher state revenues, although it is obvious that the Ukrainian government is likely to use any marginal resources less efficiently than
anybody else. Wagner's law states empirically that public revenues
(or expenditures) are correlated to the GDP per capita. Accordingly,
Ukraine should not have state revenues of 35 percent of GDP but
rather some 20 percent of GDP (see Tanzi 1999). Wagner's law could
be interpreted as a limit for how large resources a weak state can use
efficiently. As both the government and the IMF struggle so hard all
the time to keep state revenues high, it should be easy to bring them
down. Since Ukrainian social expenditures are highly regressive,
such a reduction is not likely to harm the poor. On the contrary,
smaller public expenditures should be more transparent and thus
more socially allocated.

On the back of the strong state sector, the organs of law enforcement have flourished. The main service has been the police, and
the Ministry of the Interior has 420,000 employees. Under Yuri
Kravchenko, minister of the interior from 1995 to 2001, this ministry
became a dominant clan in the president's service, and it was identified as the main source of extortion of enterprises. The second
strongest law enforcement service was actually the tax service under
Mykola Azarov, which became the base of a new oligarchic clan with
its 70,000 tax inspectors and tax policemen. The third service was the
Security Service (former KGB) with some 28,000 men. Under Minister

Leonid Derkach it rivaled the Ministry of Interior as a clan. The law-lessness of these organs made them major players in the oligarchic life of Ukraine. Strangely, when Kravchenko and Derkach were dis-missed in early 2001, both their services seem at least initially to have fallen apart into regional organizations to be controlled by the re-gional governors, clarifying the structural weakness of these seem-ingly formidable forces.

The changes that occurred in 2000 and early 2001 were amazing in their consequences, one reason being that rents tend to decline over time, and total rents in Ukraine are quite small. Rent seekers in Ukraine are not likely to extract more than perhaps 5 percent of GDP under present conditions. Since Ukraine's GDP was only $31 billion in 1999, we are discussing merely $1.5 billion a year. Therefore, the Ukrainian rent seekers seem too weak to be able to hold their own for much longer. The outside world has such a degree of leverage on Ukraine that it should be possible to effectively buy out or bid over the rent seekers. Ukraine might be closer to a breakthrough than appears possible today.

Although Ukraine applied for membership in the World Trade Organization (WTO) in 1994, it is far from becoming a member, partly because of its own policy, and partly because of the slowness and ineffectiveness of the WTO. If the staff of the WTO acted as efficiently as the staff of the IMF, Ukraine would have been a member of the WTO long ago and probably would have done a great deal to liber-alize its foreign trade, which would have diminished rents. It is a mystery how Ukraine has managed to isolate itself so much from foreign trade for so long, because traders tend to be able to trade and reduce each other's rents even under restrictive trade regimes, and Ukraine's is not all that restrictive on paper.

Conclusions

Ukraine has suffered from a poor sense of direction, a weak state, a corrupt bureaucracy, corrupt businessmen, and a weak civil society. The harm of half-hearted and delayed reform is abundantly evident. Too much of the old communist establishment persists in the Ukrai-nian state apparatus, and the most prominent new businessmen have been co-opted into corruption. An iron triangle of government, busi-nessmen, and parliament, all living off and for corruption and rent seeking long maintained an economically suboptimal equilibrium.

Ukraine was caught in a vicious circle. Piecemeal reforms bred extraordinary corruption and rent seeking. A small group of very rich people arose, and they bought political power with their wealth. They used their fortunes to maintain their fortunes by bribing politicians, bureaucrats, and parliamentarians to introduce new regulations that generate more rents. Such a vicious circle usually ends a major macroeconomic destabilization, as occurred in Bulgaria in 1996. If one does not learn from the mistakes of others, or even from one's own mistakes, one is bound to repeat them.

However, Ukraine appears to have been rocked out of this equilibrium without any major shock. Many elements contributed to the change, and it is difficult to pinpoint any decisive factor. The public understanding of market economics has greatly improved. The Russian financial crash and Ukraine's verging on default created a real sense of crisis. The party structuring of the parliament and the presidential election of 1999 clarified who was responsible. Privatization reinforced the autonomy of the oligarchs and thus facilitated their increased competition. Integration in the world economy and the purchasing by foreigners of major Ukrainian companies aggravated the elite competition. A contributing reason has been that the Ukrainian rents are small in any international comparison, while their social cost is large, and the volatility of the leading oligarchic has been striking. Yet, little could have been done without the commitment of the Prime Minister to real market reform, but he would not have accomplished much without a vicious competition among the oligarchs, driving down rents. An underlying force has been democracy, however weak it is in Ukraine, because politicians have considered the impact of their actions on public opinion.

References

Åslund, Anders, and Georges de Ménil, eds. 2000. *Ukrainian economic reform: The unfinished agenda.* Armonk, N.Y.: M. E. Sharpe.

Åslund, Anders. 1999. Why has Russia's economic transformation been so arduous? Paper presented at the World Bank's Annual Bank Conference on Development Economics, Washington, D.C., April 28–30.

Blanchard, Olivier, and Michael Kremer. 1997. Disorganization. *Quarterly Journal of Economics* 112, no. 4: 1091–1126.

Collier, Paul, and Jan Willem Gunning. 1999. Explaining African economic performance. *Journal of Economic Literature* 37, no. 1: 64–111.

Djankov, Simeon. 1999. Enterprise restructuring in Russia. In *Russian enterprise reform*, ed. Harry G. Broadman. Washington, D.C.: World Bank.

Ekelund, Robert B., and Robert D. Tollison. 1981. *Mercantilism as a rent-seeking society*. College Station: Texas A&M University Press.

European Bank for Reconstruction and Development (EBRD). 1998. *Transition Report 1998*. London: EBRD.

European Bank for Reconstruction and Development (EBRD). 2000. *Transition report 2000*. London: EBRD.

Gaddy, Clifford G., and Barry W. Ickes. 1998. Russia's virtual economy. *Foreign Affairs* 77, no. 5: 53–67.

Gwartney, James D., and Robert A. Lawson. 1997. *Economic freedom of the world*. Vancouver: Fraser Institute. Internet: ⟨http://www.fraserinstitute.ca/books/econ_free⟩.

Holmes, Kim R., Bryan T. Johnson, and Melanie Kirkpatrick. 1999. *1999 Index of Economic Freedom*. Washington, D.C.: Heritage Foundation and Wall Street Journal.

International Center for Policy Studies (ICPS). 2001. *Economic Statistics* 6 (April).

International Monetary Fund (IMF). 1993. *Economic Review: Ukraine 1993*. Washington, D.C.: International Monetary Fund.

International Monetary Fund (IMF). 1995. *Economic Review: Ukraine 1994*. Washington, D.C.: International Monetary Fund.

Johnson, Simon, Daniel Kaufmann, and Andrei Shleifer 1997. The unofficial economy in transition. *Brookings Papers on Economic Activity* 2: 159–239.

Kaufmann, Daniel. 1995. Diminishing returns to administrative controls and the emergence of the unofficial economy: A framework of analysis and applications to Ukraine. *Economic Policy* 19, suppl.: 52–69.

Konings, Jozef, and Patrick Paul Walsh. 1999. Disorganization in the process of transition. *Economics of Transition* 7, no. 1: 29–46.

Lerman, Zvi. 1999. Land reform and farm restructuring in Ukraine. *Problems of Post-Communism* (May/June): 42–55.

Maravall, Jose Maria. 1994. The myth of authoritarian advantage. *Journal of Democracy* 5, no. 4: 17–31.

Milanovic, Branko. 1998. *Income, inequality, and poverty during the transition from planned to market economy*. Washington, D.C.: World Bank.

O'Loughlin, John, and James E. Bell. 1999. The political geography of civic engagement in Ukraine. *Post-Soviet Geography and Economics* 40, no. 4: 233–66.

Palianytsia, Andri, and Serhi Segeda. 1999. Reform of the Ukrainian licensing system: One head is cut off—Two are growing. *ICPS Newsletter* 4: 1–2.

Pinto, Brian, Vladimir Drebentsov, and Alexander Morozov. 1999. Dismantling Russia's nonpayments system: Creating conditions for growth. Report by the World Bank, Moscow, September.

Shleifer, Andrei, and Daniel Treisman. 2000. *Without a map: Political tactics and economic reform in Russia.* Cambridge: MIT Press.

Shleifer, Andrei, and Robert W. Vishny. 1993. Corruption. *Quarterly Journal of Economics* 108, no. 3: 599–617.

Shleifer, Andrei, and Robert W. Vishny. 1998. *The grabbing hand: Government pathologies and their cures.* Cambridge: Harvard University Press.

Tanzi, Vito. 1999. Transition and the changing role of government. Paper presented at the International Monetary Fund Conference "A Decade of Transition: Achievements and Challenges," Washington, D.C., February 1–3.

Timoshenko, Viktor. 1998. Vse bogatye lyudi Ukrainy zarabotali svoi kapitaly na rossiiskom gaze (All rich people in Ukraine made their money on Russian gas). *Nezavisimaya gazeta*, October 16, 1998.

Transparency International. 1998. The Corruption Perceptions Index. Internet: ⟨http://www.transparency.de/documents.cpi/index.html⟩.

Van Atta, Don. 1998. Household budgets in Ukraine: A research report. *Post-Soviet Geography and Economics* 39, no. 10: 606–16.

Wise, Charles R., and Volodymyr Pigenko. 1999. The separation of powers puzzle in Ukraine: Sorting out responsibilities and relationships between president, parliament, and the prime minister. In *State and institution-building in Ukraine*, ed. Taras Kuzio, Robert S. Kravchuk, and Paul D'Anieri. New York: St. Martin's.

World Bank. 1998. *Assessing aid: What works, what doesn't and why.* New York: Oxford University Press.

13   The Economic Transition in Bulgaria, 1989–1999

Ilian Mihov

Introduction

After seven years of recurrent surges in inflation, stumbling structural reform, and a series of banking crises, in July 1997 Bulgaria
launched a comprehensive economic stabilization program. Its cornerstone is the introduction of a currency board arrangement, but
the program also includes acceleration of privatization, recovery of
the banking sector, a comprehensive tax reform, and several other
macroeconomic measures. Two years after its launch, the new stabilization package seemed remarkably successful both in reducing
inflation to single-digit numbers and in creating an environment for
the implementation of long-delayed structural reforms.

Before the start of the July 1997 program, the economic transition
in Bulgaria was a clear illustration of the pitfalls of partial reform.
The purpose of this chapter is twofold. First, it presents an overview
of key macroeconomic developments in Bulgaria from 1989 to 1999,
highlighting lessons from the delay of economic reforms and describing the exact mechanisms of economic and financial collapse. Second,
it reports the merits of introducing a currency board in Bulgaria, as
well as its sustainability in the medium and the long run.

Several stylized facts stand out as the key characteristics of the
economic transition in Bulgaria: (1) delay of economic reform—on
several occasions attempts were made to jump-start the process of
transition, but all of these programs failed except for the 1997 stabilization package; (2) considerable decline in economic activity—at
the bottom of economic collapse in 1997, Bulgarian GDP fell to
63 percent of its 1989 level; (3) several financial crises; and (4) introduction of a currency board with a comprehensive package of
reforms in 1997 and subsequent stabilization of the macroeconomic

environment.[1] The search for a coherent explanation of these facts must address one fundamental question: Why were reforms delayed? With hindsight, it is clear that economic transition in Bulgaria started without any vision for a comprehensive structural reform: Privatization, deregulation, tax reform, everything was done on an ad hoc basis until 1997. Why did successive governments fail to implement changes that would clearly have enhanced efficiency?

The question becomes even more puzzling once we consider the success of the concurrent political transition. By 1992 Bulgaria had a working constitution, the consolidation of democracy was progressing quite rapidly, and there were no significant ethnic conflicts. The public had at its disposal a well-functioning electoral system and yet it did not vote for economic reform in the first seven years of transition. Political advances did not translate into economic reforms.

These questions are quite general, and some of the answers can be found in recent models that study the political determinants of economic reforms. Theories analyze the problem of delayed reform by investigating the interaction between voters and politicians, the incentive structures, and the rules in the electoral process. Several models formalize the problem of delayed reform. Alesina and Drazen (1991) study the "war of attrition." In this model, stabilization is implemented only if both parties vote for it, and then the war starts over who should bear the costs of stabilization. Reform is delayed until one of the groups concedes. Fernandez and Rodrik (1991) introduce uncertainty about the benefits of reform and build in a conflict between two interest groups. The uncertainty leads voters who might actually gain from the reform to vote for the status quo. In a different setting, Dewatripont and Roland (1992) construct a model designed to explain the delay of restructuring in transition economies. Their key result is that gradualism in reforming state-owned enterprises might be an equilibrium outcome under the assumption of asymmetric information: Slow reform allows the government to learn workers' type, so that layoffs and restructuring are conducted in an efficient manner.

In explaining the Bulgarian case, one has to note first that the communist government in the pre-1989 period managed to avoid major economic collapses. Unlike other countries from the region, at the end of 1989 the disenchantment with the communist regime in Bulgaria had not reached its peak. The preferences of the population for preserving the old economic system were clearly manifested in the fact that in the eight years after 1989 no Bulgarian government received a clear mandate for a comprehensive market-oriented economic reform. To the contrary, large masses of the population were disappointed with the initial stages of transition, and in a crucial vote in 1994 the public gave a mandate to the socialist party to slow down the process of reform and to conduct a more "socially-oriented" policy.[2] In addition to voters' preferences, one should also take into account special interests and in particular the interests of the managers of socialist enterprises. The slow process of economic reform allowed these managers to conduct "hidden" privatization by creating parallel structures and charging the losses to the state-owned enterprises they ran while channeling the profits into their own private companies.[3]

To understand the delay of reform in Bulgaria, one needs to address the question of why the public voted continuously for the former Communist Party even though the agent of efficiency-improving market-oriented reform was the opposition. Good starting points are models with incumbents. The Bulgarian public voted for the Communist Party because it did not completely damage its image as being a competent government in that country in the 1980s.[4] At the same time, the uncertainty surrounding the competence of the opposition amplified the inherent resistance among some of the voters to bearing the short-term costs of reforms. Hence a model extending Rogoff 1990 in the direction of asymmetric uncertainty about politicians' ability to run the government and incorporating findings from the delay-of-stabilization literature will be useful in explaining the dynamics of economic reform in Bulgaria. Outlining the theoretical framework of such a model is beyond the scope of this chapter, but the basic idea seems to be compatible with the key facts: consistent support for the ex-communists and a change in the political landscape only after the incompetence of the ex-Communist Party was clearly revealed when the economy slipped into hyperinflation and a financial breakdown.[5]

Leaving now the political economy story aside, the stylized facts outlined above also raise questions about the decline of economic activity in Bulgaria: What were the mechanics of the financial and economic collapse? How much of the collapse can be explained by the slow speed of transition and how much was the inevitable cost of reforming the economy? Even a quick glance at the dynamics of output in Bulgaria suggests that the speed of transition is in part to blame for the sharp decline in economic activity. As in most of the

transition economies, output in Bulgaria declined in the first three
years of transition. Unlike countries that implemented large-scale
reforms, however, in the following five years the economy in Bulgaria failed to regain the ground it lost in the first three. Although
structural changes and improved accounting could explain the initial
decline in measured GDP, the persistence of the decline is attributed
primarily to the absence of reforms and to the inability of successive governments to create an environment conducive to economic
growth. The sequence of economic crises in Bulgaria in the 1990s can
be linked to monetary and financial developments in the economy.
Yet the main source of the protracted decline in economic activity
was the slow pace of privatization, restructuring, and deregulation,
which basically meant that loss makers had to be subsidized over a
long period. Furthermore, in the process of propping up unsustainable economic structures, the government channeled subsidies via
the banking sector by instructing some of the largest state-owned
banks to lend to loss-making enterprises knowing that these loans
were of very doubtful quality.

In addition to the sharp and protracted decline of economic activity
during 1989–1997, another key characteristic of the Bulgarian transition is the high and variable inflation prior to June 1997. Several
studies have explored the causal factors for inflation with the common finding that monetary policy does not appear to be a significant
determinant of inflation in econometric regressions.[6] One possible
explanation for this controversial result is that policy actions undertaken by the Bulgarian central bank before 1997 lacked credibility
and were not implemented in a timely manner. Indeed, this chapter
uses impulse responses from vector autoregressions to document the
puzzling dynamics of inflation after a monetary policy tightening.
This result is consistent with the argument that policy actions designed to reduce inflation might turn unsustainable ex post and,
instead of reducing inflation, may lead to faster price increases. This
argument is reminiscent of the Sargent and Wallace (1981) result that
monetary policy tightening today leads to inflation in the future if
the need to finance deficits by printing money increases.

Although the Bulgarian central bank was independent on paper,
the government intervened on several occasions in the conduct of
monetary policy. It is tempting to explain the motivation for these
interventions by using models of time inconsistency of optimal plans,

in which governments instruct the monetary authority to pursue easy policy before elections, but these explanations are probably of little relevance to the current analysis. In periods of moderate inflation, any attempt to use the Phillips curve for short-term gains is unlikely to bring significant benefits. And indeed, it is very difficult to find any evidence that a Phillips curve relationship was exploited in Bulgaria in the 1990s. A more plausible explanation for the continuous political interventions focuses on the governments' needs to finance budget deficits by printing money. Furthermore, in addition to the simple extension of direct credit from the Bulgarian National Bank (BNB) to the government, a more "sophisticated" version of seigniorage financing, was also put in place. The loss-making state-owned enterprises were directly subsidized by commercial banks, thus creating a quasi-fiscal liability of the government and indirectly of the central bank. This method of subsidizing led to high inflation and directly caused deterioration in the balance sheets of the banking sector, thus creating conditions for bank runs and financial panics.

The inconsistency of Bulgaria's macroeconomic policies threw the country into hyperinflation in early 1997. The cataclysmic developments of the first two months of that year led to a change in the government, and for the first time in the postcommunist era, a government with a clear mandate for a thorough reform was elected. Shortly after taking office, the new government started implementing a comprehensive stabilization program built around the introduction of a currency board arrangement as of July 1, 1997. The success of the new program in its first four years was quite remarkable: Inflation dropped to single-digit numbers, the banking sector recovered swiftly, any possibility of direct financing of the budget was practically eliminated, tax collection improved, and most importantly, economic behavior changed. There are still some problems, however, will the real sector be viable enough to bear the strains of the currency board straitjacket? How will the government manage deterioration in the balance of payments? Is there a need for an exit strategy discussion at this point? More generally, is there a safe exit from the currency board arrangement without financial turmoil?

Two years after the implementation of the currency board, the benefits and the costs of this institution became quite visible. On the one hand, Bulgaria enjoyed macroeconomic stability. On the other

hand, the crisis in Kosovo and the turmoil on the world financial
markets reduced capital inflows and thus significantly restricted monetary growth when the economy started recovering from the recent
crisis.

The next section provides an overview of the main economic
developments in Bulgaria from 1989 to 1999. The third section focuses
on Bulgarian monetary policy and the banking sector, discussing the
sequence of banking crises and the economic collapse of 1996–1997
and providing some econometric evidence on the effects of monetary
policy on inflation and unemployment. The stabilization package of
July 1997 and the operation of the currency board are analyzed in the
chapter's fourth section. The final section offers some conclusions.

Economic Transition in Bulgaria: The Facts

Figure 13.1 reports the dynamics of output. In addition to providing
an index of real GDP (1988 = 100), the figure documents changes in
the Bulgarian government for the given period. The frequent political
reshuffling depicted in the figure was one of the immediate reasons
for the failure of the reforms in the first eight years of transition.
The initial stabilization program in Bulgaria was introduced in February 1991 with large-scale price liberalization and restrictions on the
growth rate of money. From the figure it seems that the Bulgarian

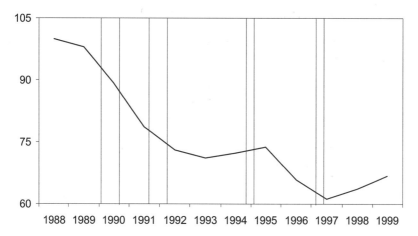

Figure 13.1
Index of real GDP in Bulgaria (1989 = 100)
Note: Vertical lines indicate when government in Bulgaria changed.

economy followed a standard adjustment of the real sector after this stabilization package, with output sharply declining to its lowest level two years after the start of the program. The dynamics resembled initially the bust-boom cycle in money-based stabilizations, but the boom, unfortunately, was never realized. The economy recovered slightly in 1994 and 1995, only to enter another tailspin in 1996. By the end of 1995 it was clear that the stabilization package of February 1991 had failed.

Of the components of GDP in Bulgaria, the sharpest decline was in investment, from 35 percent of output in the late 1980s to about 10 percent in the second half of the 1990s. One clear factor in this fall is the decline in saving. The budget deficit in Bulgaria increased dramatically in the 1990s, reaching −11 percent of GDP in certain years, causing some crowding out of investment, and private saving also declined, with consumption share rising from 59 percent in 1988 to more than 80 percent during most of the 1990s. Had the 1991 stabilization program and the structural reform in Bulgaria been successful, the return on investment at this point would have been very high and foreign capital would have stepped in. This increase in inflows would have caused current account deficits but at the same time would have filled the gap between domestic saving and investment.

For several reasons, however, new capital did not flow into Bulgaria. First and foremost, the slow pace of economic reform created general macroeconomic instability, leaving wide open the possibility of sharp depreciations. Second, in the first half of 1990 the Bulgarian government declared unilaterally a moratorium on debt repayment, thus effectively cutting the economy off from world capital markets. The negotiations and rescheduling of debt took more than three years, and according to the International Monetary Fund (IMF) country report for 1999, even by the end of 1998 Bulgaria had not regained full access to foreign capital markets. The evolution of Bulgaria's foreign debt and its structure are reported on figure 13.2.

The collapse of output in the first years of transition in Bulgaria is clearly manifested also in the sharp increase in the rate of unemployment (figure 13.3). The extent of job destruction has been quite significant, which shows that there was an initial round of restructuring. The two years of positive economic growth in the first half of the decade are also reflected in the decline of the number of unemployed during that time. One should note, however, that the figures reported in this graph understate the true unemployment rate since

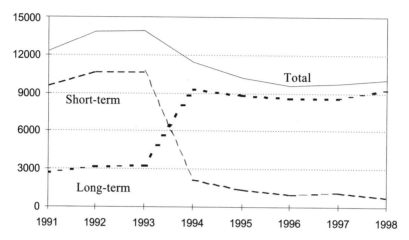

Figure 13.2
Bulgaria's foreign debt (in U.S. dollars)

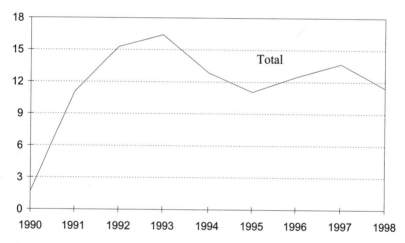

Figure 13.3
Unemployment in Bulgaria

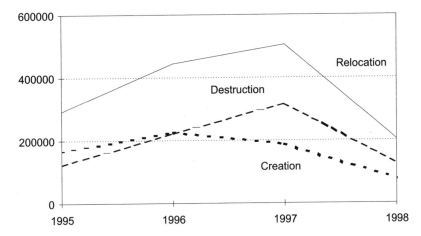

Figure 13.4
Job destruction and creation in Bulgaria

they are based on the number of registered rather than actual unemployed. Also, many workers were forced into early retirement,
which again kept the rate relatively low. A more informative metric
for evaluation of the dynamics of the labor market is the rates of job
destruction and job creation. Unfortunately, no data exist that allow
us to pin down these rates precisely, but figure 13.4 constructs total
job destruction and creation as well as relocation by assuming that
the public sector has primarily destroyed jobs, whereas the private
sector has primarily been creating jobs.[7]

Figure 13.4 presents net flows in the private sector as job creation
and net flows in the public sector as job destruction. Evidently, despite the decline in official unemployment, the net effect in 1998 was
actually a reduction in total employment. More worrisome is the fact
that the private sector was unable in 1997–1998 to absorb the workers
laid off from the public sector. One can also see that relative to the two
most turbulent years, 1996 and 1997, the last year in the figure is a
period of "chill" on the labor market, with declining destruction and
creation. The evolution of the real wage has also been disappointing,
as evidenced by figure 13.5. Currently Bulgaria has one of the lowest
wage rates in dollar terms among Central and Eastern European
(CEE) countries.

The monetary sector in Bulgaria has been instrumental in prop-
agating instability throughout the country's economic system and in

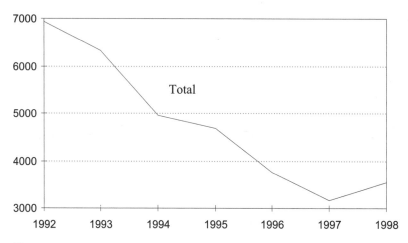

Figure 13.5
Real wages in the Bulgarian public sector (in 1994 leva)

deepening the extent of economic collapse. Through lax supervision of the banking sector and inconsistent monetary policy, the central bank has contributed significantly to the acceleration of the country's banking and financial crises. Its continuous refinancing of the country's insolvent commercial banks and its attempt to stop inflation by increasing interest rates created a vicious circle by causing a deteriorating of both the health of the banking sector and the state of government balances. (This theme will be discussed in detail in the chapter's next section.) Figures 13.6 and 13.7 report the evolution of Bulgaria's interest rates, inflation, and rate of depreciation against the U.S. dollar before the introduction of the currency board.

Fiscal policy has been more restrictive at first glance. As figure 13.8 indicates, even though the overall budget was mostly in deficit, successive governments have run primary surpluses. One of the trademarks of Bulgarian governments, however, has been the ability to redress primary deficits as bad loans of state-owned commercial banks. Indeed, the government's books suggest that subsidies declined in only two years from more than 20 percent at the start of the transition to less than 2 percent of GDP.

More generally, there were substantial changes both on the revenue side and the expenditure side during the 1990s. Total revenue declined rapidly from about 58.9 percent of GDP in 1989 to less than 32 percent in 1997, with a similar decline in expenditures. The only

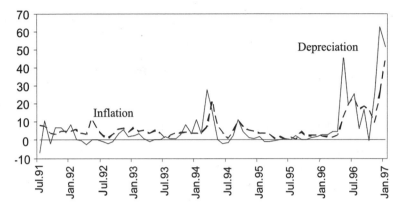

Figure 13.6
Monthly inflation and depreciation in Bulgaria

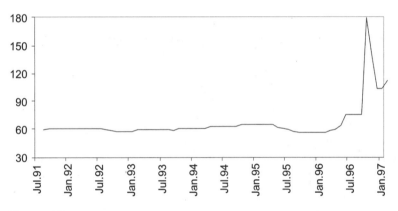

Figure 13.7
Interest rates in Bulgaria

item on the expenditure side that increased steadily until 1997 was interest expenditures, which reached 19.7 percent of GDP in 1996. The government was caught in its own trap. High interest rates imposed by the central bank meant further deterioration of the budget. Low interest rates, on the other hand, led to inflation and rapid depreciation of the currency. Deterioration in the value of the lev translated into an increase in the foreign debt burden. The inconsistency of fiscal and monetary policies was further complicated by the banking sector's involvement in implicit subsidizing of loss makers.

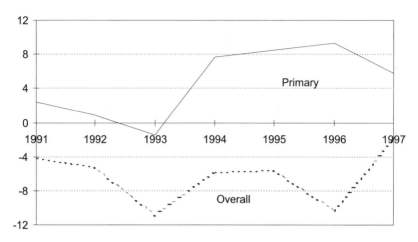

Figure 13.8
Government deficit/surplus in Bulgaria, 1991–1997

After the introduction of the comprehensive stabilization package in July 1997, the fiscal situation in Bulgaria improved dramatically. Although by the end of 1997 the overall balance was still in deficit, a trend toward improvement was clear. For the first four months of 1998, the overall balance was in surplus, with first-quarter revenues reaching 33 percent of the annual figure and expenditures reaching only 21 percent. The key factors for this turnaround were a sharp decline in interest rates and an increase in tax collection. Under a three-year agreement with the IMF, the Bulgarian government proposed a long list of fiscal policy measures targeted at further improving collection of taxes, increasing restrictions on expenses, and reforming the country's overall tax policy.

The inconsistency of fiscal and monetary policies in the period between 1993 and 1996 was an immediate result of the country's slow structural reform. The process of economic restructuring was driven primarily by a change in the ownership structure in the economy via restitution, privatization, and the emergence of private enterprises. Restitution was a transfer of ownership from the state to private citizens of commercial real estate, land, and housing, in effect a reversal of the nationalization process that took place in late 1940s and early 1950s. Ten years after the start of transition, there were still unresolved issues with the housing restitution and to a lesser degree with land restitution. The relatively undisputed denationalization of

Table 13.1
Privatization of SOEs in Bulgaria

	1993	1994	1995	1996	1997	1998
Privatization transactions	115	549	1,522	3,090	914	1,201
Proceeds (millions of U.S. dollars)	72.2	232.8	181.9	416.6	608	530

Note: As of 1993, there were 11,000 state-owned enterprises to be privatized in Bulgaria.

Table 13.2
Private sector in industrial production in Bulgaria

	1991	1992	1993	1994	1995	1996	1997	1998
Share of industry in GDP	37.4	40.5	35.0	35.4	32.7	32.4	29.4	33.0
Share of private sector in industrial output	6.5	10.7	18.3	18.9	27.7	28.7	42.7	40.0

commercial real estate led to an initial boom in the retail and other services sectors. Against the background of the slow process of privatizing state-owned enterprises, restitution was the initial spark for the creation of an entrepreneurial culture in the country and at some point the single driving factor for the growth of small private firms. Together with the creation of new private firms, restitution is the primary explanatory factor for the increase in the share of the private-services sector in GDP from 20 percent in 1991 to more than 50 percent in 1995. Privatization of state-owned enterprises, however, was lagging behind. Table 13.1 shows that, as of 1998, 20–25 percent of state-owned enterprises (SOEs) in Bulgaria were yet to be privatized. In terms of value added, these firms constituted more than 50 percent of the industrial base. Table 13.2 reports the share of the private sector in industrial production. Despite the increased importance of the private sector in GDP, industrial output was still dominated by SOEs as of the first half of 1998.

The process of privatization in Bulgaria followed complicated rules, with successive parliaments introducing a total of fifteen amendments to the 1992 Law on Privatization. Three Bulgarian agencies are in charge of privatization: branch ministries, municipalities, and the Privatization Agency (PA). The latter deals primarily with large enterprises, whereas the other two are in charge of the small and medium-sized ones. There is also a whole range of methods of privatization: (1) direct sales (via auctions; tenders; negotiations, with or without assistance of privatization consultants; sales of pools of enterprises or parts of one enterprise; and debt-equity swaps), (2) sale of a package of shares on the Bulgarian stock exchange, (3) management and employee buyouts (MEBOs), and (4) mass privatization via vouchers. When assessing the progress of privatization, however, it should be taken into account that there is an inconsistency in the way ownership is treated by the commercial code and the PA. The code specifies a range of decisions that must be made with a qualified majority of two-thirds, whereas the PA considers an enterprise privatized if the state owns less than 50 percent of it. Hence some firms that are currently considered privatized by the PA are in effect still under state control to a certain degree (IMF 1999).

Turning to the balance of payments, throughout the 1990s Bulgaria did not experience any substantial capital inflow. Not surprisingly by mid-1996 it had the lowest level of foreign direct investment (FDI) per capita of all CEE countries ($69 per capita). Most of the FDI in Bulgaria is actually in small projects for less than $1,000 (65 percent of all projects).[8] The swift reforms of 1997 returned some confidence in Bulgaria, and the capital account at the end of that year showed a surplus of U.S. $401 million compared to the deficit of U.S. $715 million in 1996. One can clearly see in the data the reversal starting from the second quarter of 1997, when capital inflows started picking up in tandem with an improvement in the trade balance. On the trade side, wars in neighboring Yugoslavia amplified the detrimental effect of the slow process of economic restructuring on the country's export performance. Even though competitiveness indices based on unit labor costs or real wages speak in favor of Bulgarian producers, it seems that these advantages have not yet been translated into solid export performance.

Monetary Policy and the Banking Sector from 1990 to July 1997

In the first years of transition, monetary policy in Bulgaria attempted to stabilize macroeconomic conditions by targeting the growth rate of monetary aggregates. The exchange rate regime was liberalized in 1991, and given the low level of reserves and the insulation from the world financial markets caused by the moratorium on debt repayment, the central bank did not have much choice in terms of the exchange rate regime. The only viable option was a floating rate, with possible interventions by the central bank targeted at smoothing large fluctuations. Although throughout the whole period the governing legislation specified that the ultimate goal of the central bank was to ensure stability of the national currency, there were several episodes in which the bank did not meet this goal in any meaningful interpretation. There were clear conflicts throughout the period between the bank and the government. For example, there was an attempt to "guide" the Bulgarian lev into a relatively mild depreciation in 1995, which necessarily required high interest rates. These rates affected the budget adversely, and the government exerted pressure on the central bank to lower the base interest rates, which led inevitably to currency substitution and an exchange rate crisis.

Despite the importance attached to exchange rate stability in the constitution of the BNB, formal rules for intervention on the foreign exchange market have never been specified. The central bank has tried on several occasions to use the exchange rate as a nominal anchor for monetary policy. Sharp depreciations of the Bulgarian lev are preceded by a running down of foreign reserves. This evidence is only suggestive but is certainly consistent with the claim that the central bank has tried on several occasions to defend the lev, with most of its attempts being unsuccessful. Alternative interpretations are also possible, of course, even though these are less plausible. For example, the reduction of the reserves could have been an endogenous response to other developments in the economy, which in turn might have also caused the depreciation of the lev.

Before the introduction of the currency board, the BNB controlled money supply via several instruments:

• *Credit ceilings.* From the very beginning of the transition period, the BNB used credit ceilings as an instrument of monetary policy. At the same time, it has used these ceilings as an operational target. Initially credit ceilings were determined on a quarterly basis and after 1992 on a monthly basis. Each bank was assigned a quota for credit expansion, and banks exceeding their quota were sanctioned with higher reserve requirements (up to the legally allowed maximum of 15 percent). As an instrument of monetary policy, this had many deficiencies. First, it was very difficult to impose discipline on banks, and the number of banks with fines increased over time. Second, government credit was not included in the aggregate target for credit extension, nor were credits to the agricultural sector.

Eventually, the central bank discontinued the use of direct credit controls as a monetary policy instrument in favor of conventional instruments of monetary policy.

• *Direct financing of budget deficits.* Despite the fact that by law the BNB is relatively independent from the legislative and executive branches of the state in its conduct of monetary policy activities, in practice the bank had to satisfy the needs of the budget on several occasions. The legal structure in Bulgaria puts the State Budget Act after only the constitution of the country. If there is a conflict between a specific law and the budget, then the conflict is automatically resolved in favor of the budget. Thus in 1991 and 1992 the State Budget Act overrode concrete articles in the law governing the BNB that specified the extent and the nature of central bank lending to the government. Direct credit to the government was predominantly extended in 1991 and 1992 and then again in 1996, when the BNB extended at least eight direct loans to the government, two of which were in direct conflict with the law that governed the bank. The loans were much larger than the budgeted amount of 5 percent of revenues and they were extended for a period of fifteen years with a five-year grace period—both the amount and the duration of these bans were in violation of the law.[9]

• *Refinancing of commercial banks.* There are four types of refinancing facilities in Bulgaria: Lombard loans, discount loans, overdrafts, and unsecured loans. In 1994 Lombard loans constituted some 80 percent of all loans to Bulgarian commercial banks. After June 1995, there was a structural break in the series for refinancing, as a result of bailouts of several commercial banks, with some 84 percent of loans being unsecured loans and overdrafts. In preparation for the currency board the BNB stopped refinancing in the beginning of 1997.

• *Open-market operations.* Open-market operations came into practice after the development of the primary and secondary market for government securities. The BNB started using this facility in 1993, and by 1995 it turned into the major instrument of monetary policy. Most of the operations (up to 90 percent) were in the form of repurchase agreements. On June 13, 1997, the central bank ceased its participation on the open market.

• *Reserve requirements.* The BNB started using reserve requirements extensively as a policy tool in 1994. In 1995, for example, there were several changes in reserve policy: First, reserve requirements were increased from 10 to 12 percent, then banks were allowed to hold up to 50 percent of required reserves in foreign exchange, and the interest rate on reserves was changed twice. Finally, in July 1995, reserve requirements were decreased to 11 percent. It is important to note that decreases in reserve requirements were accompanied by a specific requirement that the released funds would be used for purchases of government securities or as deposits in the state deposit insurance fund. The use of reserve requirements as a monetary policy instrument in the period between 1994 and 1996 was complemented with that of many other detailed requirements. For example, restrictions were placed on the amount of cash holdings qualifying as reserves and on the amount of foreign currency holdings that could be counted toward satisfying requirements, and there were continuous changes in the interest rates on deposits at the central bank.

It is difficult to evaluate the role of monetary authorities in the crises of 1994 and 1996–1997. Taken at face value, all crises in Bulgaria had a significant monetary component: Surges in inflation, banking sector instability, and sharp depreciations are the results of poor management of monetary policy. Notwithstanding this evidence against the central bank, one must acknowledge that a great deal of the blame lies with the Bulgarian government. Two main issues were pivotal in the collapse of Bulgaria's economy. First, the continuous seigniorage financing of deficits, which culminated in December 1996, was one of the main reasons for the surges in inflation. Second, the government's inability to deal with the bad loans from the socialist period and its unwillingness to restructure promptly the real sector in the economy were the key culprits in the hyperinflationary burst in the beginning of 1997. The nexus of the calamities in the two years preceding the introduction of the currency board is tied to the developments in the banking sector.

The Banking Sector

During the 1990s the banking sector in Bulgaria experienced dramatic shifts. When the transition period started, there were seven sectoral banks in charge of financing different branches of the Bulgarian economy. In addition to these seven sectoral banks, there were also two special banks: the State Savings Bank, which held the deposits of the population, and the Foreign Trade Bank, which was

Table 13.3
Commercial banks in Bulgaria

	1990	1991	1992	1993	1994	1995	1996	1997
Total	70	78	59	41	45	47	31	34
Private	2	10	14	18	25	29	15	18
Foreign	0	0	0	1	3	5	7	10

responsible for international operations. Apart from these nine banks, fifty-nine new commercial banks were created from the branches of the Bulgarian National Bank. Table 13.3 gives the evolution of the number of banks for this period. The initial proliferation of banks was later reversed mainly by means of a sequence of consolidations. In 1991 a bank consolidation company was set up with the goal of managing the consolidation of the state-owned banks as well as of promoting privatization of these banks. By the beginning of 1997, none of the banks had yet been privatized, but some progress was subsequently made in the last years of the decade, although the largest bank, Bulbank, had not been privatized as of mid-1999. The consolidation efforts of the government explain the downward trend in the number of banks for the first half of the sample. Bankruptcy legislation was underdeveloped before 1996 and did not permit any radical measures against insolvent banks, and therefore the process of closing down banks started only in 1996. By the end of 1997 some 15 banks were undergoing a process of liquidation.

The poor performance of some of the banks is in part linked to the issue of bad debts. The first governments in Bulgaria after the collapse of the communist regime underestimated the threat of bad loans to the health of the banking sector. In 1991 the government took ad hoc measures by issuing securities and swapping them for bad loans incurred on lending before 1990. This measure was partial, since it covered only some 35 percent of the bad loans in existence at the time. Only towards the end of 1993 did the parliament pass the Bad Loans Act, a comprehensive law for dealing with nonperforming loans. This act was supposed to ease the burden on commercial banks by transforming bad debts into government obligations. However, about 40 percent of these securities (called ZUNKs, based on the abbreviation of the Bad Loans Act) paid interest rates in certain times equal to only one-third of the base interest rates. This interest rate gap, which was also manifested as an interest differential between some bank assets (ZUNKs) and liabilities, for example, time deposits, aggravated the position of many of the state-owned banks because they were earning less then what they had to pay to attract depositors. Furthermore, shortly after the introduction of ZUNKs, monetary policy turned tight, thus increasing the spread between the market rates and the rates paid on these instruments. By the end of the year the central bank had to change its course of action to save the entire system from collapse. It drastically slashed interest rates from 72 to 34 percent and started widespread refinancing of the troubled commercial banks, illustrating again the inconsistency of the policy mix in Bulgaria. The monetary authority had to pursue conflicting goals: It had to keep inflation in check, which required high interest rates, and it had to be in charge of the banking sector, under the constraint that some of the banks were forced to receive on their assets only a fraction of what they had to pay as interest on their liabilities.[10]

In addition to mismanaging the bad loans in the banking sector, the government encouraged state-owned banks to extend loans to loss-making SOEs to keep the latter afloat. This was a way of giving hidden subsidies to some large enterprises. Obviously this channel of subsidizing loss makers dramatically weakened the balance sheets of the lending banks. Initially the troubled banks were continuously bailed out by the central bank. The amount of Lombard loans skyrocketed in 1994 and 1995, stopping only after the government replaced bad loans with securities in accordance with the above-mentioned Bad Loans Act. Refinancing stopped briefly, only to pick up again six months later. At this point the intricate complexity of incoherent policies was a trap for the government itself, putting the economy on an explosive path. With the issue of bonds related to the Bad Loans Act, the government doubled the amount of its outstanding debt. High interest rates then increased the budget deficit, and the BNB had to cut the interest rate in half (from 72 percent at the beginning of 1995 to 34 percent in August of that year). At the same time refinancing started again because newly issued bad loans had weakened the position of several big banks. Inflationary pressures increased, and in early 1996 the BNB raised base rates several times. This change in monetary policy stance led to a further increase in the budget deficit and to deterioration of banks' balance sheets, partly because of ZUNK holdings that were paying only a fraction of the base rate. High interest rates were needed to stop the depreciation of the currency so that external debt was easier to honor, but at the same time high interest rates led to an increase in the internal debt service. Without any option left the government was forced at the end of 1996 to ask for a long-term direct credit from the central bank in the amount of 115 billion Bulgarian leva (BGL). To put this number in perspective, the monetary base in November 1996 was BGL 193 billion. Realizing the implications of this inflationary financing, the public swiftly switched from lev-denominated deposits into foreign currency, thus accelerating the country's economic collapse.[11]

This scenario shows the importance of timely structural reform. In addition to the state-owned loss makers, private firms also had their share of bad loans. About half of the new nonperforming loans were loans to private firms. Thus the lesson is more general than simply the effects of slow restructuring. The lack of bank supervision, the inability of the BNB to act promptly and close down insolvent banks, and the implicit promise of continuous bailout led to an increase in moral hazard–type behavior. Insider lending seemed to be widespread, with the central bank being unable to control it. Only after banking supervision became well defined and the costs of failure increased did commercial banks become more prudent.

Data Analysis

Most of the narratives in the previous subsections are impossible to capture in any econometric study. Yet we can learn something about the dynamics of the Bulgarian economy in the transition period by looking more closely at the data. First, we summarize the monetary-sector developments with a vector autoregression (VAR). Over the last decade, monetary VARs have become a standard methodology for the study of monetary policy effects on the macroeconomy. To understand the basic idea of evaluating the impact of monetary policy, I start with the following framework proposed by Bernanke and Blinder (1992) and developed further by Bernanke and Mihov (1998). Suppose the "true" economic structure of a particular country is

$$\mathbf{Y}_t = \sum_{i=0}^{k} \mathbf{B}_i \mathbf{Y}_{t-i} + \sum_{i=0}^{k} \mathbf{C}_i p_{t-i} + \mathbf{A}^y \mathbf{v}_t^y \tag{13.1}$$

$$p_t = \sum_{i=0}^{k} \mathbf{D}_i \mathbf{Y}_{t-i} + \sum_{i=1}^{k} g_i p_{t-i} + v_t^p. \tag{13.2}$$

Equations (13.1) and (13.2) define an unrestricted linear dynamic model that allows both contemporaneous values and up to k lags of any variable to appear in any equation. Boldface letters are used to indicate vectors or matrices of variables or coefficients. In particular, $\mathbf{Y}$ is a vector of macroeconomic variables, and p is a variable indicating a particular policy stance, for example, a short-term nominal interest rate like the call rate in Germany or the federal funds rate in the United States.[12] The direct impact of current and past policy on the economy is captured by coefficient vectors C, whereas the dependence of macroeconomic variables on their own past values is represented by coefficient matrices B. Equation (13.2) predicts current policy stance given the impact of current and lagged values of macroeconomic variables via coefficient matrices D and lagged policy variables, whereas equation (13.1) describes a set of structural relationships in the rest of the economy. The vector $\mathbf{v}^y$ and the scalar v^p are mutually uncorrelated "primitive" or "structural" error terms. Macroeconomic shocks are propagated via matrix A^y. The goal is to find the appropriate measure of policy stance and then to trace the dynamic effects of changes in this measure on the economy.

I use monthly data for the rate of unemployment, the exchange rate, and inflation for 1991:4 to 1997:6 (ending with the introduction of the currency board). As a policy variable, I include the base interest rate. The model is estimated with two lags of each variable. The reason for this parsimonious specification is that we want to focus on the short-run relationships among the variables. Moreover, given the sample size, a longer lag length will result in a reduction in efficiency and may lead to one-time events having a very significant impact on the dynamics of the system.

The results of the analysis of the model are presented in figure 13.9. The figure depicts the responses of the four endogenous variables after a monetary policy tightening, measured as a one-standard-deviation increase in the interest rate. First, one should note the persistence of the interest rate response: The horizon of the increase is more than twelve months. Second, policy tightening leads to a statistically significant increase in unemployment.

It is difficult to calculate a sacrifice ratio from this graph, since these are responses only to unanticipated increases in the base rate. The evidence, however, is suggestive of the costs of disinflation or even of a general increase in the nominal interest rate to fight speculative runs on the currency. The figure also shows that policy tightening is

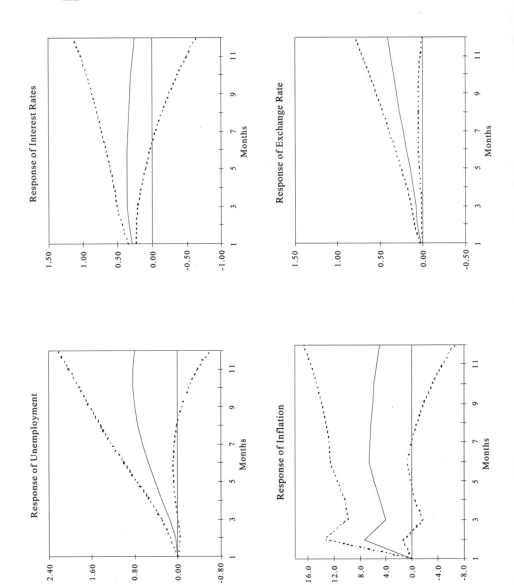

Response of Interest Rates

Response of Unemployment

Response of Exchange Rate

Response of Inflation

followed by an increase in inflation, which is certainly a paradoxical result. The history of the Bulgarian transition, however, does provide a clue as to why this might happen. One possibility is that in the presence of inflation inertia, attempts to fight inflation will give results only after two years or more. More plausibly, however, we need a better measure of expected inflation. The VAR captures only some mechanisms by which expectations are formed. If the true story is more along the lines of the "unpleasant monetarist arithmetic" modeled by Sargent and Wallace (1981), then the VAR simply captures the reaction of the public to changes in expectations of future inflation. Specifically, the tightening of monetary policy almost automatically widens the budget deficit and thus presupposes easing of policy in the future or even direct financing of the budget deficit by printing money. In this case, the public expects the value of the domestic currency to deteriorate, and money demand collapses, as demonstrated by high inflation and depreciation.

This VAR summarizes the average response to an increase in the base interest rate. It is interesting, however, to study in more detail the period of 1996–1997, when the widespread banking and economic crises led to a hyperinflationary burst. To this end, I turn to a simple decomposition of the price level into components as proposed by Bernanke and Mihov (2000). The starting point is the following tautological expression for the price level at time t:

$$P_t = \frac{P_t}{M_t} \frac{M_t}{Base_t} \frac{Base_t}{e_t{}^*Res_t} Res_t{}^*e_t$$

where

P_t = the price level (CPI)

M_t = the nominal money supply (here, M1)

$Base_t$ = the monetary base

Res_t = international reserves of the central bank (foreign asssets plus gold reserves), valued in U.S. dollars

e_t = exchange rate lev/dollar.

Figure 13.9
VAR results

This equation may be viewed as a decomposition of the price level into the following ratios:

1. *The inverse of real money balances.* Changes in this ratio are usually interpreted as reflecting changes in the quantity of real money balances that the public desires to hold. Implicitly, this interpretation relies on the assumption that prices adjust rapidly to equate the real money stock and real money demand. Changes in real money demand can arise from a variety of sources, including changes in real output, changes in expected inflation (as embodied in nominal interest rates), and changes in payments technology.

2. *The "money multiplier."* In fractional-reserve banking systems, the quantity of "inside money" (M1) is a multiple of the quantity of "outside money" (the monetary base). Sharp variations in the money multiplier—which must be associated with large changes in the ratios of currency and bank reserves to deposits—are typically associated with banking panics or at least problems in the banking system.

3. *Currency backing ratio.* An increase in this ratio can signal, for example, excessive money creation without the necessary increase in international reserves.

Figure 13.10 displays the movements in these ratios over the period from December 1995 to March 1998 as percentage changes over the previous quarter. One can clearly see on the first graph that money demand has collapsed (recall that on the graph I plot the inverse money demand) in the most severe crisis in the beginning of 1997. Given the basic shifters in this ratio, the only plausible explanation is that expected inflation changed dramatically in this period. This result is not extremely surprising, given the above-mentioned direct credit to the government of BGL 115 billion (a 66 percent increase in the monetary base). Certainly theoretical models can easily rationalize this result. Both standard models along the lines of Cagan 1956 and dynamic general equilibrium models with explicit microfoundations like that of Obstfeld and Rogoff (1995, 1996) predict that changes in future growth paths of money will lead immediately, as they become known, to a discrete jump in the price level. Hence it is not much of a surprise that in this volatile environment it is hard to find a predictive role for *past* monetary growth.

The overall assessment of monetary policy in Bulgaria in the first eight years of transition does not speak in favor of the policy pur-

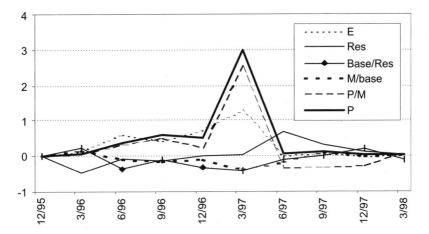

Figure 13.10
Decomposition of Bulgarian inflation

sued by the central bank. The uncertainty created by volatile inflation and the inability to supervise the banking sector led to dramatic
economic developments. Hyperinflation and the banking crises,
however, taught both the future government and the public that a
profound structural change was on the agenda. The delay in the reform only increased its cost and made a waste of the sacrifices associated with the first stabilization package of 1991.

The Currency Board

The inability of successive governments in Bulgaria to achieve macroeconomic stability showed that the country needed to take some
drastic measures. The IMF suggested replacing the central bank with
a currency board arrangement as early as the fall of 1996. It justified
this step with two simple arguments. First, governments intervened
continuously in the work of the central bank, and second, the central
bank itself was pouring funds endlessly into completely insolvent
banks. Two years after the start of the July 1997 stabilization the reform seemed to have been very successful in bringing down inflation
and restoring prospects for a robust economic recovery in Bulgaria.
The most important condition for the success of the program was a
dramatic change in economic behavior. Whether this change was a
result of the new stabilization package or a legacy of the hyperinflationary chaos of January and February 1997 is difficult to tell. Most

probably the reform's success was due to both factors, and one could only speculate what would have happened to the currency board if it had not been preceded by the country's economic and financial collapse.

Structure and Specificity

The currency board in Bulgaria has its own specificity, yet its closest cousins are the boards in Estonia and Lithuania. The BNB is preserved as an institution with functions typical of a standard central bank, including bank supervision and a limited lender-of-last-resort function. The organization of the bank is currently as follows:[13]

• *Managing Board*. The Managing Board consists of seven members: the governor of the bank, three deputy governors, and three members who are not involved in the bank's operations. The deputy governors head the three departments in the bank: Issue, Banking, and Bank Supervision. Board members are appointed for a period of six years. The initial board, however, has members whose terms expire earlier in order to ensure smooth rotation, with one member being replaced every year, except for the governor and the head of the issue department, who are replaced in the same year. The president appoints the three outside members and the parliament approves the rest.

• *Issue Department*. The issue department functions as a currency board with 100 percent backing of the currency in circulation plus commercial banks' deposits with liquid foreign assets. The asset side of the department consists of cash, deposits in foreign banks, highly liquid foreign securities, and monetary gold. It is important to note that the Bulgarian currency board has a "broad"-based backing rule. In addition to currency in circulation, it fully backs all other liquid liabilities of the central bank like commercial banks' deposits, government deposits, and the deposit of the banking department (see table 13.4).

• *Banking Department*. The banking department can serve as a lender of last resort, but only if there is a systemic risk in the banking sector and only up to the value of its deposit in the issue department. In addition, it serves as the intermediary between the IMF and the government; it is also in charge of continuous monitoring of the liquidity in the banking system as well as the conditions on the financial markets (table 13.5).

Table 13.4
Balance sheet of BNB Issue Department, December 31, 1997 (in billions of BGL)

Assets		Liabilities	
Cash and accounts in foreign currency	2,264	Currency in circulation	1,420
		Bank deposits and current accounts	858
Monetary gold	644		
Foreign securities	1,495	Government deposits and accounts	1,601
Accrued interest receivable	9		
		Other depositors' accounts	25
		Accrued interest payable	2
		Banking department deposit	506
Total	4,412	Total	4,412

Table 13.5
Balance sheet of BNB Banking Department, December 31, 1997 (billions of BGL)

Assets		Liabilities	
Nonmonetary gold and other precious metals	83	Borrowings from IMF	1,675
		Liabilities to other financial institutions	1,033
Investments in securities	283		
Loans and advances to banks	20	Accrued interest payable	1
Receivables from government	1,632	Other liabilities	10
Bulgaria's IMF quota and other IFIs	1,041		
Accrued interest receivable	1		
Equity investments in domestic entities	2		
Fixed assets	97	Capital	20
Other assets	7	Reserves	676
Deposit with the Issue Department	506	Retained profit	257
Total	3,671	Total	3,671

• *Banking Supervision Department.* The banking supervision department deals with the regulation and supervision of commercial banks. It proposes to the managing board licensing of new commercial banks, analyzes the solvency of operational commercial banks, and can initiate bankruptcy procedures.

As of July 1, 1997, the Bulgarian lev was fixed at the rate of 1,000 lev/deutsche mark (DM). There are no access restrictions, and the bank can charge a fixed fee of up to 0.5 percent on exchanges. There are special provisions in the law designed to limit the exchange rate risk for the BNB. First, the bank exchanges Bulgarian leva only for deutsche marks. Second, there are restrictions on the mismatch between amount of assets and liabilities held by the BNB denominated in any one currency. The credibility of the board is ensured in part by stipulating that the exchange rate cannot be changed by the central bank; any such change must be voted by the parliament. In early July 1999, on the basis of this provision, a monetary reform was introduced replacing 1,000 old leva for one new lev. Hence the fixed exchange rate became 1 lev = 1 DM after July 4, 1999. In addition, the Bulgarian currency board operates in a relatively transparent way. The Issue Department is required to publish its balance sheet on a weekly basis.

The currency board has retained only reserve requirements as an instrument for monetary control. So far reserve requirements have not been used to affect the country's money supply, and it is tacitly accepted that this instrument will be used rarely and only after consultation with the IMF. One specific change in the new law is that it abolished the previous ceiling on reserve requirements of 15 percent. Currently, the minimum required reserves ratio is at 11 percent, but it can be increased, without any prespecified limit, provided the conditions in the banking sector convince the IMF and the BNB to do so.

The Issue Department ensures full convertibility for a number of liabilities. It must back fully the currency in circulation and the lev deposits of commercial banks with instruments denominated in DM. It can, however, also keep assets and liabilities in other currencies. To reduce the exchange rate risk, the law stipulates that the mismatch between liabilities and assets denominated in one currency cannot exceed 2 percent in either direction. The BNB can also invest in highly liquid debt instruments issued by foreign governments, central banks, and the like as long as these instruments have one of the two highest ratings given by at least two internationally recognized rating agencies.

Although the BNB's function as lender of last resort is preserved in the current situation, it is quite limited in at least three respects:

1. *Macroeconomic conditions.* There must be sufficient evidence that there is a systemic risk in the banking sector before lender-of-last-resort credit can be extended.

2. *Credit requirements.* The bank(s) to which lender-of-last-resort credit is extended must be solvent, the maturity of the credit cannot exceed three months, and the loan must be fully collateralized with gold, foreign exchange, or other highly liquid assets.

3. *Amount.* The amount of this type of credit available is limited to the amount the Banking Department has on deposit with the Issue Department.[14]

The initial deposit of the Banking Department when the law took effect was determined to be the amount of international reserves above the monetary liabilities of the Issue Department. Every week, this deposit is determined on a residual principle after deducting, from foreign reserves, the amount of currency issued, bank reserves, and deposits of the government and other agencies. This deposit, which indicates the ability of the BNB to act as a lender of last resort, fluctuated between BGL 500 billion and 1 trillion (i.e., DM 500 million and 1 billion) in 1998–1999. To ensure that the amount does not evaporate before a crisis hits the economy, the Bulgarian government has decided, in accordance with its 1998 three-year agreement with the IMF, to establish a floor on the deposit of the Banking Department. For the first half of 1999 this floor was set at DM 630 million. To further increase the credibility of central bank policies and to reduce rent-seeking behavior, the BNB is required to consult with the IMF whenever the outstanding lending from the Banking Department to banks exceeds DM 1.8 million (i.e., when it exceeds 0.3 percent of the floor on the Banking Department deposit).

Economic Effects of Stabilization

The introduction of the currency board led immediately to positive developments in the Bulgarian economy. Figure 13.11 summarizes the evolution of some key variables in 1997.

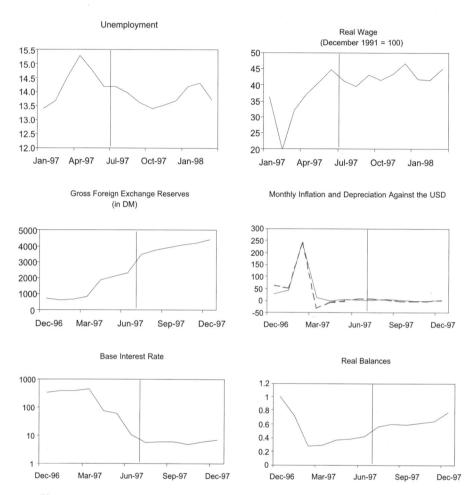

Figure 13.11
Bulgaria: Key macroeconomic variables, 1997

In a comparison of the Bulgarian case to other exchange rate–based stabilizations, it is notable that the dynamics of most macro variables in the initial months is quite similar to the developments in Argentina following the introduction of its currency board. Economic activity recovered almost immediately, with output growing at 4 percent in 1998 (see figure 13.1). Remonetization in both cases started in the year of the reform, and in Bulgaria it even preceded the introduction of the currency board, signifying that the forthcoming reform was credible. This credibility was manifested also in the fast growth of foreign exchange reserves in the central bank. Interest rates dropped for the first time to single-digit numbers, and in the first year of the currency board the interest rate differential between the yield on Bulgarian government securities and the three-month interbank offer rate in Germany fluctuated between 100 and 300 basis points. This spread has not been significantly perturbed by the crisis in Asia or by the financial turmoil in Russia. Inflation declined from 500 percent to 1 percent in the course of one year. In terms of bringing down interest rates and inflation the currency board in Bulgaria is among the most successful exchange rate–based stabilizations in economic history.

The long-term success of the July 1997 stabilization will depend on the extent of the structural reform undertaken, on fiscal discipline, and on the health of the Bulgarian banking sector. Bulgaria's economy is still quite susceptible to internal and external shocks and in particular to financial crises.[15] To evaluate the possibility of a speculative attack on Bulgaria's currency, Nenovsky and Hristov (1997) construct several popular crisis indicators. First, they construct the ratio of quasi money to the assets of the currency board. Of course, indices of this sort are hard to interpret in many cases. One would expect that a country with a well-developed banking sector could have a value for this index exceeding one without this fact suggesting any sort of risk for the system. In countries like Bulgaria, however, movements in this index might signify emerging instability. If the index exceeds one, reserves are insufficient to cover possible conversion of this quasi money into foreign assets. When the index starts falling sharply, confidence in the banking sector has clearly diminished and a banking crisis might be approaching. For the period after the introduction of the currency board, this index fluctuated mildly around one, which suggests relative stability.

Several other indicators relating broad monetary aggregates and international reserves can also be constructed. In general, all of these indicators suggest that as of 2000, four years after its institution, the currency board arrangement was quite stable. Throughout the period, reserves were sufficient to cover over 80 percent of M2. Nenovsky and Hristov also analyze the state of the banking sector by constructing balance sheet ratios, reporting the maturity of extended funds on the interbank market, and so on. The picture emerging from these indicators is that the banking sector in 1997–1998 was quite passive. The credit-to-deposit ratio has decreased dramatically, which indicates

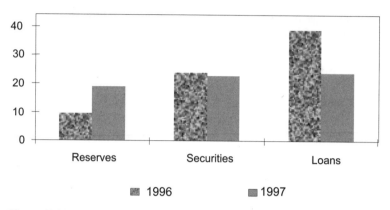

Figure 13.12
Assets of Bulgaria's commercial banks (in percent)

banks are unwilling to extend credit.[16] With the introduction of the currency board, banks' behavior changed significantly. Under the tight financial constraint, they showed a clear preference for higher liquidity (see figure 13.12), doubling the amount of reserves they maintained. At the same time claims on the nonfinancial sector declined dramatically, from 40 percent of assets to less than 25 percent. Combined with the overall decline of commercial banks' assets from 120 percent to 30 percent of GDP in 1996–1997, this means that the total share of loans in GDP collapsed from 67 percent in 1996 to 10 percent in 1997.

Figure 13.13 provides information on the credit conditions in Bulgaria by plotting the spread between the monthly interest rates on short-term loans and one-month deposits. First, we can see from the figure that the introduction of the currency board in July 1997 led to a sharp decrease in the spread. Indeed, interest rates on credit fell from about 20 percent per month to 1 percent, and since the spread is highly correlated (about 0.90) with the level of interest rates, the spread also declined. Recalling the abrupt decrease in loans as a percentage of total assets reported in figure 13.12, one is certainly tempted to invoke some story about a credit channel or credit rationing as a primary explanation of these comovements. Indeed, a simultaneous decline in interest rates (spreads) and credit activity is evidence par excellence consistent with credit rationing. But a more detailed analysis might also show that a decrease in credit demand underlay changes in total loans outstanding. Not only have loans

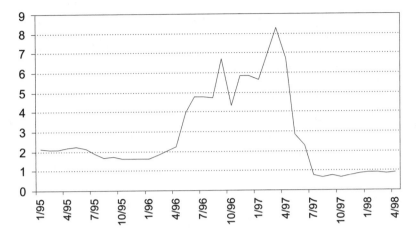

Figure 13.13
Interest rate spread in Bulgaria

decreased as a percentage of assets, but also the ratio of loans to GDP has plummeted from 67 percent in 1996 to 10 percent in 1997, as described above. It is impossible to determine the direction of causality between credit and output in this case. Yet given the dramatic decrease, it seems implausible that a story based on an endogenous fall in the demand for loans can explain why the demand for loans has declined more than five times.

Bank loans do remain a primary source of outside financing for Bulgarian firms. There is enough evidence to support a belief that the introduction of new regulations targeted at strengthening the health of Bulgaria's banking system had a significant effect on Bulgarian banks' lending practices. Banks have become extremely cautious in extending loans because (1) they are now required to report every large credit they make, (2) provisioning for loans has a very steep schedule when a loan is not performing, and this provisioning is strictly supervised, (3) the uncertainty surrounding the future of the economy increased dramatically and has not yet diminished, and (4) banks know that the lender-of-last-resort function of the central bank has been significantly curtailed, and they have therefore shown a clear preference for more liquid instruments.

Many of these shifts in banks' behavior were in fact prompted by improvements in legislation and regulation. The central bank introduced significant changes in bank supervision leading to a large number of regulations, additional personnel in charge of supervision, and simplification of the procedures for dealing with problem banks. In 1997 fifteen Bulgarian banks with poor solvency positions were declared bankrupt. The remaining thirty-four banks are closely supervised, and together with the increased soundness of banking practices, this has resulted in a dramatic improvement in the Bulgarian banking sector. In the first half of 1997, for example, banks started to improve their capital adequacy. By the year's end, the average capital adequacy ratio for Bulgarian banks was 26.86 percent, compared to 10–11 percent in the previous two years. For the first quarter of 1998 it decreased slightly to 22.6 percent, but as of that time there was no bank not fulfilling the legal requirement for capital adequacy.

Another danger for the macroeconomic stability of Bulgaria comes from the balance-of-payments dynamics. Despite the fact that inflation in Bulgaria was the same as in the EU between 1998 and 2000 and therefore the real exchange rate had not changed dramatically, the current account was in deficit both in 1999 and 2000. Initially, the lack of capital inflows combined with the current account deficit led to loss of foreign reserves by the BNB. In 2000, however, a number of successful privatization deals resulted in a surge of foreign direct investment and an overall increase in foreign reserves.

The newly emerging debate on what to do about the current account deficits in Bulgaria raises several important points. First and foremost, the deficit is a result of the discrepancy between saving and investment. Having current account deficits in the transitional period to a market economy is to be expected. The initial decline in incomes in Bulgaria after transition has led to a reduction in saving, which has translated into a sharp decline in investment.

With the return of stability, lending to the country should resume and investors should borrow from abroad to purchase capital. Second, the currency board system relies on self-adjusting mechanisms for correcting external and internal imbalances. The validity of the claim that market forces will easily restore equilibrium has yet to be tested. As long as current account deficits do not lead to persistent losses of foreign reserves, there are no immediate dangers to the economy. If, however, there are no inflows, the deficit will be financed by the central bank's reserves, which will set in motion some self-correcting mechanisms. One possibility is that the loss of reserves will lead automatically to monetary contraction and therefore to declining prices. The decline in the price level will improve the competitiveness of Bulgarian products, and this will lead eventually to the elimination of the deficit. How long it will take for this mechanism to correct the disequilibrium is still an open question. The danger, of course, is whether the self-correction will be completed before the economy sets on another explosive path.

In view of these dangers, there have been many opponents of the currency board, especially among economists, who fear that the board might turn out to be a very expensive stabilization device exactly because of the slow operation of the self-adjusting mechanisms in the wage and price setting and because monetary policy might be a very important factor in creating the appropriate environment for economic growth.[17] Periodically the "exit strategy debate" reappears on front pages of Bulgarian newspapers.[18] Three options are popularly considered as potential strategies to end the currency board arrangement: (1) a fixed or flexible exchange rate with a fully fledged central bank, (2) monetary union with the EMU members, or (3) "Euroization," that is, adopting the Euro as a legal tender without entering the EMU.

From a theoretical point of view, the first option is probably the most desirable. For practical reasons, it is also the least feasible one. The problem with this strategy seems to be the Bulgarian inability to create a truly independent central bank. Anything short of a currency board in Bulgaria leads to government intervention in monetary policy. The second option seems to be the most probable at this point. Bulgaria has very strong claims on joining the EU and eventually the EMU. The time horizon is yet unclear, but if the first two years under the currency board are any guide, then Bulgaria might join the union in the next decade. The only question related to this outcome is whether the system will resist speculative attacks and adverse developments long enough for the country to join the monetary union. Finally, the unilateral adoption of the Euro might in fact be very close to the operation of the currency board. The loss of seigniorage is often cited as a monetary cost in this case, but note that it is not clear what the overall welfare impact would be. If one has to pay a higher risk premium for the luxury of having one's own currency and no monetary policy, then it is easy to imagine that the elimination of this premium might easily outweigh the monetary cost of lost seigniorage. As to the lender of last resort and the ability to change reserve requirements, the features in the Bulgarian currency board that make it look like a central bank, it is not clear why these should necessarily disappear with the giving up of the country's own currency. The Bank Supervision Department of the BNB can be separated and given the authority to change reserve requirements. The lender-of-last-resort function can also be preserved in a separate facility or within the supervisory body. Recall that this function is limited in Bulgaria to the value of the Banking Department's deposit with the Issue Department. Hence at least theoretically there is not much of a difference between the currency board and Euroization.

Four years after the introduction of the currency board, it seems that all these options are in the distant future. Both the currency board and the financial sector are quite stable, and the trade deficits of 1999 and 2000 did not yet present a trend in external balances. One recent suggestion for dealing with current account deficits, if they persist, is to implement a one-time devaluation within the currency board arrangement. In addition to its being completely infeasible, it is hard to imagine that this policy would improve welfare because of the accompanying credibility loss. If parity changes, then it will not be long before investors or even speculators see another "sign" of coming devaluation. This sounds like a prescription for recurrent crises.

Conclusions and Challenges

Bulgaria's road to a market economy has been a very difficult one, with a cumulative decline in GDP from its 1989 level of 37 percent. I have argued in this chapter that the case of Bulgaria shows clearly the pitfalls of partial reform. Slow privatization led to piling up of losses by the SOEs. To continue operating, these enterprises had to be financed by commercial banks, and thus the inefficiency of the real economy translated into financial instability. The accumulation of bad loans in commercial banks' portfolios forced the central bank to inject extensive amounts of liquidity into the system continuously via refinancing. At the same time the BNB was somewhat concerned about inflation and rapid depreciation of the exchange rate and tried to raise interest rates on several occasions. These rate hikes further deteriorated the position of the commercial banks, thus creating more demand for refinancing. The government also saw its interest burden increasing with the high rates of interest. At some point the system broke down and ended in hyperinflation.

With the introduction of the currency board in July 1997, the country started the process of transition (privatization, deregulation, etc.) all over again. Over the last few years, the board has been quite successful in curbing inflation, closing down the big loss makers, insulating the banking sector from unproductive SOEs, and improving that sector's balances. In a truly decisive break with past practices, the reforms of 1997 were implemented consistently and with sound strategic considerations in mind. The commercial banks are privatized with a couple of exceptions, privatization is almost fully completed, and as of 2001 the macroeconomic stability of Bulgaria is beyond question. In terms of monetary institutions, it is widely recognized that the currency board in Bulgaria has operated very successfully over the last four years. But is this the arrangement Bulgaria wants to keep in the future? If the real exchange rate appreciates and the current account turns into a deficit without sizable foreign investment in the economy, then the necessary equilibrium adjustment will be very painful (in terms of unemployment). The monetary base will have to shrink, and prices must then adjust downward. Historical evidence shows that deflationary adjustment is usually related to deep and prolonged recessions or even depressions. The question then is, how long will the public be willing to endure this adjustment? It seems clear from the experience of Singapore in the early 1970s that it is not a disaster if one abandons a currency board from a position of strength. As with any fixed exchange rate arrangement, however, leaving the currency board at a time of recession is bound to cause economic calamity. Overall, it seems that the Bulgarian economy has recovered succesfully from the collapse of 1996–1997, despite exogenous shocks like worldwide financial crises or the war in neighboring Yugoslavia. The question is, will it continue to grow at its potential level in the next four or five years when the currency board might become a restrainer instead of a stabilizer?

References

Alesina, A., and A. Drazen. 1991. Why are stabilizations delayed? *American Economic Review* 81: 1170–88.

Avramov, R. 1996. The Bulgarian economy: Transition in the transition. Occasional paper no. 45, Woodrow Wilson Center, Washington, D.C.

Avramov, R. 1999. The role of a currency board in financial crises: The case of Bulgaria. Discussion paper 6/99, Bulgarian National Bank, Sofia, Bulgaria.

Bernanke, B., and A. Blinder. 1992. The federal funds rate and the channels of monetary transmission. *American Economic Review* 82: 901–21.

Bernanke, B., and I. Mihov. 1998. Measuring monetary policy. *Quarterly Journal of Economics* 113, no. 3: 869–902.

Bernanke, B., and I. Mihov. 2000. Deflation and monetary contraction in the Great Depression: An analysis by simple ratios. In Essays on the Great Depression, ed. B. Bernanke, 108–60. Princeton: Princeton University Press.

Bristow, J. 1996. *The Bulgarian economy in transition*. Cheltenham: Edward Elgar.

Burns, A., and W. Mitchell. 1946. *Measuring business cycles*. New York: National Bureau of Economic Research.

Cagan, P. 1956. The monetary dynamics of hyperinflation. In *Studies in the quantity theory of money*, ed. M. Friedman, 25–117. Chicago: University of Chicago Press.

Christov, L. 1997. A role for independent central bank in transition? The case of Bulgaria. In *The Bulgarian economy: Lessons from reform during early transition*, ed. D. Jones and J. Miller, 129–59. Aldershot, U.K.: Ashgate.

Cukierman, A., S. Webb, and B. Neyapti. 1992. Measuring the independence of central banks and its effects on policy outcome. *World Bank Economic Review* 6: 353–98.

Davis, S., and J. Haltiwanger. 1992. Gross job creation, gross job destruction, and employment reallocation. *Quarterly Journal of Economics* 107, no. 3: 819–63.

Dewatripont, M., and G. Roland. 1992. Economic reform and dynamic political constraints. *Review of Economic Studies* 59, no. 4: 703–30.

Fernandez, R., and D. Rodrik. 1991. Resistance to reform: Status quo in the presence of individual-specific uncertainty. *American Economic Review* 81: 1146–55.

Ganev, G. 1999. Reflections on the elusive Bulgarian growth. Mimeographed.

Ganev, V. 1999. State and networks in post-communist Bulgaria. Ph.D. diss., University of Chicago.

Gulde, A.-M. 1999. The role of the currency board in Bulgaria's stabilization. Policy discussion paper 99/3, International Monetary Fund, Washington, D.C.

Hillman, A., L. Mitov, and R. K. Peters. 1995. The private sector, state enterprises, and informal economic activity. In *Financing government in transition: Bulgaria*, ed. Z. Bogetic and A. Hillman, 47–70. Washington, D.C.: World Bank.

International Monetary Fund (IMF). 1999. *Bulgaria: Recent economic developments and statistical appendix*. Washington, D.C.: IMF.

Lucas, R. 1977. *Understanding business cycles*. Carnegie-Rochester Conference Series on Public Policy. North-Holland: Elsevier.

Minassian, G. 1997. Inflation in a transition economy: The case of Bulgaria. In *The Bulgarian economy: Lessons from reform during early transition*, ed. D. Jones and J. Miller, 53–62. Aldershot, U.K.: Ashgate.

Nenovsky, N., and K. Hristov. 1997. Criteria for evaluation of the systemic risk under currency board. Bulgarian National Bank, Sofia, Bulgaria. Mimeographed.

Obstfeld, M., and K. Rogoff. 1995. Exchange rate dynamics redux. *Journal of Political Economy* 103: 624–60.

Obstfeld, M., and K. Rogoff. 1996. *Foundations of international macroeconomics*. Cambridge: MIT Press.

Organisation for Economic Cooperation and Development (OECD). 1997. *Economic surveys: Bulgaria*. Paris: OECD.

Rogoff, K. 1990. Equilibrium political budget cycles. *American Economic Review* 80: 21–36.

Sargent, T., and N. Wallace. 1981. Some unpleasant monetarist arithmetic. *Federal Reserve Bank of Minneapolis Quarterly Review* (Fall): 1–17.

Wyzan, M. 1998. The political economy of Bulgaria's peculiar post-communist business cycle. *Comparative Economic Studies* (Spring): 5–42.

Yotzov, V., N. Nenovsky, K. Hristov, I. Petrova, and B. Petrov. 1998. The first year of the currency board in Bulgaria. Discussion paper 1/98, Bulgarian National Bank, Sofia, Bulgaria.

14

Strain and Economic Adjustment: Romania's Travails and Pains

Daniel Daianu

Almost ten years' time of postcommunist transition have elapsed. Much of the initial euphoria and illusions are gone. People, including academic professionals, realize that this historical endeavor is a very complex and complicated affair. The current state of transition compels one to scrutinize more carefully the process of change, to go beyond stereotypes, myths, and oversimplifications. As a World Bank official working on postcommunist countries stated, a few years ago, one should judge a policy on its own merits by skewing intellectual prejudices (Gelb 1996, 2). This prodding was strongly reinforced recently by J. Stiglitz (1995).[1]

This chapter discusses economic change in Romania and links it to two major issues: the legacy of resource misallocation, or what can be termed inherited structure, and institutional fragility. The legacy of resource misallocation leads to very intense strain in the system when there is a brutal and dramatic change of relative prices to market-clearing levels. At the new prices resources should flow from low- to high-productivity areas, a process that can generate much pain and friction in a real economy. The strain or tension involved explains why there is much opposition to change and why coalitions of interests emerge to hinder deep restructuring. Strain also explains why large quasi-fiscal deficits are a feature of postcommand economies, creating an endemic proclivity to high inflation.

Some analysts relate inflation primarily to the breakdown of the political process and rent-seeking activities by old elites (Boone and Hoerder 1998). Although this explanation is not implausible, the approach adopted in this chapter emphasizes the magnitude of the required resource reallocation required in transition, which is sometimes so large that it undermines attempts to achieve durable stabilization. It is arguable that the success of the leading transition economies is due, primarily, to policy's ability to deal with the magnitude of required resource reallocation while not being "captured" by vested interests.

Institutional fragility is another dimension of the transformation process that underlines the complicated nature of change, restructuring included. The lack of institutions, of organized markets, in a command economy as it undertakes transition hinders a smooth reallocation of resources and has a negative effect on performance at both the micro and macroeconomic levels; it also helps to explain the intense friction in the system, especially rising transaction costs, that arises during the passage between two regimes. This line of reasoning finds substantial analytical support in recent work (Blanchard 1997).

Together with strain, institutional fragility helps to explain stop-go policies as well as many of the setbacks and inconsistencies in the transition process. Fuzziness and a lack of transparency characterize the realm of public finance. For example, banks are frequently the vehicle for the granting of subsidies. Primitive banking systems, in the grip of redundant structures, are likely to perpetuate much of the old pattern of resource allocation (or misallocation) and engage in significant quasi-fiscal operations, with the latter showing up in high rates of inflation or of bank failures. Romania's experience is a highly relevant example of how strain and institutional fragility condition macroeconomic stabilization.

In the following analysis of economic developments in Romania during 1990–1998, stop-go policies, resurgent inflation, and macro disequilibria, as well as bank failures, all emerge as an inevitable outcome of a feeble pace of restructuring and fragile institutions. The analysis emphasizes that without large inflows of foreign direct investment (FDI) and the creation of appropriate institutions, the Romanian economy is unlikely to be able to escape from the grip of the old structures. It is also clear that a more rapid rate of privatization would help to increase the inflow of foreign capital to Romania. The slow pace of restructuring has maintained an intense strain in the system and has led to bad "path dependency." Romania started the transition process at a disadvantage, with significantly worse initial conditions than those prevailing in the leading reform countries,[2] which suggests that its policymakers have also had less room to maneuver.[3] Nonetheless, the end result is that those policymakers have not yet been able to find a clear way forward to a well-functioning market economy. Under the current unfavourable conditions in the world economy it will be increasingly difficult for the Romanian economy to escape from this path dependency.

The first part of the chapter deals with two major underplayed issues: institutional fragility and the magnitude of the required resource reallocation, which engenders the so-called strain. The second part focuses on economic developments in Romania between 1990 and 1998. The third part offers final conclusions.

Two Major Underplayed Issues in Transition

Two issues are of utmost importance for coming to grips, analytically and operationally, with the reality of postcommunist transformation; both, in my view, have been underestimated. One issue regards the relative backwardness of the former command systems and a related institutional fragility; the other refers to the magnitude of required resource reallocation in relation to the new relative prices dictated by liberalization and opening of the economy.

The Legacy of Backwardness

Knowledgeable professionals can often be heard making judgments on the transformation process while seeming to neglect the legacy of backwardness of most of the societies undergoing transformation, a state of affairs that goes back well into history. A note of caution is nevertheless required. The postcommunist societies of Europe are societal entities that show common (structural) traits but also major discrepancies; the latter can be linked with different precommunist legacies (the former Czechoslovakia, as a leading industrial country during the interwar period, is the most conspicuous example) and different brands of national central planning, in terms of relaxation of direct controls and economic policy choices. The different histories explain widely different incomes per capita (with Romania as one of the poorest postcommunist countries in Europe), why market institutions vary qualitatively among the national environments, and why macro and micro disequilibria differed among these countries on the eve of 1989. Undoubtedly, Hungary, the former Czechoslovakia, and Poland had a substantial competitive edge in starting the process of managing transition. Unsurprisingly, all these countries have fared better than the rest in their stabilization programs, although their recipes were not similar, as some would argue.

Backwardness should be seen as bearing considerably on the potential for societies with poor institutional arrangements to overcoming their performance deficits; on one hand, it points to the lack of specific knowledge of individuals and of society as a whole and at the constraints for genuine institutional change and, on the other hand, it suggests that there is much scope for a system to get outside what can be conceived as an ideal tunnel of evolution. The stress put on the burden of the past is meant to warn against its dragging effects and an unfavorable path dependency, from which it may not be easy to break away.

Backwardness makes it harder for a society to overcome the fragility of its emerging market institutions and enhances the potential for the dynamics of change to get out of control. Institutional fragility in transition countries has been much underestimated by policymakers and their advisers.[4]

Similarly inadequate is the neglect of the extreme complexity of the process under way. Gross oversimplifications and reductionism of the type "black vs. white" (with no shades in between) and a lack of understanding of how interests are socially articulated, particularly in a transition period, can only obscure real processes and lead to hasty and inadequate decisions. "The elite failed to understand that society was a far more complex organism than what they had thought, that simple, well-meaning declarations were not effective in politics, that ideas and programs would have to be sold to the public, and that institutions were necessary for the routinised exercise of power" (Schopflin 1994, 130). Besides, "[i]mperfect and costly information, imperfect capital markets, imperfect competition: these are the realities of market economies—aspects that must be taken into account by those countries embarking on the choice of an economic system" (Stiglitz 1995, 267). The implication is clear in the sense of the stringent need to consider how market economies actually function. On a more general level it is high time that we take cognizance of an extremely important fact: The postcommunist countries are in a period when the basic constructs of the future systems are put in place and this can be seen as a historic opportunity for designing viable societal aggregates.

The syntagma of institutional fragility has already been implied. Apart from the insufficient analytical attention paid to the institutional buildup in the transforming societies in Europe, one has to consider the seeds of instability produced by this fragility. The poor capacity of immature institutions to perform needs to be mentioned in this context. For example, the debate on universal versus narrow banks (on whether and how banks should be involved in resource allocation) is quite relevant for the concern immature market institutions create in terms of enhancing instability and uncertainty in the system.[5]

From a broader perspective one can pose the issue of the governance capabilities of the political and economic elites of these countries and to what extent these elites are capable of inducing and managing change (transformation) when so much fuzziness, volatility, and uncertainty is prevailing. One can also assume that institutional fragility will bear significantly on the nature of capitalism in the region.

The Magnitude of Resource Reallocation: The Emergence of Strain

Another issue that is not sufficiently highlighted in the professional and public debate is the dimension of the inherited misallocation of resources in transition economies—that is, the sheer scale of disequilibria, at the new relative prices, that indicates the magnitude of required restructuring, as compared to the ability of the system to undergo wide-ranging and quick change. The structure of the economy and the legacy of resource misallocation have put the system under exceptional strain once the combination of internal shocks (engineered by reforms or simply triggered by the uncontrolled processes of system dissolution) and external shocks occurred. Appendix 14.1 provides an analytical explanation of strain buttressed by an empirical analysis done by Organisation for Economic Cooperation and Development (OECD) experts.

At dramatically changed relative prices and should financial discipline be strictly imposed, many enterprises (the inefficient ones) in transition economies would have to be out of the economic circuit; they might try to survive by reducing X-inefficiency (Leibenstein 1966), but in the end, should potential efficiency gains be evenly distributed (ubiquitous), they would have to bow out. To put it in short, the array of structurally inefficient enterprises in a country forms a silent "conspiracy" against change in that country; they represent entrenched personal stakes, which oppose restructuring for obvious reasons. Together with other factors (including insufficient policy credibility) the lack of a capacity to pay triggers a chain reaction of interenterprise debt, of arrears. The latter can be seen as temporary quasi-inside money, which undermines the effectiveness of monetary policy.[6] Appendix 14.2 uses a simple model to illustrate how arrears affect stabilization policy. Arrears reduce the relevance of low official budget deficits, since quasi-fiscal deficits are large. It should be noted that quasi-fiscal deficits have loomed ominously over economic policy in Romania during the years of transformation.

What are the major implications of strain? One is that economies under strain can easily become exceedingly unstable and that their capacity to absorb shocks is quite low; these economies have a high degree of vulnerability! Another implication is that policymakers face extremely painful trade-offs and that, in most cases, unless policy is clever and sufficient external support is available, their room for maneuvering is in practice quite limited. Finally, macroeconomic stabilization in certain countries hides deeply seated tensions that sooner or later come into the open unless deep restructuring takes place.

Strain needs to be seen in relationship to unemployment. First, unemployment rates in the transforming economies are not exceedingly high in comparison with the European levels of the mid-1990s, and this could reduce the perception of strain. The yardstick used is itself questionable, however, taking into account the unemployment problem in Western Europe. Second, the weakness of safety nets acquires particular significance in the poorer postcommunist countries, where the consequences of a "new type of poverty" could be extremely serious.[7] Another factor is the fact that restructuring of large companies in transition countries, which need mostly to shed labor to become profitable, is very slow or, in practice, not taking place; this means that significant increases in unemployment may still be ahead.

Strain should be linked also with an intense distribution struggle and an erosion of the consensus for societal change when many individuals appear as losers—once market forces start to reward people in accordance with merit, effort, good ideas, and inspiration, and also as a result of some workers' misfortune to have jobs in bad (unprofitable) enterprises. This also explains why some governments see inflation as a redistribution device when strain is extreme.

Another dimension to this distribution struggle needs to be highlighted for its exceptional character in human history and for its effects on system transformation: the process of privatization, which means a massive (total) redistribution of state assets. As we know, economics textbooks take as a given the initial distribution of assets among individual private owners; this distribution is almost God given, and it underpins such textbooks' entire reasoning on how best to allocate resources and achieve Pareto optimality (highest welfare). In the case of postcommunist countries, "God" has decided to come down from heaven, for what we are witnessing currently is an extraordinary process, without precedent in the history of mankind. In the next few years, the fate of tens, if not hundreds, of millions of living individuals (and of their descendants) is going to be shaped by the mechanics and dynamics of privatization. What took many hundreds of years in the advanced capitalist countries is supposed to occur, through various procedures (more or less legal), in the postcommunist countries in a snapshot on the scale of history. It is not, therefore, surprising that everything surrounding this process is so highly charged emotionally—why so many hopes, dreams, reckless and ruthless actions, misbehavior, and delusions are linked to it. All individuals want to be on the winning side, but markets cannot make them all happy.

The nature of capitalism in the postcommunist countries will be decisively influenced by the actual results of privatization as a process. If privatization results in the development of a strong middle class as the social backbone of the new economic system, stability and vigor will be secured, and democratic institutions will develop. Otherwise, the new system in the making will be inherently unstable.

One particular feature of communism needs to be emphasized to explain better the social tension engendered by postcommunist transformation and the intensity of the distribution struggle. Communism, as an economic system, functioned as a kind of poor and steadily declining (suffering from economic euthanasia) but nonetheless "premature welfare state" (Kornai 1994). As in Western countries, where powerful vested interests exist that oppose economic adjustment, in postcommunist countries those who cannot compete in the markets have turned into a coalition of interests that can retard or even arrest reforms. This mass of individuals is most likely to fall prey to populist slogans. Robert Gilpin's (1987) observation that adjustment is very difficult in welfare states applies mutatis mutandis in the case of postcommunist countries.

Judging Romania's Economic Transition

The Burden of the Past

In comparative analyses of the transition economies insufficient attention has been paid to the initial conditions prevailing when the transformation process got under way.[8] Communist Romania, particularly in the 1970s and 1980s, provides an interesting and instructive case of "immiserizing growth" caused by the logic of the system, in particular, the rush to speed up industrial growth and to increase ties with market economies on a very weak functional basis (by totally ignoring market mechanisms). This phenomenon is explained in the literature by the existence of various price distortions that harm resource allocation, worsen the terms of trade, and reduce welfare (Bhagwati 1958; Johnson 1967). But it can also be argued that it was the way the economy functioned as a whole (including the genesis of wrong industrial choices) that constituted *the* distortion that led to immiserizing growth. It has been shown that the inner dynamics of the system—its incapacity to cope with increasing complexity and its inability to assimilate and generate technological progress—led to a "softening" of output characterized by its expansion with a strong bias toward low value-added industrial goods, which led to a steady deterioration of the terms of trade (Daianu 1985).

Since "immiserizing growth" limited the potential to increase exports, the targeted trade surpluses in the 1980s—required to pay back the external debt—were achieved through very large cuts in hard-currency imports. Apart from the reduced level of investment, growth possibilities were also impaired by a sharp reduction in imports of machinery and equipment from Western countries. The heavy overtaxation of domestic absorption that took place during this period subsequently resulted in lower growth rates of production, reduced welfare (consumption), and bigger domestic imbalances (both visible and hidden). In addition, shortages were increasing in both production and consumption. The immiserizing nature of "growth" in communist Romania is well illustrated by its income per capita (which has remained one of the lowest in Europe) and the very high energy intensity of its GDP.[9] Another telling fact is that whereas the GDP in Romania grew—allegedly—by almost 28 percent during the 1980s, the country's exports decreased over the same period.

The structure of Romanian industry before transition also reveals a strong bias toward the creation of gigantic units, with no regard for the important sources of flexibility in an economy, namely, the small and medium-sized enterprises. Thus in Romania in 1989, 1,075 enterprises with more than 1,000 employees each represented more than 51 percent of all units, provided jobs for 87 percent of all industrial workers, and supplied almost 85 percent of all industrial output; enterprises with more than 3,000 workers (which accounted for about 16 percent of the total) supplied more than 50 percent of total industrial output and provided jobs for 53 percent of all employees in industry. At the same time, small and medium-sized enterprises (with less than 500 employees) accounted for 4 percent of all workers and 6 percent of total industrial output.

The forced reduction of the external debt in Romania in the 1980s (actually a sui generis shock therapy) accentuated the decline in the competitiveness of the country's economy, exacerbated imbalances among sectors, increased shortages, and generally lowered the welfare of the people.

The High-Inflation Period, 1990–1993

The early years of postcommunism in Romania were marred by severe economic difficulties, including a very large decline in output (table 14.1), an institutional interregnum (see Kozul-Wright and Rayment 1997), and "systematic" policy incoherence. Institutional hiatus refers to the melting down of much of the old institutional structures without a rapid buildup of market-based institutions. This obviously contributed in Romania to increasing uncertainty, fuzziness, and volatility in the national economic environment. At this stage the entrenched structures are being broken and changed, which means that the quantity of friction in the system increases considerably and important energies (resources) are consumed to accommodate change. A lot boils down to a change in the organizational behavior of actors, to the buildup of new organizational capital. In this phase of transition there exists a territory over which market coordination failures combine with an "abandoned-child" feeling of

Table 14.1
Macroeconomic indicators in Romania, 1990–1998

Indicators	1990	1991	1992	1993	1994	1995	1996	1997	1998
GDP (annual change)	-5.6	-12.9	-8.8	1.5	3.9	7.1	3.9	-6.6	-5.4
Unemployment rate (end of period)	—	3.0	8.2	10.4	10.9	9.5	6.6	8.8	10.3
Inflation									
average	5.1	170.2	210.4	256.1	136.7	32.3	38.8	154.8	59.1
Dec./Dec.	37.7	222.8	199.2	295.5	61.7	27.8	56.9	151.4	40.6
M₂ (end of period) growth rate	22	101.2	79.6	141	138.1	71.6	66	104.9	48.9
Nominal devaluation									
average	50.3	240.5	303.1	146.8	117.8	22.8	51.6	132.5	23.8
Dec./Dec.	140.4	444.5	143.3	177.4	38.4	45.9	56.5	98.8	36.5
M₂/GDP	55.7	27.4	20.1	13.8	13.3	18.1	20.5	18.1	—
Budget deficit[a]/GDP	1.0	3.3	-4.6	-0.4	-1.9	-2.6	-3.9	-3.7	-3.3
Current account/GDP	-8.5	-3.5	-8	-4.5	-1.4	-5	-7.4	-7.2	-7.2
Real wage index	5.1	-18.3	-13.0	-16.7	0.4	212.6	9.5	-22.2	6.0

Source: National Bank of Romania.
Note: All figures are percentages.
[a] Consolidated budget (including privatization revenues)
[b] Exchange rate variation deflated by the ratio between Romanian Producer Price Index (PPI) and US PPI.

many enterprises that are no longer able to rely on central allocation of resources and customers. In Romania, information and transaction costs for these enterprises skyrocketed (Daianu 1994b; see also Estrin, Dimitrov, and Richet 1998, 249).

In spite of its tortuous path some institutional change did take place during the early years of postcommunism in Romania through spontaneous processes such as massive land privatization and the emergence of a private sector (which preceded Law 54 of 1990 on the setting up of private enterprises)[10] as well as measures "from above" initiated by the Romanian government. Among the latter were the implementation of a two-tiered banking system (in 1990), the commercialization of state-owned enterprises (Law 15 of 1990), and the Law 58 of 1991, dealing with privatization, which aimed at giving 30 percent of the equity of commercial companies to Romanian citizens.[11] What happened with the privatization law is symptomatic of the vacillations and inconsistencies of Romanian reform policies during that period; Law 58 created much confusion regarding the actual structure of property rights and the need for enhanced management of assets. What was lacking was a concern for building institutionally organized markets for factors of production.

Overall and in a formal sense, it can be said that policymakers in Romania practiced a sort of "institutional mimetism" by trying to adopt, although in a highly inconsistent way, institutions found in the Western world. One problem with institutional mimetism, however, is that it cannot deal with the fine print of reforms (institutional change) and frequently lacks substance, since the real functioning of institutions is driven by vested interests.

After December 1989 there was tremendous pressure from below in Romania to consume tradables and to reduce exports and boost imports of both consumer and intermediate goods, after the severe deprivation of the 1980s. The switch in consumption in favor of tradables was almost instantaneous and virtually unstoppable; it was also strengthened by a "shunning of domestic goods" syndrome. A boost in consumption in Romania in 1990 was financed primarily by dissaving (the depletion of foreign exchange reserves).

Another side of the story needs to be highlighted, however, namely, that Romanian policymakers complicated the state of the economy both by commission and omission. They did so by commission in that they faltered in the face of pressures from below and were influenced also by the prospect of elections in May 1990. This resulted in the concession of large wage increases[12] and the introduction of the five-day workweek, despite the fact that output was plummeting, together with the continuation of wide-ranging price controls, a greatly overvalued exchange rate, and mismanagement of the country's foreign exchange reserves. Policymakers also complicated the state of the economy by omission, for they made no serious attempts to deal with macroeconomic imbalances before November 1990. Events during that year revealed a fundamental flaw in the transformation process in Romania, namely, the considerable decision-making power enterprises have when they do not face hard budget constraints.

As policymakers were confronted with a rapid deterioration of the economy and unable to contain growing disequilibria (unsustainable trade deficits, rising prices, vanishing investment) a stabilization plan, supported by the International Monetary Fund (IMF), was introduced in Romania at the start of 1991 (see Demekas and Khan 1991). The middle-of-the-road, gradualistic stabilization program that took shape included the following: a tightening of fiscal and monetary policy (although real interest rates remained highly negative), a tax-based income policy, a new devaluation, and introduction of a two-tier exchange rate system (through the initiation of an interbank foreign exchange auction system in February 1991). The program failed to stop inflation.

At the end of 1991 tensions in the system were growing: for example, an overvalued official exchange rate, artificially low prices for energy and raw materials that encouraged their overconsumption, and insufficient inflows of foreign capital to compensate for the low levels of domestic saving and the weakness of fixed investment. Many exporters and importers found a way out of the impasse through making barter deals, which introduced an implicit exchange rate into the functioning of the economy; this rate mitigated the pernicious effects of overvaluation but entailed considerable information and transaction costs. However, capital flight and insufficient exports were becoming matters of major concern.

In the spring of 1992 Romanian policymakers were compelled to act. Interest rates were raised considerably, with the refinancing rate of the National Bank of Romania reaching 80 percent; the exchange rate was devalued substantially; and exporters were granted full retention rights in the hope of overcoming their mistrust of policymakers and encouraging the repatriation of capital. The full-retention measure was thought necessary since enterprises still had a vivid memory of the "confiscation" of their hard-currency holdings at the end of 1991. But the policy turnaround was incomplete, and interest rates remained negative as a result of a large array of preferential credits and very low deposit rates, the latter reflecting a high propensity to shun the domestic currency in favor of the dollar. Political factors resulting from the elections of September 1992 also weakened the government's determination to pursue a consistent policy.

A Policy Breakthrough, 1993–1994: The Interest Rate Shock

Rising inflation and the persistence of a large trade imbalance eventually forced a reconsideration of policies in Romania. A breakthrough occurred in the last quarter of 1993 when several key decisions were made to contain and reverse the dynamics of inflationary expectations, to start the remonetization of the economy, and to create a transparent, functioning foreign exchange market. The major omission in the whole strategy, however, was privatization, which would have had a major influence on the size of capital inflows and on the scope and intensity of restructuring.

The main decision made at this time, a dramatic increase in nominal interest rates, led to positive real interest rates. Thus the National Bank of Romania's average refinancing rate rose from an annual rate of 59.1 percent in September 1993 to 136.3 percent in January 1994 and remained at that level for another three months. Commercial banks' lending rates followed suit with a two-month lag. This decision had two major consequences: First, it stemmed the flight from the leu and started a rapid rate of remonetization; and second, it greatly helped in the formation of a transparent foreign exchange market and thereby strengthened the potential for an export drive. The scale of remonetization explains why the policy shock of 1994 did not lead to a decline of output, as was the case in 1997 (when the economy was subject to a credit crunch).

Another key decision was the substantial devaluation (in several stages) of the official (interbank market) exchange rate, which lowered it to more or less the rate prevailing on the gray market; this also increased the transparency of the foreign exchange market, which in turn reduced considerably the entry costs for those in need of foreign exchange.

The third decision involved a stricter control of base money and consequently a reduced rate of money creation. And finally, the country's fiscal stance was tightened to aim at a low budget deficit when corrected for the removal of explicit and implicit subsidies.[13]

The results of this policy breakthrough were much as expected. Inflation fell to an annual rate of 62 percent (December on December) in 1994, and the trade deficit was greatly reduced, to $411 million.[14] The economy absorbed the shock of high positive real interest rates and of the exchange rate unification, which meant the suppression of some implicit and explicit subsidies to inefficient producers, and there was no decline in output. The removal of implicit subsidies explains why the budget deficit rose to 4.3 percent in 1994, with a large part of the financing for the deficit being obtained from external sources.

The export drive played a major role in the recovery, but it cannot explain why so many enterprises in the weak sectors also did well in 1993, especially as arrears did not appear to be rising sharply in 1994.[15] Several explanations for this phenomenon can be suggested. One is the existence of important market imperfections, such as monopolies, that can extract rents and operate in the less efficient sectors. Another is that there were huge amounts of X-inefficiency in the system, meaning that potential microefficiency gains are ubiquitous and that, when under pressure, even firms in the backward sectors can realize some of these gains and cope with the situation. But accepting this explanation requires an evaluation of the resilience of organizational routines in the system. One implication of the X-inefficiency explanation is that the pressure for fundamental restructuring begins to bite only when most of the efficiency reserves are exhausted. A third explanation is that there was more reliance on self-financing, although in fact many companies were plagued by a lack of working capital. Last but not least, unwarranted bank lending (rollover of loans) may have played a significant role in supporting the weaker enterprises.

Fragile Growth and Relapse into Inflation, 1995–1996

In 1995 GDP grew rapidly in Romania, to 7.1 percent against just under 4 percent in 1994 and under 2 percent in 1993; at the same time the inflation rate at the end of 1995 was about 28 percent. The remonetization of the economy continued, as indicated by the expansion of the money supply (71 percent), far exceeding the rate of inflation (table 14.1). Although exports continued to grow rapidly (by over 20 percent), imports increased by more than 30 percent, causing the trade imbalance to increase again to more than $1,200 million and putting pressure on the foreign exchange (interbank) market.

What caused the trade imbalance to deteriorate again, bearing in mind that the real exchange rate did not appreciate in 1995 (although it did so in the second half of 1994) and that there were no major changes in the terms of trade in this period? One explanation is that an import and consumer-spending boom started in the last months of 1994 that arguably might have been encouraged by perceptions that the exchange rate was unsustainable. But this explanation would have to be reconciled with the fact that in 1994 the trade and current account imbalances improved dramatically and the foreign exchange reserves of the banking system (including the central bank) increased substantially, which might have suggested that the exchange rate was in fact sustainable.

It is also possible that the various economic agents in Romania were unaccustomed to stability of the nominal exchange rate and therefore anticipated an inevitable depreciation, which paradoxically may not have been justified by the economic fundamentals. Another conjecture is that some of the improvement in the trade balance in 1994 was caused by temporary factors; their removal in the following year then put additional pressure on an exchange rate that was already overvalued. Without dismissing these factors, the more important explanation is probably that the higher growth rate of the economy, driven by highly import-dependent branches, led to overheating and the rapid growth of imports.

In 1996 there was a clear link between inflation in Romania and the way the country's budget deficit was financed. Whereas the target for the consolidated budget deficit was 2.2 percent, the actual figure turned out to be 5.7 percent, on an accrual basis. More significant was that its financing was inflationary as a result of the commercial banks' buying an increasing volume of three-month T-bills. The scale of inflationary financing was augmented by the injection of base money to cover the quasi-fiscal deficit that arose because of the losses of agriculture and of the *régies autonomes*. Together with the quasi-fiscal deficit, the fiscal imbalance reached 8.4 percent (on an accrual basis) in 1996 (table 14.2).

The process of remonetization had supported the Romanian government's efforts to subdue inflation in 1994 and 1995. Regarding remonetization, several aspects should be emphasized:

Table 14.2
Fiscal and quasi-fiscal deficits in Romania (as percentage share in GDP)

	1993	1994	1995	1996	1997
Budget balance					
Total					
Cash	−0.4	−1.9	−2.6	−3.9	−4.5
Accruals	−0.4	−1.9	−3.0	−5.8	−3.5
Primary					
Cash	80.6	−0.5	−1.2	−2.2	−0.5
Accruals	0.6	−0.5	−1.6	−4.1	0.5
Quasi-fiscal deficit NBR refinancing	−3.1	−3.6	−0.3	−2.6	0.0
Budget balance including quasi-fiscal deficit					
Total					
Cash	−3.5	2−5.5	−2.9	−6.5	−4.5
Accruals	−3.5	−5.5	−3.3	−8.4	−3.5
Primary					
Cash	−2.5	−4.1	−1.5	−4.8	−0.5
Accruals	−2.5	−4.1	−1.9	−6.7	0.5
Memorandum item:					2
Interest payment	0.9	1.4	1.4	1.7	4

Source: National Bank of Romania.

1. It facilitated the subsidization of various sectors of the economy (agriculture, energy) from the central bank's resources, allowing the central bank to pursue simultaneously the reduction of inflation. The sectoral financing mirrored the existence of major structural disequilibria in the economy.

2. It "helped" the government put off dealing resolutely with two failed banks: Dacia Felix and Credit Bank; more then 1,700 billion lei (about $400 million) were injected into the two through special credits during 1995–1996. If money demand had not grown for most of 1995 and 1996, the size of the special credits would have certainly fueled inflation. The reason for this injection was that there was no insurance scheme for small depositors, and so it was felt necessary to forestall a run on the banks and therefore a possible systemic crisis.

3. It involved the expansion of base money through the increase of net domestic assets and not through the accumulation of net foreign assets. Ideally, remonetization should have taken place as an outcome of an increase in net foreign assets—that is, as a result of capital

inflows or of net exports—and not primarily via base money injections that supported the expansion of domestic credit.

4. It can be argued that this remonetization slowed down the development of monetary policy instruments, namely open-market operations, because the central bank did not face the pressure to cope with a surge of liquidity as it would have with substantial capital inflows. The main reasons why such inflows did not occur are the feeble pace of Romanian privatization during 1994–1996, the poor functioning of the domestic capital markets, and the credibility problem surrounding domestic policies in Romania.

By the end of 1996 several worrisome tendencies had emerged: a very sharp rise in the monthly inflation rate, which was in double digits in the last quarter of the year; a sharp rise in the trade and current account deficits, although the growth rate of GDP was lower than in 1995 (3.9 percent as against 7.1 percent); and still greater distortions in relative prices due especially to the delay in adjusting energy prices and to administrative control of the exchange rate. Overall, the Romanian macroeconomic stabilization program was losing steam. The inflation rate at the end of the year was 57 percent. Furthermore, in spite of heavy borrowing (more than $1.5 billion) on the international capital markets,[16] the foreign exchange reserves of the National Bank of Romania stood at about $700 million at the end of 1996. The country's external debt was increasing rapidly, with peak payments looming in the following years. In addition, the policy mix being pursued by the Romanian government (multiple exchange rates, price controls, subsidies, etc.) was making it unlikely that it would be possible to reach a new arrangement with the IMF. Such developments were clearly leading to a dead end, and a policy change was urgently needed.

The events of 1995 and 1996 in Romania underscored the importance of privatization for inducing autonomous capital inflows and for enhancing restructuring as well as the danger of "populist macroeconomics."[17]

The Policy Shock of 1997 and Its Consequences, 1997–1998

At the end of 1996 the economic situation in Romania was as follows: The monthly inflation rate was more than 10 percent; the consolidated budget deficit and the quasi-fiscal operations of the central bank were in excess of 8 percent of GDP; the current account deficit was about 7.4 percent of GDP; and foreign exchange reserves were down to some U.S. $700 million—less than a month's imports—in spite of the large loans than had been raised in the international capital market. At the same time, financial indiscipline (total arrears) had reached a magnitude that was causing serious concern (about 34 percent of GDP), whereas the steps being taken toward privatization and restructuring were inadequate. Last but not least, remonetization of the economy had allowed massive subsidies to be given to agriculture and other sectors in 1995 and 1996 without raising inflation; as the remonetization process came to a halt in the latter half of 1996, maintaining subsidies without igniting inflation proving an impossible endeavor.

What happened in 1997? The new government's first step was to liberalize the country's foreign exchange market (which led to a large depreciation of the leu) and the prices of certain goods, which were still administratively regulated. Paradoxically, in a year when efforts to achieve macroeconomic stabilization were renewed, the expected annual inflation rate, 90 percent, was set much higher than in 1996 (57 percent). The explanation of this paradox lies in the magnitude of the effect of liberalizing prices and the anticipated devaluation of the leu.[18] Nevertheless, the assault on several of the major imbalances led to some positive results: Romania's foreign exchange market began to function adequately; the consolidated budget deficit (including formerly quasi-fiscal operations) was reduced to 3.7 percent of GDP;[19] the current account deficit shrank a little, from 7.2 percent to 6.6 percent of GDP; and the central bank's foreign exchange reserves soared to about $2.6 billion.[20] The size of this fiscal adjustment should also be seen against the backdrop of the sharp decline in the country's output, which greatly reduced its tax base. But despite all this, there was another side to the coin: The actual inflation rate was 151 percent, and GDP declined by much more than expected (6.6 percent as against 2 percent). Both demand and supply shocks were behind the decline of the Romanian economy in 1997.

One consequence of the 1997 program that is not often mentioned was its severe impact on the emerging private sector. The strong contraction of real credit diminished the prospects for many small and medium-sized companies considerably and was a major factor in the reduction in the country's output in that year. Thus total real credit (in domestic and foreign currency) declined by 52.5 percent and its nongovernment component by as much as 61.3 percent. This should be set against the growth of real credit in previous years, when the nongovernment component increased (by 19.7 percent, 35.6 percent, and 4.1 percent in 1994, 1995, and 1996, respectively).[21] In many sectors, sales declined by 20–25 percent. This development generated the growing chorus of demands in Romania's private sector for fiscal relaxation, demands that became very intense during 1998. Ironically, a program that was meant to advance reforms affected the emerging entrepreneurial class negatively and encouraged the expansion of the underground economy because of the degree of austerity involved.

Several factors explain Romania's high rate of inflation in 1997. First, the corrective component of inflation (price decontrol plus a rise in some administered prices) came strongly into play in March, when inflation reached almost 30 percent. Second, the overshooting of the leu was a factor. Third, the government's program underestimated the role of monopolies and the slow response of supply as sources of inflation. Another factor lay in the economic policy slippage in the latter half of the year when monetary policy was relaxed prematurely: There was an extensive and abrupt indexation of wages, redundancy payments were granted to laid-off workers, and large amounts of money were pumped into banks that were in difficulty. The macroeconomic policy mix was obviously not well balanced and the supply side response clearly had been greatly overestimated.

Belated moves were made in 1997 to restructure some of the major "producers" of arrears, delayed because of the problems inherent in undertaking such an operation in a year when the economy was in steep decline: On the one hand, the overall measures aimed at restructuring implied the need for layoffs, but on the other hand, the troubles confronting small and medium-sized enterprises in the private sector, a direct consequence of the austerity measures, were discouraging the creation of new job opportunities. Privatization of large enterprises dragged on at a snail's pace, and as for bank privatization, its various projects were left in abeyance. Such a situation could neither provide incentives for FDI nor promote restructuring.

In the last months of 1997 the tremendous losses of Romania's state banks, accumulated over a long period and mirroring the state of the real economy, attracted increasing attention. In the last quarter of the year, the central bank and the Ministry of Finance converted 8,000 billion lei (U.S. $1 billion) in poor credit granted by Banca

Agricola and Bancorex into government bonds as a way of recapitalizing the two banks. Whereas the Dacia Felix and the Credit Bank failures were caused by large-scale fraud and embezzlement, the failure of the state banks resulted primarily from a chronic misallocation of resources and poor performance in a number of large economic sectors, which in turn was due to slow restructuring and feeble capital inflows.[22]

GDP continued to decline in Romania in 1998, according to preliminary data, by almost 7 percent. At the end of the year unemployment stood at about 10 percent (as against 6.6 percent in December 1996). Inflation in December (year-on-year) fell to 40.6 percent, and the consolidated budget deficit with privatization revenues was kept to 3.3 percent. The latter should be seen against the background of a further reduction of the tax base (because of the decline in output) and the implications for government spending of the rescue package for the two state-owned banks. Actually, the budget deficit was kept under control by a very severe cut in public expenditure undertaken in August.

Real interest rates stayed high in 1998[23] as a result of the tight monetary conditions and a lack of sufficient credibility in the country's macroeconomic policy. The level of interest rates indicated how little room policymakers had to maneuver. Interestingly, real credit started to grow again in Romania in 1998, although output did not. Between December 1997 and November 1998 real domestic credit rose by some 24 percent, with the nongovernment component increasing even more. A note of caution should be injected here, however, since over the same period, the net foreign assets of the Romanian banking system declined by almost a half and the real money supply shrank (see table 14.1), which indicates no resumption of remonetization.

Based on consumer prices, the exchange rate appreciated in real terms by about 30 percent between mid-1997 and the end of 1998 (after the sharp devaluation at the start of 1997), which helps to explain the rising trade and current account deficits in 1998. The foreign exchange reserves of the National Bank of Romania declined to less than 1.9 billion at the end of 1998, a result of its interventions to stem the fall of the leu. It should also be mentioned that excessively lax income policies also help explain the magnitude of domestic absorption in a year when output contracted further. Real wages actually grew by about 6 percent to December 1998 (see table 14.1).

The fallout from the 1998 financial crisis in Russia led to the postponement of new external bond issues in Romania and cast doubt on the possibility that a portion of the country's external debt could be rolled over in 1999. Because of the size of payments due in 1999 (about U.S. $2.9 billion) the threat of a financial crisis and default loomed unless an agreement with the international financial organizations could be reached early in 1999. This threat explains the considerable efforts to in Romania conclude privatization deals at the end of 1998 (Romtelecom, Romanian Development Bank, etc.) and the attempt to close down large loss-making companies.

A Comparison of the Two Stabilization Programs, 1994–1995 and 1997–1998

Several features differentiate the two attempts at macroeconomic stabilization in Romania in 1994–1995 (hereafter policy A) and in 1997–1998 (policy B). These differences help explain why output grew, albeit on a very fragile basis, during the first attempt whereas it declined in 1997 and 1998. It should be stressed that in both cases the pace of restructuring was feeble.

Both policies were accompanied by interest rate shocks. Policy A, however, did not involve a credit crunch; on the contrary, M2 grew rapidly and so did lending, due, as was mentioned already, to the rapid remonetization of the economy, which was enhanced by a psychological factor: For the first time people found it worthwhile to put their savings into banks (because of positive real interest rates). Consequently, bank deposits grew rapidly. The psychological-cum-savings reorientation factors were no longer strong by the second period, and the sharp rise in interest rates (in 1997) could not be accompanied by remonetization. Policy B, as a matter of fact, involved a major credit crunch.

It should also be emphasised that the process of remonetization came to a halt in the second half of 1996, which created a major constraint for policy in 1997. The increase in the velocity of money forced policymakers to consider a much tighter monetary policy. The issue at stake was how much tighter it should be.

Policy B involved exchange rate unification via a large overshooting of the leu, which magnified inflation and the decline of money balances in real terms. Policy A included multiple exchange rates and controls on key prices such as energy. Unlike policy A, policy B involved a major fiscal adjustment, including a large reduction in explicit and implicit subsidies, which affected certain sectors more heavily than others. Policy B used base money (which actually recovered its 1996 December level in the second quarter of 1997) as a nominal anchor, whereas policy A was quite eclectic, relying on both control of the money supply and a certain degree of stability in the exchange rate[24] during the phase of intense remonetization.

Macroeconomic imbalances persisted, or even developed, in Romania over the 1994–1996 period. Arrears rose to more than 34 percent of GDP in 1996 (from an average of 22–23 percent in previous years), which was increasingly worrisome since, as the economy had been growing, restructuring should have been encouraged. A factor here is that policymakers ignored the need for a restructuring policy, an industrial policy they conceived of as a damage control device.[25] The growth in arrears crippled the country's economic growth. The rising trade deficits in 1995 and 1996 were financed by substantial compensating capital inflows, which created a dangerous situation for the following years. With the benefit of hindsight, one can imagine various scenarios against the backdrop of the world financial crisis.

Policy B tried to speed up privatization and used the Romanian stock market to this end. This explains the large inflows of portfolio capital in the first half of 1997 and the accumulation of foreign exchange reserves by the central bank. For the first time in 1997 Romania received substantial autonomous capital inflows, which tested the sterilization capacity of the central bank. These flows later subsided as policy reached an impasse.

An apparent puzzle emerges from comparing the two programs. In 1994–1996 Romania's trade and current account deficits rose in the wake of the expanding economy. With the very severe compression of domestic absorption in 1997 and 1998, an improvement in the current account deficit might have been expected. The deficit did decrease slightly in 1997 (as against 1996), but it started to grow again in 1998. The fact is that, after a fall in GDP of more than 12 percent in just two years, the current account deficit remained in the vicinity of 7 percent of GDP. The immediate explanation is that this was due to the real appreciation of the exchange rate and the lax income policy in 1998.

Whether the decline in output in 1997 could have been smaller, or even avoided, can only be a matter for speculation. It is clear nonetheless that, owing to very tight credit conditions, a continuation of growth in Romania was hardly possible, and this is why the program anticipated a decline of 2 percent in GDP. One policy issue for analysis is the appropriateness of the nominal reduction of base money in the first quarter of 1997, instead, for instance, of keeping M0 fixed for a while. The reasons for the reduction—a rising velocity of money and the desire to mitigate the size of the correction in the price level—are plausible but not indisputable. The appropriateness of moving at the same time on two tracks, cutting M0 and floating the exchange rate, can also be questioned. It is possible to conceive of a sequence of moves such that the floating of the exchange rate would have followed the correction of the inflationary surge that had been set off by the too rapid expansion of base money in late 1996. The size of tariff reductions proposed for agriculture might also have been scrutinized more closely and more critically. The conclusion is that Romania's policymakers at the time underestimated the scale and extent of supply rigidities in the country's economy.

As for the 1994–1995 program, it should again be emphasized that the slow pace of privatization and restructuring in the country at the time damaged the program's effectiveness. A faster rate of privatization, and consequently greater capital inflows, especially of FDI, could have changed the structure of the economy significantly. Even if the government at the time had not allowed the official exchange rate to float, a dual system—a commercial rate with rationing and a free rate for financial transactions—could have created an exit window for potential foreign investors in the local equity market. The government might also have used the favorable circumstances of an expanding economy to deal with large loss-making units. Its failure to do so represents a missed opportunity.

What Next?

At the beginning of 1999 Romania faced three major interlinked threats and policy challenges: the risk of an external payments default;[26] the danger of a banking crisis owing to the scale of bad loans in the banking system and the size of the foreign exchange reserves of the central bank, which were less than base money and insufficient to stem a run on the country's banks;[27] and a possible financial crisis as a result of persistently high real interest rates and the consequences of a further bailout of Bancorex (about $400 million in December 1998). Other important constraints on policy were social and policy fatigue[28] and an increasingly unfavorable external environment.

In February 1999 the Romanian parliament approved a budget that envisaged a deficit of 2 percent of GDP and relied on an increase in taxation and further cuts in expenditure.[29] The letter of intent signed with the IMF in April of that year condoned a bigger deficit, of 2.7 percent. The big unknown in the whole picture, however, was the real quasi-fiscal deficit in the economy, which was hidden by arrears and the accumulation of bad loans to enterprises. What happened with Bancorex and Banca Agricola was an illustration of the result of years of weak restructuring, which showed up in the balance sheets of the banks[30] and, ultimately, in the consolidated budget deficit when the "day of reckoning" could not be postponed any longer.

In 1999, in order to avoid default on external payments, it was essential for the government to reach an agreement with the IMF and the World Bank. The difficulties of concluding such agreements stemmed from requirements imposed by these two organizations for further drastic cuts in the consolidated budget deficit and for finding resources to finance substantial restructuring in a year when GDP was expected to fall again. As already mentioned, a very critical challenge for Romanian policy at the time was to avert a banking crisis. Eventually, the full-blown banking and financial crisis was averted in 1999, which represented a success for the government. Over the longer term, the government needed to design a strategy that would help the export orientation of the Romanian economy, lead to better management of the country's external debt, and create conditions in the country for sustainable economic growth.

Concluding Remarks

A command system allocates resources inefficiently because it makes economic calculation impossible. Consequently, the freeing of prices and the functional opening of the economy put the latter under tremendous strain when resource reallocation cannot take place quickly enough and without friction. Such strain is augmented by congenital institutional fragility.

The magnitude of the resource reallocation required for economic transformation can seriously undermine a country's attempt to pursue a low inflation rate in the short run, particularly if the lack of capital markets, the presence of large and growing budget deficits, low saving rates, and meager foreign capital inflows and external aid are taken into account. In a system subject to substantial strain, strong forces create a high propensity to generate inflation as a way of diffusing tension by spreading out, or putting off, the costs of adjustment; another effect of strain is massive interenterprise arrears, which appear as a sui generis and unintended financial innovation and create a structural trap for stabilization policy. The inflation tax and negative real interest rates are implicit subsidies for those unable to make ends meet financially in a competitive environment.

Analysts have frequently highlighted the relatively tighter financial discipline in countries such as Hungary, Poland, and the Czech Republic as compared with the Russian Federation, Ukraine, or Romania. It has been suggested that an explanation for these differences in financial discipline is provided by looking at the structure of the former economies,[31] their ability to export to Western markets and to attract foreign investment, their size, their economic policies, and not least, their geography. Furthermore, structure is influenced by whether or not there is a history of partial reforms in the country (that in some cases brought about several of the ingredients of a market environment), the degree of concentration of industry, and the prior existence of a private sector. Policy credibility can be singled out as a major explanatory factor, but a policy's credibility itself depends on how much structural adjustment can be brought about by that policy over a stated period, and the capacity to adjust is influenced by the initial structure and the scale of resource misallocation that it contains.

If it is accepted that the roots of financial indiscipline are to be sought in structure, however multifaceted, and the strain to which an economy is subjected, the obvious conclusion is that to correct that indiscipline both structure and strain must be targeted by policy. Dealing with structure involves focusing on both property rights and corporate governance. Attention must also be paid to the development of appropriate and effective market institutions and to finding ways to erode the existing economic power structure and to change enterprise behavior. Strain, which reflects the scale of the required resource reallocation, should be approached by starting with the simple truth that structural adjustment is always difficult, even in an advanced market-based economy and even when reform is credible (Bruno 1992).

The Romanian experience is a glaring example of the importance of structural reforms, of reducing the structural distortions in the economy to achieve durable macroeconomic stabilization. At the same time, it is proof of the pains inflicted by such reforms. Unless financial discipline is imposed (in the form of hard budget constraints), the pressure on the central bank and on the banking sector in general becomes a constant feature of the way the system functions, which also proliferates into wide-ranging rent seeking (demand for cheap credit). Here one sees the pressure exerted by those who cannot pay at the new relative prices combine with that of those who do not wish to pay because "it pays not to pay" (the moral hazard issue). Another lesson of the Romanian experience are the links among privatization, capital inflows, and restructuring. With the benefit of hindsight it can be asserted that the magnitude of resource reallocation required for transformation assigns a special role to foreign capital in helping reallocate resources and in imposing financial discipline in the system.

Where policy is inconsistent, privatization is slow, and FDI is nonsignificant, high strain persists, undermining macroeconomic stabilization and preserving the flow problem of the banking industry. Here a dangerous vicious circle can be at work between macroeconomic policy and the state of the banking system. Thus unless there is deep restructuring of the economy, both tightening and expansionary policies can be ambivalent as to their impact on banks; expansions can be accompanied by poor lending and unsustainable trade imbalances (as happened in Romania in the second half of 1995 and in 1996), whereas high real interest rates (as during 1997–1998 in that country) can damage the payment capacity of banks and enterprises and unleash mounting pressure for forgiveness.

Unless authorities can create and maintain a momentum of policy steadiness, the feeling of overall uncertainty and volatility is unlikely to be mitigated. Although stop-and-go measures can hardly be avoided under the circumstances, large policy fluctuations are detrimental to the economy; they entail large income transfers among economic sectors and groups of population and unnerve expectations instead of stabilizing them. Think only about the dynamic of inflation in Romania in the 1990s: from about 200 percent and 295 percent in 1992 and 1993, respectively, to about 62 percent in 1994, 28 percent in 1995, 57 percent in 1996, 151 in 1997, and 40.6 percent in 1998.[32] This dynamic was accompanied by dramatic shifts in interest rates: from highly negative during 1990–1993 to highly positive levels in 1994 and in subsequent years.

If the level of positive real interest rates in Romania continues to be quite high (in the absence of substantial restructuring and of a reduction of the fuzziness of the environment), this will be detrimental to long-term investments in the country and will skew the composition of foreign capital inflows in favor of short-term capital. It will also damage the longer-term prospects for banks, since large spreads do not help their clients and intensify adverse selection.

Without deep restructuring of the Romanian economy, high real interest rates will maintain intense strain in the country's economic system and make it prone to instability. In this context, the situation of enterprises that are potentially viable but burdened with heavy debts should be considered more creatively. It should be kept in mind that many companies are heavily in debt because they were undercapitalized (without working capital) by design, and not by choice, as was the case of firms in Southeast Asia. Tight monetary conditions and high real interest rates can kill even potentially viable companies. One way of reducing this risk would be to distinguish between past and current payments. On past debts the interest rate paid could be composed of two elements—the registered inflation rate and the real interest prevailing on international markets— whereas current interest rates should apply only to current payments.[33] Something along this line could mitigate the plight of many potentially sound companies.

Apart from the extraordinary pressure exerted by strain, the fuzziness of a country's economic environment has an impact on people's behavior and causes short-termism. Fuzziness and uncertainty also explain why banks have a very low propensity to provide long-term credit, a phenomenon enhanced by low domestic savings.[34]

Large policy fluctuations in a country can easily lead to a boom-and-bust evolution of its economy. The economic dynamics in post-communist Romania show the difficulty the policymakers had in setting a corridor of policy steadiness and their reactive stance most of the time.

A country's institutions ultimately determine its economic performance. Institutions, understood as socially accepted rules and procedures, determine the quality of economic policy in a country and of its choices as well. Institutions cannot, however, be created by "hocus pocus economics"; particularly in the case of postcommunist economies, one can detect tension between constructivism and organicism in fostering institutional change.

Romania's experience shows that *natura non facit saltus*, that making institutions function properly takes time, and that the grip of *structure*—as the product of history—is hard to loosen. It would be naive to assume that the institutions of the postcommunist economies can quickly and easily perform according to the various role models of Western Europe or North America; they need time to develop to perform effectively. Realism is needed not only in designing policies, but also in making balanced judgments as to what constitutes good performance and what is to be done next.

Appendix 14.1   Strain in a Transforming Economy: A Formal Analysis

In a transforming economy, the origin of strain can be traced to two main sources: the fragility of institutions in the making and the magnitude of the required reallocation of resources (Daianu 1994a, 1997). The following analysis puts the focus on the second factor, namely, the system's ability to react rapidly, via resource reallocation, to a new set of market-clearing prices.

The magnitude of the resource reallocation required in transformation can be illustrated by the ratio

$$J = \frac{\sum p_i^* |q_i^* - q_i|}{\sum p_i^* q_i^*}, \tag{14A.1}$$

where p^* and q^* refer to equilibrium values and p and q correspond to the current (distorted) resource allocation. J can be viewed as a measure of aggregate disequilibrium (in the system) as against the vector of equilibrium prices and quantities.

The size of the above ratio measures the strain within the system and reflects the magnitude of aggregate disequilibrium. It can be assumed that the potential level of unemployment is related to the degree of strain in the system: The higher is strain (resource misallocation), the higher would be the unemployment brought about by the required resource reallocation—when job creation is not intense.

This is a major reason behind the temptation for governments to tolerate high inflation rates as a way to diffuse tension within a system. Strain can be mitigated by interenterprise arrears, monopoly pricing, explicit and implicit subsidies, spillover effects, the elimination of negative value–added activities, learning, the efficiency reserves of producers, and by exporting it. The more numerous are those who would lose their jobs because of the resource reallocation needed for restructuring, the more intense would be the opposition to it.

Another way of portraying strain is to focus on the scope of the required process of overall income (wages) readjustment, which should fit the new market-clearing prices. The modified form of J (J') that builds on wages is

$$J' = \frac{\sum n_i |w_i^* - w_i|}{\sum n_i w_i}, \tag{14A.2}$$

where n denotes labor in sector i and w_i^* and w_i refer to equilibrium and actual wage, respectively, for sector i. $\sum n_i = N$, where N refers to all labor resources. For inefficient, subsidized (explicitly or implicitly) sectors, actual wage exceeds the marginal productivity of labor: $w_i > dq_i/dn_i$. The higher is J', that is, the higher is strain, the more fierce would be the distribution struggle. The difference between equilibrium and actual wages reflects the resource transfer (subsidies) practiced by the system; the higher is this difference, the stronger will be the forces that oppose change.

OECD 1998 compares the level of strain in labor market adjustment in Romania with that in other countries (table 14A.1). The equilibrium level was defined, in a somewhat arbitrary way, as the structure of relative wages (on the price side) and employment (on the quantity side) in the United Kingdom for the year 1994 (the latest data available at the time). Another benchmark country could have been used; the essential results would not have changed dramatically if, for example, France had been chosen instead of the United Kingdom. The results suggest four main points:

1. As expected, the distance between the United Kingdom and the transition countries, in particular Romania, is much higher than the distance between it and a country like France. It is important to confirm this basic and intuitive result before pursuing further any interpretation of the indicator.

Table 14A.1
Levels of strain in labor market adjustment

	Romania		Hungary	
	1990	1995	1992	1995
Relative wages (average monthly earnings = 100)				
Agriculture and forestry	104.2	81.6	68.9	76.8
Industry	98.6	107.6	99.0	104.0
Constructions	110.9	106.4	90.2	84.4
Trade, hotel, and restaurant	86.1	78.2	97.0	90.0
Transport, communications	108.5	121.0	105.8	106.5
Financial banking and insurance, real estate, and other services	109.3	126.8	144.7	137.4
Education, health, and social assistance	96.5	85.3	93.5	86.5
Public administration and defense, other branches	88.9	88.6	118.0	111.3
Index of "strain" on prices (excluding agriculture)	23.0	9.8	24.1	19.7
	21.2	12.9	26.0	21.3
Employment shares (percent)				
Agriculture and forestry	29.0	34.4	11.4	8.1
Industry	36.9	28.6	30.2	27.1
Constructions	6.5	5.0	5.4	6.0
Trade, hotel, and restaurant	6.87	10.4	14.8	15.9
Transport, communications	7.0	5.9	8.6	8.8
Financial banking and insurance, real estate, and other services	3.9	4.2	5.2	5.9
Education, health and social assistance	6.7	8.1	13.6	15.6
Public administration and defense, other branches	3.1	3.4	10.6	12.5
Index of "strain" on quantities (excluding agriculture)	91.4	76.6	47.6	37.2
	76.4	57.5	41.5	33.7
Indicator of total "strain" (excluding agriculture)	94.2	77.2	53.3	42.1
	79.3	59.0	49.0	39.9

Source: OECD Economic Surveys, Romania, Paris, 1998, p. 171.
Note: Dashes indicate data are not available.

Table 14A.1
(continued)

Czech Republic		Slovakia		Slovenia				France	U.K.
1992	1995	1991	1995	1991	1995	1993	1995	1992	1994
82.3	90.6	97.2	84.2	99.7	81.7	105.3	95.5	72.5	77.9
98.7	108.9	104.5	99.2	101.4	104.3	84.9	85.0	111.1	116.5
106.1	92.5	106.2	108.0	102.4	104.8	83.0	82.5	98.6	109.2
90.3	88.9	85.8	88.2	89.3	94.0	102.2	99.8	90.9	69.9
102.1	101.2	102.1	100.7	102.1	108.4	115.0	110.9	105.4	144.6
147.7	137.3	99.9	130.7	103.9	131.4	143.8	124.6	128.0	136.8
86.9	81.7	93.2	91.2	97.6	87.2	111.8	109.6	75.8	53.0
115.7	108.9	88.5	103.8	103.4	102.5	127.8	132.7	91.0	93.6
18.3	17.0	21.1	19.1	23.8	17.2	33.9	33.1	11.7	—
22.9	18.1	21.2	20.0	24.0	18.6	34.5	34.8	12.0	—
25.5	22.6	12.1	6.6	15.8	9.2	10.7	10.4	5.2	2.0
25.2	25.9	41.0	33.2	35.9	30.3	38.7	38.0	20.6	20.2
6.6	6.1	5.7	9.2	8.2	8.6	5.4	5.1	7.2	6.4
10.7	13.6	7.8	15.7	8.1	13.1	14.6	15.4	17.4	20.8
5.5	5.8	9.0	7.7	5.5	7.8	6.5	5.9	5.8	5.8
1.3	2.0	5.4	6.7	5.4	5.8	4.6	6.1	10.8	12.5
13.1	13.3	13.8	12.1	16.5	14.5	10.2	11.4	6.9	14.5
12.1	10.7	5.1	8.8	4.6	10.7	9.2	7.6	26.2	17.9
60.4	56.7	68.1	47.1	68.7	45.9	62.2	56.7	13.8	—
46.0	42.4	63.1	44.4	63.4	43.2	52.9	48.3	21.8	—
63.1	59.2	71.3	50.8	72.6	49.0	70.9	65.6	18.1	—
51.4	46.1	66.6	48.7	67.8	47.0	63.2	59.5	24.9	—

2. The level of strain in Romania is much higher for the employment structure than for relative wages. Somewhat surprisingly, Romania had by 1995 a much closer relative wage structure to that of the United Kingdom than that of other countries in transition.

3. The overall required adjustment, however, combining the price and quantity sides, is the highest in Romania among the countries covered in the analysis.

4. Finally, without the agricultural sector, the structure of the Romanian economy would appear much closer to that of the other countries in transition.

This strain indicator confirms some features of the Romanian economy. Notably, the legacy of the previous economic structure appears to be particularly heavy in Romania, at least when compared with other that in transition countries in Central and Eastern Europe. This may explain why there has been so much resistance to structural change in Romania and also why inflation and interenterprise arrears became a way of diffusing the pressure in the system when unemployment was not allowed to exceed a certain upper limit (for political reasons) and when noninflationary means for financing the budget were hardly available.

Appendix 14.2   A Symptom of Systemic Strain: Interenterprise Arrears

Interenterprise arrears reflect strain in a postcommand economy. As temporary quasi-inside money, interenterprise arrears endogenize money supply growth in a perverse way and significantly emasculate monetary policy. Other explanations for interenterprise arrears in postcommand economies can be highlighted: the fuzzy state of property rights (Clifton and Khan 1993), the primitive state of the financial system (Ickes and Rytermann 1992), the real credit squeeze (Calvo and Coricelli 1992), and the lack of policy credibility (Rostowski 1994). In what follows I use a very simple model to emphasize strain in explaining interenterprise arrears.

Let us suppose that the output g of an agent i is an increasing function of market discipline visualized as a public good or as a positive externality—as a means for easing the efficient allocation of resources. Market (financial) discipline emerges as a public good and as a positive externality because of collective (generalized) good behavior. The state does not supply it, though it can influence its production by enforcing bankruptcy procedures and providing other institutional means of law enforcement. Nonetheless, the state action (policy) of enforcement becomes irrelevant when collective good behavior is impossible for various reasons, and, as is my contention, because of strain in the main.

Were market discipline perfect and resource reallocation fast enough, interenterprise arrears would not exist; any inefficiency would be promptly penalized. Should interenterprise arrears arise, however, they would harm creditors, a fact that would be reflected by their output. Taking as a working hypothesis immediate resource reallocation, it can be assumed that the production of agent i is

$q_i = q + c \cdot g$,   for the agents who do not cause arrears (where c is a
             constant)

$= q$,   for the agents who cause arrears.

Another assumption is that the level of financial discipline (g), seen as a positive externality, is determined by $n \cdot t$, where t indicates whether agents pay their debts and n refers to those who do not cause arrears. A final assumption is that $c < 1 < N$, where $N > (1/c)$. N is a threshold number of agents.

Multiple equilibrium situations can be imagined, depending on agents' behavior and the existence of financial discipline as a public good. If agents pay their debts in due time, their incomes show up as $q + (c \cdot g) - t$, whereas if they produce arrears, their earnings appear as simply q. An enterprise decides to cause arrears if $c \cdot g = c \cdot nt < t$ or $n < (1/c)$, that is, when the number of those who pay in due time is low. It follows that when policy credibility is low and financial discipline is widely disregarded, agents are tempted to produce arrears. Instead, if $n = N$, agent N is stimulated to pay debts, since $n = N > (1/c)$, as our assumption says.

It would seem that everything boils down to policy credibility, to the functioning of market discipline. However, a critical question arises: What is going to happen, and what can be done, if the number of those who do not pay is high and, what is even more important, nonpayment is the result of the lack of capacity to pay? This means that nonpayment is not an opportunistic response to the existing circumstances concerning market (financial) discipline or low policy credibility. Consequently, whichever is the determinant of the policy course decision makers choose to pursue, the sheer number of those who cannot pay makes $n < (1/c)$—and thus, the vicious circle of arrears comes into being.

Moreover, the working hypothesis should be made more realistic by assuming that resource reallocation is slow. In this case, a complete exit of inefficient but still positive value–added enterprises would mean that output is substantially less than if arrears emerge in the system. Consequently, the short-run production function of an agent could be redefined as

$q_i = q + c \cdot g$ no arrears and immediate resource reallocation

$\quad = q$ arrears and no or very slow reallocation of resources

$\quad = q - k$ no arrears and no or very slow reallocation of resources (the case of an efficient agent)

$\quad = 0$ no arrears (full exit) and no resource reallocation (the case of an inefficient agent)

where k indicates the decline in output when there is full exit. Clearly, under the circumstances, the second situation (which includes arrears) appears as a preferred solution for the short term. It should be stressed that the choice of agents is influenced, in most cases, by their wage fund–centered goal function.

Therefore, when resource reallocation is very slow and when the number of those who cannot pay—because of their lack of capacity to pay—is high, policy credibility cannot be the main factor behind the growth of arrears; the main factor is represented by the large number of enterprises that, at the new equilibrium prices, would have to get out of the economic circuit. Since such a huge exit is impossible, interenterprise arrears emerge as a symptom of strain in the system and as a way to diffuse that strain.

References

Bhagwati, J. 1958. Immiserising growth—A geometrical note. *Review of Economic Studies* 25 (June): 201–05.

Blanchard, O. 1997. *The economics of post-communist transition.* Oxford: Clarendon.

Boone, P., and J. Hoerder. 1998. Inflation: Causes, consequences, and cures. In *Emerging from communism: Lessons from Russia, China and Eastern Europe*, ed. P. Boone, S. Gomulka, and R. Layard, 42–72. Cambridge: MIT Press.

Bruno, M. 1992. Stabilization and reform in Eastern Europe: A preliminary evaluation. *IMF Staff Papers* 39, no. 4: 741–77.

Calvo, G., and F. Coricelli. 1992. Output collapse in Eastern Europe. The role of credit. IMF working paper, August.

Carrare, C., and E. R. Perotti. 1997. The evolution of bank credit quality in Romania since 1991. In *Lessons from the economic transition*, ed. S. Zecchini, 301–14. Dordrecht, the Netherlands: Kluwer Academic.

Clifton, E. V., and M. S. Khan. 1993. Interenterprise arrears in transforming economies: The case of Romania. *IMF Staff Papers* 40, no. 3: 680–96.

Daianu, D. 1985. A case of immiserising growth (in Romanian). *Revista Economica* 20: 19–20.

Daianu, D. 1992. Transformation and the legacy of backwardness. *Économies et Sociétés*, no. 44 (May): 181–206.

Daianu, D. 1994a. Inter-enterprise arrears in a post-command economy: Thoughts from a Romanian perspective. Working paper no. 94/54, International Monetary Fund, Washington, D.C.

Daianu, D. 1994b. The changing mix of disequilibria during transition: A Romanian background. Working paper no. 94/73, International Monetary Fund, Washington, D.C.

Daianu, D. 1997. The economic explorations of strains. In *Issues of transformation theory*, ed. J. G. Backhaus and G. Krause, 41–61. Marburg: Metropol.

Daianu, D. 1999a. Romania. In *Economic Survey of Europe*, 70–81. Geneva: United Nations/Economic Commission for Europe.

Daianu, D. 1999b. What to do about high real interest rates (in Romanian). *Ziarul Financiar*, March 24.

Demekas, D. G., and M. S. Khan. 1991. The Romanian economic reform program. Occasional paper no. 89, International Monetary Fund, Washington, D.C.

Earle, J. S., and C. Pauna, 1996. Incidence and duration of unemployment in Romania. *European Economic Review* 40: 829–37.

Estrin, S., M. Dimitrov, and X. Richet. 1998. State enterprise restructuring in Bulgaria, Albania and Romania. *Economic Analysis* 1, no. 3: 239–55.

European Bank for Reconstruction and Development (EBRD). 1995. *Transition report 1995*. London: EBRD.

Feldstein, M. 1998. All is not lost for the won. *Wall Street Journal*, June 4.

Gelb, A. 1996. From plan to market: A twenty-eight country adventure. *Transition* 7, nos. 5–6: 2–4.

Gilpin, R. 1987. *The political economy of international relations*. Princeton: Princeton University Press.

Ickes, B., and R. Rytermann. 1992. Inter-enterprise arrears and financial underdevelopment in Russia. Mimeographed. September.

International Monetary Fund (IMF). 1997. Romania—Recent economic developments. Staff country reports no. 97/46, International Monetary Fund, Washington, D.C.

Johnson, H. 1967. The possibility of income losses from increased efficiency of factor accumulation in the presence of tariffs. *Economic Journal* 77: 151–54.

Kornai, J. 1994. Lasting growth as a top priority. Discussion paper no. 7. Collegium, Institute for Advanced Study, Budapest.

Kozul-Wright, R., and P. Rayment. 1997. The institutional hiatus in economies in transition and its policy consequences. *Cambridge Journal of Economics* 21, no. 5: 641–61.

Liebenstein, H. 1966. Allocative efficiency vs. X-efficiency. *American Economic Review* 56, no. 3: 392–410.

Minsky, H. 1997. A theory of systemic fragility. In *Financial crises: Institutions and markets in a fragile environment*, ed. E. I. Altman and A. W. Semetz. New York: John Wiley and Sons.

Organisation for Economic Cooperation and Development (OECD). 1998. Romania—Macroeconomic stabilisation and restructuring, social policy, 169–72. OECD Economic Surveys, OECD, Paris.

Rostowsky, J. 1994. Inter-enterprise debt explosion in the former Soviet Union. Causes, consequences, cures. IMF working paper, August.

Rutland, P. 1994–95. Has democracy failed Russia? *National Interest* (Winter): 11.

Schopflin, G. 1994. Post-communism: The problems of democratic construction. *Daedalus* 123, no. 3: 130.

Stiglitz, J. 1995. *Whither socialism?* Cambridge: MIT Press.

Stiglitz, J. 1999. Whither reform? Ten years of transition. Paper presented at the annual World Bank Conference on Development Economics, World Bank, Washington, D.C., April 28–30.

15   Transition Economies

Jacques de Larosière

Transition toward a market economy involves, by definition, an element of change: moving from a planned and more or less centralized economy to a decentralized market system in which decisions are made by economic agents in an open and competitive environment. To a large degree, transition transcends planned economies. Even market economies are subject to changes. They are continuously adapting, notably to technological innovations, to the revolution in information, and to the growing globalization of the world economy. But transition in Central and Eastern European countries presents a specific challenge given the nature of their starting point. The complexity of their task is amplified by the fact that the world has changed since 1980, continues to change, and becomes more and more demanding for small and medium-sized economies (globalization of the international financial system, concentration in the financial industry, etc.) as time goes on.

I would like, in closing this volume, to underline a few common threads that have been highlighted by the chapters and that come out of my own experience. I divide my remarks here into two sections, each dealing with a single broad concept:

• The initial success of transition in a country very much depends on the combination of structural reforms it chooses and macroeconomic stabilization.

• The ongoing success of transition in a country depends on a coherent legal environment and on the building of strong institutions.

Initial Success of Transition: Structural Reforms and Macroeconomic Stabilization

Structural Reforms

Price Liberalization

Price controls are an inherent tool in a centralized and planned economy. They are instrumental in allocating resources, in enacting the priorities set by the economic plan, and in shaping up the income structure. Price controls were indeed often used as a proxy for social safety nets in such economies. But as we all know, controlled prices do not allow consumers to express their needs and wishes. They give only a blurred message to producers. Scarcities are translated not into higher prices but into queues or the black market.

Price liberalization is therefore a key element in the establishment of a market economy in a transition country. But price liberalization involves consequences that must be understood. Given the scarcities existing in a centralized economy, price liberalization inevitably leads, at least initially, to price increases. Because energy, consumer goods, rents, and so on were maintained at artificially low levels under the previous regime, liberalization tends initially to change relative prices and to raise the level of prices structurally. The challenge for a country at that particular juncture is to avoid creating, through budget subsidies and deficits, "compensatory" increases in income. If this compensation were to take place, it would trigger an inflationary process that could eventually annihilate the benefit of price liberalization. Therefore, budgetary, monetary, and income discipline are essential albeit difficult, particularly in that phase of the transition.

Opening to Foreign Trade

Such relative price reshapings from price liberalization will be all the more tolerable once the country's economy is more open and external reserves are sufficient to permit the development of imports. But in many cases, such opening can only be gradual, given the lack of reserves, the weak current account position, and the limited borrowing capacity of the countries in question. But a move toward foreign trade liberalization is essential to the success of transition. Opening a country's borders is indeed the most effective way of introducing competition, which is the essence of a market economy.

Opening to Capital Markets

In particular, Capital liberalization should be approached prudently. Experience has shown how short-term capital inflows (and outflows) can be disruptive for small or medium-sized economies. Although foreign direct investment is generally positive, short-term flows can be disruptive, especially if the country's financial sector and the fiscal policy are weak and exchange rates do not look credible. Flows of foreign direct investment should therefore be carefully watched (central bank monitoring of the external position of banks and corporations should be considered as a prudential method and not as a form of exchange control).

Freedom of Enterprise

Whereas in a centralized economy, the state is the owner of the means of production means and the plan is the allocator of resources, in a market economy enterprises become the actors: They are confronted by the market, in which prices give them messages on supply and demand and in which they must compete with other—foreign or local—enterprises. This implies that monopolies are dismantled and that the state privatizes not only small enterprises but also large public concerns. It also implies that new enterprises are free to establish themselves, but also to disappear in case of difficulties. And it also implies that the state stops subsidizing or granting credits to loss-making enterprises.

Macroeconomic Stabilization

Why Does Inflation Kill Economic Reforms?

I alluded above to the notion that liberalization of prices inevitably creates an initial structural upward change in prices. Therefore, the setting of a tight framework, in terms of monetary and fiscal policy, is of the essence in a transition economy. After the initial structural upward adjustment in prices, a first "equilibrium level" tends to be attained, and no "conjunctural shocks" must be allowed to compound the structural shock. At a minimum, such increases should be carefully limited. If not, high or hyperinflation—another way of blurring price messages and distorting incomes—could well destroy the benefits of economic reform.

Setting Up a New Monetary Policy

In the old planned system, money played only a limited role: It was there to "accompany" the circulation of the physical goods and services allocated by the plan. As prices, wages, and so on were fixed, inflation was, by definition, a nonproblem.

The formation of capital is not influenced by interest rates and savings but by discretionary decisions. In the new economic context in transition economies, money becomes a reality in itself and reflects tensions between supply and demand. If the state, through its central bank, prints too much currency to finance large budget deficits or to subsidize or allocate credit to loss-making enterprises, inflation rises, and the deterioration—domestic and external—of the currency becomes in turn a source of instability with severe economic implications. Therefore, a noninflationary monetary policy is of the essence from the start of transition. This is one the conditions necessary to foster domestic savings and attract foreign direct investment, both of which are crucial for growth.

The beginning of transition that I have tried to describe above is one of the most difficult economic policy actions conceivable: Indeed, structural reforms and macroeconomic stabilization must go hand in hand. If not adequately supported by budgetary and monetary disciplines, too rapid liberalization can easily end up in high inflation. Conversely, macroeconomic discipline can be short-lived if loss-making companies are allowed to survive and if the nerve of competition is not permitted to fully operate.

On the whole, the experience of the last ten years or so shows that those transition countries that have, from the very start, decidedly moved forward on the structural and macroeconomic fronts have obtained the best results. Those that have delayed for too long some crucial efforts of adjustment (bankruptcy laws, elimination of subsidies to loss-making enterprises, openness to foreign direct investment, fiscal discipline) have been significantly less successful.

It is difficult to make normative judgments on the best course and sequence of actions for a country entering transition. Much depends on the starting points and on the cohesiveness of governments. It is clear, for instance, that countries with massive concentrations of obsolete heavy industries in some regions have greater social and political problems to resolve than other countries. Of course, the results of policies are also different from country to country, and no superficial generalization should be made. But, on the whole, one can say, in the light of the European Bank for Reconstruction and Development's (EBRD's) last *Transition Reports*, that the process is now well advanced in a number of countries:

• Substantial progress toward price liberalization has been made (state procurement at nonmarket prices has been largely phased out).

• Trade liberalization is now well on its way: Quantitative and administrative import and export restrictions (apart from those on agriculture) have been removed in most countries.

• Privatization of small and medium-sized enterprises is complete. As far as large public enterprises are concerned, more than 25 percent are in private hands, and the process is continuing. On average, 60 to 70 percent of the GDP of the region can be considered private. But as I will stress later, the way privatization is executed is perhaps more important than privatization itself.

• Large problems remain in the financial sector. As far as macroeconomic stabilization is concerned, results are mixed. After the initial period of high price increases due to structural shocks (300 percent average yearly in inflation over 1991 to 1993 in Central and Eastern Europe), inflation has receded and is now relatively under control at average levels, around 10 percent in Central and Eastern Europe (except for Romania) and around 20 percent for the Commonwealth of Independent States countries.

The fiscal policies implemented have often been often faulty, and monetary policy has had to bear the brunt of stabilization, with the consequential interest rate and exchange rate problems. Slow progress to reduce fiscal deficits challenges the viability of fixed exchange rates.

Concerning growth, there has been a deep fall in output since the first moves toward transition, because "nondesired" goods are less in demand and the productive sector cannot instantly adapt to new demand. The supply response requires capital investment, organization, management, and real enterpreneurship, and that takes time. Therefore, it is inevitable that a reduction in output, a fall in real incomes, and increasing unemployment will characterize the first phase of transition.

But it is important and encouraging to note that after the three first years (1990 to 1993) of severe negative growth, most Central

European countries have resumed positive growth since 1994 and have reached on average over the last four years rates of growth on the order of 4 to 5 percent per year. But this is not the case in countries like Russia and Ukraine.

Ongoing Success of Transition: A Coherent Legal Environment and Building Strong Institutions

Structural reforms and macroeconomic stabilization are, as I have just noted, indispensable pillars of transition. But the more a country moves on from the initial phase of transition, the more new challenges come to the forefront. All countries, whatever their progress on economic reform, face a common problem: the task of improving market-oriented governance. This has many interrelated aspects, which I will try to briefly summarize.

Legal Setting

A well-functioning market economy requires a clear definition of rights and obligations. This includes civil and criminal laws and their enforceability by independent courts as well as an effective and respected police. More specifically, in economic terms, this effort requires good company laws, including the establishment of joint-stock companies, the registration of shares, corporate governance (duties and responsibilities of managers and directors), and the protection of rights granted to shareholders.

Most countries have now active legislation in this field. But progress is still needed, in particular, concerning, in a number of countries, pledge and bankruptcy laws. In those countries, the registration and the enforcement of security over movable assets have been inadequately addressed and commercial legal rules remain often unclear. These matters are of great importance for attracting local and foreign investors. The rules of the game must be clear and applied evenhandedly.

Tax legislation, which is part of the legal context, is still in need of improvement in many countries: Tax systems are often complex, sometimes poorly applied, and in some cases confiscatory. Experience shows that tax systems are all the more effective to the extent that they are simple, equitable, and broadly based with few exceptions and that their rates are moderate.

I should add that adequate policies on the environment, including impact assessments, are now an integral element of modern economies. The enforcement of such rules should be strengthened in transition economies.

The Role of Government

There is often a misunderstanding with respect to the role of government in transition economies. Some people think that after years of overwhelmingly potent governments, the state should almost disappear from the economic scene in transition countries. This, of course, is not true. The state must not only reduce its size and scope (the process has started, but not enough has been accomplished) but also change its focus from detailed intervention in the daily functioning of the economy to designing broad legislation and controlling systems that allow a market to function in a regulated, transparent, and evenhanded way.

Transformation of the government's role from intervention to strategy and supervision is perhaps one of the most delicate and difficult challenges of transition. And I can tell you that that challenge is not only limited to former planned economies. Many countries in the world face the same problem.

One of the facets on this new regulatory role consists in institution building. As Grzegorz Kolodko says in chapter 3: "The institutional arrangements in an economy are the most important factor in determining its progress toward durable growth." Let me offer a few examples.

Monetary Policy

Experience shows—and this is now well recognized in theory and in practice—that monetary policy is best conceived and conducted by independent central banks that are at arm's-length distance from governmental interference. It is remarkable to observe how many former centrally planned economies are moving in that direction, given that it took so long for a number of free-market economies that were not subject to communism to do so.

Regulation of Utilities

It is one thing to privatize public utilities; it is another thing entirely—and every bit as important—to see to it that the new owners or operators of utilities or former monopolies act in a transparent fashion and in a way that protects the interests of the community as a whole, including private clients and households. This requires the establishment of independent regulators, whose role is to set the framework in which the utilities operate, and supervisors, whose role is to ensure that the operators apply the rules in a fair way.

Thus we see how fine and important is this new definition of the state's responsibility. The state sets the system; in some cases, it assumes the regulatory role, whereas the surveillance of the system is more and more carried out by independent authorities. In some cases, independent authorities are also in charge of regulation.

These authorities, of course, operate within market forces. But they have to operate according to clear rules of the game, which must be independently surveyed. These are evolving notions. The more the market advances, alongside privatization of utilities, the more the state has to reinforce its regulatory role and to strengthen the independence of supervisory authorities to guard against the risks of cartels, private oligopolies, and the temptation of misusing public goods.

Corporate Governance and Enterprise Structure

Severe budget constraints have motivated many of the privatizations that have occurred in transition economies. However, the reduction of budget subsidies to loss-making public enterprises has often been accompanied by an increase in off-budget subsidies. This has weakened financial discipline and reduced economic efficiency. Enterprise restructuring has also been slowed by the ineffective implementation of bankruptcy laws in many countries. The various methods used for privatization (vouchers without injection of equity versus open tenders and sales to strategic investors) have also played a role in influencing the effectiveness of privatization.

A key factor in this respect has been the extent of ownership transferred to existing managers or to preferred insiders versus strategic investors. In a number of cases the privatization process has led to insider-controlled enterprises, and this has favored neither the transparency and effectiveness of the process nor the intensification of competition. Too many privatized companies are still loss makers. They often take advantage of subsidies or soft budgetary constraints (like tolerance of tax arrears and weak enforcement of bankruptcy laws).

Financial Institutions

As we all know, financial institutions, and banks in particular, have a major role to play in collecting savings and allocating them to productive and well-selected investments. This was not the case in the formerly planned economies, where banks had no selective role to play in the choice of investments.

After an initial period of unregulated expansion of financial institutions at the beginning of transition, there is now a general recognition in transition countries of the need to consolidate, strengthen, increase the independence of, and better supervise the financial sector. In spite of some notable progresses, the banking system in most transition economies remains weak and vulnerable to external shocks, especially when ill-conceived pegs prevail.

Recapitalization, treatment of bad loans, independence and competence of management, and quality of supervision are all recognized as indispensable in rehabilitation of the financial sector in these economies. This will take time and resources. I should remark that opening the equity of banks to foreign institutions is also a powerful way of strengthening local financial institutions. Foreign investors not only carry the financial backing of their parent companies but also bring to the investee company a wealth of good governance and risk management practices.

I should add as well that securities markets and nonbank financial institutions are still even less developed than banks in most transition economies. Institutions in this field are far from fulfilling their key function in the transition process, which is to develop capital markets as alternatives to the financing of the private sector and to offer savers a good and liquid market for their portfolio instruments.

The supervision of banks, the strengthening of financial institutions, the enhancement of capital markets in transition countries will take time, but they are an essential challenge.

Conclusion

As one can see from these cursory remarks, much has been done in postcommunist countries in terms of economic transition but also in terms of building a democratic, pluralistic system. If one looks at the Western European countries ten years after the end of World War II, one observes that they had achieved much less in terms of economic and financial liberalization at a comparable point in their transitions. Price and exchange controls were still in existence in a number of those countries as late as the 1970s, thirty years later. Now many of these countries are converging toward European Union.

It is remarkable that in a number of Central and Eastern European countries, the financial crises in Southeast Asia, Russia, and South American did not really affect economic and financial stability. But it is also true that much remains to be done in many fields, some of which I have tried to highlight. And this will take time, more time than was thought initially by most economists.

I should also observe that in a number of countries the human costs of transition have been high, for instance, in terms of male life expectancy (with a significant decline in Russia and to a lesser extent in Ukraine and the Baltic states), rising income inequalities, and increased poverty. This calls, in my view, for more focus on social policies and safety nets than has the been the case up to now.

And as has been the theme of this chapter Central and Eastern European countries are clearly now facing the "second wave" of transition, in which the focus is on better microeconomic management, restructuring, transparency, and institution building. This part of the journey is an essential element toward their eventual integration into the European Union. It also offers tremendous opportunities to multilateral financial institutions, like the World Bank, the International Finance Corporation, and the EBRD, in terms of restructuring and catalyzing foreign private investment.

To conclude, let me take up the following question: Why do we see, in a number of countries (but this is not true for all) so little respect for general interests in the conduct of economic reforms? Political freedom has advanced, but corruption, rent seeking, insider privileges, and industrial-financial pressure groups are prospering in some countries. What is the future and the meaning of institution building in such a context? No good answers have been provided. My hunch—perhaps because I am fundamentally optimistic—is that education and openness to world information will eventually help the people of those countries attain better governance.

Notes

1 A Decade of Transition in a Variety of Settings: A Comparison of Country Experiences

1. See, for example, EBRD 1999; Fischer and Sahay 2000; Wyplosz 2000.

2 Ten Years of Transition in Central Europe and the Former Soviet Union: The Good News and the Not-So-Good News

The author is grateful for the inputs and comments by Ricardo Martin and Marcelo Selowsky. The views expressed are those of the author and do not necessarily represent the views of the World Bank.

1. GDP estimates in Central Europe and the former Soviet Union remain notoriously unreliable, principally due to an underrecording of informal-sector activities. As a result GDP growth rates for these areas tend to be underestimated, and the drops in GDP experienced in the region tend to be substantially overestimated.

2. Comparisons of nominal GDP in the region need to be interpreted with caution for the same reasons mentioned in note 1 as well as because of distortions in the nominal exchange rates. Nonetheless, they do provide a rough indication of the dramatic shifts in the relative economic sizes of the countries concerned.

3 Postcommunist Transition and Post-Washington Consensus: The Lessons for Policy Reforms

The author was Poland's First Deputy Premier and Minister of Finance from 1994 to 1997. This chapter was written when he was a senior visiting scholar in the Economic Policy Department of the World Bank and in the Fiscal Affairs Department of the International Monetary Fund in 1998–1999.

1. From this angle, the Chinese reforms in the late 1990s go along a different line than the earlier Eastern European reforms. China now accepts open unemployment, which in 1998 officially exceeded 4 percent.

2. Direct communication between the authors.

3. This alternative regards policy reorientation executed under the medium-term transition and development program "Strategy for Poland" (Kolodko 1996), when the author was Poland's First Deputy Premier and Minister of Finance (1994–1997). The outline and implementation of this program compared with earlier policies are described as "the Polish alternative" in Kolodko and Nuti 1997.

4. Including those of transitional economies, of course.

5. That was a declaration (and, unfortunately, a way of dealing) of the Minister of Industry and Trade of the Polish government at the time of "shock therapy," which turned out to be shock without therapy.

4   East Germany: Transition with Unification, Experiments, and Experiences

1. See von Hagen 1997 for a description of the initial conditions of East Germany's transition. We begin our analysis with 1991, since it is the first one for which complete data are available for the East German economy.

2. Separate data for the uses of GDP in East and West Germany have not been published in official documents since 1994.

3. For a review of the monetary union and its macroeconomic effects see von Hagen 1993.

4. Groebel works with data from the East German statistical office based on pre-unification prices and accounting rules. Her sectoral shares are therefore not comparable to the shares calculated by the West German statistical office today. Nevertheless, her results indicate the importance of the effect, which prevails in the new statistical data.

5. Theoretical models emphasize the role of unemployment benefits in determining the level of structural unemployment (e.g., Driffill and Miller 1998). Empirical findings strongly confirm that high income replacement rates in combination with their "long-term" duration causes high levels of structural unemployment, particularly if no effective active labor market policies are in place bringing people back to work (see Nickell 1997).

6. A literature overview and additional evidence is provided in Hübler 1997 and Berthold and Fehn 1997.

7. Most alternative proposals suggested letting the market determine wages and paying transfers to employees who could not support themselves or their families at the market wage rate instead of tying transfers to unemployment. This would have helped overcome the inherited labor market distortions and would have kept unemployment low in the first place (see Akerlof et al. 1991; Sinn and Sinn 1991).

8. See Schneider 1998 for a similar calculation. Schneider starts from the observation that the average employment rate in East Germany was only marginally lower than that in West Germany in 1998, namely, 59.7 percent compared to 60.8 percent.

9. According to table 4.14, between DM 50 billion and DM 56 billion per year cannot be ascribed to any of these transfer categories; this amount includes wage compensation for public employees and other transfers.

10. Government employment rose drastically because of this reshuffling of institutions. For example, in some cities that formerly had an administrative staff of 250 to 300 employees, the staff number rose to 4,000 or 5,000, or even 10,000 in Erfurt, between 1990 and 1991 (Wollmann 1996, 128).

11. For example, coordination problems among small communities induced the excessive construction of water-clearing facilities and industrial areas, because each community wanted to create its own facility irrespective of the actual demand and the efficiency of the measures (see Bizer and Scholl 1998, 44, and the literature cited there).

12. An overview is provided in Bizer and Scholl 1998 (71–72). Saxonia, for example, had about 120 different funding programs on which local governments could draw to finance capital expenditures. (Schneider 1993, 23). Apart from grants, special arrangements were made with regard to the calculation of taxes shared among different layers of government. For example, local communities received their share of income tax revenues according to the number of inhabitants instead of the local income until 1996 because the data were reliable (see Rensch 1997 for his and other special arrangements).

13. Therefore, revenue figures do not add up to 100 percent when local governments ran deficits. On the expenditure side only the most significant spending categories are depicted. Figures do not add to 100 percent because of the missing resource flows, such as purchases.

14. For details see Bizer and Scholl 1998 and the literature cited there.

15. These constraints were somewhat outweighed, because the local governments did not have to forward parts of the profit tax to the Länder government (Bohley 1995, 208).

16. The following discussion is based on Bizer and Scholl 1998 (184–88).

17. The following discussion is largely based on Deutsche Bundesbank 1996 (42).

5 Ten Years of Polish Economic Transition, 1989–1999

1. The Balcerowicz group's proposal was the most radical among many others that were the subject of debate. Even this proposal, however, did not go beyond the boundaries of market socialism (because it did not propose privatization of the public sector). See Balcerowicz et al. 1981.

2. In fact Poland was the first country (before Mexico) to announce default on its foreign debt (in the spring of 1981).

3. This law functioned in 1990 only when the wage level in the enterprise sector was kept under relatively tough control. In the near-hyperinflationary situation in 1989, the government could not catch up to the nominal wage level in the enterprise sector. The law was suspended in every year's budget starting from spring 1991. Sejm (the Polish parliament) and the Polish senate finally replaced this law with another regulation at the end of 1994.

4. The official declaration of the Ministry of Finance and the NBP about the convertibility of zloty according to Article 8 of the IMF's Articles of Agreement was made only at the end of May 1995.

5. It was kept at this level until the zloty was devalued in mid-May 1991. Beginning in October 1991, a preannounced crawling-peg formula was adopted, which was con-

verted into a crawling band in May 1995. In February 1998 the process of moving towards a floating exchange rate started.

6. *Popiwek* was introduced in 1982 and existed throughout the 1980s, though the details of the construction of this instrument and even the formal name of the tax were changed almost every year.

7. Many technical aspects of the tax on excess wages were changed permanently. The most important change (which took place on January 1, 1991) was connected with moving from controlling the total wage bill of enterprise to controlling the average wage.

8. As in other postcommunist countries, official statistics overestimate the transition output decline. A detailed discussion of this question would go far beyond the topic and limited size of this chapter. Briefly, in the case of Poland, the initial GDP level (that is, prior to the beginning of transition, in 1988 and 1989) was overestimated (mainly because of problems connected with GDP deflators under very high inflation and problems with recording inventories) and GDP for the transition years was underestimated. For more extensive discussion of this issue in relation to the Polish economy, see Bratkowski 1993.

9. A few weeks before Poland implemented its stabilization program, the former Yugoslavia also undertook a strong anti-inflationary program, which initially succeeded. Unfortunately, because the political disintegration of the Yugoslav federation had in fact already started in 1990, the positive effect of this program was very short lived.

10. It is particularly favorable compared to that of Hungary, which started from a moderate level of inflation in 1990 (33.4 percent) that was actually steadily decreasing, though rather slowly, then reversed the trend in 1995, when inflation jumped to 28 percent. Inflation in Hungary then decreased again to 19.8 percent in 1996, 18.4 percent in 1997, and 10.3 percent in 1998.

11. Periods between each threshold were defined as the annualized three-month inflation rates. A country was classified as having crossed a particular threshold when its inflation rate first fell below that threshold and remained there for a year, provided the 12-month inflation rate fell below that same threshold level during the following year without rising above it again in that same year. (The latter part of the rule was not applied to countries that crossed the threshold during 1997, the final year of the analysis.)

12. Dates for the beginning of a country's stabilization program were assumed to be the dates of the beginning of IMF-supported programs (usually stand-by arrangements or systemic transformation facilities). In the case of Poland, January 1990 was taken as the starting point.

13. For early empirical observations of this phenomenon, see Belka et al. 1994.

14. The high fiscal costs of sterilization in Poland were confirmed by Cukrowski and Janecki (1998).

15. However, A backward-looking indexation of pensions and wages in the so-called budgetary sphere contributes, to a certain extent, to strengthening an inflationary inertia.

16. For transition economies, see Antczak and Górski 1998 and Tomczynska 1998.

17. In 1999, one could observe the new wave of agriculture protectionism inspired by the aggressive pressure of the farmers' trade unions.

18. In the following part of this section, I draw extensively from Blaszczyk 1999. I want to express my acknowledgment to the author of this comprehensive study on the Polish privatization process for her kind permission to use statistical data and some other information from her study for the purposes of this chapter.

6 Fiscal Foundations of Convergence to the European Union

1. The ACs are the Czech Republic, Estonia, Hungary, Poland, and Slovenia.

2. This is one of the topics of Barabás, Hamecz and Neményi 1998.

3. To avoid currency and debt crises, the Hungarian government launched a complex set of harmonized fiscal and monetary measures in March 1995. See Bokros and Dethier 1998.

4. Credit, bank, and debtor consolidation programs in 1992–1994. The off-budget obligations stemming from these programs (the stock of long-run government securities issued for this purpose) amounted to more than HUF 500 billion Hungarian Forints (HUF) (around 10 percent of GDP). The restructuring of commercial banks required an additional HUF 150 billion in 1998.

5. The liquidity of ten-year maturity bonds is not high, but the introduction of this instrument activated the five-year bond market.

6. See Csajbók and Neményi 1998.

7. Real depreciation, ceteris paribus, opens up a development-level gap. Nominal and real exchange rate volatility is an argument to use purchasing power parity for international comparisons. This parity can deviate from the equilibrium exchange rate substantially and systematically, which leads to undesired consequences. Halpern and Wyplosz (1997) deal with the details.

8. The Forint has been pegged to a basket, whose composition was changed several times during the nineties. Since January 1, 2000, the peg is to 100 percent Euro basket.

9. See Surányi and Vincze 1998.

10. See Jakab and Szapáry 1998.

11. See details in Bokros and Dethier 1998.

12. See Easterly 1999 on the illusionary role of such factors, such as privatization, in fiscal adjustment.

13. All the computations in the table refer to monetary seigniorage. Inclusion of opportunity cost approach would result in somewhat higher figures.

14. Barabás, Hamecz, and Neményi 1998 introduced net seigniorage as the central bank has paid interest on mandatory reserves, which reduced the amount of seigniorage acquired by the state.

15. In the 1960s, the average gross debt-to-GDP ratio of the small open European economies (Austria, Belgium, Finland, the Netherlands, Norway, and Sweden) was

around 20 percent. Excluding Belgium, whose gross debt-to-GDP ratio was around 50 percent, the average value was 15 percent.

16. The sequencing and timing necessary to undertake the commitment of Exchange Rate Mechanism (ERM) II is beyond the scope of this chapter. The consequences of targeting an ERM II membership in the medium term for the exchange rate policy are analyzed in Kopits 1999.

17. See Halpern and Wyplosz 1998.

18. For Hungary, trend real appreciation is estimated by Kovács and Simon 1998 to be between 2 and 2.5 percent a year.

19. This is probably the main reason why the Irish debt rate decreased from 61.3 to 52.1 percent within one year in 1998.

20. See further arguments in Buiter 1992 and Buiter, Corsetti, and Roubini 1992.

21. See Buti, Franco, and Ongena 1998.

7   The Czech Republic: Ten Years of Transition

1. For particularly interesting opinions on the problems encountered in the Czech transition, see Blanchard 1996 and Winiecki 1995.

2. To quantify the impact of the separation is not easy. According different sources it seems that in the three years after 1992, economic growth in the Czech Republic could have been higher by 0.5–1.0 percent.

3. Even with the application of the vouchers, the reality was more complicated: The demand side of privatization was generated by distributing the vouchers; the supply side, however, was generated by the preparation of so-called privatization projects, and the government played an essential role in this process. During the selection and approval of the privatization projects, many companies were implicitly restructured.

4. The Association Agreement signed by Czechoslovakia, Poland, and Hungary with at that time the European Community in Brussels in December 1991 had an important impact. The so-called asymmetric concessions of that agreement provided the Central European economies with faster access to EU markets than vice versa.

5. The low unemployment was definitely not caused solely by slow restructuring. A high participation rate at the end of central planning, together with successful privatization in the retail sector and service and tourist industries, was the main reason for low Czech unemployment, at least in 1991–1994. Since then, however, the absorption capacity of newly created firms has diminished, and low unemployment has been maintained mainly because of the slower restructuring.

6. The core reasons for this slowdown are many and complex. Most of them are political in nature; some are based on false economic beliefs. These strictly political issues are not discussed in this chapter.

7. This does not mean that giving restructuring priority over privatization should be advocated. An omnipotent central planner would have distorted the restructuring process on the microeconomic level before privatization, which could have been critical in the economy, with its excessive share of heavy industries. At the same time,

several scholars have recently argued that the large Czech banks were nothing more than a prolonged arm of the government. This is not true either: There was no direct governmental involvement in the decision process concerning credits; it was the synergy between the interest of banks, funds, and enterprises, together with weak corporate governance, that was decisive in the slow adjustment.

8. For a general discussion of these operations, see Calvo, Sahay, and Végh 1995.

9. It must be remembered, however, that the notion of a consolidated budget—given the IMF suggestion—was formally introduced only since 1996.

10. According some estimates, up to one-tenth of the Czech trade deficit in 1994 and 1995 can be attributed to imports of foreign technology for the desulfurization of lignite power plants and for the building of the MERO pipeline to diversify oil imports.

11. Jonáš 1995 covers these issues for the precrisis period.

12. To make the situation even worse, the country was hit by extreme floods in July 1997.

13. It is fair to say that the present political forces in the Czech Republic are making some progress in this area, namely in the privatization of the country's banks, the legislative framework, bankruptcy procedures, and so on.

14. The central bank can hardly be held responsible for this policy, which is an inevitable step in approaching the Bank for International Settlement (BIS) standards.

8 Croatia in the Second Stage of Transition: 1994–1999

At the time of the writing of this chapter, Velimir Šonje was the Executive Director for Research and Statistics of the Croatian National Bank. Boris Vujčić is the Director of Research at the same institution. All views expressed in this chapter are entirely the authors' responsibility and in no way necessarily reflect the official views of the Croatian National Bank.

1. Most of the statistics from that period are quite unreliable.

2. The reasons, however, are different for the two countries. In Slovakia, the lack of structural adjustment probably turned most of the strain of transition into budget demands. In Slovenia, the average deficit in the second stage is still low (among the three lowest, together with that of the Czech Republic and Croatia), and the increase occurred because of a fiscal surplus in the initial stage (Slovenia was unique in this respect).

3. This was largely because of the divorce from Slovakia.

4. The simple average of openness for the eight countries increased from 37 percent in the first stage to 42 percent in the second stage. When Bulgaria, Romania, and Slovakia are excluded from the sample, the simple average increases from 34 percent to 42 percent.

5. The advanced transition countries gained access to the private international financial markets in the mid-1990s. Most of them, including Croatia, received the investment grade. They had easy access to foreign savings at a time of high optimism/confidence in the international financial markets. Investors' attitudes changed after the

East Asian and Russian crises, which caused large swings in capital flows out of the "emerging markets." Considerable FDI and portfolio inflows also occurred in the advanced transition countries in the mid-1990s, when large privatization projects gained momentum and domestic financial markets began to develop rapidly. No new inflows comparable to the initial inflows are likely to occur in the medium run, at least in some of the advanced transition countries, which have already privatized their most valuable companies. This is not the case in Croatia, however, where large-scale privatization started later due to the war. Croatia is now in the midst of large privatization programs. Inflows were not important at all during the early 1990s because most of them began during 1993–1994 in the most advanced countries. Therefore, the fact that we omit 1992 for the transition countries does not impair the relevance of the data and conclusions.

6. Šonje, Kraft, and Dorsey (1996) and Babić, Jurković, and Šonje (1999) point out the historical reasons behind inefficient banking in Croatia. Lending to related parties was actually promoted in the former Yugoslav system of self-management because enterprises/debtors formally owned the banks.

7. Jankov's (1999) estimate is higher (29 percent of GDP) because he used another denominator—GDP in the year when the bond issue occurred—and added up the shares. Babić, Jurković, and Šonje (1999) added up the U.S. dollar values of the bond issues (converted at current exchange rates) and divided the sum by Croatia's 1997 GDP.

8. An explicit limited deposit insurance scheme was introduced as of July 1997. Only deposits from the household sector are insured, for up to 100,000 Croation Kuna (HRK) (13,000 Euros (EUR)) per depositor in a single bank. The maximum insurable amount is determined by the Minister of Finance, who increased it to the current limit following parliamentary discussion in 1998. The insurance fund is managed by a governmental agency that collects (linear) premiums of 0.2 percent per quarter, but it can be financed additionally from the central budget.

9. Measurement of the costs of banking crises is very imprecise, either because of a lack of data or because various methodologies are employed (see Frydl 1999). Moreover, most methodologies rely on static estimates of fiscal costs, which can seriously overestimate actual costs because they calculate no returns on bank rescue operations and these returns can be substantial (Lovegrove 1998). In compiling the list in the chapter, we used the highest estimates where several estimates were available (e.g., Chile).

10. Until March 1999, only a transfer of deposits took place, because deposits in aggregate did not drop. In March and April, however, overall FX deposits fell by 2.2 percent and 2.5 percent, respectively. The pace of withdrawals slowed in May 1999.

11. The central bank can, however, be held responsible for its excessively liberal licensing of banks and, especially, bank managers.

12. Note that the rates of change in table 8.9 are annualized. Because it has such a narrow band of fluctuation, some authors have labeled the Croatian exchange rate regime "quasi-fixed."

13. The highest net inflows occurred in two countries with notably different exchange rate regimes (the Czech Republic and Hungary). Slovenia had a regime similar to that of Hungary, but it had the lowest net capital inflows, because it did not abandon capital controls.

14. Theoretically, currency substitution leads to suboptimality of monetarist rule (Vegh 1989).

15. Such problems are not limited to emerging economies.

16. It is, however, reasonable to assume that tax evasion has become less widespread (more difficult) since the introduction of the value-added tax at the beginning of 1998.

17. These are, in fact, intersectoral arrears. The biggest creditor is the banking sector, with approximately 40 percent of all claims, followed by the government with 30 percent. "Pure" interenterprise arrears constitute the rest of the claims.

18. The problem/extent of interenterprise arrears is the most difficult one to quantify. It consists of debts to the banking sector, to the government, and among enterprises themselves. Many of these debts have piled up simply because of the interest accrual over time in the absence of bankruptcies. There is no doubt, however, that the extent of the problem is large.

19. "Foreign savings" is in quotation marks here because inflows were initially based mainly on the repatriation of residents and the diaspora's foreign exchange savings. See "Banks and Capital Flows," above.

20. An initial liquidity effect occurred the first time the VAT was paid. It took some time for agents to learn to optimize liquidity in the VAT environment. For example, it took some time for agents to request VAT returns after the VAT was paid on imports for the first time.

21. Pension system beneficiaries represented 23 percent of the population in Croatia in the late 1990s.

22. Widening the deficit deepens the recession.

23. The role of fiscal policy should be investigated using appropriate statistical techniques. This is why the word "might" is used here.

24. Anecdotal evidence indicates that arrears were decreasing during the first half of the year, so it is possible that the stock of arrears at the December level remained unchanged during 1998.

25. Potential growth announcements undermined credibility in general as they introduced confusion about what regime Croatia was actually using. The fact that policymakers (the Minister of Finance and CNB governor) informally but publicly announced inflation targets for the year as a whole while at the same time emphasizing (relative) exchange rate stability created a lot of noise. Hence it was never clear if the regime was targeting inflation or the exchange rate. On top of this, the ministry made nominal GDP growth announcements.

26. See Ghosh 1997 for proof of the very high inflationary elasticity of the demand for money in transition countries.

27. If the GDP is adjusted upward for the extent of the unrecorded economy, however, the ratio of the current account deficit to GDP drops below the rule-of-thumb level of 5 percent.

28. In this chapter, when we refer to Central and Eastern European countries, we particularly have in mind countries in that region that have an association agreement with the EU.

29. The increase in unemployment in the Czech Republic seems to have been not circumvented but delayed. Many analysts ascribe this delay to the delayed restructuring in that country.

30. This is primarily because many people register to obtain welfare or war-related benefits.

31. There is, however, a question of the complete comparability of the ILO surveys. In Croatia, the 1997 ILO survey was conducted in June, when the unemployment rate is somewhat lower than average because of seasonal factors.

32. The desirable long-run target for a structural change was defined as being congruent to the EU employment structure.

9   Fiscal Impulse of Transition: The Case of Slovenia

I thank the Ministry of Finance, the Bank of Slovenia, the Tax Administration, and the Agency for Payment System for access to data necessary for this analysis. I thank Stane Vencelj for providing early data on consolidated general government as well as for discussions of some methodological issues. For data transfer help, thanks to Katarina Koler and Slaven Mićković.

1. On the concept of "controllability" versus "sustainability" as an appropriate indicator of healthy public finances, see Perotti, Strauch, and von Hagen 1997.

2. Several simple measures are used for appraising the fiscal impulse: for example, the Blanchard, the Organisation for Economic Cooperation and Development (OECD), and the International Monetary Fund (IMF) measures (see, for example, Blanchard 1990; Alesina and Perotti 1995; and Alesina, Perotti, and Tavares 1998).

3. On conceptual and measurement problems of budget deficit, see Tanzi 1993 and Blejer and Cheasty 1991. On structural effects and fiscal adjustment, see, for example, Perotti 1996 and Alesina and Perotti 1997; on structural effects on growth, see Tanzi and Zee 1997.

4. See, for example, Tanzi 1995.

5. See also Mencinger 1998.

6. See Bole 1997 and Korže 1994.

7. See Bole 1997.

8. See Bole 1997 and Korže 1994. The effects of disorganization, known from some other economies in transition, were minor (on disorganization, see Blanchard and Kremer 1997).

9. See Stanovnik and Kukar 1995 or Ministry for Labour, Family and Social Security 1997.

10. See Stanovnik 1998 and Vodopivec 1995.

11. See Korže 1994.

12. See Bole 1999.

13. In 1995 the difference between interest rates on transitional debt and total government debt made fiscal costs of interest 0.1 percent of GDP higher.

14. See "Balances of the Banking Sector," internal data of the Slovenian central bank.

15. See Bole 1999.

16. See Vodopivec 1996 and Stanovnik 1998.

17. On similar developments in other transition countries, see, for example, Blanchard 1997.

18. There were ninety-six types of subsidies offered by the Slovenian government in 1998.

19. In Poland in 1992, business sector subsidies reached about 3.3 percent of GDP, and in the Czech Republic in the same year, about 5 percent of GDP. See Schaffer 1995.

20. See, for example, Bole 1999.

21. See Tanzi 1995 and Zee 1996.

22. See, for example, Schaffer 1995.

23. See, for example, OECD 1999.

24. Many economists advocate just the opposite sequencing. See, for example, Lindbeck 1994 and Perotti 1996.

25. On the scale and reasons for significant tax erosion in some transition economies, see IMF 1995.

26. See Schaffer 1995.

27. The same conclusion is reached for other, more developed transitional economies; see Schaffer 1995.

28. See IMF 1997 and Rebrica 1998.

29. After 1997, when basic restructuring of the most distressed firms had come to an end, the basic purpose of the fund was redefined towards promoting and accelerating technology restructuring of enterprises.

30. See Korže 1994.

31. See Ministry of Finance 1999.

32. The volume of special credit facilities for banks in rehabilitation in the first years of rehabilitation reached a level of more than 15 percent of base money.

33. See, for example, Stanovnik and Kukar 1995 and Bole 1998.

34. As noted above, in 1998 96 types of subsidies were in use by Slovenia's government.

10   The Legacy of the Socialist Economy: The Macro- and Microeconomic Consequences of Soft Budget Constraints

1. The issue of postsocialist transition in countries that commenced economic reforms at an early stage of industrial development, with the share of those employed in the agricultural sector above 75 percent of GDP (China, Vietnam, and Laos) is not examined in this chapter on account of the fundamental differences between industrial and industrializing economies.

2. Czechoslovakia and Hungary were least affected by these problems, but even in these countries price liberalization was attended by a significant leap in inflation rates.

3. Bearing in mind the substantial differences between transition economies and stably functioning market economies, in which modern macroeconomic theory emerged with the debates between monetarists and Keynesians, the use of the term "monetarist" here is not precise. Here and later on I use this term both because it has taken root in debates on transition economies and because in the fundamental issue of the desirability of supporting stable, low nominal monetary growth rates to halt high levels of inflation, the monetary policy in the countries that implemented rapid disinflation indeed followed monetarist recommendations. A key characteristic of populist economic policy is the lack of monetarist constraints. Economic policy in countries that disinflated slowly falls into the "populist" category.

4. Of course in both the first and the second group of countries there was a real battle over the course of economic policy, and in the process of transition, fiscal and monetary policies underwent significant changes, but in this chapter I am interested only in the general result of the interaction of these factors for the policy that was actually realized.

5. See Gaidar 1997.

6. The most competent exposition of this viewpoint, which was rather widespread at the start of the transformation recession, can be found in Calvo and Coricelli 1992.

7. In this chapter I focus on the general features of the development of events during the postsocialist recession and the boom that follows. Upheavals in the international economy and domestic economic policy exert a significant influence on the development of events in specific countries.

8. Janos Kornai (1980) introduced the concept of hard and soft budget constraints in his classic work *The Economics of Shortage*.

9. See, for example, Gedeon 1987 and Tyson 1977.

10. See Dombrovsky 1996; Hemmins, Cheasry, and Lahiri 1997; and Gaidar 1997c.

11. A typical example is the case of the two largest Polish shipyards: Szceczin and Gdansk. The Szceczin shipyard started a major restructuring program back in 1990, cutting costs and personnel. Currently it is the sixth largest shipbuilding enterprise in the world, is financially efficient, and is working at capacity to fulfill export orders. The Gdansk shipyard, from which Polish president Lech Walesa launched his political career, is a classic example of a postsocialist enterprise with powerful political connections and soft budget constraints. The enterprise refused to implement a restructuring program, conducted a policy of protecting jobs and accumulated debts to the budget. In 1996 the enterprise was declared bankrupt. See OECD 1997, 79–80.

12. For more detail see Gaidar 1997b.

13. See Cagan 1956 and Sargent 1982.

14. See Tanzi 1978.

15. The development of the financial crisis in Russia is described in detail in IEPPP 1999.

11   Belarus: A Command Economy without Central Planning

This chapter is based on a paper presented at the Fifth Dubrovnik Conference on Transition Economies: "Ten Years of Transition: What Have We Learned and What Lies Ahead," June 23–25, 1999. An earlier and much shorter draft was presented at an international conference, "The Belarusian Economy: Growth Factors and Sustainable Development," held February 25, 1999, in Minsk by the Council of Ministers of Belarus and the World Bank. The writer was economic adviser to the presidential administration of Belarus from January through September 1998, under World Bank auspices, and in 1999 has been involved in the EU-TACIS (Technical Assistance to the Commonwealth of Independent States) project for the publication of *Belarus Economic Trends*, but the views expressed here are purely personal and should not necessarily be associated with any of these organizations. Financial support from ESRC (Economic and Social Research Project) Project L213 25 2003, within the "One Europe or Several" program, is gratefully acknowledged.

12   Problems with Economic Transformation in Ukraine

1. Statistics provided by Daniel Kaufmann at the World Bank.

2. Holubcheko seems to have lost out in the summer of 1999.

3. Information obtained from Ukraine's Minister of Finance, June 4, 1999.

13   The Economic Transition in Bulgaria, 1989–1999

I would like to thank Roumen Avramov, Nikolay Nenovsky, Pieter Stek, and participants at the Fifth Dubrovnik Conference on Transition Economies, Dubrovnik, Croatia, for helpful discussions. The staff of the Centre for Liberal Strategies, Sofia, has been extremely helpful throughout the project.

1. Certainly, there are also other candidates for "key facts." Wyzan (1998) argues that the burden of foreign debt is a key leitmotif in the Bulgarian transition and that the International Monetary Fund's (IMF's) policy has been instrumental in creating business cycles. First of all, I think it is a little unclear how one should interpret the "business cycles" in Bulgaria, since the comovements of macroeconomic variables do not fit the standard definition of Burns and Mitchell (1946) or that of Lucas (1977). Second, I consider the reaction of the IMF largely endogenous to the macroeconomic policy in Bulgaria. Third, foreign debt is a key economic parameter, but its effects are largely determined by governmental policy in Bulgaria, and in particular by the declaration of a moratorium on debt repayments in early 1990.

2. Bristow (1996) reports results from surveys conducted in the first four years of transition. Bristow's tables clearly show that between 55 and 66 percent of the public approved of the old economic system throughout the period.

3. See V. Ganev 1999 for a recent discussion of transfer pricing. Hillman, Mitov, and Peters (1995) provide one of the first accounts of the linkage between private and state-owned firms in Bulgaria.

4. "Competence" is used here in the sense of Rogoff (1990).

5. An alternative explanation for the slow speed of reforms in Bulgaria and the collapse of economic activity based on the insufficient level of social capital is provided by G. Ganev (1999).

6. See, for example, Minassian 1997.

7. Under certain conditions this measure is equivalent to the one in Davis and Haltiwanger 1992.

8. See OECD 1997.

9. Christov (1997) calculates the index of central bank independence for the BNB and finds that formally the BNB is as independent as the Greek central bank and more independent than the Danish one. In fact, among central banks in the set of developing countries considered initially by Cukierman, Webb, and Neyapti (1992), the BNB is one of the most independent banks.

10. See OECD 1997 for further details on the bad-loans issue.

11. See also Avramov 1996 for an analysis of the difficulties in Bulgarian banking.

12. This discussion follows somewhat that of Bernanke and Mihov (1998). They, however, allow the correct measure of monetary policy to be a combination of several policy variables.

13. There are many articles describing the operations of the currency board arrangement in Bulgaria and its impact on the economy in its first years. See Avramov 1999; Gulde 1999; and Yotzov et al. 1997, among others.

14. As of June 4, 1999, this deposit stood at BGL 806 billion.

15. For a comprehensive analysis of Bulgaria's internal and external vulnerability, see Avramov 1999.

16. Below I mention alternative theories that can also explain this trend.

17. The canonical example is Argentina in 1995. After the Mexican peso crisis, the tequila effect overwhelmed most of Latin America. Only Argentina, because of the currency board constraint, saw a collapse in its output of the same magnitude as in Mexico.

18. See again Avramov 1999 for a lucid discussion of the exit strategy debate.

14   Strain and Economic Adjustment: Romania's Travails and Pains

This chapter relies heavily on the author's previous research and his work for the United Nations/ECE in early 1999. In this respect see Daianu 1999a. I wish to thank Arntraud Hartmann, Pieter Stek, and J. de Beaufort Wijnholds for their comments during the Dubrovnik conference. Certainly, full responsibility for the content of the chapter rests with the author.

1. Stiglitz remarked that the failures of reforms "are not just due to sound policies being poorly implemented ... failures go deeper, to a misunderstanding of the foundations of a market economy as well as a misunderstanding of the basics of an institutional reform process" (1). One need not fully agree with Stiglitz to see that he has a point.

2. Romania practiced late Stalinism until the very end of the communist regime. Initial conditions can be related to the magnitude of resource misallocation, the institutional ingredients of a market environment, the existence of a private sector, a certain industrial culture, and so on.

3. See also Estrin, Dimitrov, and Richet 1998. These authors conclude that "when one looks at differences in terms of progress of restructuring it seems likely that these can best be explained by preconditions rather than current progress in reforms" (250).

4. As Peter Rutland (1994–95) rightly points out, "in a travesty of Hayekian logic, it was assumed that market institutions would be self-generating" (11).

5. One can talk about an enhanced "financial instability hypothesis," in the vein Minsky 1977.

6. If the equation of exchange $(PY = MV)$ is put in a dynamic form by using logarithms: $\dot{p} + \dot{y} = \dot{m} + \dot{v}$, where $\dot{p}$, $\dot{y}$, $\dot{m}$ and $\dot{v}$ are the rates of change of prices, output, money supply, and money velocity, respectively. When monetary policy is tightened, $\dot{m} = 0$, and $(\dot{p} + \dot{y})$ is above zero, $\dot{v}$ needs to be positive to alleviate the expected decline of output. In this case, arrears appear as if they modify money velocity. If arrears are considered temporary quasi-inside money and velocity is kept constant, the relationship becomes $\dot{p} + \dot{y} = \dot{m}(c, a)$, where c is cash and bank credit and a represents arrears. When $\dot{c} = 0$ because of the dear money policy, $\dot{p} + \dot{y} = \dot{a}$. See Daianu 1994a. For the history of arrears in Romania, see also Clifton and Khan 1993. Carare and Perotti (1997) argue that arrears in Romania are a result of inconsistent reform policies and the underdevelopment of financial makets. Consequently, they argue in favor of hardening budget constraints. But like other analysts, they do not explain why reform policy is inconsistent and the structure of incentives for banks so hard to change. Thence comes the relevance of strain.

7. About labor hysteresis and its implications for Romania see Earle and Pauna 1996.

8. IMF 1997 acknowledges that "Romania emerged from communism with an economy that was suffering from considerably more deep-seated structural problems than most former communist countries in the region" (7).

9. The energy consumption per unit of GDP in Romania is twice as high as in Hungary and more than four times the OECD average (EBRD 1995, 77).

10. In 1991 the number of private companies in Romania rose quickly to 72,277; these companies operated mainly in trade and services. By the end of 1995 the number had risen to almost half a million. It should be recalled that, in contrast to that in Hungary or Poland, the communist regime in Romania did not allow any form of private property.

11. It should be noted that commercial companies represented only 60 percent of state assets; the rest belonged to the so-called *régies autonomes*, which were created according to the French model.

12. This development should be seen in the context of the elections in May 1990. Measured real wages rose by 11 percent between December 1989 and October 1990, while output continued to fall. The removal of price controls began in November 1990.

13. The budget deficit was actually higher in 1994 (4.3 percent) than in 1993 (1.7 percent), but many implicit and explicit subsidies had been removed, which was a key objective.

14. It can be argued, however, that the ceteris paribus condition does not apply in this assessment, since there were favourable external "shocks" as well.

15. Caution is required with the numbers, since arrears can be obscured by inefficient activities being kept afloat by bank lending (via rollovers). Ultimately, these "hidden" arrears will show up in a deterioration in the portfolios of the banks. This appears to be what happened in 1996 and thereafter.

16. During 1995 Romania was rated BB– by the principal Western rating agencies (and BB+ by JCRA, the Japanese Credit Rating Agency), which helped in the raising of money on the international capital markets. These accommodating capital inflows fended off a major balance-of-payments crisis in 1996.

17. The elections of 1996 clearly had an impact on macroeconomic policy and subsequently on the performance of the economy.

18. From some 4,000 lei/dollar at the end of December 1996, the rate rose sharply to about 9,000 lei/dollar in late February 1997, after which a nominal appreciation took place and the rate stabilized at around 7,000 lei/dollar.

19. This is an overstatement to the extent that arrears stood at a high level and even increased. The bailout of Banca Agricola and Bancorex in 1997 indicated how serious the problem of arrears was and how arrears can obscure quasi-fiscal deficits.

20. Significant amounts of portfolio capital entered the country, which tested the ability of the central bank to sterilize such capital when base money represented no more than 4.6–4.7 percent of GDP.

21. National Bank of Romania data.

22. Behind these developments was the slow pace of privatization, which therefore failed to attract capital inflows and thereby help restructuring.

23. In the second half of the year ex post U.S. dollar returns on three-month T-bills hovered at about 50 percent.

24. De facto quasi unification of the rates occurred during 1994. The relative stability of the rates helped the stabilization effort at that time.

25. I advocated an industrial policy, seen as managing the gradual phasing out of chronically inefficient companies, in Daianu 1992.

26. Although Romania had only a moderate level of external debt as of 1999 (which did not exceed 30 percent of GDP), its debt nevertheless was increasing rapidly. Questions can therefore be raised about the country's management of its external debt, with a peak payment approaching $2.9 billion in 1999.

27. At the start of 1998 the $500 limit in Romania on the purchase of hard currency by individuals was lifted. This measure may increase the risk of a run on the banking system. The lack of a collective experience of a banking system collapse, however, can act as a cushion against such a run.

28. This fatigue was the result of an austerity policy underway for two years in which GDP had fallen by more than 13 percent.

29. Particularly worrisome were the low shares in the state budget of expenditure on education and health care and the plunging share of capital expenditure (especially on infrastructure).

30. According to data made public by the National Bank of Romania, nonperforming loans accounted for more than 60 percent of total outstanding loans in June 1998, with much of the total belonging to large state-owned banks.

31. A World Bank study showed the median number of employees in a sample of firms in Romania to be 1,327, whereas in other countries it was very low: Slovenia, 213; Poland, 820; Hungary, 241; Bulgaria, 291.

32. Inflation rates are recorded at the end of the year.

33. See Daianu 1999b. Martin Feldstein (1998) has proposed something similar for Asian companies hurt by the high real interest rates resulting from austerity measures.

34. In 1998 aggregate savings in Romania were about 16 percent of GDP.

Index